PRACTICING TO TAKE THE

GRE®
GENERAL
TEST – No. 8

INCLUDES:

- Three official GRE General Tests administered in 1989-90
- One additional official GRE General Test complete with explanations
- Instructions and answer sheets
- Percent of examinees answering each question correctly

AN OFFICIAL PUBLICATION OF THE GRE BOARD

Published by Educational Testing Service
for the Graduate Record Examinations Board

The Graduate Record Examinations Program offers a General Test measuring developed verbal, quantitative, and analytical abilities and Subject Tests measuring achievement in the following 16 fields:

Biochemistry, Cell and Molecular Biology	Economics	Literature in English	Political Science
Biology	Education	Mathematics	Psychology
Chemistry	Engineering	Music	Sociology
Computer Science	Geology	Physics	
	History		

The tests are administered by Educational Testing Service under policies determined by the Graduate Record Examinations Board, an independent board affiliated with the Association of Graduate Schools and the Council of Graduate Schools.

The Graduate Record Examinations Board has officially made available for purchase two practice books, each containing three General Tests, of which this book is one. The Board has also made available for purchase practice books for 15 of the 16 Subject Tests each containing a full-length test. A practice book is currently not available for the Biochemistry, Cell and Molecular Biology Test. The Subject Test practice books and *Practicing to Take the General Test — No. 7* may be purchased by using the order form on page 303.

Individual booklets describing each test and including sample questions are available free of charge for all 16 Subject Tests. The *GRE Information Bulletin,* is also available free of charge. Copies of the *Bulletin* and the Subject Test Descriptive Booklets may be requested by writing to:

Graduate Record Examinations
Educational Testing Service
P.O. Box 6014
Princeton, NJ 08541-6014

TABLE OF CONTENTS

Practicing to Take the GRE General Test 4

Test-Taking Strategy 5

Procedures for Practicing 6

How to Score Your Practice Test................................ 7

Evaluating Your Performance 7

Additional Information 8

Test Preparation Material 8

    Purpose of the GRE General Test.............................. 8

    How the Test Is Developed 9

    Description of the General Test 9

        Verbal Ability 10

        Quantitative Ability 20

        Analytical Ability 34

GRE General Test GR90-13 45

    Answer Key and Percentages of Examinees Answering Each Question

    Correctly 89

    Score Conversion Table 90

GRE General Test GR86-1 (with explanations) 93

    Answer Key and Percentages of Examinees Answering Each Question

    Correctly 203

    Score Conversion Table 204

GRE General Test GR90-14 205

    Answer Key and Percentages of Examinees Answering Each Question

    Correctly 247

    Score Conversion Table 248

GRE General Test GR90-15 249

    Answer Key and Percentages of Examinees Answering Each Question

    Correctly 293

    Score Conversion Table 294

General Test Average Scores for Seniors and
Nonenrolled College Graduates, Classified by
Intended Graduate Major Field Group 294

Answer Sheets... 295

Order Form 303

PRACTICING TO TAKE THE GRE® GENERAL TEST

The General Test is intended to measure verbal, quantitative, and analytical skills. Although a brief review will not dramatically change the abilities you have acquired over years, use of this book may help you evaluate your ability level and identify areas for further study before you take the General Test.

This practice book contains the three GRE® General Tests that were given at GRE test centers in October 1989, December 1989, and February 1990 and an additional full-length test with questions, answers, and explanations. The tests are complete except for the single section of trial questions in each test that was not counted in the scoring. The location of the nonscored section varies from test to test. The order of the verbal, quantitative, and analytical abilities sections may vary; therefore, when you take the General Test to earn scores, you may find that these sections are not in the same order as they appear in these tests.

The practice book also contains detailed descriptions of the nine general types of questions used in the General Test and suggested strategies for answering them. Forty-eight sample questions with explanations illustrate these strategies.

On the following pages are suggestions for the use of this practice book. To obtain maximum benefit, try the following:

- Take the first test, score it, and compare your scores with the scores of other people who took the test by referring to the table on page 90.

- Read the practice material on pages 8-43.

- Then work through the test with explanations.

- Take the second test, score it, and compare these scores with your scores on the first test to note your improvement and/or any persistent areas of weakness.

- Review again the sample questions and explanations related to the areas where you have answered questions incorrectly. This will help guide you to further study.

- When you are ready, take the third test. The scores you earn on this test are the best estimate of what your performance might be if you take the General Test under standard conditions in the near future.

- Be sure to observe the time limits for each section.

TEST-TAKING STRATEGY

Your test-taking strategy may affect your scores. In preparing to take the General Test, it is important that you become thoroughly familiar with the directions in the practice tests because they are the same as those in the actual test. You have probably taken tests that contain questions similar to those found in the verbal and quantitative sections of the General Test. The question types found in the analytical section may be less familiar. You are strongly urged to review the directions for these questions and to work through some of the practice questions, particularly if you have not encountered them previously. The same is true for any of the verbal or quantitative question types that are not familiar to you. Research suggests that practicing unfamiliar question types results in improved performance and decreases the likelihood of inaccurately low scores. You should still read the directions for each group of questions carefully during the actual test administration.

Work as rapidly as you can without being careless. Check frequently to make sure you are marking your answers in the appropriate rows on your answer sheet. Since no question carries greater weight than any other, do not waste time pondering individual questions you find extremely difficult or unfamiliar.

You may find it advantageous to go through a section of the General Test a first time quite rapidly, stopping only to answer those questions of which you are confident. Then go back and answer the questions that require greater thought, concluding with the very difficult questions, if you have time.

Your scores on the General Test will be determined by the number of questions for which you select the best answer from the choices given. Questions for which you mark no answer or more than one answer are not counted in scoring. Nothing is subtracted if you answer a question incorrectly. Therefore, to maximize your scores, it is better for you to guess at the answer than not to respond at all.

Some sections of the General Test contain test questions with four response options (A through D). All GRE answer sheets contain response positions for five responses (A through E). If an E response is marked for a four-option question, it will be ignored. That is, an E response for a four-option question is treated the same as no response (omitted).

During the actual administration of the General Test, you may work *only* on the section the supervisor designates and only for the time allowed. You may *not* go back to an earlier section of the test after the supervisor announces, "Please stop work" for that section. The supervisor is authorized to dismiss you from the center for doing so.

PROCEDURES FOR PRACTICING

To get an idea of your performance at this time, before further review, take the first practice test under conditions that simulate those at an actual test administration and evaluate the results.

Allow 30 minutes to complete each section of the test. Work on only one section of the test during each 30-minute time period. Do not go back to a previous section or work on a subsequent section. (If you do so at an actual test administration, you may be dismissed from the test.) Once you have completed the third section of the test, you may take a 10- to 15-minute break.

Do not use books, compasses, rulers, slide rules, calculators, (including watch calculators), pamphlets, protractors, highlighter pens, stereos, or radios with headphones, watch alarms (including those wth flashing lights or alarm sounds), dictionaries, keyboards, or paper of any kind, since you will not be permitted to use them at a test center.

When you are ready to begin the test:

- Remove an answer sheet from the back of this book.

- Read the back cover of the test book (page 88) and complete the identification portion of the answer sheet.

- Read the inside back cover of the test book (page 87).

- Note the time and begin testing.

Once you have completed the test, determine your score and evaluate your performance, following the procedures outlined in the following two sections. If you find you are not doing well on any of the question types, review the relevant sample questions and explanations. Once this process is completed, review the full-length test with explanations. The explanations provide a basis for the underlying logic of the correct or best answer choices. Rationales are provided for all possible answer choices for the analytical and verbal tests. For the quantitative tests, the best answer choices are accompanied by solutions or quantitative explanations. When you are ready, take the second test following the same procedures as you did with the first. Repeat the process of scoring and evaluation to determine if your practice proved beneficial. If you still note weaknesses, review again those sample questions and explanations and undertake whatever further study and review you consider necessary. When you are ready to take the third test, again try to simulate actual testing conditions. Take the test, score your answer sheet, and convert the scores. These scores are the best estimate of what your performance might be if you take the General Test in the near future.

Research on the General Test shows that scores often rise by 20 to 30 points as a result of taking the test more than once, although scores of some examinees do decline. The possible significance of this finding is tempered by the observation that repeaters are typically a self-selected group who believe that repeating the test will increase their scores. However, by preparing to take the General Test as suggested here, you may be able to do better than you would if you took the test without any initial preparation.

HOW TO SCORE YOUR PRACTICE TEST

On the page following each test is a list of the correct answers. Match your answer to each question against the answer given in the list, crossing out questions you answered incorrectly or omitted. For test GR90-13, add the number of your correct answers in Sections 3 and 6 to obtain your raw verbal score, in Sections 1 and 4 to obtain your raw quantitative score, and in Sections 2 and 5 to obtain your raw analytical ability score. For test GR90-14, add the number of your correct answers in Sections 1 and 7 to obtain your raw verbal score, in Sections 2 and 5 to obtain your raw quantitative score, and in Sections 3 and 4 to obtain your raw analytical ability score. For GR90-15, add the number of your correct answers in Sections 3 and 5 to obtain your raw verbal score, in Sections 2 and 6 to obtain your raw quantitative score, and in Sections 1 and 4 to obtain your raw analytical ability score. In the conversion table for each test, you will find the scaled scores that correspond to your raw scores on the test. Convert your raw scores to scaled scores.

EVALUATING YOUR PERFORMANCE

To evaluate your performance, you may compare your scaled scores with those of others who have taken the General Test at GRE test centers between October 1, 1986, and September 30, 1989. The score conversion tables on pages 90, 248, and 294 indicate for each scaled score shown, the percentages of examinees who earned lower scores. For example, in the table on page 90, in the percent column next to the verbal ability scaled score 460 is the percent 44. This means that 44 percent of the examinees tested between October 1986 and September 1989 earned verbal ability scores below 460. For each score you earned on this practice test, note the percent of GRE examinees who earned lower scores. This is a reasonable indication of your rank among GRE General Test examinees if you follow the test-taking suggestions in this practice book.

The P+ number to the right of each correct answer is based on the percent of examinees who actually took that edition of the test and answered the question correctly. (This percent, however, has been adjusted so that it is an estimate of the P+ that would have been obtained if all examinees tested between October 1986 and September 1989 had had the opportunity to answer the question.) This information enables you to see how other examinees performed on each question. It can also help identify content areas in which you need more practice and review.

It is important to realize that ability patterns differ for people who have different interests and experience. The second table on page 294 shows you the average scores for people in various categories of intended graduate major fields. You can see that those whose interests lie in the physical sciences, which are highly mathematical, generally have relatively high scores in quantitative ability, whereas those interested in the humanities generally have relatively high verbal scores. Find the major field category most closely related to your career goal to see how your performance compares with that of others who are striving for similar goals.

ADDITIONAL INFORMATION

If you have any questions about any of the information in this book, please write to:

Graduate Record Examinations
Educational Testing Service
P.O. Box 6000
Princeton, NJ 08541-6000

TEST PREPARATION MATERIAL

Purpose of the GRE General Test

The GRE General Test measures certain developed verbal, quantitative, and analytical abilities that are important for academic achievement. In doing so, the test necessarily reflects the opportunities and efforts that have contributed to the development of those abilities.

The General Test is only one of several means of evaluating likely success in graduate school. It is not intended to measure inherent intellectual capacity or intelligence. Neither is it intended to measure creativity, motivation, perseverance, or social worth. The test does, however, make it possible to compare students with different backgrounds. A GRE score of 500, for example, has the same meaning whether earned by a student at a small, private liberal arts college or by a student at a large public university.

Because several different forms (or editions) of the test are in active use, all students do not receive exactly the same test edition. However, all editions measure the same skills and meet the same specifications for content and difficulty. The scores from different editions are made comparable to one another by a statistical procedure known as equating. This process makes it possible to assure that all reported scores of a given value denote the same level of developed ability regardless of which edition of the test is taken.

Since students have wide-ranging backgrounds, interests, and skills, the *verbal sections* of the General Test use questions from diverse areas of experience. The areas range from the activities of daily life to broad categories of academic interest such as the sciences, social studies, and the humanities. Knowledge of high school level arithmetic, plane geometry, and algebra provides adequate preparation for the *quantitative sections* of the test. Questions in the *analytical sections* measure analytical skills developed in virtually all fields of study. No formal training in logic or methods of analysis is needed to do well in these sections.

How the Test is Developed

The General Test is composed of questions formulated by specialists in various fields. Each question is reviewed by several independent critics and revised if necessary. New questions are pretested in actual tests under standard testing conditions.

Questions appearing in a test for the first time are analyzed for usefulness and weaknesses; they are not used in computing scores. Questions that perform satisfactorily become part of a pool from which a new edition of the General Test will be assembled at a future date. Those that do not perform well are discarded or are rewritten to correct the flaws and tried out again.

When a General Test has been assembled, it is reviewed by other subject matter and test specialists from inside and outside ETS. After any problems raised in these reviews have been resolved, the test goes to a test editor, who may make further suggestions for change. Individual test questions and the test as a whole are reviewed to eliminate language, symbols, or content considered to be potentially offensive or inappropriate for major subgroups of the test-taking population, or serve to perpetuate any negative attitude that may be conveyed to these subgroups.

All reviewers except the editors, copyreaders, and proofreaders must attempt to answer each question without the help of the answer key. Thus, each reviewer "takes the test," uninfluenced by knowledge of what the question writer or test assembler believed each answer should be. The answer key is certified as official only after the reviewers have agreed independently on the best answer for each question.

The extensive procedure described above has been developed to assure that every question in the General Test is appropriate and useful and that the combination of questions is satisfactory. Even so, the appraisal is not complete until after the new edition has been administered and subjected to a rigorous item analysis to see whether each question yields the expected results.

This analysis may reveal that a question is ambiguous, requires knowledge beyond the scope of the test, or is inappropriate for the total group or a particular subgroup of examinees taking the test. Answers to such a question are not used in computing scores.

Description of the General Test

In this description, several examples of each type of question included in the verbal, quantitative, and analytical measures of the GRE General Test are discussed, and explanations of the correct answers are provided.

Verbal Ability

The verbal ability measure is designed to test one's ability to reason with words in solving problems. Reasoning effectively in a verbal medium depends primarily upon the ability to discern, comprehend, and analyze relationships among words or groups of words and within larger units of discourse such as sentences and written passages. Such factors as knowledge of words and practice in reading will, of course, define the limits within which one can reason using these tools.

The verbal measure consists of four question types: analogies, antonyms, sentence completions, and reading comprehension sets. The examples of verbal questions in this section do not reflect precisely the difficulty range of the verbal measure. A greater number of difficult questions than would be encountered in the test have been included to provide practice in approaching more complex verbal questions.

Analogies

Analogy questions test the ability to recognize relationships among words and the concepts they represent and to recognize when these relationships are parallel. The process of eliminating four incorrect answer choices requires one to formulate and then analyze the relationships linking six pairs of words (the given pair and the five answer choices) and to recognize which answer pair is most nearly analogous to the given pair. Some examples of relationships that might be found in analogy questions are kind, size, contiguity, or degree.

Some approaches that may be helpful in answering analogy questions:

- Before looking at the answer choices, try to establish a precise relationship between the words in the given pair. It is usually helpful to express that relationship in a phrase or sentence; for example, the relationship between the word pair THRIFTY : MISERLY could be expressed as "to be *miserly* is to be *thrifty* to an excessive degree." Next, look for the answer choice with the pair of words whose relationship is closest to that of the given pair and can be expressed in a similar fashion.

- Occasionally, more than one of the answer choices may seem at first to express a relationship similar to that of the given pair. Go back to the given pair and try to state the relationship more precisely or identify some aspect of the relationship between the given pair of words that is paralleled in only *one* answer choice pair.

- Remember that a single word can have several different meanings. If you are unable to establish a relationship between the given pair or to find a parallel relationship among the answer choice pairs, check to be sure you have not overlooked a possible second meaning for one of the words.

- *Never* decide on the best answer without reading *all* the answer choices. If you do not read all the answer choices, you may miss an answer choice that would have appeared superior to the choice you made or might have prompted you to reevaluate your understanding of the question.

■ Practice recognizing and formulating relationships between word pairs. You can do this with the following sample questions and with the analogy questions in the practice test in this booklet.

Directions: In each of the following questions, a related pair of words or phrases is followed by five lettered pairs of words or phrases. Select the lettered pair that best expresses a relationship similar to that expressed in the original pair.

1. COLOR : SPECTRUM ::   (A) tone : scale   (B) sound : waves
   (C) verse : poem   (D) dimension : space   (E) cell : organism

The relationship between *color* and *spectrum* is not merely that of part to whole, in which case (E) or even (C) might be defended as correct. A *spectrum* is made up of a progressive, graduated series of colors, as a *scale* is of a progressive, graduated sequence of tones. Thus, (A) is correct. Here, the best answer must be selected from a group of fairly close choices.

2. ABDICATION : THRONE ::   (A) paradox : argument
   (B) competition : match   (C) defeat : election
   (D) bequest : will   (E) resignation : office

The relationship between *abdication* and *throne* is easy to perceive and only the correct answer, (E), expresses a similar relationship. (C) is incorrect because *defeat* is not voluntary, as are *abdication* and *resignation* and because *election,* the process of attaining a particular status, is not parallel to *throne* and *office.*

3. DESICCATE : MOISTURE :: (A) pulverize : dust   (B) varnish : deterioration
   (C) shatter : shards   (D) bend : contents   (E) darken : light

To *desiccate* an object is to cause it to dry up by depriving it of *moisture.* Among the answer choices, only (E) has a similar relationship between its two words: to *darken* an object is to make it darker by depriving it of *light.* In the other four choices, the first words, *pulverize, varnish, shatter,* and *bend,* are parallel to *desiccate* in that they describe actions that alter the condition of an object, but the second word is not something of which an object is deprived as a result of the action the first word describes. In (A) and (C), the second words, *dust* and *shards,* are the results of pulverizing and shattering, respectively. *Deterioration* in (B) may be prevented through varnishing, and *contents* in (D) bears no relationship to bending that resembles the relationship between *desiccate* and *moisture.*

4. HEADLONG : FORETHOUGHT ::   (A) barefaced : shame
   (B) mealymouthed : talent   (C) heartbroken : emotion
   (D) levelheaded : resolve   (E) singlehanded : ambition

The difficulty of this question probably derives primarily from the complexity of the relationship between *headlong* and *forethought* rather than from any inherent difficulty in the words. Analysis of the relationship between *headlong* and *forethought* reveals the following: an action or behavior that is *headlong* reveals lack of *forethought.* Only answer choice (A) displays the same relationship between its two terms.

Antonyms

Although antonym questions test knowledge of vocabulary more directly than do any of the other verbal question types, the purpose of the antonym questions is to measure not merely the strength of one's vocabulary but also the ability to reason from a given concept to its opposite. Antonyms may require only rather general knowledge of a word or they may require one to make fine distinctions among answer choices. Antonyms are generally confined to nouns, verbs, and adjectives; answer choices may be single words or phrases.

Some approaches that may be helpful in answering antonym questions:

- Remember that you are looking for the word that is the most nearly *opposite* to the given word; you are *not* looking for a synonym. Since many words do not have a precise opposite, you must look for the answer choice that expresses a concept *most nearly* opposite to that of the given word. For this reason, antonym questions are not measures of rote vocabulary knowledge; rather, these questions ask you to evaluate shades of meaning and the interaction of meaning between words.

- In some cases more than one of the answer choices may appear at first to be opposite to the given word. Questions that require you to make fine distinctions among two or more answer choices are best handled by defining more precisely or in greater detail the meaning of the given word.

- It is often useful, in weighing answer choices, to make up a sentence using the given word; if you do not know the precise dictionary meaning of a word but have a general sense of how the word might be used, try to make up a phrase or sentence with the word. Substituting the answer choices in the phrase or sentence and seeing which best "fits," in that it reverses the meaning or tone of the sentence or phrase, may help you determine the best answer.

- Remember that a particular word may have more than one meaning, so if you are unable to find an answer choice that appears opposite to the given word, examine all the words for possible second meanings.

- Use your knowledge of root, prefix, and suffix meanings to help you determine the meanings of words with which you are not entirely familiar.

Directions: Each question below consists of a word printed in capital letters followed by five lettered words or phrases. Choose the lettered word or phrase that is most nearly *opposite* in meaning to the word in capital letters. Since some of the questions require you to distinguish fine shades of meaning, be sure to consider all the choices before deciding which one is best.

5. DIFFUSE : (A) concentrate   (B) contend   (C) imply
    (D) pretend   (E) rebel

The answer is (A). *Diffuse* means to permit or cause to spread out; only (A) presents an idea that is in any way opposite to *diffuse*.

6. COINCIDENCE: (A) depletion (B) incongruity (C) pessimism (D) ill fortune (E) lack of ideas

One meaning of *coincidence* is being in harmony or accord; another is corresponding in nature, character, or function. *Incongruity,* the correct answer, means lack of harmony or lack of conformity. Answer choice (D) may seem plausible at first glance since a *coincidence* of events is often a pleasant chance occurrence ("good luck" as opposed to "bad luck"), but careful reflection reveals that a *coincidence* is not necessarily a positive phenomenon.

7. MULTIFARIOUS: (A) deprived of freedom (B) deprived of comfort (C) lacking space (D) lacking stability (E) lacking diversity

Multifarious means having or occurring in great variety, so the correct answer is (E). Even if one is not entirely familiar with the meaning of *multifarious*, it is possible to use the clue provided by "multi-" to help find the right answer to this question.

8. PARSIMONIOUS: (A) initial (B) vegetative (C) prodigal (D) affluent (E) impromptu

The answer to this question is (C); *parsimonious* means frugal to the point of stinginess, and *prodigal,* which means extravagant to the point of wastefulness, is the only answer choice opposite in meaning. At first, answer choice (D), *affluent,* may seem plausible in that it may be thought that wealth is an opposite concept to frugality — but it is well known that not all wealthy persons are generous.

Sentence Completions

The purpose of the sentence completion questions is to measure the ability to recognize words or phrases that both logically and stylistically complete the meaning of a sentence. In deciding which of five words or sets of words can best be substituted for blank spaces in a sentence, one must analyze the relationships among the component parts of the incomplete sentence. One must consider each answer choice and decide which completes the sentence in such a way that the sentence has a logically satisfying meaning and can be read as a stylistically integrated whole.

Sentence completion questions provide a context within which to analyze the function of words as they relate to and combine with one another to form a meaningful unit of discourse.

Some approaches that may be helpful in answering sentence completion questions:

■ Read the entire sentence carefully before you consider the answer choices; be sure you understand the ideas expressed in the sentence and examine the sentence for possible indications of tone (irony, humor, and the like).

- Before reading the answer choices you may find it helpful to fill in the blanks with a word or words of your own that complete the meaning of the sentence. Then examine the answer choices to see if any of them parallels your own completion of the sentence.

- Pay attention to grammatical clues in the sentence. For example, words like *although* and *nevertheless* indicate that some qualification or opposition is taking place in the sentence, whereas *moreover* implies an intensification or support of some idea in the sentence. Pay attention also to the style of, and choice of words in, the sentence; sometimes determining the best answer depends in whole or in part on considerations of stylistic consistency among the parts of the sentence.

- If a sentence has two blanks, be sure that *both* parts of your answer choice fit logically and stylistically into the sentence. Do not choose an answer on the basis of the fit of the first word alone.

- When you have chosen an answer, read the complete sentence through to check that it has acquired a logically and stylistically satisfying meaning.

Directions: **Each sentence below has one or two blanks, each blank indicating that something has been omitted. Beneath the sentence are five lettered words or sets of words. Choose the word or set of words for each blank that *best* fits the meaning of the sentence as a whole.**

9. **Early ------- of hearing loss is ------- by the fact that the other senses are able to compensate for moderate amounts of loss, so that people frequently do not know that their hearing is imperfect.**

   (A) discovery . . indicated
   (B) development . . prevented
   (C) detection . . complicated
   (D) treatment . . facilitated
   (E) incidence . . corrected

The statement that the other senses compensate for partial loss of hearing indicates that the hearing loss is not *prevented* or *corrected*; therefore, choices (B) and (E) can be eliminated. Furthermore, the ability to compensate for hearing loss certainly does not facilitate the early *treatment* (D) or the early *discovery* (A) of hearing loss. It is reasonable, however, that early *detection* of hearing loss is *complicated* by the ability to compensate for it. The correct answer is (C).

10. **The ------- science of seismology has grown just enough so that the first overly bold theories have been -------.**

   (A) magnetic . . accepted
   (B) fledgling . . refuted
   (C) revolutionary . . analyzed
   (D) predictive . . protected
   (E) exploratory . . recalled

At first reading, there may appear to be several answer choices that "make sense" when substituted in the blanks of the sentence. (A) and (D) can be dismissed fairly readily when it is seen that *accepted* and *protected* are not compatible with *overly bold* in the sentence. The sentence yielded by (C) is logically more acceptable but not as strong as the sentences yielded by (B) and (E). Of these two latter choices, (B) is superior on stylistic grounds: theories are not *recalled* (E), and *fledgling* (B) reflects the idea of growth present in the sentence.

11. If her characters are still being written about as unfathomable riddles, it is to be attributed more to a human passion for ------- than to dubious complexities of her art.

(A) conundrums **(B) platitudes** **(C) scapegoats**
(D) euphemisms **(E) stereotypes**

The answer to this question is (A). While any of the answer choices may be argued to be an object of human passion, only *conundrums* enables the sentence *as a whole* to acquire a coherent meaning. It is necessary, in choosing an answer, to complete the sentence in such a way as to make clear why the writer's characters are seen as *unfathomable riddles*. A human penchant for *conundrums*, or puzzling questions whose answers can only be conjectural, will account for this.

Reading Comprehension

The purpose of the reading comprehension questions is to measure the ability to read with understanding, insight, and discrimination. This type of question explores the examinee's ability to analyze a written passage from several perspectives, including the ability to recognize both explicitly stated elements in the passage and assumptions underlying statements or arguments in the passage as well as the implications of those statements or arguments. Because the written passage upon which reading comprehension questions are based presents a sustained discussion of a particular topic, there is ample context for analyzing a variety of relationships; for example, the function of a word in relation to a larger segment of the passage, the relationships among the various ideas in the passage, or the relation of the author to his or her topic or to the audience.

There are six types of reading comprehension questions. These types focus on (1) the main idea or primary purpose of the passage; (2) information explicitly stated in the passage; (3) information or ideas implied or suggested by the author; (4) possible application of the author's ideas to other situations; (5) the author's logic, reasoning, or persuasive techniques; and (6) the tone of the passage or the author's attitude as it is revealed in the language used.

In each edition of the General Test, there are two relatively long reading comprehension passages, each providing the basis for answering seven or eight questions, and two relatively short passages, each providing the basis for answering three or four questions. The four passages are drawn from four different subject matter areas: the humanities, the social sciences, the biological sciences, and the physical sciences.

Some approaches that may be helpful in answering reading comprehension questions:

■ Since reading passages are drawn from many different disciplines and sources, you should not expect to be familiar with the material in all the passages. However, you should not be discouraged by encountering material with which you are not familiar; questions are to be answered on the basis of the information provided in the passage, and you are not expected to rely on outside knowledge, which you may or may not have, of a particular topic. You may, however, want to save for last a passage that seems particularly difficult or unfamiliar.

■ There are different strategies for approaching reading comprehension questions; you must decide which works most effectively for you. You might try different strategies as you do the reading comprehension questions in the practice test in this booklet. Some different strategies are: reading the passage very closely and then proceeding to the questions; skimming the passage, reading quickly through the questions, and then rereading the passage closely; and reading the questions first, then reading the passage closely. You may find that different strategies work better for different kinds of passages; for example, it might be helpful with a difficult or unfamiliar passage to read through the questions first.

■ Whatever strategy you choose, you should analyze the passage carefully before answering the questions. As with any kind of close and thoughtful reading, you should be sensitive to clues that will help you understand less explicit aspects of the passage. Try to separate main ideas from supporting ideas or evidence; try also to separate the author's own ideas or attitudes from information he or she is simply presenting. It is important to note transitions from one idea to the next and to examine the relationships among the different ideas or parts of the passage: Are they contrasting? Are they complementary?, for example. You should consider both the points the author makes and the conclusions he or she draws and also how and why those points are made or conclusions drawn.

■ You may find it helpful to underline or mark key parts of the passage. For example, you might underline main ideas or important arguments or you might circle transitional words that will help you map the logical structure of the passage (*although, nevertheless, correspondingly,* and the like) or descriptive words that will help you identify the author's attitude toward a particular idea or person.

■ Read each question carefully and be certain that you understand exactly what is being asked.

- *Always* read all the answer choices before selecting the best answer.

- The best answer is the one that most accurately and most completely answers the question being posed. Be careful not to pick an answer choice simply because it is a true statement; be careful also not to be misled by answer choices that are only partially true or only partially satisfy the problem posed in the question.

- Answer the questions on the basis of the information provided in the passage and do not rely on outside knowledge. Your own views or opinions may sometimes conflict with the views expressed or the information provided in the passage; be sure that you work within the context provided by the passage. You should not expect to agree with everything you encounter in reading passages.

Directions: **The passage is followed by questions based on its content. After reading the passage, choose the best answer to each question. Answer all questions following the passage on the basis of what is *stated* or *implied* in the passage.**

Picture-taking is a technique both for annexing the objective world and for expressing the singular self. Photographs depict objective realities that already exist, though only the camera can disclose them. And they depict an individual
(5) photographer's temperament, discovering itself through the camera's cropping of reality. That is, photography has two antithetical ideals: in the first, photography is about the world and the photographer is a mere observer who counts for little; but in the second, photography is the instrument of intrepid,
(10) questing subjectivity and the photographer is all.

These conflicting ideals arise from a fundamental uneasiness on the part of both photographers and viewers of photographs toward the aggressive component in "taking" a picture. Accordingly, the ideal of a photographer as observer is
(15) attractive because it implicitly denies that picture-taking is an aggressive act. The issue, of course, is not so clear-cut. What photographers do cannot be characterized as simply predatory or as simply, and essentially, benevolent. As a consequence, one ideal of picture-taking or the other is always being rediscovered
(20) and championed.

An important result of the coexistence of these two ideals is a recurrent ambivalence toward photography's means. Whatever the claims that photography might make to be a form of personal expression on a par with painting, its originality is
(25) inextricably linked to the powers of a machine. The steady growth of these powers has made possible the extraordinary informativeness and imaginative formal beauty of many photographs, like Harold Edgerton's high-speed photographs of a bullet hitting its target or of the swirls and eddies of a tennis

(30) stroke. But as cameras become more sophisticated, more
automated, some photographers are tempted to disarm
themselves or to suggest that they are not really armed, prefer-
ring to submit themselves to the limits imposed by premodern
camera technology because a cruder, less high-powered

(35) machine is thought to give more interesting or emotive results,
to leave more room for creative accident. For example, it has
been virtually a point of honor for many photographers, including Walker Evans and Cartier-Bresson, to refuse to use modern
equipment. These photographers have come to doubt the value

(40) of the camera as an instrument of "fast seeing." Cartier-
Bresson, in fact, claims that the modern camera may see too
fast.

This ambivalence toward photographic means determines
trends in taste. The cult of the future (of faster and faster

(45) seeing) alternates over time with the wish to return to a purer
past — when images had a handmade quality. This nostalgia
for some pristine state of the photographic enterprise is
currently widespread and underlies the present-day enthusiasm
for daguerreotypes and the work of forgotten nineteenth-

(50) century provincial photographers. Photographers and viewers
of photographs, it seems, need periodically to resist their own
knowingness.

12. According to the passage, the two antithetical ideals of photography
differ primarily in the

(A) value that each places on the beauty of the finished product
(B) emphasis that each places on the emotional impact of the finished
product
(C) degree of technical knowledge that each requires of the
photographer
(D) extent of the power that each requires of the photographer's
equipment
(E) way in which each defines the role of the photographer

The answer to this question is (E). Photography's two ideals are presented in
lines 6-10. The main emphasis in the description of these two ideals is on the
relationship of the photographer to the enterprise of photography, with the
photographer described in the one as a passive observer and in the other as an
active questioner. (E) identifies this key feature in the description of the two
ideals — the way in which each ideal conceives or defines the role of the
photographer in photography. (A) through (D) present aspects of photography
that are mentioned in the passage, but none of these choices represents a primary
difference between the two ideals of photography.

13. **According to the passage, interest among photographers in each of photography's two ideals can be described as**

    (A) rapidly changing
    (B) cyclically recurring
    (C) steadily growing
    (D) unimportant to the viewers of photographs
    (E) unrelated to changes in technology

This question requires one to look for comments in the passage about the nature of photographers' interest in the two ideals of photography. While the whole passage is, in a sense, about the response of photographers to these ideals, there are elements in the passage that comment specifically on this issue. Lines 18-20 tell us that the two ideals alternate in terms of their perceived relevance and value, that each ideal has periods of popularity and of neglect. These lines support (B). Lines 21-22 tell us that the two ideals affect attitudes toward "photography's means," that is, the technology of the camera; (E), therefore, cannot be the correct answer. In lines 43-46, attitudes toward photographic means (which result from the two ideals) are said to alternate over time; these lines provide further support for B. (A) can be eliminated because, although the passage tells us that the interest of photographers in each of the ideals fluctuates over time, it nowhere indicates that this fluctuation or change is rapid. Nor does the passage say anywhere that interest in these ideals is growing; the passage *does* state that the powers of the camera are steadily growing (lines 25-26), but this does not mean that interest in the two ideals is growing. Thus (C) can be eliminated. (D) can be eliminated because the passage nowhere states that reactions to the ideals are either important or unimportant to viewers' concerns. Thus (B) is the correct answer.

14. **Which of the following statements would be most likely to begin the paragraph immediately following the passage?**

    (A) Photographers, as a result of their heightened awareness of time, are constantly trying to capture events and actions that are fleeting.
    (B) Thus the cult of the future, the worship of machines and speed, is firmly established in spite of efforts to the contrary by some photographers.
    (C) The rejection of technical knowledge, however, can never be complete and photography cannot for any length of time pretend that it has no weapons.
    (D) The point of honor involved in rejecting complex equipment is, however, of no significance to the viewer of a photograph.
    (E) Consequently the impulse to return to the past through images that suggest a handwrought quality is nothing more than a passing fad.

Answering this question requires one to think about where the discussion in the passage as a whole is moving and in particular where the final paragraph points. The last two paragraphs discuss the effect of the two ideals of photography on photographers' attitudes toward the camera. The final paragraph describes two such attitudes, or trends in taste (one in which the technology of today's camera is valued and one in which it is seen as a handicap), and tells us that these two attitudes alternate, with the second currently predominating. (B) and (E) can be eliminated because they both suggest that the first attitude will prevail, thus contradicting information in the last paragraph. (A) is not connected in any way to the discussion of attitudes toward the use of the present-day camera and so is not a good choice. (D) appears related to the previous material in the passage in that it discusses the second attitude; however, it introduces an idea — consideration of the viewer — that has not been developed in the passage. (C), the correct answer, is superior not only because it comments on the second attitude but also because it reiterates the idea that neither attitude will prevail. (C) is strengthened through its stylistic relation to earlier elements in the passage: the use of the word *weapons* recalls the references in lines 31 and 32 to photographers as *armed* with cameras.

Quantitative Ability

The quantitative sections of the General Test are designed to measure basic mathematical skills, understanding of elementary mathematical concepts, and ability to reason quantitatively and to solve problems in a quantitative setting. The mathematics required does not extend beyond that assumed to be common to the mathematics background of almost all examinees. The questions include three broad content areas: arithmetic, algebra, and geometry. Although a question in these areas may be posed in either English or metric units of measure, neither the knowledge required for converting units in one system to units in another system, nor the ability to convert from one unit to another in the same system, is tested. If an answer to a question is expected to be in a unit of measure different from the unit in which the question is posed, a relationship between the units is provided unless the relationship is a common one, such as minutes to hours.

Arithmetic

Questions classified as *arithmetic* include those involving the following topics: arithmetic operations (addition, subtraction, multiplication, division, and nonnegative powers) on rational numbers, estimation, percent, average, interpretation of graphs and tables, properties of numbers (such as those relating to odd and even integers, primes, and divisibility), factoring, and elementary counting and probability.

Some facts about numbers that might be helpful. An odd integer power of a negative number is negative, and an even integer power is positive; for example, $(-2)^3 = -8$, but $(-2)^2 = 4$.

Squaring a number between 0 and 1 (or raising it to a higher power) results in a smaller number; for example, $\left(\dfrac{1}{3}\right)^2 = \dfrac{1}{9}$, and $(0.5)^3 = 0.125$.

The sum and product of even and odd integers will be even or odd depending on the operation and the kinds of integers; for example, the sum of an odd integer and an even integer is odd.

If an integer P is a divisor (or a factor) of another integer N, then N is the product of P and another integer, and N is said to be a multiple of P; for example, 3 is a divisor (or a factor) of 6, and 6 is a multiple of 3.

A *prime* number is an integer that has only two distinct positive divisors, 1 and itself; for example, 2, 3, 5, 7, and 11 are primes, but 9 is not a prime because it has three positive divisors: 1, 3, and 9.

The sum and product of signed numbers will be positive or negative depending on the operation and the kinds of numbers; for example, the product of a negative number and a positive number is negative.

For any two numbers on the number line, the number on the left is less than the number on the right; for example, $2 < 3$ and $-4 < -3$.

The radical sign "$\sqrt{}$" means "the nonnegative square root of." For example, $\sqrt{0} = 0$ and $\sqrt{4} = 2$.

If n is a positive integer, then "x^n" denotes the product of n factors of x; for example, 3^4 means $3 \cdot 3 \cdot 3 \cdot 3 = 81$.

Note also that $3^0 = 1$, and that division by zero is undefined; that is, $\dfrac{5}{0}$ has no meaning.

Algebra

Questions classified as *algebra* include those involving operations with radical expressions, factoring and simplifying algebraic expressions, equations and inequalities, and absolute value. The skills required include the ability to solve first and second degree equations and inequalities, and simultaneous equations; the ability to read a word problem and set up the necessary equations or inequalities to solve it; and the ability to apply basic algebraic skills to solve unfamiliar problems. In general, the algebra required does not extend beyond that usually covered in a first-year high school course, and it is expected that examinees will be familiar with conventional symbolism, such as:
$x < y$ (x is less than y), $x \neq y$ (x is not equal to y),
and $|x|$, which is equal to x if $x \geq 0$ and $-x$ if $x < 0$; for example,
$|8| = 8$ and $|-8| = -(-8) = 8$. Nonstandard notation is used only when it is explicitly defined in a particular question.

Some facts about algebra that might be helpful. If $ab = 0$, then either $a = 0$ or $b = 0$; for example, if $(x - 1)(x + 2) = 0$, it follows that either $x - 1 = 0$ or $x + 2 = 0$. Therefore, $x = 1$ or $x = -2$.

Adding a number to or subtracting a number from both sides of an equation preserves the equality. Similarly, multiplying or dividing both sides of an equation by a nonzero number preserves the equality. Similar rules apply to inequalities, with the exception that in the case of multiplying or dividing by a *negative* number, the inequality reverses. For example: multiplying the inequality $3x - 4 > 5$ by 4 yields the inequality $12x - 16 > 20$. However, multiplying that same inequality by -4 yields $-12x + 16 < -20$.

The following rules for exponents are useful. If r, s, x, and y are positive integers, then

(a)	$x^r \cdot x^s = x^{r+s}$	; e.g.	$3^2 \cdot 3^4 = 3^6 = 729$
(b)	$x^r \cdot y^r = (xy)^r$	; e.g.	$3^4 \cdot 2^4 = 6^4 = 1,296$
(c)	$(x^r)^s = x^{rs}$	; e.g.	$(2^3)^4 = 2^{12} = 4,096$
(d)	$\dfrac{x^r}{x^s} = x^{r-s}$	; e.g.	$\dfrac{4^5}{4^2} = 4^3 = 64$

Geometry

Questions classified as *geometry* include those involving the following topics: properties associated with parallel lines, circles and their inscribed and central angles, triangles, rectangles, other polygons, measurement-related concepts of area, perimeter, volume, the Pythagorean Theorem, and angle measure in degrees. Knowledge of simple coordinate geometry and special triangles such as isosceles, equilateral, and $30° - 60° - 90°$ triangles are also tested. The ability to construct proofs is not measured.

It is expected that examinees will be familiar with the conventional symbolism used in elementary geometry, such as the following: $\parallel$ (this means *is parallel to*), $\perp$ (this means *is perpendicular to*), and

(this means that $\angle ABC$ is a right angle).

Some facts about geometry that might be helpful. If two lines intersect, the vertical angles are equal; for example, in the figure

, $x = y$.

If two parallel lines are intersected by a third line, some of the angles formed are equal; for example, in the figure

where $\ell_1 \parallel \ell_2$, $y = x = z$.

The number of degrees of arc in a circle is 360; for example, in the figure

 if $x = 60$, then the length of arc ABC is $\dfrac{60}{360}$ of the circumference of the circle.

The sum of the degree measures of the angles of a triangle is 180.

The volume of a rectangular solid or of a right circular cylinder is the product of the area of the base and the height; for example, the volume of a cylinder with base of radius 2 and height 5 is $\pi (2^2)(5) = 20\pi$.

The square of the length of the hypotenuse of a right triangle is equal to the sum of the squares of the lengths of the two legs.

The coordinates of a point (x,y) give the location of the point in the coordinate plane; for example, the point $(2, -3)$ is located in the fourth quadrant 2 units to the right of the Y-axis and 3 units below the X-axis.

The sides of a $45° - 45° - 90°$ triangle are in the ratio $1 : 1 : \sqrt{2}$, and the sides of a $30° - 60° - 90°$ triangle are in the ratio $1 : \sqrt{3} : 2$.

Drawing in lines that are not shown in a figure can sometimes help in solving a geometry problem; for example, by drawing the dashed lines in the pentagon

, the number of degrees in the pentagon can be found

by adding up the number of degrees in the three triangles.

The quantitative measure employs three types of questions: quantitative comparison, discrete quantitative, and data interpretation. Pacing yourself on all of these question types is important. Do not spend an excessive amount of time pondering over problems you find difficult. Go on to the next question and, if time permits, come back to the difficult questions when you have completed the section.

The following information on numbers and figures applies to all questions in the quantitative sections.

Numbers: **All numbers used are real numbers.**

Figures: **Position of points, angles, regions, etc., can be assumed to be in the order shown, and angle measures can be assumed to be positive.**

Lines shown as straight can be assumed to be straight.

Figures can be assumed to lie in a plane unless otherwise indicated.

Figures that accompany questions are intended to provide information useful in answering the questions. However, unless a note states that a figure is drawn to scale, you should solve these problems NOT by estimating sizes by sight or by measurement, but by using your knowledge of mathematics.

Quantitative Comparison

The quantitative comparison questions test the ability to reason quickly and accurately about the relative sizes of two quantities or to perceive that not enough information is provided to make such a decision. To solve a quantitative comparison problem, you compare the quantities given in two columns, Column A and Column B, and decide whether one quantity is greater than the other, whether the two quantities are equal, or whether the relationship cannot be determined from the information given. Some questions only require some manipulation to determine which of the quantities is greater; other questions require you to reason more or to think of special cases in which the relative sizes of the quantities reverse.

The following strategies might help in answering quantitative comparison questions.

- Do not waste time performing needless computations in order to eventually compare two specific numbers. Simplify or transform one or both of the given quantities only as much as is necessary to determine which quantity is greater or whether the two quantities are equal. Once you have determined that one quantity is greater than the other, do not take time to find the exact sizes of the quantities. Answer and go on to the next question.

- If both quantities being compared involve no variables, then the correct answer can never be (D), which states that the relationship cannot be determined. The answer is then reduced to three choices.

- Consider all kinds of numbers before you make a decision. As soon as you establish that quantity A is greater in one case while quantity B is greater in another case, choose answer (D) immediately and move on to the next comparison.

- Geometric figures may not be drawn to scale. Comparisons should be made based on knowledge of mathematics rather than appearance. However, you can sometimes find a clue by sketching another figure in your test book. Try to visualize the parts of a figure that are fixed by the information given and the parts that are collapsible and changeable. If a figure can flow into other shapes and sizes while conforming to given information, the answer is probably (D).

Directions for quantitative comparison questions and some examples with explanations follow.

Directions: Each of the following questions consists of two quantities, one in Column A and one in Column B. You are to compare the two quantities and choose

- **A   if the quantity in Column A is greater;**
- **B   if the quantity in Column B is greater;**
- **C   if the two quantities are equal;**
- **D   if the relationship cannot be determined from the information given.**

Note: **Since there are only four choices, NEVER MARK (E).**

In a question, information concerning one or both of the quantities to be compared is centered above the two columns. A symbol that appears in both columns represents the same thing in Column A as it does in Column B.

	Column A	Column B	Sample Answers
Example 1:	2×6	$2 + 6$	● Ⓑ Ⓒ Ⓓ Ⓔ

Examples 2-4 refer to $\triangle PQR$.

| **Example 2:** | **PN** | **NQ** | Ⓐ Ⓑ Ⓒ ● Ⓔ |

(since equal measures cannot be assumed, even though PN and NQ appear equal)

| **Example 3:** | x | y | Ⓐ ● Ⓒ Ⓓ Ⓔ |

(since N is between P and Q)

| **Example 4:** | w + z | 180 | Ⓐ Ⓑ ● Ⓓ Ⓔ |

(since PQ is a straight line)

	Column A	Column B
15.	**9.8**	$\sqrt{100}$

$\sqrt{100}$ denotes 10, the positive square root of 100. (For any positive number x, $\sqrt{x}$ denotes the *positive* number whose square is x.) Since 10 is greater than 9.8, the correct answer is B. It is important not to confuse this question with a comparison of 9.8 and x where $x^2 = 100$. The latter comparison would yield D as the correct answer because $x^2 = 100$ implies that either $x = \sqrt{100}$ or $x = -\sqrt{100}$, and there is no way to determine which value x actually would have. However, this question asks for a comparison of 9.8 and $\sqrt{100}$, and $9.8 < \sqrt{100}$ for the reasons previously given.

Column A	Column B

16. $(-6)^4$ $(-6)^5$

Since $(-6)^4$ is the product of four negative factors and the product of an even number of negative numbers is positive, $(-6)^4$ is positive. Since the product of an odd number of negative numbers is negative, $(-6)^5$ is negative. Therefore $(-6)^4$ is greater than $(-6)^5$ since any positive number is greater than any negative number. The correct answer is A. Do not waste time determining that $(-6)^4 = 1,296$ and that $(-6)^5 = -7,776$. This information is not needed to make the comparison.

$$x + y = 10$$

$$x - y = 2$$

17. $x^2 - y^2$ **19**

Since $x^2 - y^2 = (x + y)(x - y)$ and, from the information given, $(x + y)(x - y) = 10 \cdot 2 = 20$, which is greater than 19, the correct answer is A. The two equations could be solved for x and y, giving $x = 6$ and $y = 4$, and then $x^2 - y^2$ could be computed, but this solution is more time-consuming.

18.   **The area of an equilateral triangle with side 6**   **The area of a right triangle with legs $\sqrt{3}$ and 9**

The area of a triangle is one-half the product of the lengths of the base and the altitude. In column A, the length of the altitude must first be determined. A sketch of the triangle may be helpful.

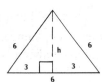

The altitude h divides the base of an equilateral triangle into two equal parts. From the Pythagorean Theorem, $h^2 + 3^2 = 6^2$ or $h = 3\sqrt{3}$. Therefore the area of the triangle in column A is $\frac{1}{2} \cdot 6 \cdot 3\sqrt{3} = 9\sqrt{3}$. In column B, the base and the altitude of the right triangle are the two legs, and therefore the area is $\frac{9\sqrt{3}}{2}$. Since $9\sqrt{3}$ is greater than $\frac{9\sqrt{3}}{2}$, the correct answer is A.

Column A	Column B

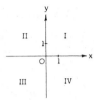

A point (x,y) is in region III.

19.   x   y

From the fact that point (x,y) is in region III, it is clear that x and y are both negative. However, since the location of the point within the region is not known, the relative sizes of x and y cannot be determined; for example, if the point is $(-3, -6)$, x > y but if the point is $(-6, -3)$, x < y. Thus the answer is D.

$$(273 \times 87) + q = 29,235$$
$$(273 \times 87) + p = 30,063$$

20.   p   q

It is not necessary to do a lot of computation to solve this problem. The sum of a number and q is less than the sum of the same number and p. Therefore q < p, and the answer is A.

$$x^2 = y^2 + 1$$

21.   x   y

From the given equation, it can be determined that $x^2 > y^2$; however, the relative sizes of x and y cannot be determined. For example, if y = 0, x could be 1 or –1 and, since there is no way to tell which number x is, the answer is D.

Discrete Quantitative

Each discrete question contains all the information needed for answering the question except for the basic mathematical knowledge assumed to be common to the backgrounds of all examinees. Many of these questions require little more than manipulation and very basic knowledge; others require the examinee to read, understand, and solve a problem that involves either an actual or an abstract situation.

The following strategies might be helpful in answering discrete quantitative questions.

- Read each question carefully to determine what information is given and what is being asked.

- Before attempting to answer a question, scan the answer choices; otherwise you may waste time putting answers in a form that is not given (for example, putting an answer in the form $\frac{\sqrt{2}}{2}$ when the options are given in the form $\frac{1}{\sqrt{2}}$ or finding the answer in decimal form, such as 0.25, when the choices are given in fractional form, such as $\frac{1}{4}$).

- For questions that require approximations, scan the answer choices to get some idea of the required closeness of approximation; otherwise, you may waste time on long computations when a short mental process would be sufficient (for example, finding 48 percent of a number when taking half of the number would give a close enough approximation).

Directions for discrete quantitative questions and some examples with explanations follow.

Directions: Each of the following questions has five answer choices. For each of these questions, select the best of the answer choices given.

22. **The average of x and y is 20. If z = 5, what is the average of x, y, and z?**

   (A) $8\frac{1}{3}$ (B) **10**   (C) $12\frac{1}{2}$ (D) **15**   (E) $17\frac{1}{2}$

Since the average of x and y is 20, $\frac{x+y}{2} = 20$ or x + y = 40. Thus x + y + z = x + y + 5 = 40 + 5 = 45 and therefore $\frac{x+y+z}{3} = \frac{45}{3} = 15$. The correct answer is D.

23. **Several years ago, Minnesota produced $\frac{2}{3}$ and Michigan $\frac{1}{6}$ of all the iron ore produced in the United States. If all the other states combined produced 18 million tons in a year, how many million tons did Minnesota produce that year?**

   (A) **27**   (B) **36**   (C) **54**   (D) **72**   (E) **162**

Since Minnesota produced $\frac{2}{3}$ and Michigan $\frac{1}{6}$ of all the iron ore produced in the United States, the two states together produced $\frac{5}{6}$ of the iron ore. Therefore the 18 million tons produced by the rest of the United States was $\frac{1}{6}$ of the total production. Thus the total United States production was $6 \cdot 18 = 108$ million tons, and Minnesota produced $\frac{2}{3}(108) = 72$ million tons. The correct answer is D.

24. Into how many segments, each 20 centimeters long, can a segment 5 meters long be divided? (1 meter = 100 centimeters)

(A) 20   (B) 25   (C) 45   (D) 50   (E) 80

Using the given information that there are 100 centimeters in a meter, it can be determined that there are 500 centimeters in 5 meters. The number of segments, each 20 centimeters long, into which a 500-centimeter segment can be divided is $\frac{500}{20} = 25$. The answer is B.

25. If $\dfrac{x}{3} - \dfrac{x}{6} + \dfrac{x}{9} - \dfrac{x}{12} = 1 - \dfrac{1}{2} + \dfrac{1}{3} - \dfrac{1}{4}$, then x =

(A) 3   (B) 1   (C) $\dfrac{1}{3}$ (D) $-\dfrac{1}{3}$ (E) –3

This problem can be solved without a lot of computation by factoring $\frac{x}{3}$ out of

the expression on the left side of the equation $\dfrac{x}{3} - \dfrac{x}{6} + \dfrac{x}{9} - \dfrac{x}{12} = \dfrac{x}{3}(1 - \dfrac{1}{2} + \dfrac{1}{3} - \dfrac{1}{4})$
and substituting the factored expression into the equation, obtaining
$\dfrac{x}{3}(1 - \dfrac{1}{2} + \dfrac{1}{3} - \dfrac{1}{4}) = 1 - \dfrac{1}{2} + \dfrac{1}{3} - \dfrac{1}{4}$. Dividing both sides of the equation by
$1 - \dfrac{1}{2} + \dfrac{1}{3} - \dfrac{1}{4}$ (which is not zero) gives the resulting equation, $\dfrac{x}{3} = 1$. Thus x = 3
and the answer is A.

26. In the figure above, if AE = ED = DC and the area of the shaded region is 5, what is the area of △ ABC?

(A) 10   (B) 12.5   (C) 15   (D) 20   (E) 25

In this geometry problem, the shaded triangular region has a base that is $\frac{1}{3}$ the base of $\triangle ABC$ and has the same height as $\triangle ABC$. Therefore, the area of the shaded region is $\frac{1}{3}$ the area of $\triangle ABC$, and hence the area of $\triangle ABC = 3(5) = 15$. The answer is C.

27. Joan earned twice as much as Bill, and Sam earned $3 more than half as much as Bill. If the amounts earned by Joan, Bill, and Sam are j, b, and s, respectively, which of the following is a correct ordering of these amounts?

(A) $j < b < s$ (B) $j < s < b$ (C) $b < j < s$ (D) $b < s < j$
(E) It cannot be determined from the information given.

From the first sentence the following two equations can be written: $j = 2b$ and $s = \frac{1}{2}b + 3$. The first equation implies that j is greater than b $(j > b)$. The second equation, however, does not imply anything about the relationship between s and b; for example, if $b = 2$, $s = \frac{1}{2}(2) + 3 = 4$ and $s > b$ but if $b = 8$, $s = \frac{1}{2}(8) + 3 = 7$ and $s < b$. Thus E is the best of the choices given.

Data Interpretation

The data interpretation questions, like the reading comprehension questions in the verbal measure, usually appear in sets. These questions are based on data presented in tables or graphs and test one's ability to synthesize information, to select appropriate data for answering a question, or to determine that sufficient information for answering a question is not provided.

The following strategies might help in answering sets of data interpretation questions.

■ Scan the set of data briefly to see what it is about, but do not attempt to grasp everything before reading the first question. Become familiar with it gradually, while trying to answer the questions. Be sure to read all notes related to the data.

■ If a graph has insufficient grid lines, use the edge of the answer sheet as a grid line to help read more accurately.

- When possible, try to determine averages by visualizing a line through the important values and estimating the midpoint rather than reading off each value and then computing the average. Remember the average must be somewhere between the least value and the greatest value.

- If a question is too long and involved to take in at one time, break it down into parts and substitute the values from the graph for each part. Then reread the question and attempt to answer it.

- If the numbers are large, estimate products and quotients instead of performing involved computations.

- Remember that these questions are to be answered only on the basis of the data given, everyday facts (such as the number of days in a year), and your knowledge of mathematics. Do not make use of specific information that you recall that may seem to relate to the particular situation on which the questions are based unless that information is derivable from the data provided.

The directions for data interpretation questions are the same as those for the discrete questions. Some examples of data interpretation questions with explanations follow.

Questions 28-30 **refer to the following table:**

**PERCENT CHANGE IN DOLLAR AMOUNT OF SALES
IN CERTAIN RETAIL STORES FROM 1977 TO 1979**

Store	Percent Change	
	From 1977 to 1978	**From 1978 to 1979**
P	+10	−10
Q	−20	+9
R	+5	+12
S	−7	−15
T	+17	−8

28. In 1979 which of the stores had greater sales than any of the others shown?

(A) P (B) Q (C) R (D) S
  (E) It cannot be determined from the information given.

Since the only information given in the table is the percent change from year to year, there is no way to compare the amount of sales for the stores in any one year. The best answer is E.

29. In store T, the sales for 1978 amounted to approximately what percent of the sales for 1979?

(A) 86% (B) 92% (C) 109% (D) 117% (E) 122%

If A is the amount of sales for store T in 1978, then 0.08 A is the amount of decrease and A – 0.08 A = 0.92 A is the amount of sales for 1979. Therefore the desired result can be obtained by dividing A by 0.92 A, which equals $\dfrac{1}{0.92}$ or approximately 109%. The best answer is C.

30. If sales in store P amounted to $800,000 in 1977, what did the sales amount to in that store in 1979?

   (A) $727,200 (B) $792,000 (C) $800,000
     (D) $880,000 (E) $968,000

If sales in store P amounted to $800,000 in 1977, then in 1978 they amounted to 110 percent of that; i.e., $880,000. In 1979 sales amounted to 90 percent of $880,000; i.e., $792,000. Note that an increase of 10 percent in one year and a decrease of 10 percent in the following year does not result in the same amount as the original amount of sales because the base used in computing the percents changes from $800,000 to $880,000. The correct answer is B.

Questions 31-34 **refer to the following data.**

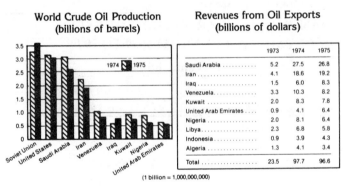

	1973	1974	1975
Saudi Arabia	5.2	27.5	26.8
Iran	4.1	18.6	19.2
Iraq	1.5	6.0	8.3
Venezuela.	3.3	10.3	8.2
Kuwait	2.0	8.3	7.8
United Arab Emirates	0.9	4.1	6.4
Nigeria	2.0	8.1	6.4
Libya.	2.3	6.8	5.8
Indonesia	0.9	3.9	4.3
Algeria	1.3	4.1	3.4
Total	23.5	97.7	96.6

31. How many of the countries shown produced more crude oil in 1975 than in 1974?

   (A) None (B) One (C) Two (D) Three (E) Four

To answer this question, one needs only to examine the bar graph that deals with production and count the number of countries for which the solid bar is taller than the lined bar. The Soviet Union and Iraq are the only such countries; therefore, the answer is C.

32. In 1974, for which of the following countries were revenues from oil exports most nearly equal to 20 percent of the total for all the countries listed?

(A) Iran (B) Iraq (C) Kuwait (D) Saudi Arabia (E) Venezuela

For this question, only the table is needed. Since 20 percent of the total (97.7) is a little less than 20, and 18.6, the revenue for Iran, is the only 1974 entry that is a little less than 20, the answer is A.

33. The country that had the greatest percent decrease in crude oil production from 1974 to 1975 had how many billions of dollars of revenue from oil exports in 1974?

(A) $27.5 (B) $18.6 (C) $10.3 (D) $8.1 (E) $4.1

This question requires the use of both the bar graph and the table. From the bar graph, it can be seen that there are seven countries that had a decrease in production; however, it would be very time-consuming to compute all of the percents. If the percent decrease is to be the greatest, then the difference between the two bars must be larger in relation to the height of the lined bar than any of the others. Some countries, such as the United States and United Arab Emirates, can be ruled out because the heights of the bars are so nearly the same. Venezuela and Kuwait can be ruled out because they have smaller differences but taller lined bars than Nigeria. Iran can be ruled out because it has about the same difference as Nigeria but a much taller lined bar. That leaves only Saudi Arabia and Nigeria and one would suspect that the ratio of the difference to the height of the lined bar is smaller for Saudi Arabia. A quick check shows that $\frac{0.5}{3}$ is less than $\frac{0.2}{0.9}$ and, therefore, Nigeria had the greatest percent decrease. From the table, Nigeria had 8.1 billions of dollars of revenue, and the best answer is D.

34. Which of the following can be concluded from the data?

   I. In 1974, Iraq exported four times as many barrels of oil as in 1973.
  II. In 1974, Iran exported three times as much oil as Iraq.
 III. In 1975, the combined crude oil production of the Soviet Union, the United States, and Saudi Arabia was more than half of the total production of all nine countries shown.

(A) I only (B) II only (C) III only (D) I and II (E) II and III

In this question, you have to decide whether each of three statements can be concluded from the data. Statement I cannot be concluded since no information is given about numbers of barrels exported in either year or about revenue per barrel in any given year. Although Iran's revenue in 1974 was approximately three times that of Iraq, no information is given about the cost per barrel in each of the countries; therefore, Statement II cannot be concluded. Note that it cannot be assumed that the price per barrel is the same in Iran and Iraq (although it might seem to be a reasonable assumption on the basis of outside knowledge) because no such information is provided in the data. In 1975 the combined production of the Soviet Union, the United States, and Saudi Arabia was about 9 billion barrels. Iran's production was about 2 billion and the remaining 5 countries produced less than 1 billion each, giving a total of less than 7 billion barrels for these countries. Therefore Statement III can be concluded, and the answer is C.

Analytical Ability

Each analytical section includes two kinds of questions:

- analytical reasoning questions in groups of three or more questions, with each group based on a different set of conditions describing a fictional situation, and

- logical reasoning questions, usually with each question based on a separate short prose passage, but sometimes with two or three questions based on the same passage.

These sections of the General Test are designed to measure the ability to think analytically. Analytical reasoning questions focus on the ability to analyze a given structure of arbitrary relationships and to deduce new information from that structure, and logical reasoning questions focus on the ability to analyze and critique argumentation by understanding and assessing relationships among arguments or parts of an argument.

The directions for all the questions in the analytical ability sections are the same and are as follows:

Directions: **Each question or group of questions is based on a passage or set of conditions. In answering some of the questions, it may be useful to draw a rough diagram. For each question, select the best answer choice given.**

Analytical Reasoning

Analytical reasoning questions test the ability to understand a given structure of arbitrary relationships among fictitious persons, places, things, or events, and to deduce new information from the relationships given. Each analytical reasoning group consists of (1) a set of about three to seven related statements or conditions (and sometimes other explanatory material) describing a structure of relationships, and (2) three or more questions that test understanding of that structure and its implications. Although each question in a group is based on the same set of conditions, the questions are independent of one another; answering one question in a group does not depend on answering any other question.

No knowledge of formal logic or mathematics is required for solving analytical reasoning problems. Although some of the same processes of reasoning are involved in solving both analytical reasoning problems and problems in those specialized fields, analytical reasoning problems can be solved using knowledge, skills, vocabulary, and computational ability (simple addition and subtraction) common to college students.

Each group of analytical reasoning questions is based on a set of conditions that establish relationships among persons, places, things, or events. These relationships are common ones such as temporal order (X arrived before Y but after Z), spatial order (City X is west of point Y and point Z), set membership (If Professor Green serves on the committee, then Professor Brown must also serve), and cause and effect (Event Q always causes event R). The conditions should be read carefully to determine the exact nature of the relationship or relationships involved. Some relationships are fixed or constant (The second house on the block belongs to P). Other relationships are variable (Q must be assigned to either campsite 1 or campsite 3). Some relationships that are not given can be easily deduced from those given. (If one condition about books on a shelf specifies that book L is to the left of book Y, and another specifies that book P is to the left of book L, then it can be deduced that book P is to the left of book Y.)

The following strategies may be helpful in answering analytical reasoning questions:

- In general, it is best to answer first those questions in a group that seem to pose little difficulty and then to return to those that seem troublesome. It is best not to start one group before finishing another because much time can be lost later in returning to an analytical reasoning group and reestablishing familiarity with its relationships. Do not avoid a group merely because its conditions look long or complicated.

- In reading the conditions, it is important not to introduce unwarranted assumptions; for instance, in a set establishing relationships of height and weight among the members of a team, do not assume that a person who is taller than another person must weigh more than that person.

- Since it is intended that the conditions be as clear as possible, avoid interpreting them as if they were designed to trick you by means of hidden ambiguities or other such devices. When in doubt, read the conditions in their most obvious, common-language sense. This does not mean, however, that the language in the condition is not intended to be read for precise meaning. It is essential, for instance, to pay particular attention to function words that describe or limit relationships, such as *only, exactly, never, always, must be, cannot be,* and the like. The result of the thorough reading described above should be a clear picture of a structure of relationships, including what kind or kinds of relationships are involved, who or what the participants in the relationships are, and what is and is not known about the structure of the relationships. For instance, at this point it can often be determined whether only a single configuration of relationships is permitted by the conditions or whether alternatives are permitted.

- Many examinees find it useful to underline key points in the conditions or to draw a simple diagram, as the directions for the analytical sections suggest.

■ Even though some people who solve analytical reasoning problems find diagrams to be helpful, other people seldom resort to them. And among those who do regularly use diagrams, there is by no means universal agreement on which kind of diagram is best for which problem or in which cases a diagram is most useful. Therefore, do not be concerned if a particular problem in the test seems to be best approached without the use of diagrams.

■ Each question should be considered separately from the other questions in its group; no information, except what is given in the original conditions, should be carried over from one question to another. In many cases a question will simply ask for conclusions to be drawn from the conditions as originally given. An individual question can, however, add information to the original conditions or temporarily suspend one of the original conditions for the purpose of that question only.

Sample Questions with Explanations

Questions 35-36

A half tone is the smallest possible interval between notes.
Note T is a half tone higher than note V.
Note V is a whole tone higher than note W.
Note W is a half tone lower than note X.
Note X is a whole tone lower than note T.
Note Y is a whole tone lower than note W.

35. **Which of the following represents the relative order of the notes from the lowest to the highest?**

    (A) X Y W V T   (B) Y W X V T   (C) W V T Y X
    (D) Y W V T X   (E) Y X W V T

The answer to this question can be determined by reading the six given statements and understanding the relationships among them. The relationships may be clarified by drawing a simple illustrative diagram:

$$T$$
$$V$$
$$X$$
$$W$$

$$Y$$

The diagram shows the relative order of the notes; since the question asks for the order from the lowest note to the highest, the correct answer is (B).

36. **Which of the following statements about an additional note, Z, could NOT be true?**

    (A) Z is higher than T.   (B) Z is lower than Y.   (C) Z is lower than W.
    (D) Z is between W and Y.   (E) Z is between W and X.

Since W and X are a half tone apart, and since a half tone is the smallest possible interval between notes, Z cannot be between W and X. The best answer is therefore (E).

Questions 37-39

F, H, I, J, K, L, M, and N spoke, but not necessarily in that order. Only one person spoke at a time.

F spoke after L and took more time than H.

I spoke before M and after H, and took less time than K.

J spoke after N and before H, and took less time than N and more time than K.

N spoke after F and took less time than H.

37. Of the following, which spoke first?

   (A) H   (B) I   (C) J   (D) L   (E) N

38. Of the following, which took the most time?

   (A) F   (B) H   (C) J   (D) K   (E) N

39. Which of the following must be true?

   (A) F was the second speaker and gave the third lengthiest speech.
   (B) H spoke before I and took more time than N.
   (C) I spoke last and gave the shortest speech.
   (D) J spoke after M and took less time than F.
   (E) N spoke after L and took more time than F.

These questions may be answered by making two lists of the speakers, as follows:

   Order of appearance: L F N J H I M
   Length of speech: F H N J K I

From these two lists the answers to all three questions emerge. The answer to 37 is (D), to 38 (A), and to 39 (B). For question 39, it is necessary to note that although (A) could be true, there is insufficient information provided to establish that it must be true.

Questions 40-42

To apply to college a student must see the school counselor, obtain a transcript at the transcript office, and obtain a recommendation from Teacher A or Teacher B.

A student must see the counselor before obtaining a transcript.

The counselor is available only Friday mornings and Tuesday, Wednesday, and Thursday afternoons.

The transcript office is open only Tuesday and Wednesday mornings, Thursday afternoons, and Friday mornings.

Teacher A is available only Monday and Wednesday mornings.

Teacher B is available only Monday afternoons and Friday mornings.

40. Maria, a student, has already seen the counselor and does not care from which teacher she obtains her recommendation. Which of the following is a complete and accurate list of those days when she could possibly complete the application process in one day?

(A) Friday   (B) Monday, Wednesday   (C) Monday, Friday
   (D) Wednesday, Friday   (E) Monday, Wednesday, Friday

To complete the application process in one day, the student has to obtain a transcript and a recommendation on the same day. This will be possible on Wednesdays, when both the transcript office and teacher A are accessible, and on Fridays, when both the transcript office and teacher B are accessible, and at no other time. The only other day that a teacher recommendation can be obtained is Monday, but on Mondays no transcripts can be obtained. Thus, the correct answer is (D).

41. John, a student, completed his application procedure in one day. Which of the following statements must be true?

   I.   He obtained his recommendation from Teacher A.
  II.   He obtained his recommendation from Teacher B.
 III.   He completed the procedure in the morning.

(A) I only   (B) II only   (C) III only
   (D) I and III only   (E) II and III only

If a student completed the entire application procedure in a single day, that day must have been a Friday. It could not have been a Monday, since on Mondays neither counselor nor transcript office is accessible. It could not have been either a Tuesday or a Thursday, because on neither of these days would a teacher have been available for a recommendation. And it could not have been a Wednesday because on Wednesdays one cannot see the counselor before obtaining a transcript. Now, given that the student in question must have done everything on a Friday, I must be false since teacher A is not available on Fridays, II must be true since teacher B is both available on Fridays and the only teacher to be so available, and III must also be true since on Fridays all of the relevant business can only be conducted in the morning. Therefore, the correct answer is (E).

42. Anne, a student, has already obtained her transcript and does not care from which teacher she obtains her recommendation. Which of the following is a complete and accurate list of those days when she could possibly complete the application process?

(A) Friday   (B) Monday, Wednesday   (C) Monday, Friday
   (D) Wednesday, Friday   (E) Monday, Wednesday, Friday

If the student has already obtained her transcript, she must have seen the counselor, too, since seeing the counselor must precede receipt of a transcript. This means that obtaining a recommendation from a teacher is all that is left to do. Since it does not matter which teacher the recommendation is from, the application process can be completed on any day that either teacher A or teacher B is available. Those days are Monday, when both are available, Wednesday, when A is available, and Friday, when B is available. The correct answer, therefore, is (E).

Questions 43-44

A farmer plants only five different kinds of vegetables — beans, corn, kale, peas, and squash. Every year the farmer plants exactly three kinds of vegetables according to the following restrictions:

If the farmer plants corn, the farmer also plants beans that year.
If the farmer plants kale one year, the farmer does not plant it the next year.
In any year, the farmer plants no more than one of the vegetables the farmer planted in the previous year.

43. **Which of the following is a possible sequence of combinations for the farmer to plant in two successive years?**

    (A) **Beans, corn, kale; corn, peas, squash**
    (B) **Beans, corn, peas; beans, corn, squash**
    (C) **Beans, peas, squash; beans, corn, kale**
    (D) **Corn, peas, squash; beans, kale, peas**
    (E) **Kale, peas, squash; beans, corn, kale**

Options (A) and (D) are not possible because corn appears as a vegetable without beans in a given year. Option (E) is not possible because kale appears in two successive years. Option (B) is not possible because two vegetables are repeated in two successive years. Option (C) contains a possible sequence of combinations.

44. **If the farmer plants beans, corn, and kale in the first year, which of the following combinations must be planted in the third year?**

    (A) **Beans, corn, and kale**
    (B) **Beans, corn, and peas**
    (C) **Beans, kale, and peas**
    (D) **Beans, peas, and squash**
    (E) **Kale, peas, and squash**

Beans, peas, and squash are planted in the second year, since kale may not be repeated two consecutive years and since corn cannot be repeated without repeating beans (only one vegetable can be repeated in consecutive years). In the third year, corn and kale must be planted (only one of the second year vegetables may be repeated). Beans are planted whenever corn is planted, so (A) is the correct answer choice.

Logical Reasoning

Logical reasoning questions test the ability to understand, analyze, and evaluate arguments. Some of the abilities tested by specific questions include recognizing the point of an argument, recognizing assumptions on which an argument is based, drawing conclusions and forming hypotheses, identifying methods of argument, evaluating arguments and counterarguments, and analyzing evidence.

Each question or group of questions is based on a short argument, generally an excerpt from the kind of material graduate students are likely to encounter in their academic and personal reading. Although arguments may be drawn from specific fields of study such as the humanities, social studies, and the physical sciences, materials from more familiar sources such as political speeches, advertisements, and informal discussions or dialogues also form the basis for some questions. No specialized knowledge of any particular field is required for answering the questions, however, and no knowledge of the terminology of formal logic is presupposed.

Specific questions asked about the arguments draw on information obtained by the process of critical and analytical reading described above.

The following strategies may be helpful in answering logical reasoning questions:

- The passage on which a question (or questions) is based should be read very carefully with close attention to such matters as (1) what is said specifically about a subject, (2) what is not said but necessarily follows from what is said, (3) what is suggested or claimed without substantiation in what is said. In addition, the means of relating statements, inferences, and claims — the structure of the argument — should be noted. Such careful reading may lead to the conclusion that the argument presented proceeds in an unsound or illogical fashion, but in many cases there will be no apparent weakness in the argument. It is important, in reading the arguments given, to attend to the soundness of the method employed and not to the actual truth of opinions presented.

- It is important to determine exactly what information the question is asking for; for instance, although it might be expected that one would be asked to detect or name the most glaring fault in a weak argument, the question posed may actually ask for the selection of one of a group of other arguments that reveals the same fault. In some cases, questions may ask for a negative response, for instance, a weakness that is NOT found in an argument or a conclusion that CANNOT be drawn from an argument.

45. **If Ruth was born in New York State, then she is a citizen of the United States.**

    The statement above can be deduced logically from which of the following statements?

    (A) Everyone born in New York State is a citizen of the United States.
    (B) Every citizen of the United States is a resident either of one of the states or of one of the territories.
    (C) Some people born in New York State are citizens of the United States.
    (D) Ruth was born either in New York or in California.
    (E) Ruth is a citizen either of the United States or of Sweden.

The question here is which of (A) through (E), if true, would guarantee that Ruth cannot have her birthplace in New York State without being a United States citizen. Since, crucially, the relationship between birthplace and citizenship is at stake, any statement that concerns itself with birthplace alone, like (D), or citizenship alone, like (E), or with the relationship between residence and citizenship, like (B), will be unsuitable for providing any such guarantee. This leaves (A) and (C), both of which deal with the relationship at issue here. Of these, (C) makes the weaker claim: It leaves open the possibility that there might be people born in New York State who are not United States citizens, and it leaves open whether or not Ruth is one of those people. (A), on the other hand, rules out any possibility of anyone being born in New York State and yet not being a United States citizen. Therefore, (A) rules out that possibility for Ruth also, and (A) is thus the correct answer.

46. **There is no reason to rule out the possibility of life on Uranus. We must, then, undertake the exploration of that planet.**

    The argument above assumes that

    (A) life exists on Uranus
    (B) Uranus is the only other planet in the solar system capable of supporting life
    (C) Uranian life would be readily recognizable as life
    (D) the search for life is a sufficient motive for space exploration
    (E) no one has previously proposed the exploration of Uranus

The argument is based on the weak claim that there is a possibility that life may exist on Uranus and not on the stronger claim that life on Uranus actually exists; since logically weak claims do not presuppose logically stronger claims, (A) is not an assumption. (B) is likewise readily eliminated since the author's argument is presented as independent of any comparison of Uranus with other planets. (E) is also clearly not the correct answer: There is no hint in the argument that its author takes it to be a novel one or takes its conclusion to be a novel one. (C) comes closer to being an assumption of the argument: If the mere possibility of the existence of life on Uranus is taken as an impetus for exploration, we can safely conclude that a major aim of any such exploration would be to ascertain whether or not there actually was life on Uranus. But this search for life does not presuppose that the techniques scientists on earth have for detecting life will be adequate for recognizing possibly alien life forms in every case. Even less is it presupposed that this task will be relatively easy. So (C) cannot be an assumption of the argument. The correct answer is (D), for, if (D) is true, the mere possibility of there being life on Uranus is indeed a compelling reason for the exploration of the planet.

47. **The rush to use distilled grains as petroleum substitutes poses potential market problems. By 1995, the value of corn as alcohol will exceed the value of corn as food. Alcohol produced from grain will displace some imported oil, and the price of oil will begin to dictate the price of corn.**

    If the claims made in the passage above are true, which of the following draws the most reliable inference about the effect of a reduction in the price of imported oil after 1995?

    (A) Some corn would be diverted from energy markets into food markets.
    (B) A downward pressure would be exerted on the price of corn.
    (C) An upward pressure would be exerted on the worldwide demand for corn.
    (D) Farmers would have an incentive to grow more corn.
    (E) Energy companies would have an incentive to produce more domestic oil.

If the price of oil is beginning to dictate the price of corn, then one would expect that a decrease in the price of imported oil will exert some downward pressure on the price of corn. This much can reliably be inferred, and (B) is, therefore, the correct answer. None of (A), (C), (D), or (E) can be inferred with a similar degree of confidence. (A) could perhaps be inferred if, as a result of the decrease in the price of imported oil, the value of corn as food once more exceeded the price of corn as alcohol; but we lack any information on this point. The worldwide demand for corn might increase if corn as alcohol proved to be a relatively inexpensive alternative to oil; but a drop in the price of oil makes oil more, not less, price-competitive, so (C) cannot be inferred. (D) might be inferred if corn prices could be expected to rise; but corn prices are liable to fall, so (D) cannot be inferred. (E) might be inferred if the price of imported oil had increased; but we are considering a situation in which the price of imported oil is reduced, so (E) cannot be inferred.

48. **Offshore blasting in oil exploration does not hurt fishing; blasting started this year, and this year's salmon catch has been the largest in a long time.**

   All of the following statements, if true, are valid objections to the argument above EXCEPT:

   (A) The salmon is only one of many species of fish that might be affected by the blasts.

   (B) The rapid changes of water pressure caused by the blasts make salmon mate more frequently.

   (C) The noise of the blasts interferes with the food chain salmon depend on.

   (D) Factors that have nothing to do with the well-being of salmon may significantly affect the size of one year's catch.

   (E) Vibrations from the blasts destroy fish eggs.

The given argument draws a general conclusion on the basis of a seemingly relevant particular observation. The question takes for granted that the general conclusion drawn is not adequately supported by the evidence cited and asks for a discrimination between the kinds of factual observations that would actually show the argument to be flawed and the kinds of factual observations that would not do so. (A) points out that some other kinds of fish may be hurt even if salmon are not. (D) points out that the size of the catch depends on other factors, like the number of people trying to catch fish. (C) and (E) both revolve around the fact that the argument seems to assume that any effects of offshore blasting would have immediate impact on fishing; both point out facts that are reasonably construed as implying negative effects of the blasts in the long run. (B), on the other hand, is most naturally construed as suggesting that the salmon population may well increase, which in turn should help fishing rather than hurt it. So (B) is most readily interpreted as making the conclusion of the argument more likely to be true. Since no statement that supports the conclusion of an argument will, under ordinary circumstances, constitute a valid objection to that argument, (B) is the correct answer.

THE GRADUATE RECORD EXAMINATIONS

General Test

*Do not break the seal
until you are told to do so.*

*The contents of this test are confidential.
Disclosure or reproduction of any portion
of it is prohibited.*

THIS TEST BOOK MUST NOT BE TAKEN FROM THE ROOM.

SECTION 1
Time—30 minutes
30 Questions

Numbers: All numbers used are real numbers.

Figures: Position of points, angles, regions, etc. can be assumed to be in the order shown; and angle measures can be assumed to be positive.

Lines shown as straight can be assumed to be straight.

Figures can be assumed to lie in a plane unless otherwise indicated.

Figures that accompany questions are intended to provide information useful in answering the questions. However, unless a note states that a figure is drawn to scale, you should solve these problems NOT by estimating sizes by sight or by measurement, but by using your knowledge of mathematics (see Example 2 below).

Directions: Each of the Questions 1-15 consists of two quantities, one in Column A and one in Column B. You are to compare the two quantities and choose

    A if the quantity in Column A is greater;
    B if the quantity in Column B is greater;
    C if the two quantities are equal;
    D if the relationship cannot be determined from the information given.

Note: Since there are only four choices, NEVER MARK (E).

Common Information: In a question, information concerning one or both of the quantities to be compared is centered above the two columns. A symbol that appears in both columns represents the same thing in Column A as it does in Column B.

	Column A	Column B	Sample Answers
Example 1:	2×6	$2 + 6$	● Ⓑ Ⓒ Ⓓ Ⓔ

Examples 2-4 refer to $\triangle PQR$.

	Column A	Column B	Sample Answers
Example 2:	PN	NQ	Ⓐ Ⓑ Ⓒ ● Ⓔ (since equal measures cannot be assumed, even though PN and NQ appear equal)
Example 3:	x	y	Ⓐ ● Ⓒ Ⓓ Ⓔ (since N is between P and Q)
Example 4:	$w + z$	180	Ⓐ Ⓑ ● Ⓓ Ⓔ (since PQ is a straight line)

46

GO ON TO THE NEXT PAGE.

A if the quantity in Column A is greater;
B if the quantity in Column B is greater;
C if the two quantities are equal;
D if the relationship cannot be determined from the information given.

	Column A	Column B			Column A	Column B

Column A   Column B

$$xy < 0$$

1. x y

2. $(0.3)^{20}$ $(0.03)^{50}$

$$x > 3$$

3. $\dfrac{1}{x+3}$ $\dfrac{1}{x-2}$

The circumference of circle P is greater than the circumference of circle Q.

4. The radius of circle P The diameter of circle Q

In Town X the population increased from 20,000 in 1960 to 30,000 in 1980. In Town X, the population under age ten in 1960 was 2,500, and in 1980 the population under age ten was 10 percent of the population.

5. The increase in the   600
   population under age
   ten in Town X from
   1960 to 1980

Column A   Column B

$$s + t = 6$$

6. $s + 2t$ $2s + t$

John is exactly 3 years younger than Sue, and Sue is exactly 4 years older than Kim.

7. John's age now   Kim's age one year
                           from now

8. x y

$$24x = 18y$$

9. $4x$ $3y$

GO ON TO THE NEXT PAGE.

47

A if the quantity in Column A is greater;
B if the quantity in Column B is greater;
C if the two quantities are equal;
D if the relationship cannot be determined from the information given.

Column A   Column B

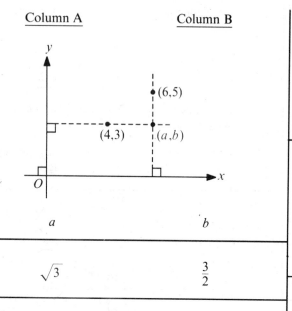

10. a b

11. $\sqrt{3}$ $\dfrac{3}{2}$

The perimeter of the rectangle is 16.

12. The area of the rectangular   12
     region

Column A   Column B

The average (arithmetic mean) of 10 numbers is 52. When one of the numbers is discarded, the average of the remaining numbers becomes 53.

13. The discarded number   51

Circles R, S, and T are in the same plane, have a common center, and have radii r, s, and $r + s$, respectively, where $0 < r < s$.

14. The area of the region πs^2
     whose boundary consists
     of circles R and T

n is an even integer.

15. The number of different   The number of differ-
     prime factors of n ent prime factors of $2n$

GO ON TO THE NEXT PAGE.

48

Directions: Each of the Questions 16-30 has five answer choices. For each of these questions, select the best of the answer choices given.

16. A dresser drawer contains 15 garments. If 40 percent of those garments are blouses, how many are <u>not</u> blouses?

(A) 6
(B) 8
(C) 9
(D) 10
(E) 12

17. $1 + \frac{1}{2} + \frac{1}{3} + \frac{1}{4} + \frac{1}{5} =$

(A) $\frac{32}{25}$ (B) $\frac{117}{60}$ (C) $\frac{52}{25}$ (D) $\frac{109}{50}$ (E) $\frac{137}{60}$

18. The length of a rectangular floor is 16 feet and its width is 12 feet. If each dimension were reduced by s feet to make the ratio of length to width 3 to 2, what would be the value of s?

(A) 0
(B) 2
(C) 4
(D) 6
(E) 8

19. If $y = 2^{(x-1)^2}$ and $x = 3$, then $y =$

(A) 8
(B) 16
(C) 32
(D) 64
(E) 128

20. How many even integers are between $\frac{17}{4}$ and $\frac{47}{2}$?

(A) Nine
(B) Eight
(C) Six
(D) Five
(E) Four

GO ON TO THE NEXT PAGE.

Questions 21-25 refer to the following graphs.

DISTRIBUTION OF EARNINGS AND REVENUES FOR COMPANY *X*, 1978-1983
ELECTRONIC AND NONELECTRONIC OPERATIONS

(1 billion = 1,000,000,000)

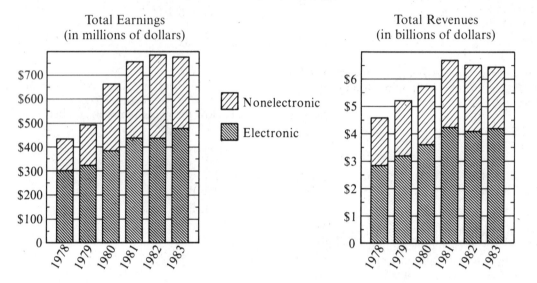

Total Earnings
(in millions of dollars)

Total Revenues
(in billions of dollars)

Nonelectronic

Electronic

Distribution of Earnings from Nonelectronic Operations, 1983
(in millions of dollars)

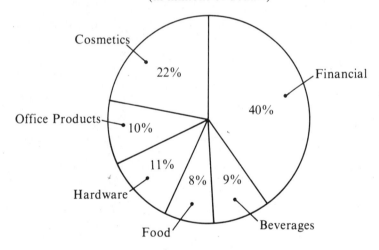

Cosmetics 22%

Financial 40%

Office Products 10%

11%

Hardware

Food 8%

9%

Beverages

Note: Drawn to scale.

GO ON TO THE NEXT PAGE.

21. Total earnings from operations in 1982 were approximately how much more than total earnings from operations in 1978 ?

   (A) $100 million
   (B) $125 million
   (C) $180 million
   (D) $340 million
   (E) $475 million

22. For the year in which earnings from electronic operations first exceeded $400 million, total revenues were approximately

   (A) $2.8 billion
   (B) $4.5 billion
   (C) $5.2 billion
   (D) $5.8 billion
   (E) $6.7 billion

23. In 1979, total earnings for Company X were approximately what percent of total revenues?

   (A)   1%
   (B)   5%
   (C) 10%
   (D) 15%
   (E) 60%

24. For the two years in which earnings from electronic operations were most nearly equal, the combined earnings from nonelectronic operations were most nearly

   (A) $340 million
   (B) $520 million
   (C) $670 million
   (D) $780 million
   (E) $1,520 million

25. In 1983 earnings from financial nonelectronic operations accounted for approximately how many millions of dollars?

   (A) 312
   (B) 300
   (C) 180
   (D) 140
   (E) 120

GO ON TO THE NEXT PAGE.

26. If k is an integer and $5^k < 20,000$, what is the greatest possible value of k ?

(A) 6   (B) 7   (C) 8   (D) 9   (E) 10

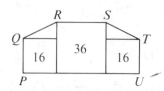

27. In the figure above, region $PQRSTU$ consists of three square regions and two triangular regions. If the square regions have areas 16, 36, and 16, what is the perimeter of $PQRSTU$?

(A) $22 + 4\sqrt{5}$

(B) $28 + 2\sqrt{5}$

(C) $28 + 4\sqrt{5}$

(D) $34 + 2\sqrt{5}$

(E) $34 + 4\sqrt{5}$

28. If x is a nonzero integer, which of the following must be a negative integer?

   I. $-(3x^2 + 4)$

  II. $-(-x)$

 III. $(-x)^3$

(A) None
(B) I only
(C) III only
(D) I and III only
(E) I, II, and III

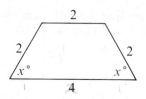

29. What is the area of the quadrilateral shown above?

(A) $2\sqrt{3}$

(B) $3\sqrt{3}$

(C) $6\sqrt{3}$

(D) 6

(E) 8

30. If the length of each of the sides of three square garden plots is increased by 50 percent, by what percent is the sum of the areas of the three plots increased?

(A) 375%
(B) 200%
(C) 150%
(D) 125%
(E) 50%

STOP

IF YOU FINISH BEFORE TIME IS CALLED, YOU MAY CHECK YOUR WORK ON THIS SECTION ONLY.
DO NOT TURN TO ANY OTHER SECTION IN THE TEST.

SECTION 2

Time—30 minutes

25 Questions

Directions: Each question or group of questions is based on a passage or set of conditions. In answering some of the questions, it may be useful to draw a rough diagram. For each question, select the best answer choice given.

Questions 1-5

An old painting portrays a seated jury of exactly six persons arranged in two parallel rows of three persons each. Each person in the back row is directly behind one person in the front row. The positions of the six jurors, numbered 1 through 6 by historians, appear in the painting as follows:

Back row, left to right—4 5 6
Front row, left to right—1 2 3

Inscribed on the back of the paintings are the names of exactly five persons—Urquart, Vere, Winters, Young, and Zeno. The historians know that each of these five persons is a juror portrayed in the painting. The name of the sixth person in the painting is unknown. The only additional information that historians have comes from letters of the time, which indicate the following:

Zeno is in position 5.
Young is directly behind Winters.
Urquart is not in the same row as Vere.

1. If the jury's front row is made up, from left to right, of Urquart, the juror whose name is unknown, and Winters, which of the following must be true?

    (A) Vere is in position 4.
    (B) Vere is in position 5.
    (C) Vere is in position 6.
    (D) Young is in position 4.
    (E) Young is in position 5.

2. If one of the two rows is made up, from left to right, of Winters, the juror whose name is unknown, and Vere, then Urquart must be in position

    (A) 1
    (B) 2
    (C) 3
    (D) 4
    (E) 6

3. If Urquart is directly in front of Zeno, which of the following must be true?

    (A) Vere is in position 4.
    (B) Vere is directly behind the juror whose name is unknown.
    (C) The juror whose name is unknown is in position 1.
    (D) The juror whose name is unknown is in position 6.
    (E) The juror whose name is unknown is directly behind Vere.

4. Which of the following jurors must be in the same row as Zeno?

    (A) Urquart
    (B) The juror whose name is unknown
    (C) Vere
    (D) Winters
    (E) Young

5. Which of the following, if it could be established, would allow historians to determine the positions of all other jurors portrayed in the painting?

    (A) The juror whose name is unknown is in position 1.
    (B) Vere is in position 2.
    (C) Vere is in position 3.
    (D) Winters is in position 1.
    (E) Young is in position 6.

GO ON TO THE NEXT PAGE.

6. The average after-tax income for a household was 2.4 percent higher in 1983 than in 1982. At the same time, average after-tax income declined for households at the lower- and middle-income levels.

Which of the following can be most reasonably inferred from the information above?

(A) There were more households overall in 1983 than in 1982.
(B) There were fewer households at the upper-income level in 1983 than in 1982.
(C) Total after-tax income for all households at the lower- and middle-income levels was higher in 1983 than in 1982.
(D) Average after-tax income for households at the upper-income level rose by more than 2.4 percent between 1982 and 1983.
(E) Average after-tax income for households at the lower- and middle-income levels was declining prior to 1982.

7. A study of attitudes toward new cars showed that cars that were identical in every respect except color received widely differing ratings for quality from potential buyers. Therefore, in future advertisements for cars of high quality, we can expect to see no variety in the color of car featured.

Which of the following is an assumption made in the passage above?

(A) If a car in a preferred color is not available, a buyer is usually willing to accept the car in another color.
(B) New cars differ significantly from each other with respect to quality.
(C) There is a single color generally associated with the highest quality rating in the study.
(D) An advertisement for a particular car should display all of its significant advantages.
(E) Potential buyers give more weight to color than to price in making a decision about a car.

8. Sometime during the 1950's, rock music permanently ousted jazz from the music scene. This is evident from the behavior of youths of that time. In crowded nightclubs they would applaud rock acts enthusiastically. But when a jazz act began, they went outside and got refreshments. They came back in only when the jazz set was finished.

Which of the following statements, if true, is a valid objection to the conclusion drawn above?

(A) Jazz is the most important musical contribution of the United States to world culture.
(B) Although some young people who attended nightclubs in the 1950's did try to listen to jazz, they eventually became bored with it.
(C) Since the 1960's, rock music has not only provided youths with recreation but has, as well, become a rallying point for making social statements.
(D) Although by 1960 jazz performances were less popular, there has since been a revival of interest in jazz among middle-class professionals.
(E) Jazz steadily increased in popularity between the 1930's and the 1950's.

GO ON TO THE NEXT PAGE.

Questions 9-14

In a city, the public transportation system consists of one subway line and one bus line.

The subway goes from station T to R to S to G to H to I, stopping at each station, and then returns, making the same stops in the reverse order.

The bus goes from station R to W to L to G to F, stopping at each station, and then returns, making the same stops in the reverse order.

On each line, there are frequent buses or trains that make each stop along the route.

During rush hour, there is also an express bus on the bus line that stops only at R, L, and F and returns, making the same three stops in the reverse order.

A passenger can transfer from the subway or bus line to the other line wherever the bus and subway both stop at a station with the same name.

It is not possible to transfer from an express bus to a nonexpress bus.

There is no other means of transportation available on the public transportation system.

9. To make a trip on public transportation from S to I, a passenger must pass through which of the following additional stops?

(A) G and H only
(B) F, G, and H only
(C) H, L, and W only
(D) F, H, L, and W only
(E) G, H, L, and R only

10. Using buses only, a passenger CANNOT go on public transportation from

(A) F to W
(B) G to R
(C) L to H
(D) L to R
(E) W to L

11. To go on public transportation from F to T, a passenger must

(A) transfer at G
(B) transfer at R
(C) take a vehicle to or through R
(D) take a vehicle to or through S
(E) take a vehicle to or through W

12. If a fire temporarily closes the subway tracks at R to subway trains but the subway still runs from I to S and the bus still stops at R, it will be IMPOSSIBLE for any passenger to go on public transportation to

(A) F
(B) I
(C) L
(D) R
(E) T

13. To make a trip on public transportation from I to W during rush hour, a passenger must do which of the following?

(A) Transfer to a bus at G.
(B) Ride the subway only.
(C) Board a nonexpress bus.
(D) Ride a bus past L.
(E) Go through S on the subway.

14. If all nonexpress buses are halted during rush hour by equipment failures, is it possible during rush hour for a passenger to board an express bus at L and then go to G ?

(A) It is not possible.
(B) It is possible, but only if the passenger transfers at R.
(C) It is possible, but only if the passenger transfers at F.
(D) It is possible, but only if the passenger goes through both F and R.
(E) It is possible, but only if the passenger takes a bus that stops at W.

GO ON TO THE NEXT PAGE.

Questions 15-18

Internal audits in the Goodcrop Corporation are overseen by a panel of exactly five staff members. Panelists are drawn from the company's divisions: Fertilizers, Pesticides, and Seeds. There is a standard way of referring to the composition of any panel: the member with the longest current term of service on the panel is listed first, then the others in decreasing order of current term of service, and the letters F, P, or S are added as subscripts to each name to indicate whether a panelist works in Fertilizers, Pesticides, or Seeds, respectively. At the beginning of each month, exactly one panelist is rotated off the panel and a new panelist is appointed as a replacement. The monthly rotation is subject to the following conditions:

> If the panelist being rotated off is from Fertilizers, his or her replacement must either also be from Fertilizers or be from Seeds.
> If the panelist being rotated off is from Pesticides, his or her replacement must be from Fertilizers.
> If the panelist being rotated off is from Seeds, his or her replacement must be from Pesticides.
> The panelist being rotated off must be the one with the longest current term of service on the panel.

15. If the list of panel members for May begins with "Ms. Liang$_P$," which of the following must be true of the list of panel members for June?

  (A) It begins with the name of a staff member from Fertilizers.
  (B) It begins with the name of a staff member from Pesticides.
  (C) It begins with the name of a staff member from Seeds.
  (D) It ends with the name of a staff member from Fertilizers.
  (E) It ends with the name of a staff member from Seeds.

16. If the April panel is listed as "Ms. Medeiros$_P$, Mr. Liu$_F$, Ms. Ortiz$_S$, Mr. Giro$_S$, and Mr. Rossi$_F$," which of the following will happen at the beginning of July?

  (A) Mr. Liu will be rotated off and replaced by someone from Seeds.
  (B) Mr. Liu will be rotated off and replaced by someone else from Fertilizers.
  (C) Ms. Ortiz will be rotated off and replaced by someone from Pesticides.
  (D) Ms. Ortiz will be rotated off and replaced by someone else from Seeds.
  (E) Mr. Giro will be rotated off and replaced by someone from Pesticides.

17. If all the members of the March panel are from Pesticides, which of the following is the earliest month in which the panel members could all be from Fertilizers?

  (A) July
  (B) August
  (C) September
  (D) October
  (E) November

18. If the members of the July panel are listed, from first to last, as being from divisions F, P, S, F, and S, respectively, the members of the October panel could be, respectively, from divisions

  (A) F, F, P, S, and P
  (B) F, P, S, P, and F
  (C) F, S, F, F, and P
  (D) P, S, S, F, and P
  (E) S, F, S, P, and S

GO ON TO THE NEXT PAGE.

Questions 19-22

The officers of Renco Manufacturing are analyzing their company's chances of winning a large contract to manufacture equipment for the state highway department. Renco is one of five companies competing for the contract: the others are Selway, Inc., Tate Industries, Upshaw Corp., and Velco. The contract will be awarded on the basis of points given in three categories: cost, amount of experience on similar contracts, and quality of equipment. In each category, the company that is best in that category will receive five points, the second best, 4 points, and so on down to 1. There will be no ties within any of the categories. The company that receives the highest total number of points will be awarded the contract. In the event of a tie, the company with the higher number of 5's will be awarded the contract; if the number of 5's is the same, additional criteria will be used to break the tie.

19. The highest total number of points that any of the competing companies can receive is

(A) twelve
(B) fourteen
(C) fifteen
(D) twenty
(E) twenty-five

20. If no one company is given the same number of points in any two categories, the highest possible winning total is

(A) eleven
(B) twelve
(C) thirteen
(D) fourteen
(E) fifteen

21. If the five companies tie with nine points each, which of the following CANNOT be the distribution of points received by any of the companies?

(A) Three 3's
(B) Two 4's and a 1
(C) A 5 and two 2's
(D) A 4, a 3, and a 2
(E) A 5, a 3, and a 1

22. If Selway, Inc. and Velco between them receive all of the 1's and 2's and each of the remaining three competitors receives a 5, Renco would need to receive how many points in addition to its 5 to be awarded the contract without having first been tied for total number of points?

(A) Four
(B) Five
(C) Six
(D) Seven
(E) Eight

---

23. Persons imprisoned for violent street crimes often commit the same crimes again after being released. Persons imprisoned for white-collar crimes such as receiving bribes or embezzlement, however, typically do not, after being released, repeat the crimes for which they have been imprisoned. It is fair to conclude that imprisonment, while it often fails to change the behavior of violent street criminals, does succeed in making white-collar criminals unwilling to repeat their crimes.

Which of the following, if true, would most seriously weaken the conclusion stated above?

(A) Statistics show that persons convicted of committing white-collar crimes rarely have a prison record.
(B) The percentage of those who commit white-collar crimes and are imprisoned for doing so is lower than the percentage of those who commit violent street crimes and are imprisoned for doing so.
(C) White-collar criminals whose prison sentences are shortened return to criminal activities at a slightly higher rate than white-collar criminals who serve their full sentences.
(D) Persons released from prison after white-collar crimes are seldom given high positions or access to other people's money.
(E) Persons who commit violent street crimes seldom commit white-collar crimes, and vice versa.

GO ON TO THE NEXT PAGE.

24. Industrial solvents, which can damage the liver, kidneys, and nervous system, often drain into public water supplies. Currently, tested water is considered pure if the amount of solvent an individual is exposed to through drinking one-half gallon of water per day—roughly what a typical adult drinks per day—does not pose a significant threat to human health. But many toxicologists claim that the standard set by this method does not adequately protect the public.

Which of the following, if true, would best support the claim of the toxicologists mentioned above?

(A) The figure of one-half gallon a day includes water contained in beverages such as soft drinks, which are often bottled at locations distant from where they are consumed.
(B) Some industrial solvents have less toxic but more expensive analogues that industry has not adopted for use.
(C) Water treatment centers usually filter out bacteria and other organisms before the water is pumped into public supply systems.
(D) Industrial polluters are rarely fined or punished, even when they knowingly allow toxic chemicals to enter water supplies.
(E) More solvent enters the body through skin absorption, during washing and bathing, than through drinking.

25. Many behavioral studies of the psychological capacities of animals reveal hardly any difference between rats and chimpanzees. The most reasonable explanation for such results is that the studies themselves are inadequate.

The argument above relies on the unstated premise that

(A) rats and chimpanzees do not have highly developed psychological capacities
(B) the results of psychological studies of animals are often misinterpreted by biased experimenters
(C) there is no way to measure objectively the psychological capacities of animals
(D) there is considerable difference between the psychological capacities of rats and those of chimpanzees
(E) examining the brain of an animal is a better means of determining its psychological capacity than is a study of the animal's behavior

STOP

IF YOU FINISH BEFORE TIME IS CALLED, YOU MAY CHECK YOUR WORK ON THIS SECTION ONLY.
DO NOT TURN TO ANY OTHER SECTION IN THE TEST.

SECTION 3

Time—30 minutes

38 Questions

Directions: Each sentence below has one or two blanks, each blank indicating that something has been omitted. Beneath the sentence are five lettered words or sets of words. Choose the word or set of words for each blank that best fits the meaning of the sentence as a whole.

1. Many artists believe that successful imitation, far from being symptomatic of a lack of -------, is the first step in learning to be creative.

   (A) elegance   (B) resolution   (C) goodness
   (D) originality   (E) sympathy

2. As serious as she is about the bullfight, she does not allow respect to ------- her sense of whimsy when painting it.

   (A) inspire   (B) provoke   (C) suppress
   (D) attack   (E) satisfy

3. No one is ------- about Stephens; he inspires either uncritical adulation or profound ------- in those who work for him.

   (A) neutral. .antipathy
   (B) infuriated. .aversion
   (C) worried. .anxiety
   (D) enthusiastic. .veneration
   (E) apprehensive. .consternation

4. Before about 1960, virtually all accounts of evolution assumed most adaptation to be a product of selection at the level of populations; recent studies of evolution, however, have found no ------- this ------- view of selection.

   (A) departures from. .controversial
   (B) basis for. .pervasive
   (C) bias toward. .unchallenged
   (D) precursors of. .innovative
   (E) criticisms of. .renowned

5. The new biological psychiatry does not deny the contributing role of psychological factors in mental illnesses, but posits that these factors may act as a catalyst on existing physiological conditions and ------- such illnesses.

   (A) disguise   (B) impede   (C) constrain
   (D) precipitate   (E) consummate

6. During periods of social and cultural stability, many art academies are so firmly controlled by ------- that all real creative work must be done by the -------.

   (A) dogmatists. .disenfranchised
   (B) managers. .reactionaries
   (C) reformers. .dissatisfied
   (D) imposters. .academicians
   (E) specialists. .elite

7. The First World War began in a context of jargon and verbal delicacy and continued in a cloud of ------- as ------- as language and literature, skillfully used, could make it.

   (A) circumlocution. .literal
   (B) cliché. .lucid
   (C) euphemism. .impenetrable
   (D) particularity. .deliberate
   (E) subjectivity. .enthralling

GO ON TO THE NEXT PAGE.

59

Directions: In each of the following questions, a related pair of words or phrases is followed by five lettered pairs of words or phrases. Select the lettered pair that best expresses a relationship similar to that expressed in the original pair.

8. THERMOMETER : TEMPERATURE ::
   (A) plane : thickness
   (B) wrench : torque
   (C) camera : exposure
   (D) compass : direction
   (E) grindstone : sharpness

9. FOOLPROOF : FAIL :: (A) translucent : filter
   (B) viscous : smear   (C) volatile : explode
   (D) airtight : leak   (E) taut : break

10. SUFFOCATE : OXYGEN :: (A) restrict : supplies
    (B) rob : money   (C) inhibit : drives
    (D) imprison : freedom   (E) starve : nutrients

11. ORCHESTRA : MUSIC :: (A) vocalist : song
    (B) poet : anthology   (C) actor : cues
    (D) choreographer : ballet   (E) troupe : drama

12. BIRD : SNARE :: (A) lion : den   (B) fish : seine
    (C) lamb : shears   (D) scorpion : sting
    (E) lobster : claw

13. RESOLUTENESS : WILL :: (A) zeal : conviction
    (B) honor : restitution   (C) esteem : adoration
    (D) anguish : hesitation   (E) sorrow : compassion

14. MILLER : GRAIN :: (A) carpenter : awl
    (B) forger : furnace   (C) tanner : hide
    (D) vintner : wine   (E) mason : cement

15. DIDACTIC : INSTRUCT ::
    (A) pedantic : contend   (B) comic : amuse
    (C) theatrical : applaud   (D) imperative : obey
    (E) rhetorical : recite

16. GARRULOUS : TALKATIVE ::
    (A) suspicious : unreliable
    (B) cantankerous : obtuse
    (C) cloying : sweet
    (D) reflective : insightful
    (E) prudent : indecisive

GO ON TO THE NEXT PAGE.

Directions: Each passage in this group is followed by questions based on its content. After reading a passage, choose the best answer to each question. Answer all questions following a passage on the basis of what is <u>stated</u> or <u>implied</u> in that passage.

Geologists have long known that the Earth's mantle is heterogeneous, but its spatial arrangement remains unresolved—is the mantle essentially layered or irregularly heterogeneous? The best evidence for the layered-
Line
(5) mantle thesis is the well-established fact that volcanic rocks found on oceanic islands, islands believed to result from mantle plumes arising from the lower mantle, are composed of material fundamentally different from that of the midocean ridge system, whose source, most geolo-
(10) gists contend, is the upper mantle.

Some geologists, however, on the basis of observations concerning mantle xenoliths, argue that the mantle is not layered, but that heterogeneity is created by fluids rich in "incompatible elements" (elements
(15) tending toward liquid rather than solid state) percolating upward and transforming portions of the upper mantle irregularly, according to the vagaries of the fluids' pathways. We believe, perhaps unimaginatively, that this debate can be resolved through further study, and that the underexplored midocean ridge system is the key.

17. Which of the following best expresses the main idea of the passage?

(A) Current theories regarding the structure of the Earth's mantle cannot account for new discoveries regarding the composition of mantle xenoliths.

(B) There are conflicting hypotheses about the heterogeneity of the Earth's mantle because few mantle elements have been thoroughly studied.

(C) Further research is needed to resolve the debate among geologists over the composition of the midocean ridge system.

(D) There is clear-cut disagreement within the geological community over the structure of the Earth's mantle.

(E) There has recently been a strong and exciting challenge to geologists' long-standing belief in the heterogeneity of the Earth's mantle.

18. According to the passage, it is believed that oceanic islands are formed from

(A) the same material as mantle xenoliths
(B) the same material as the midocean ridge system
(C) volcanic rocks from the upper mantle
(D) incompatible elements percolating up from the lower mantle
(E) mantle plumes arising from the lower mantle

19. It can be inferred from the passage that the supporters of the "layered-mantle" theory believe which of the following?

I. The volcanic rocks on oceanic islands are composed of material derived from the lower part of the mantle.
II. The materials of which volcanic rocks on oceanic islands and midocean ridges are composed are typical of the layers from which they are thought to originate.
III. The differences in composition between volcanic rocks on oceanic islands and the midocean ridges are a result of different concentrations of incompatible elements.

(A) I only
(B) III only
(C) I and II only
(D) II and III only
(E) I, II, and III

20. The authors suggest that their proposal for determining the nature of the mantle's heterogeneity might be considered by many to be

(A) pedestrian
(B) controversial
(C) unrealistic
(D) novel
(E) paradoxical

GO ON TO THE NEXT PAGE.

Many literary detectives have pored over a great puzzle concerning the writer Marcel Proust: what happened in 1909 ? How did *Contre Saint-Beuve*, an essay attacking the methods of the critic Saint-
Line
(5) Beuve, turn into the start of the novel *Remembrance of Things Past*? A recently published letter from Proust to the editor Vallette confirms that Fallois, the editor of the 1954 edition of *Contre Saint-Beuve*, made an essentially correct guess about the relationship of the essay
(10) to the novel. Fallois proposed that Proust had tried to begin a novel in 1908, abandoned it for what was to be a long demonstration of Saint-Beuve's blindness to the real nature of great writing, found the essay giving rise to personal memories and fictional developments, and
(15) allowed these to take over in a steadily developing novel.

Draft passages in Proust's 1909 notebooks indicate that the transition from essay to novel began in *Contre Saint-Beuve*, when Proust introduced several examples to show the powerful influence that involuntary memory
(20) exerts over the creative imagination. In effect, in trying to demonstrate that the imagination is more profound and less submissive to the intellect than Saint-Beuve assumed, Proust elicited vital memories of his own and, finding subtle connections between them, began
(25) to amass the material for *Remembrance*. By August, Proust was writing to Vallette, informing him of his intention to develop the material as a novel. Maurice Bardèche, in *Marcel Proust, romancier*, has shown the importance in the drafts of *Remembrance* of sponta-
(30) neous and apparently random associations of Proust's subconscious. As incidents and reflections occurred to Proust, he continually inserted new passages altering and expanding his narrative. But he found it difficult to control the drift of his inspiration. The very richness
(35) and complexity of the meaningful relationships that kept presenting and rearranging themselves on all levels, from abstract intelligence to profound dreamy feelings, made it difficult for Proust to set them out coherently. The beginning of control came when he saw how to connect
(40) the beginning and the end of his novel.

Intrigued by Proust's claim that he had "begun and finished" *Remembrance* at the same time, Henri Bonnet discovered that parts of *Remembrance's* last book were actually started in 1909. Already in that year, Proust
(45) had drafted descriptions of his novel's characters in their old age that would appear in the final book of *Remembrance*, where the permanence of art is set against the ravages of time. The letter to Vallette, drafts of the essay and novel, and Bonnet's researches establish in
(50) broad outline the process by which Proust generated his novel out of the ruins of his essay. But those of us who hoped, with Kolb, that Kolb's newly published complete edition of Proust's correspondence for 1909 would document the process in greater detail are disappointed. For
(55) until Proust was confident that he was at last in sight of a viable structure for *Remembrance*, he told few correspondents that he was producing anything more ambitious than *Contre Saint-Beuve*.

21. The passage is primarily concerned with

(A) the role of involuntary memory in Proust's writing
(B) evidence concerning the genesis of Proust's novel *Remembrance of Things Past*
(C) conflicting scholarly opinions about the value of studying the drafts of *Remembrance of Things Past*
(D) Proust's correspondence and what it reveals about *Remembrance of Things Past*
(E) the influence of Saint-Beuve's criticism on Proust's novel *Remembrance of Things Past*

22. It can be inferred from the passage that all of the following are literary detectives who have tried, by means of either scholarship or criticism, to help solve the "great puzzle" mentioned in lines 1-2 EXCEPT

(A) Bardèche
(B) Bonnet
(C) Fallois
(D) Kolb
(E) Vallette

23. According to the passage, in drafts of *Contre Saint-Beuve* Proust set out to show that Saint-Beuve made which of the following mistakes as a critic?

I. Saint-Beuve made no effort to study the development of a novel through its drafts and revisions.
II. Saint-Beuve assigned too great a role in the creative process to a writer's conscious intellect.
III. Saint-Beuve concentrated too much on plots and not enough on imagery and other elements of style.

(A) II only
(B) III only
(C) I and II only
(D) I and III only
(E) I, II, and III

GO ON TO THE NEXT PAGE.

24. Which of the following best states the author's attitude toward the information that scholars have gathered about Proust's writing in 1909 ?

(A) The author is disappointed that no new documents have come to light since Fallois's speculations.
(B) The author is dissatisfied because there are too many gaps and inconsistencies in the drafts.
(C) The author is confident that Fallois's 1954 guess has been proved largely correct, but regrets that still more detailed documentation concerning Proust's transition from the essay to the novel has not emerged.
(D) The author is satisfied that Fallois's judgment was largely correct, but feels that Proust's early work in designing and writing the novel was probably far more deliberate than Fallois's description of the process would suggest.
(E) The author is satisfied that the facts of Proust's life in 1909 have been thoroughly established, but believes such documents as drafts and correspondence are only of limited value in a critical assessment of Proust's writing.

25. The author of the passage implies that which of the following would be the LEAST useful source of information about Proust's transition from working on *Contre Saint-Beuve* to having a viable structure for *Remembrance of Things Past?*

(A) Fallois's comments in the 1954 edition of *Contre Saint-Beuve*
(B) Proust's 1909 notebooks, including the drafts of *Remembrance of Things Past*
(C) Proust's 1909 correspondence, excluding the letter to Vallette
(D) Bardèche's *Marcel Proust, romancier*
(E) Bonnet's researches concerning Proust's drafts of the final book of *Remembrance of Things Past*

26. The passage offers information to answer which of the following questions?

(A) Precisely when in 1909 did Proust decide to abandon *Contre Saint-Beuve*?
(B) Precisely when in 1909 did Proust decide to connect the beginning and the end of *Remembrance of Things Past*?
(C) What was the subject of the novel that Proust attempted in 1908 ?
(D) What specific criticisms of Saint-Beuve appear, in fictional form, in *Remembrance of Things Past*?
(E) What is a theme concerning art that appears in the final book of *Remembrance of Things Past*?

27. Which of the following best describes the relationship between *Contre Saint-Beuve* and *Remembrance of Things Past* as it is explained in the passage?

(A) Immediately after abandoning *Contre Saint-Beuve*, at Vallette's suggestion, Proust started *Remembrance* as a fictional demonstration that Saint-Beuve was wrong about the imagination.
(B) Immediately after abandoning *Contre Saint-Beuve*, at Vallette's suggestion, Proust turned his attention to *Remembrance*, starting with incidents that had occurred to him while planning the essay.
(C) Despondent that he could not find a coherent structure for *Contre Saint-Beuve*, an essay about the role of memory in fiction, Proust began instead to write *Remembrance*, a novel devoted to important early memories.
(D) While developing his argument about the imagination in *Contre Saint-Beuve*, Proust described and began to link together personal memories that became a foundation for *Remembrance*.
(E) While developing his argument about memory and imagination in *Contre Saint-Beuve*, Proust created fictional characters to embody the abstract themes in his essay.

GO ON TO THE NEXT PAGE.

63

Directions: Each question below consists of a word printed in capital letters, followed by five lettered words or phrases. Choose the lettered word or phrase that is most nearly opposite in meaning to the word in capital letters.

Since some of the questions require you to distinguish fine shades of meaning, be sure to consider all the choices before deciding which one is best.

28. FREQUENT: (A) contain   (B) restore   (C) sever   (D) visit rarely   (E) defend eagerly

29. COMPOUND: (A) reveal   (B) concentrate   (C) activate   (D) conserve   (E) separate

30. CRASS: (A) demanding   (B) florid   (C) refined   (D) intrepid   (E) fair

31. PLASTICITY: (A) tightness   (B) contiguity   (C) stasis   (D) rigidity   (E) order

32. CONVOKE: (A) forgive   (B) eradicate   (C) adjourn   (D) omit   (E) abridge

33. COMMODIOUS: (A) calm   (B) careless   (C) reticent   (D) enclosed   (E) cramped

34. CORROBORATE: (A) complicate   (B) controvert   (C) conflate   (D) condone   (E) counterfeit

35. MACULATED: (A) unobserved   (B) unfocused   (C) unplanned   (D) unfeigned   (E) unspotted

36. ESOTERIC: (A) unsophisticated   (B) worthless   (C) lasting   (D) generally known   (E) well expressed

37. FRUSTRATE: (A) expand   (B) enjoy   (C) nullify   (D) abet   (E) prepare

38. ASPERSIONS: (A) qualms   (B) apologies   (C) rewards   (D) vexation   (E) flattery

STOP

IF YOU FINISH BEFORE TIME IS CALLED, YOU MAY CHECK YOUR WORK ON THIS SECTION ONLY.
DO NOT TURN TO ANY OTHER SECTION IN THE TEST.

Section 4 starts on page 66.

SECTION 4
Time—30 minutes

30 Questions

Numbers: All numbers used are real numbers.

Figures: Position of points, angles, regions, etc. can be assumed to be in the order shown; and angle measures can be assumed to be positive.

Lines shown as straight can be assumed to be straight.

Figures can be assumed to lie in a plane unless otherwise indicated.

Figures that accompany questions are intended to provide information useful in answering the questions. However, unless a note states that a figure is drawn to scale, you should solve these problems NOT by estimating sizes by sight or by measurement, but by using your knowledge of mathematics (see Example 2 below).

Directions: Each of the Questions 1-15 consists of two quantities, one in Column A and one in Column B. You are to compare the two quantities and choose

         A   if the quantity in Column A is greater;
         B   if the quantity in Column B is greater;
         C   if the two quantities are equal;
         D   if the relationship cannot be determined from the information given.

Note: Since there are only four choices, NEVER MARK (E).

Common
Information: In a question, information concerning one or both of the quantities to be compared is centered above the two columns. A symbol that appears in both columns represents the same thing in Column A as it does in Column B.

	Column A	Column B	Sample Answers
Example 1:	2×6	$2 + 6$	● Ⓑ Ⓒ Ⓓ Ⓔ

Examples 2-4 refer to $\triangle PQR$.

	Column A	Column B	Sample Answers
Example 2:	PN	NQ	Ⓐ Ⓑ Ⓒ ● Ⓔ

(since equal measures cannot be assumed, even though PN and NQ appear equal)

	Column A	Column B	Sample Answers
Example 3:	x	y	Ⓐ ● Ⓒ Ⓓ Ⓔ

(since N is between P and Q)

	Column A	Column B	Sample Answers
Example 4:	$w + z$	180	Ⓐ Ⓑ ● Ⓓ Ⓔ

(since PQ is a straight line)

GO ON TO THE NEXT PAGE.

A if the quantity in Column A is greater;
B if the quantity in Column B is greater;
C if the two quantities are equal;
D if the relationship cannot be determined from the information given.

Column A	Column B

$$k + n = 13$$
$$n + 3 = 8$$

1. k n

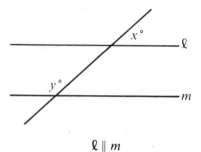

$$\ell \parallel m$$

2. $x + y$ 180

Last year Pat earned \$700 per month for each of the first 7 months of the year and \$800 per month for each of the last 5 months of the year.

3. Pat's average (arithmetic   \$750
   mean) monthly earnings
   last year

x copies of sports magazine X cost a total of \$12.

4. The total cost, in dollars, $\dfrac{12m}{x}$
   of m copies of fashion
   magazine M

$$x = 2 \text{ and } y = 3.$$

5. $x + 2y$ x^y

Column A	Column B

6. x y

7. $\dfrac{10}{\dfrac{1}{2}}$ $\dfrac{1}{2}(10)$

$$x > 0$$

8. $\dfrac{1}{1 + \dfrac{1}{x}}$ 1

$$x^2 + 3 = 19$$
$$x < 0$$

9. x -4

GO ON TO THE NEXT PAGE.

67

A if the quantity in Column A is greater;
B if the quantity in Column B is greater;
C if the two quantities are equal;
D if the relationship cannot be determined from the information given.

Column A	Column B

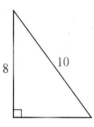

10. The area of the triangular region   40

$$\frac{3}{7} < \frac{n}{21}$$

11. n 7

12. The area of a circular region with diameter $2k$ The area of a square region with side $2k$

Column A	Column B

n is a positive integer.

13. $(-1)^{n-1}$ 0

$$0 < m < n$$

14. $n - m$ $\dfrac{n + m}{2}$

RS is a diameter of a circle.

15. The ratio of the length of diameter RS to the length of semicircular arc RS $\dfrac{2}{3}$

GO ON TO THE NEXT PAGE.

68

Directions: Each of the Questions 16-30 has five answer choices. For each of these questions, select the best of the answer choices given.

16. If $6x - 4y = 2$ and $x = 3$, then $x + y =$

(A) 4
(B) 5
(C) 7
(D) 12
(E) 19

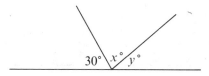

17. In the figure above, if $x = 2y$, then $y =$

(A) 50
(B) 40
(C) 30
(D) 20
(E) 10

18. Sue drives 10 miles from home to work. If she could average 50 miles per hour, how many minutes would it take her to drive from home to work?

(A) 20
(B) 18
(C) 15
(D) 12
(E) 10

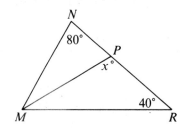

19. In the figure above, if MP bisects $\angle NMR$, then $x =$

(A) 80
(B) 90
(C) 100
(D) 110
(E) 120

20. If $x + 2y = 2x - y$, then $x =$

(A) $-y$

(B) $\dfrac{y}{3}$

(C) y

(D) $2y$

(E) $3y$

GO ON TO THE NEXT PAGE.

Questions 21-25 refer to the following data.

UNION MEMBERSHIP IN THE LABOR FORCE, 1968-1980

Labor Force

Year	Workers (in millions)
1968	75.9
1970	78.6
1972	81.7
1974	85.9
1976	87.5
1978	94.4
1980	96.5

Union Membership as a Percent
of the Labor Force

Chicago Tribune.

Distribution of Union Membership
by Economic Sector

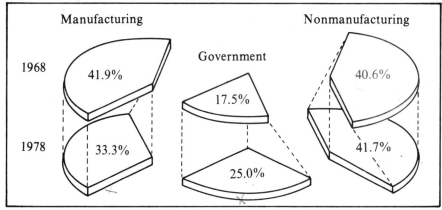

Manufacturing   Government   Nonmanufacturing

1968 — 41.9%   17.5%   40.6%

1978 — 33.3%   25.0%   41.7%

Chicago Tribune.

Note: Drawn to scale.

GO ON TO THE NEXT PAGE.

21. Over which of the following two-year periods was there the greatest increase in the number of workers in the labor force?

    (A) 1968-1970
    (B) 1970-1972
    (C) 1972-1974
    (D) 1974-1976
    (E) 1976-1978

22. In 1974 approximately how many million workers were members of a labor union?

    (A) 17.2   (B) 19.2   (C) 21.1

    (D) 24.5   (E) 85.9

23. From 1968 to 1980, the size of the labor force increased by approximately what percent?

    (A) 20%
    (B) 21%
    (C) 27%
    (D) 73%
    (E) 80%

24. In 1978 there were approximately 21 million union members. Approximately how many million more of these were in the manufacturing sector than in the government sector?

    (A) 8.6
    (B) 7.8
    (C) 6.9
    (D) 5.2
    (E) 1.7

25. In 1968 the number of union members in the non-manufacturing sector was approximately what percent of the total labor force?

    (A) 10%
    (B) 15%
    (C) 25%
    (D) 30%
    (E) 41%

GO ON TO THE NEXT PAGE.

71

26. In the equation $kx + y = 16$, k is a constant. If $y = 6$ when $x = 2$, what is the value of y when $x = 4$?

    (A) -8 (B) -4 (C) $\frac{11}{4}$ (D) 5   (E) 12

27. The greatest prime factor of 162 is

    (A) 2
    (B) 3
    (C) 29
    (D) 31
    (E) 81

28. If the cost of x gallons of unleaded gasoline priced at \$1.24 per gallon equals the cost of $x + 2$ gallons of regular gasoline priced at \$1.16 per gallon, then $x =$

    (A) 29.0
    (B) 24.0
    (C) 16.5
    (D) 14.5
    (E) 12.0

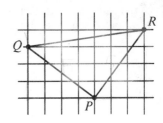

29. In the figure above, the grid consists of unit squares and P, Q, and R are points of intersection of the grid as shown. What is the perimeter of triangular region PQR?

    (A) 15

    (B) 17

    (C) 20

    (D) $5 + 5\sqrt{2}$

    (E) $10 + 5\sqrt{2}$

30. If a and b are integers and $a - b = 6$, then $a + b$ CANNOT be

    (A) 0
    (B) less than 6
    (C) greater than 6
    (D) an even integer
    (E) an odd integer

STOP

IF YOU FINISH BEFORE TIME IS CALLED, YOU MAY CHECK YOUR WORK ON THIS SECTION ONLY. DO NOT TURN TO ANY OTHER SECTION IN THE TEST.

SECTION 5

Time—30 minutes

25 Questions

Directions: Each question or group of questions is based on a passage or set of conditions. In answering some of the questions, it may be useful to draw a rough diagram. For each question, select the best answer choice given.

Questions 1-3

Four lifeguards—F, G, H, and J—work at a swimming pool that is open six days a week, Monday through Saturday. Each day exactly one lifeguard is on duty. The pool manager assigns guard duty each week according to the following conditions:

   Each lifeguard is assigned duty at least one day a week.
   No lifeguard is assigned duty on two consecutive days.

1. If during one week F is assigned duty on Monday and Saturday only, which of the following must be true of the assignments for that week?

   (A) One other lifeguard besides F is assigned duty on two days.
   (B) The lifeguard assigned duty on Wednesday cannot be assigned duty on Friday.
   (C) H is assigned duty on the day immediately before the day on which G is assigned duty.
   (D) Either G or H is assigned duty on Tuesday.
   (E) Either H or J is assigned duty on Friday.

2. If during one week H is assigned duty on exactly two days and G and J are each assigned duty on days earlier in the week than the first day on which H is assigned duty, H could be assigned duty on which of the following pairs of days?

   (A) Monday and Wednesday
   (B) Tuesday and Thursday
   (C) Tuesday and Saturday
   (D) Wednesday and Saturday
   (E) Friday and Saturday

3. If during one week F is assigned duty on Tuesday and two other days, which of the following CAN-NOT be true?

   (A) F is assigned duty on Saturday.
   (B) F and H are assigned duty on consecutive days.
   (C) G and H are assigned duty on consecutive days.
   (D) G and H are assigned duty on days before Thursday.
   (E) F is assigned duty on a day immediately before a day on which G is assigned duty and on a day immediately before a day on which J is assigned duty.

GO ON TO THE NEXT PAGE.

73

4. Because of rules imposed by the Federal Drug Administration restricting the sale of thalidomide, many people who have trouble sleeping turn to barbiturates. Yet each year barbiturate-alcohol interactions cause the deaths of over a thousand people who probably would have lived had they used thalidomide instead of barbiturates, even without changing their alcohol consumption.

Which of the following statements about thalidomide is best supported by the statements above?

(A) Thalidomide alone poses no serious health risks.
(B) Barbiturates alone are more dangerous than alcohol alone.
(C) Thalidomide is a more effective sleeping aid than barbiturates.
(D) In some cases, the thalidomide-barbiturate interaction would be less dangerous than the barbiturate-alcohol interaction.
(E) In some cases, the thalidomide-alcohol interaction would be less life-threatening than the barbiturate-alcohol interaction.

5. Existing United States landfills are rapidly approaching the limits of their capacity. Landfills can leach toxins into groundwater, polluting it. Instead of creating more landfills, solid-waste managers should recycle as much trash as possible and then incinerate the remainder. This will keep future environmental damage to a minimum.

Which of the following is an assumption on which the argument made above is based?

(A) Future landfills will pollute the environment more than do those that already exist.
(B) After existing landfills reach the limit of their capacity, they are closed, and the leaching of toxins from these sites decreases.
(C) Reducing the volume of trash through recycling will not lessen future environmental danger unless the remaining trash is subsequently incinerated.
(D) The environmental damage caused by the proposed incineration of trash would be less than that caused by the leaching of toxins from new landfills into groundwater.
(E) No new landfill sites can be found in order to increase the total capacity of landfills in the United States.

6. According to a 1980 survey, ten percent of all United States citizens over the age of sixteen are functionally illiterate. Therefore, if the projection that there will be 250 million United States citizens over sixteen in the year 2000 is correct, we project that 25 million of these citizens will be functionally illiterate.

Which of the following, if true, would most weaken the conclusion drawn by the author of the passage above?

(A) The percentage of high school graduates who do not go on to college has grown steadily over the past two decades.
(B) From 1975 to 1980 there was a three-percent decrease in the rate of functional illiteracy among United States citizens over the age of sixteen.
(C) Many United States citizens included in the 1980 survey would also be included in a survey conducted in the year 2000.
(D) Surveys that are improperly designed usually provide inaccurate results.
(E) In 1980 sixty-five percent of all United States citizens were over the age of sixteen.

GO ON TO THE NEXT PAGE.

Questions 7-13

In an office there are exactly seven employees—N, P, Q, R, S, T, and U. An employee can pass along any memoranda written by that employee as well as any memoranda received from others, but only according to specific rules:

> Memoranda can be passed in either direction between P and Q, in either direction between R and U, and in either direction between S and T.
> Memoranda can be passed from N to S, from Q to R, from S to P, from U to N, and from U to Q.

7. Which of the seven employees can pass memoranda directly to the greatest number of employees?

   (A) N
   (B) Q
   (C) R
   (D) S
   (E) U

8. If a memorandum written by P is to reach S, and is to be passed to no more employees than necessary, it must be passed to a total of how many employees other than P and S?

   (A) 1
   (B) 2
   (C) 3
   (D) 4
   (E) 5

9. A memorandum from Q that eventually reaches T must have been passed to all of the following employees EXCEPT

   (A) N
   (B) P
   (C) R
   (D) S
   (E) U

10. If R is absent from the office for a day, it is still possible for a memorandum to be passed on that day all the way along a route from

   (A) N to Q
   (B) P to S
   (C) P to U
   (D) Q to S
   (E) T to U

11. If S is absent from the office for a day, which of the following employees CANNOT receive any memoranda from any other employee on that day?

   (A) N
   (B) P
   (C) Q
   (D) R
   (E) T

12. A memorandum can travel along two alternative routes that have no employees in common except the writer and the final recipient if the writer and the final recipient, respectively, are

   (A) P and R
   (B) P and T
   (C) Q and T
   (D) S and U
   (E) U and P

13. A memorandum being passed along which of the following routes must reach each of the seven employees at least once?

   (A) N to P and then to U
   (B) R to Q and then to T
   (C) T to Q and then to U
   (D) U to P and then to S
   (E) U to T and then to N

GO ON TO THE NEXT PAGE.

Questions 14-19

A gardener has to plant exactly four varieties of flowers in a flower bed, one variety in each of four rows in an ascending order of height from the first row to the fourth row. The seven varieties available to the gardener are, in ascending order of height, red begonias, pink petunias, orange marigolds, red geraniums, white snapdragons, yellow zinnias, and pink cosmos. The following restrictions on color arrangements apply:

No two varieties of the same color can be planted. Orange flowers cannot be planted in a row immediately adjacent to a row of yellow flowers.

14. Which of the following is a color arrangement, from first row to fourth row, that the gardener can select for the flower bed?

    (A) Pink, red, white, pink
    (B) Pink, orange, white, red
    (C) Red, orange, yellow, pink
    (D) Red, white, yellow, pink
    (E) Red, pink, yellow, white

15. If the gardener plants the geraniums in the third row and the snapdragons in the fourth row, then which of the following must also be planted?

    (A) The begonias and the petunias
    (B) The begonias and the marigolds
    (C) The petunias and the marigolds
    (D) The petunias and the zinnias
    (E) The petunias and the cosmos

16. If the gardener plants the zinnias in the third row, then which of the following can be planted in the second row?

    (A) The begonias
    (B) The petunias
    (C) The marigolds
    (D) The geraniums
    (E) The cosmos

17. Flowers of which of the following colors CANNOT be planted in the third row?

    (A) Orange
    (B) Pink
    (C) Red
    (D) White
    (E) Yellow

18. If the gardener plants the begonias and the petunias, then which of the following must also be planted?

    (A) The marigolds
    (B) The geraniums
    (C) The snapdragons
    (D) The zinnias
    (E) The cosmos

19. If the gardener does not plant any red flowers, then the total number of acceptable arrangements of the flower garden is

    (A) one
    (B) two
    (C) three
    (D) four
    (E) five

GO ON TO THE NEXT PAGE.

Questions 20-22

Exactly seven people—Q, R, S, T, X, Y, and Z—serve on an advisory board. Q, R, S, and T have been elected to the board, and X, Y, and Z have been appointed to the board. Three-person or four-person panels are sometimes drawn from the board to study proposals. Each panel must include at least one elected and at least one appointed board member, but no panel can consist of equal numbers of elected and appointed members. Each panel is chaired by a person who is a member of the group of board members (elected or appointed) whose representatives are in the minority on that panel. Any panel must also conform to the following conditions:

    If Q serves on a panel, T cannot serve on that panel.
    If R serves on a panel, X cannot serve on that panel.
    T and Y cannot serve on a panel unless they serve together.
    If Z serves on a panel, X must also serve on that panel.

20. Which of the following could be a panel drawn from the advisory board?

  (A) Q, R, S
  (B) S, X, Z
  (C) T, Y, Z
  (D) Q, S, T, Y
  (E) R, T, X, Y

21. If R serves on a panel, it must be true that

  (A) it is a three-person panel
  (B) it is a four-person panel
  (C) R chairs the panel
  (D) T chairs the panel
  (E) Y chairs the panel

22. Each of the following could chair a panel EXCEPT

  (A) S
  (B) T
  (C) X
  (D) Y
  (E) Z

23. On the basis of figures it compiles, a citizens' group argues that congressional members of Party X authorize the spending of more taxpayer dollars than do congressional members of Party Y. The group's figures are based on an analysis of the number of spending bills for which members of Congress vote.

The figures of the citizens' group will be unreliable as a gauge of which party in Congress spends more taxpayer dollars if which of the following is true?

  (A) The group weighs all votes for spending bills equally, no matter how much taxpayer money is involved in each bill.
  (B) The group counts votes for all spending bills, including bills concerning the salaries of members of Congress.
  (C) Most spending bills that are introduced in Congress are passed by Congress.
  (D) Most spending bills that members of Party X vote for are written and sponsored by members of Party X.
  (E) All spending bills, before being voted on by Congress, must be approved by committees in which members of both parties participate.

GO ON TO THE NEXT PAGE.

24. Statistics over four consecutive years showed that four percent more automobile accidents happened in California during the week following the switch to daylight saving time and during the week following the switch back to standard time than occurred the week before each event. These statistics show that these time changes adversely affect the alertness of California drivers.

The conclusion in the argument above is based on which of the following assumptions?

(A) Drivers in California as well as those in the rest of the United States have similar driving patterns.
(B) The observed increases in accident rates are due almost entirely to an increase in the number of minor accidents.
(C) Four years is not a sufficiently long period of time over which to judge the phenomenon described.
(D) There are no other factors such as school vacations or holiday celebrations that cause accident rates to rise during these weeks.
(E) A time change at any other time of year would not produce a similar increase in accident rates.

25. Since 1945 there have been numerous international confrontations as tense as those that precipitated the Second World War, and yet no large-scale conflict has resulted. To explain this, some argue that fear of enormous destruction such as the Second World War produced has had a dramatic deterrent effect.

Which of the following, if true, most seriously weakens the deterrent theory mentioned above?

(A) After the First World War, the fear of great future destruction was as intense as it was after the Second World War.
(B) Psychologists have determined that the fear of retaliation tends to temper aggressiveness among human beings.
(C) The Second World War was far less destructive than most people generally believe.
(D) Fear of repeating the levels of destruction that the Second World War produced is as pervasive today as it was forty years ago.
(E) Many of the international confrontations that have occurred since 1945 have involved countries that participated in the Second World War.

STOP

**IF YOU FINISH BEFORE TIME IS CALLED, YOU MAY CHECK YOUR WORK ON THIS SECTION ONLY.
DO NOT TURN TO ANY OTHER SECTION IN THE TEST.**

SECTION 6

Time—30 minutes

37 Questions

Directions: Each sentence below has one or two blanks, each blank indicating that something has been omitted. Beneath the sentence are five lettered words or sets of words. Choose the word or set of words for each blank that best fits the meaning of the sentence as a whole.

1. Because no comprehensive ------- exist regarding personal reading practices, we do not know, for example, the greatest number of books read in an individual lifetime.

   (A) records
   (B) instincts
   (C) remedies
   (D) proposals
   (E) commercials

2. In our corporation there is a ------- between male and female ------- because 73 percent of the men and 34 percent of the women polled believe that our company provides equal compensation to men and women.

   (A) contrast. .stereotypes
   (B) difference. .perceptions
   (C) variation. .salaries
   (D) resemblance. .employees
   (E) similarity. .aspirations

3. The wonder of De Quincey is that although opium dominated his life, it never ------- him; indeed, he turned its use to ------- when he published the story of its influence in the *London Magazine*.

   (A) overcame. .altruism
   (B) intimidated. .triumph
   (C) distressed. .pleasure
   (D) conquered. .gain
   (E) released. .necessity

4. The reduction of noise has been ------- in terms of ------- its sources, but the alternative of canceling noise out by adding sound with the opposite wave pattern may be more useful in practice.

   (A) justified. .diffusing
   (B) accomplished. .tracking
   (C) conceived. .concealing
   (D) explained. .isolating
   (E) approached. .eliminating

5. While Parker is very outspoken on issues she cares about, she is not -------; she concedes the ------- of opposing arguments when they expose weaknesses inherent in her own.

   (A) fickle. .validity
   (B) arrogant. .restraint
   (C) fanatical. .strength
   (D) congenial. .incompatibility
   (E) unyielding. .speciousness

6. Hampshire's assertions, far from showing that we can ------- the ancient puzzles about objectivity, reveal the issue to be even more ------- than we had thought.

   (A) adapt. .pressing
   (B) dismiss. .relevant
   (C) rediscover. .unconventional
   (D) admire. .elusive
   (E) appreciate. .interesting

7. Usually the first to spot data that were inconsistent with other findings, in this particular experiment she let a number of ------- results slip by.

   (A) inaccurate
   (B) verifiable
   (C) redundant
   (D) salient
   (E) anomalous

GO ON TO THE NEXT PAGE.

Directions: In each of the following questions, a related pair of words or phrases is followed by five lettered pairs of words or phrases. Select the lettered pair that best expresses a relationship similar to that expressed in the original pair.

8. TORNADO : AIR ::
   (A) whirlpool : water
   (B) sinkhole : ground
   (C) forest : fire
   (D) gusher : oil
   (E) thunderbolt : lightning

9. SINGER : CHOIR :: (A) flower : bouquet
   (B) leaf : forest (C) flute : reed
   (D) line : sculpture (E) rhythm : time

10. PIGMENT : COLOR :: (A) sizing : fabric
    (B) spice : flavor (C) steel : alloy
    (D) fertilizer : soil (E) rock : energy

11. LABYRINTH : TORTUOUS ::
    (A) ornament : decorative (B) editorial : refutable
    (C) portrait : accurate (D) poster : startling
    (E) pageant : retrospective

12. PRATE : SPEAK :: (A) digress : conclude
    (B) probe : examine (C) soar : travel
    (D) wheedle : coax (E) saunter : walk

13. PERTURB : SERENITY ::
    (A) caress : affection
    (B) protect : security
    (C) harangue : bombast
    (D) annoy : consideration
    (E) reassure : doubt

14. FURTIVE : STEALTH ::
    (A) loquacious : intelligence
    (B) immoral : contrition
    (C) pontifical : reverence
    (D) whimsical : caprice
    (E) arduous : endurance

15. TENDER : ACCEPTANCE ::
    (A) publish : wisdom
    (B) exhibit : inspection
    (C) scrutinize : foresight
    (D) authorize : approval
    (E) declare : observation

16. PLUTOCRACY : WEALTH ::
    (A) democracy : freedom
    (B) aristocracy : land
    (C) gerontocracy : age
    (D) technocracy : ability
    (E) autocracy : birth

GO ON TO THE NEXT PAGE.

Directions: Each passage in this group is followed by questions based on its content. After reading a passage, choose the best answer to each question. Answer all questions following a passage on the basis of what is <u>stated</u> or <u>implied</u> in that passage.

Traditional research has confronted only Mexican and United States interpretations of Mexican-American culture. Now we must also examine the culture as we
Line
(5) Mexican Americans have experienced it, passing from a sovereign people to compatriots with newly arriving settlers to, finally, a conquered people—a charter minority on our own land.

When the Spanish first came to Mexico, they intermarried with and absorbed the culture of the indigenous
(10) Indians. This policy of colonization through acculturation was continued when Mexico acquired Texas in the early 1800's and brought the indigenous Indians into Mexican life and government. In the 1820's, United States citizens migrated to Texas, attracted by land suitable for cotton.
(15) As their numbers became more substantial, their policy of acquiring land by subduing native populations began to dominate. The two ideologies clashed repeatedly, culminating in a military conflict that led to victory for the United States. Thus, suddenly deprived of our parent
(20) culture, we had to evolve uniquely Mexican-American modes of thought and action in order to survive.

17. The author's purpose in writing this passage is primarily to

(A) suggest the motives behind Mexican and United States intervention in Texas
(B) document certain early objectives of Mexican-American society
(C) provide a historical perspective for a new analysis of Mexican-American culture
(D) appeal to both Mexican and United States scholars to give greater consideration to economic interpretations of history
(E) bring to light previously overlooked research on Mexican Americans

18. The author most probably uses the phrase "charter minority" (lines 6-7) to reinforce the idea that Mexican Americans

(A) are a native rather than an immigrant group in the United States
(B) played an active political role when Texas first became part of the United States
(C) recognized very early in the nineteenth century the need for official confirmation of their rights of citizenship
(D) have been misunderstood by scholars trying to interpret their culture
(E) identify more closely with their Indian heritage than with their Spanish heritage

19. According to the passage, a major difference between the colonization policy of the United States and that of Mexico in Texas in the 1800's was the

(A) degree to which policies were based on tradition
(B) form of economic interdependency between different cultural groups
(C) number of people who came to settle new areas
(D) treatment of the native inhabitants
(E) relationship between the military and the settlers

20. Which of the following statements most clearly contradicts the information in this passage?

(A) In the early 1800's, the Spanish committed more resources to settling California than to developing Texas.
(B) While Texas was under Mexican control, the population of Texas quadrupled, in spite of the fact that Mexico discouraged immigration from the United States.
(C) By the time Mexico acquired Texas, many Indians had already married people of Spanish heritage.
(D) Many Mexicans living in Texas returned to Mexico after Texas was annexed by the United States.
(E) Most Indians living in Texas resisted Spanish acculturation and were either killed or enslaved.

GO ON TO THE NEXT PAGE.

This passage was adapted from an article published in 1982.

Until about five years ago, the very idea that peptide hormones might be made anywhere in the brain besides the hypothalamus was astounding. Peptide hormones,
Line
(5) scientists thought, were made by endocrine glands and the hypothalamus was thought to be the brains' only endocrine gland. What is more, because peptide hormones cannot cross the blood-brain barrier, researchers believed that they never got to any part of the brain other than the hypothalamus, where they were simply
(10) produced and then released into the bloodstream.

But these beliefs about peptide hormones were questioned as laboratory after laboratory found that antiserums to peptide hormones, when injected into the brain, bind in places other than the hypothalamus, indi-
(15) cating that either the hormones or substances that crossreact with the antiserums are present. The immunological method of detecting peptide hormones by means of antiserums, however, is imprecise. Cross-reactions are possible and this method cannot determine whether
(20) the substances detected by the antiserums really are the hormones, or merely close relatives. Furthermore, this method cannot be used to determine the location in the body where the detected substances are actually produced.

(25) New techniques of molecular biology, however, provide a way to answer these questions. It is possible to make specific complementary DNA's (cDNA's) that can serve as molecular probes to seek out the messenger RNA's (mRNA's) of the peptide hormones. If brain cells
(30) are making the hormones, the cells will contain these mRNA's. If the products the brain cells make resemble the hormones but are not identical to them, then the cDNA's should still bind to these mRNA's, but should not bind as tightly as they would to mRNA's for the
(35) true hormones. The cells containing these mRNA's can then be isolated and their mRNA's decoded to determine just what their protein products are and how closely the products resemble the true peptide hormones.

(40) The molecular approach to detecting peptide hormones using cDNA probes should also be much faster than the immunological method because it can take years of tedious purifications to isolate peptide hormones and then develop antiserums to them. Roberts,
(45) expressing the sentiment of many researchers, states: "I was trained as an endocrinologist. But it became clear to me that the field of endocrinology needed molecular biology input. The process of grinding out protein purifications is just too slow."

(50) If, as the initial tests with cDNA probes suggest, peptide hormones really are made in the brain in areas other than the hypothalamus, a theory must be developed that explains their function in the brain. Some have suggested that the hormones are all growth regula-
(55) tors, but Rosen's work on rat brains indicates that this cannot be true. A number of other researchers propose that they might be used for intercellular communication in the brain.

82

21. Which of the following titles best summarizes the passage?

(A) Is Molecular Biology the Key to Understanding Intercellular Communication in the Brain?
(B) Molecular Biology: Can Researchers Exploit Its Techniques to Synthesize Peptide Hormones?
(C) The Advantages and Disadvantages of the Immunological Approach to Detecting Peptide Hormones
(D) Peptide Hormones: How Scientists Are Attempting to Solve Problems of Their Detection and to Understand Their Function
(E) Peptide Hormones: The Role Played by Messenger RNA's in Their Detection

22. The passage suggests that a substance detected in the brain by use of antiserums to peptide hormones may

(A) have been stored in the brain for a long period of time
(B) play no role in the functioning of the brain
(C) have been produced in some part of the body other than the brain
(D) have escaped detection by molecular methods
(E) play an important role in the functioning of the hypothalamus

23. According to the passage, confirmation of the belief that peptide hormones are made in the brain in areas other than the hypothalamus would force scientists to

(A) reject the theory that peptide hormones are made by endocrine glands
(B) revise their beliefs about the ability of antiserums to detect peptide hormones
(C) invent techniques that would allow them to locate accurately brain cells that produce peptide hormones
(D) search for techniques that would enable them to distinguish peptide hormones from their close relatives
(E) develop a theory that explains the role played by peptide hormones in the brain

GO ON TO THE NEXT PAGE.

24. Which of the following is mentioned in the passage as a drawback of the immunological method of detecting peptide hormones?

    (A) It cannot be used to detect the presence of growth regulators in the brain.
    (B) It cannot distinguish between the peptide hormones and substances that are very similar to them.
    (C) It uses antiserums that are unable to cross the blood-brain barrier.
    (D) It involves a purification process that requires extensive training in endocrinology.
    (E) It involves injecting foreign substances directly into the bloodstream.

25. The passage implies that, in doing research on rat brains, Rosen discovered that

    (A) peptide hormones are used for intercellular communication
    (B) complementary DNA's do not bind to cells producing peptide hormones
    (C) products closely resembling peptide hormones are not identical to peptide hormones
    (D) some peptide hormones do not function as growth regulators
    (E) antiserums cross-react with substances that are not peptide hormones

26. Which of the following is a way in which the immunological method of detecting peptide hormones differs from the molecular method?

    (A) The immunological method uses substances that react with products of hormone-producing cells, whereas the molecular method uses substances that react with a specific component of the cells themselves.
    (B) The immunological method has produced results consistent with long-held beliefs about peptide hormones, whereas the molecular method has produced results that upset these beliefs.
    (C) The immunological method requires a great deal of expertise, whereas the molecular method has been used successfully by nonspecialists.
    (D) The immunological method can only be used to test for the presence of peptide hormones within the hypothalamus, whereas the molecular method can be used throughout the brain.
    (E) The immunological method uses probes that can only bind with peptide hormones, whereas the molecular method uses probes that bind with peptide hormones and substances similar to them.

27. The idea that the field of endocrinology can gain from developments in molecular biology is regarded by Roberts with

    (A) incredulity
    (B) derision
    (C) indifference
    (D) pride
    (E) enthusiasm

GO ON TO THE NEXT PAGE.

Directions: Each question below consists of a word printed in capital letters, followed by five lettered words or phrases. Choose the lettered word or phrase that is most nearly <u>opposite</u> in meaning to the word in capital letters.

Since some of the questions require you to distinguish fine shades of meaning, be sure to consider all the choices before deciding which one is best.

28. ORIENT: (A) hasten (B) defile (C) menace
   (D) confuse (E) decline

29. UNIMPEACHABLE:
   (A) irritable (B) preventable
   (C) unused to conflict (D) open to question
   (E) available for discussion

30. EXPEND: (A) proceed toward (B) take away
   (C) place upon (D) hold to (E) store up

31. SEAMY:
   (A) decent and respectable
   (B) jagged and irregular
   (C) strict and authoritarian
   (D) ornate and adorned
   (E) subtle and dangerous

32. LUCID: (A) unrecognized (B) limited
   (C) murky (D) improbable (E) inconsistent

33. LASSITUDE:
   (A) a fear of discovery
   (B) a feeling of vigor
   (C) a twinge of embarrassment
   (D) a want of seriousness
   (E) a sense of superiority

34. HALLMARK:
   (A) grave defect
   (B) valueless object
   (C) unfortunate incident
   (D) uncharacteristic feature
   (E) untimely event

35. DIATRIBE: (A) sermon (B) discourse
   (C) eulogy (D) lecture (E) oration

36. SEDULITY:
   (A) lack of industriousness
   (B) abundance of supporters
   (C) contradiction of doctrine
   (D) rejection of analysis
   (E) depletion of resources

37. APPOSITE: (A) malevolent (B) implicit
   (C) disorganized (D) avoidable (E) irrelevant

STOP

IF YOU FINISH BEFORE TIME IS CALLED, YOU MAY CHECK YOUR WORK ON THIS SECTION ONLY.
DO NOT TURN TO ANY OTHER SECTION IN THE TEST.

NO TEST MATERIAL ON THIS PAGE

NO TEST MATERIAL ON THIS PAGE

THE GRADUATE RECORD EXAMINATIONS
GENERAL TEST

You will have 3 hours and 30 minutes in which to work on this test, which consists of seven sections. During the time allowed for one section, you may work only on that section. The time allowed for each section is 30 minutes.

Each of your scores will be determined by the number of questions for which you select the best answer from the choices given. Questions for which you mark no answer or more than one answer are not counted in scoring. Nothing is subtracted from a score if you answer a question incorrectly. Therefore, to maximize your scores, it is better for you to guess at an answer than not to respond at all.

You are advised to work as rapidly as you can without losing accuracy. Do not spend too much time on questions that are too difficult for you. Go on to the other questions and come back to the difficult ones later.

There are several different types of questions; you will find special directions for each type in the test itself. Be sure you understand the directions before attempting to answer any questions.

For each question several answer choices (lettered A-E or A-D) are given from which you are to select the ONE best answer. YOU MUST INDICATE ALL YOUR ANSWERS ON THE SEPARATE ANSWER SHEET. No credit will be given for anything written in this examination book, but to work out your answers you may write in the book as much as you wish. After you have decided which of the suggested answers is best, fill in completely the corresponding space on the answer sheet. Be sure to:

- Use a soft black lead pencil (No. 2 or HB).

- Mark only one answer to each question. No credit will be given for multiple answers.

- Mark your answer in the row with the same number as the number of the question you are answering.

- Carefully and completely fill in the space corresponding to the answer you select for each question. Fill the space with a dark mark so that you cannot see the letter inside the space. Light or partial marks may not be read by the scoring machine. See the example of proper and improper answer marks below.

- Erase all stray marks. If you change an answer, be sure that you completely erase the old answer before marking your new answer. Incomplete erasures may be read as intended answers.

Example: Sample Answer

What city is the capital of France?   Ⓐ ● Ⓒ Ⓓ Ⓔ   BEST ANSWER PROPERLY MARKED

  (A) Rome   Ⓐ ⓧ Ⓒ Ⓓ Ⓔ
  (B) Paris   Ⓐ ⓑ Ⓒ Ⓓ Ⓔ
  (C) London   Ⓐ ⬤ Ⓒ Ⓓ Ⓔ   IMPROPER MARKS
  (D) Cairo   Ⓐ ⬤ Ⓒ Ⓓ Ⓔ
  (E) Oslo

Do not be concerned that the answer sheet provides spaces for more answers than there are questions in the test. Some or all of the passages for this test have been adapted from published material to provide the examinee with significant problems for analysis and evaluation. To make the passages suitable for testing purposes, the style, content, or point of view of the original may have been altered in some cases. The ideas contained in the passages do not necessarily represent the opinions of the Graduate Record Examinations Board or Educational Testing Service.

CLOSE YOUR TEST BOOK AND WAIT FOR FURTHER INSTRUCTIONS FROM THE SUPERVISOR.

I

NOTE: To ensure the prompt and accurate processing of test results, your cooperation in following these directions is needed. The procedures that follow have been kept to the minimum necessary. They will take a few minutes to complete, but it is essential that you fill in all blanks <u>exactly</u> as directed.

GENERAL TEST

A. Print and sign your full name in this box:

PRINT: _____
(LAST)   (FIRST)   (MIDDLE)
SIGN: _____

B. Side 1 of your answer sheet contains areas that will be used to ensure accurate reporting of your test results. It is essential that you carefully enter the requested information.

    [1] through [5] YOUR NAME, DATE OF BIRTH, SOCIAL SECURITY NUMBER, REGISTRATION NUMBER, and ADDRESS: <u>Print</u> all the information requested in the boxes and then fill in completely the appropriate oval beneath each entry.

- For date of birth, be sure to enter a zero before a single digit (e.g., if you were born on the third day of the month, you would enter "03" for the day). Use the last two digits of the year of your birth (for 1966, enter 66).

- Copy the registration number from your admission ticket.

    [6] TITLE CODE: Copy the numbers shown below and fill in completely the appropriate spaces beneath each entry as shown. When you have completed item 6, check to be sure it is identical to the illustration below.

    [7] TEST NAME: Copy _____General_____ in the box.

         FORM CODE: Copy _____GR 90 - 13_____ in the box.

    [8] TEST BOOK SERIAL NUMBER: Copy the serial number of your test book in the box. It is printed in red at the upper right on the front cover of your test book.

    [9] <u>Print</u> the requested information and enter the test center number in the boxes.

    [10] CERTIFICATION STATEMENT: In the boxed area, <u>WRITE</u> (do not print) the following statement: "I certify that I am the person whose name appears on this answer sheet. I also agree not to disclose the contents of the test I am taking today to anyone." Sign and date where indicated.

When you have finished, wait for further instructions from the supervisor. DO NOT OPEN YOUR TEST BOOK UNTIL YOU ARE TOLD TO DO SO.

FOR GENERAL TEST, FORM GR90-13 ONLY
Answer Key and Percentages* of Examinees Answering Each Question Correctly

VERBAL ABILITY

Section 3			Section 6		
Number	Answer	P+	Number	Answer	P+
1	D	93	1	A	98
2	C	78	2	B	74
3	A	65	3	D	66
4	B	72	4	E	59
5	D	65	5	C	59
6	A	53	6	B	64
7	C	41	7	E	31
8	D	92	8	A	84
9	D	88	9	A	89
10	E	78	10	B	76
11	E	46	11	A	51
12	B	57	12	E	42
13	A	54	13	E	35
14	C	40	14	D	28
15	B	38	15	B	21
16	C	21	16	C	25
17	D	43	17	C	79
18	E	82	18	A	76
19	C	47	19	D	69
20	A	39	20	E	48
21	B	62	21	D	68
22	E	50	22	C	64
23	A	39	23	E	43
24	C	45	24	B	70
25	C	39	25	D	70
26	E	16	26	A	41
27	D	49	27	E	58
28	D	92	28	D	87
29	E	85	29	D	61
30	C	75	30	E	67
31	D	71	31	A	60
32	C	37	32	C	62
33	E	34	33	B	50
34	B	42	34	D	45
35	E	26	35	C	36
36	D	33	36	A	29
37	D	39	37	E	25
38	E	29			

QUANTITATIVE ABILITY

Section 1			Section 4		
Number	Answer	P+	Number	Answer	P+
1	D	93	1	A	92
2	A	84	2	C	92
3	B	83	3	B	82
4	D	74	4	D	83
5	B	79	5	C	89
6	D	72	6	C	78
7	C	71	7	A	79
8	A	67	8	B	78
9	C	71	9	C	74
10	A	73	10	B	70
11	A	55	11	A	72
12	C	53	12	B	63
13	B	49	13	D	61
14	A	44	14	D	44
15	C	36	15	B	38
16	C	82	16	C	84
17	E	81	17	A	83
18	C	76	18	D	77
19	B	77	19	D	66
20	A	66	20	E	69
21	D	87	21	E	85
22	E	66	22	C	58
23	C	59	23	C	48
24	C	59	24	E	57
25	E	29	25	A	39
26	A	53	26	B	76
27	C	50	27	B	54
28	B	36	28	A	44
29	B	31	29	E	39
30	D	22	30	E	36

ANALYTICAL ABILITY

Section 2			Section 5		
Number	Answer	P+	Number	Answer	P+
1	A	83	1	A	86
2	E	77	2	D	85
3	B	68	3	C	62
4	E	76	4	E	83
5	C	42	5	D	77
6	D	67	6	B	52
7	C	61	7	E	75
8	D	44	8	D	53
9	A	91	9	B	74
10	C	87	10	A	58
11	C	28	11	E	75
12	E	86	12	E	35
13	C	30	13	E	25
14	B	53	14	D	61
15	D	39	15	C	68
16	C	52	16	D	49
17	B	55	17	B	46
18	C	47	18	C	53
19	C	76	19	E	39
20	B	59	20	B	58
21	A	42	21	E	18
22	E	29	22	E	19
23	D	37	23	A	34
24	E	43	24	D	56
25	D	42	25	A	48

*Estimated P+ for the group of examinees who took the GRE General Test in a recent three-year period.

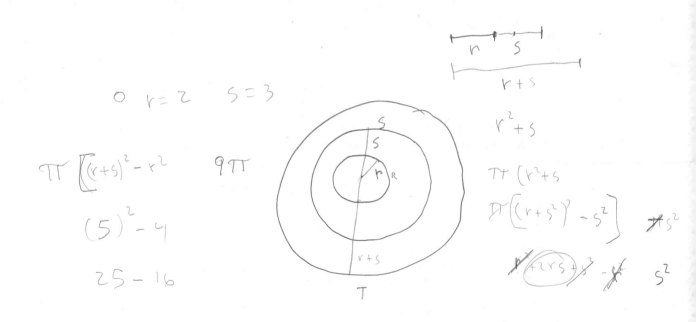

89

SCORE CONVERSIONS AND PERCENTS BELOW*
FOR GRE GENERAL TEST, Form GR90-13 ONLY

Raw Score	Verbal Score	% Below	Quantitative Score	% Below	Analytical Score	% Below	Raw Score	Verbal Score	% Below	Quantitative Score	% Below	Analytical Score	% Below
72-75	800	99					40	460	44	560	49	700	90
71	790	99					39	450	41	550	48	680	87
70	780	99					38	440	38	530	42	670	85
69	760	99					37	430	36	520	40	660	83
68	750	98					36	420	33	510	37	640	79
67	740	98					35	410	30	500	35	630	76
66	730	97					34	410	30	490	32	620	74
65	720	96					33	400	26	480	30	600	69
64	710	95					32	390	24	470	28	590	67
63	690	94					31	380	22	460	26	580	64
62	680	93					30	370	20	450	24	560	58
61	670	92					29	370	20	440	22	550	55
60	660	90	800	97			28	360	16	430	20	530	49
59	650	89	800	97			27	350	14	420	18	520	46
58	640	87	800	97			26	350	14	410	16	510	43
57	630	85	800	97			25	340	12	400	14	490	38
56	620	84	780	94			24	330	10	390	13	480	35
55	610	82	770	93			23	320	9	380	12	460	31
54	600	80	750	89			22	310	7	370	10	450	27
53	590	78	740	88			21	290	5	360	9	440	24
	580	76	720	84			20	280	4	350	7	420	20
	570	74	710	82			19	270	3	340	6	410	18
	560	72	690	78	800	99	18	260	2	330	5	390	15
	540	67	680	77	800	99	17	250	1	320	5	380	13
	530	64	660	72	800	99	16	240	1	310	4	360	10
	520	61	650	70	800	99	15	230	1	300	3	350	9
46	520	61	640	68	780	98	14	220	0	290	2	330	6
45	500	56	620	63	770	97	13	210	0	280	2	310	4
44	490	54	610	61	750	96	12	200	0	260	1	300	4
43	480	51	600	59	740	95	11	200	0	240	1	280	2
42	470	48	580	54	720	92	10	200	0	230	0	260	1
41	460	44	570	51	710	91	9	200	0	210	0	240	1
							8	200	0	200	0	220	0
							0-7	200	0	200	0	200	0

*Percent scoring below the scaled score based on the performance of 923,359 examinees who took the General Test between October 1, 1986, and September 30, 1989.

90

01

THE GRADUATE RECORD EXAMINATIONS

General Test
(with explanations)

NO TEST MATERIAL ON THIS PAGE

SECTION 1
30 Questions

Numbers: All numbers used are real numbers.

Figures: Position of points, angles, regions, etc., can be assumed to be in the order shown; and angle measures can be assumed to be positive.

Lines shown as straight can be assumed to be straight.

Figures can be assumed to lie in a plane unless otherwise indicated.

Figures that accompany questions are intended to provide information useful in answering the questions. However, unless a note states that a figure is drawn to scale, you should solve these problems NOT by estimating sizes by sight or by measurement, but by using your knowledge of mathematics (see Example 2 below).

Directions: Each of the <u>Questions 1-15</u> consists of two quantities, one in Column A and one in Column B. You are to compare the two quantities and choose

     A   **if the quantity in Column A is greater;**
     B   **if the quantity in Column B is greater;**
     C   **if the two quantities are equal;**
     D   **if the relationship cannot be determined from the information given.**

Note: Since there are only four choices, NEVER MARK (E).

Common
Information: In a question, information concerning one or both of the quantities to be compared is centered above the two columns. A symbol that appears in both columns represents the same thing in Column A as it does in Column B.

	Column A	**Column B**	**Sample Answers**
Example 1:	2×6	$2 + 6$	● Ⓑ Ⓒ Ⓓ Ⓔ

**Examples 2-4
refer to $\triangle PQR$.**

Example 2:	PN	NQ	Ⓐ Ⓑ Ⓒ ● Ⓔ

(since equal measures cannot be assumed, even though *PN* and *NQ* appear equal)

Example 3:	x	y	Ⓐ ● Ⓒ Ⓓ Ⓔ

(since *N* is between *P* and *Q*)

Example 4:	$w + z$	180	Ⓐ Ⓑ ● Ⓓ Ⓔ

(since *PQ* is a straight line)

A if the quantity in Column A is greater;
B if the quantity in Column B is greater;
C if the two quantities are equal;
D if the relationship cannot be determined from the information given.

Column A	Column B

$$S = 6 + 7 + 8 + 9$$
$$T = 9 + 8 + 7 + 6$$

1. $S + T$ $4(15)$

Ⓐ Ⓑ Ⓒ Ⓓ Ⓔ

Adding the two equations gives:

$$
\begin{aligned}
S &= 6 + 7 + 8 + 9 \\
+T &= 9 + 8 + 7 + 6 \\
\hline
S + T &= 15 + 15 + 15 + 15 = 4(15)
\end{aligned}
$$

The answer is C

2. $\dfrac{332}{999}$ $\dfrac{1}{3}$

Ⓐ Ⓑ Ⓒ Ⓓ Ⓔ

Since $\dfrac{1}{3} = \dfrac{333}{999}$, and $\dfrac{333}{999}$ is greater than $\dfrac{332}{999}$, it follows that $\dfrac{1}{3}$ must be greater than $\dfrac{332}{999}$.

The answer is B

Each of w and x is less than 5 and greater than 2.
Each of y and z is less than 2 and greater than 1.

3. $w + x$ $y + z$

Ⓐ Ⓑ Ⓒ Ⓓ Ⓔ

Since w and x are each greater than 2,

$$w + x > 4.$$

Since y and z are each less than 2,

$$y + z < 4.$$

Therefore, $w + x > y + z$.

The answer is A

Column A	Column B

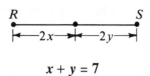

$$x + y = 7$$

4. The length of　　　　　　　　　　　**14**
　　segment *RS*

The length of segment *RS* is $2x + 2y$, which equals $2(x + y)$. Since $x + y = 7$, the length of *RS* is $2(x + y) = 2(7) = 14$.

The answer is C

$$2x + y = 6$$
$$y = x$$

5.　　　　　　$x + y$　　　　　　　　　　$3x - 2$

Ⓐ Ⓑ Ⓒ Ⓓ Ⓔ

Since $y = x$, x can be substituted for y in the first equation giving

$$2x + x = 6$$
$$3x = 6$$
$$x = 2$$

Since $y = x$, y also equals 2; therefore, by substitution:

$$x + y = 2 + 2 = 4$$
$$\text{and} \quad 3x - 2 = 3(2) - 2 = 4$$

The answer is C

For a different solution, see below:

Subtract the second equation from the first.

$$
\begin{aligned}
2x + y &= 6 \\
- \quad\quad y &= x \\
\hline
2x \quad\quad &= 6 - x \\
3x &= 6 \\
x &= 2
\end{aligned}
$$

Therefore, $y = 2$, and so forth, as in the previous solution.

A   if the quantity in Column A is greater;
B   if the quantity in Column B is greater;
C   if the two quantities are equal;
D   if the relationship cannot be determined from the information given.

<u>Column A</u>   <u>Column B</u>

Coins are put into 5 pockets so that each pocket contains at least one coin, but no two pockets contain the same number of coins.

6. **The least possible**   **16**
   total number of coins
   in the 5 pockets

Since each of the five pockets must contain at least 1 coin, and no two pockets contain the same number of coins, the smallest possible number of coins would be

$$1 + 2 + 3 + 4 + 5 = 15,$$

and 16 is greater than 15.

The answer is B

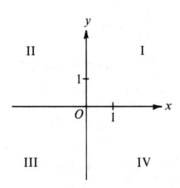

Points $(x, 3)$ and $(3, y)$ are in quadrants II and IV, respectively.

7. x y

Since $(x,3)$ is in quadrant II, x must be negative. Since $(3,y)$ is in quadrant IV, y must be negative. Since we have no other information regarding the values of x and y, we cannot determine which is larger.

The answer is D

Column A	**Column B**

$$n > 0$$

8. $\quad \dfrac{10^n}{10^{n+1}}$ $\qquad\qquad\qquad\qquad\qquad$ $\dfrac{10^{n+1}}{10^{n+2}}$

Ⓐ Ⓑ Ⓒ Ⓓ Ⓔ

Since multiplying by 1 does not change the value of an expression, we can multiply

$$\frac{10^n}{10^{n+1}} \ \text{ by } \ \frac{10}{10} \ \text{ and get}$$

$$\frac{10^n}{10^{n+1}} \bullet \frac{10^1}{10^1} = \frac{10^{n+1}}{10^{n+1+1}} = \frac{10^{n+1}}{10^{n+2}}$$

The answer is C

For a different solution, see below.

Simplify each expression as follows:

$$\frac{10^n}{10^{n+1}} = 10^{n-(n+1)} = 10^{-1}$$

$$\frac{10^{n+1}}{10^{n+2}} = 10^{n+1-(n+2)} = 10^{-1}$$

The answer is C

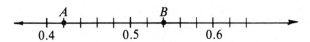

Note: Drawn to scale.

A and B are points on the number line.

9. **The length of** $\qquad\qquad\qquad\qquad$ **0.11**
   segment *AB*

Ⓐ Ⓑ Ⓒ Ⓓ Ⓔ

The line segment between 0.4 and 0.5 has length 0.1, and it is subdivided into 5 segments of equal length. Each of the smaller segments, therefore, has length $\frac{1}{5}(0.1) = 0.02$. Segment *AB* is composed of 6 such segments. Therefore, the length of segment *AB* is

$$6(0.02) = 0.12,$$

which is greater than 0.11.

The answer is A

A   if the quantity in Column A is greater;
B   if the quantity in Column B is greater;
C   if the two quantities are equal;
D   if the relationship cannot be determined from the information given.

Column A   **Column B**

The circle with center *O* and the circle with center *P* are tangent at *Q*.

10. The area of the   Four times the area
    circular region   of the circular region
    with center *O*   with center *P*

Ⓐ Ⓑ Ⓒ Ⓓ Ⓔ

Let the radius of the smaller circular region (center at *P*) be called *r*. Then the radius of the larger circular region (center at *O*) is 2*r*.

The area of the smaller circular region = πr^2.

The area of the larger circular region = $\pi (2r)^2 = 4\pi r^2$.

Therefore, 4 times the smaller area is
$$(4)(\pi r^2) = 4\pi r^2,$$
which equals the larger area.

The answer is C

Brand *R* coffee costs $3.25 per pound and brand *T* coffee costs $2.50 per pound.

11. The number of pounds   1.2
    of brand *R* in a mixture
    of brands *R* and *T* that
    costs $3.00 per pound

Ⓐ Ⓑ Ⓒ Ⓓ Ⓔ

Let
   r = the number of pounds of brand *R* in a mixture of brands *R* and *T* that costs
      $3.00 per pound, and
   t = the number of pounds of brand *T* in that same mixture.

Since the price of brand *R* is $3.25 per pound and the price of brand *T* is $2.50 per pound, we get the following equation by expressing the value of the mixture in two different ways:

$$3.25r + 2.50t = 3.00(r + t)$$

The equation reduces to $r = 2t$. We need to compare the value of r to 1.2. However, all we know is that the $3.00 mixture has 2 parts R to 1 part T. Without knowing the value of t, we cannot find r. Therefore, there is not enough information given to make the comparison.

The answer is D

Column A   **Column B**

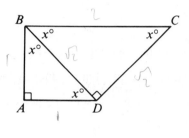

$$AB = 1$$

12. **The perimeter of**   6
   quadrilateral $ABCD$

   Ⓐ Ⓑ Ⓒ Ⓓ Ⓔ

Since right triangle ABD is isosceles, $AB = AD = 1$. By the Pythagorean Theorem, $(BD)^2 = (1)^2 + (1)^2 = 2$. Therefore, $BD = \sqrt{2}$.

Right triangle BCD is also isosceles, so $BD = CD$, and hence $CD = \sqrt{2}$.

Again by the Pythagorean Theorem, $(BC)^2 = (\sqrt{2})^2 + (\sqrt{2})^2 = 4$, so $BC = 2$.
The perimeter of $ABCD$ is therefore

$$AB + BC + CD + AD = 1 + 2 + \sqrt{2} + 1 = 4 + \sqrt{2}$$

Since $\sqrt{2} < 2$, it follows that $4 + \sqrt{2} < 6$

The answer is B

13. **The value of the**   **The value of the**
   units' digit in 6^{47}   **units' digit in 5^{77}**

The number 6 raised to any positive integer power ends in 6 because every multiplication involves two integers whose units' digit is 6, which in turn will produce a product whose units' digit is 6. Using similar reasoning, 5 raised to any positive integer power ends in 5.

Therefore, the units' digit for 6^{47} is 6, and the units' digit for 5^{77} is 5.

The answer is A

A if the quantity in Column A is greater;
B if the quantity in Column B is greater;
C if the two quantities are equal;
D if the relationship cannot be determined from the information given.

Column A	Column B

For all numbers r and s, where $s \neq 0$, $r \odot s = \dfrac{10r}{s}$.

14. $(0.01) \odot (0.01)$ 1

Ⓐ   Ⓑ   Ⓒ   Ⓓ   Ⓔ

According to the definition of the symbol $\odot$, $r \odot s$ tells us to multiply the left-hand number (r) by 10 and then divide that product by the right-hand number (s).
Therefore, $(0.01) \odot (0.01) = \dfrac{10\,(0.01)}{0.01}$, which equals 10.
The answer is A

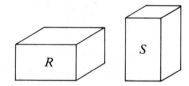

The volume of block R is equal to the volume of block S.

15. The total surface area of R   **The total surface area of S**

Ⓐ   Ⓑ   Ⓒ   Ⓓ   Ⓔ

The dimensions of blocks R and S are not given. If the dimensions for R and S were exactly the same, it is clear that the blocks would have equal surface area as well as equal volume. One way to proceed, assuming that the dimensions of blocks R and S are not exactly the same, though the volumes are equal, is to try some numbers. For example, if the dimensions for R were 3 by 4 by 5, and the dimensions for S were 3 by 2 by 10, the volumes would be equal (both 60), but the total surface areas would not be equal.

Total surface area for R = 2[(3)(4) + (3)(5) + (4)(5)] = 94.
Total surface area for S = 2[(3)(2) + (3)(10) + (2)(10)] = 112.

Although this is only one example, it is sufficient to indicate that there is not enough information given to compare the two surface areas.

The answer is D

16. A certain photocopying machine can make 10 copies every 4 seconds. At this rate, how many copies can the machine make in 6 minutes?

(A) 900
(B) 600
(C) 360
(D) 240
(E) 150

Ⓐ Ⓑ Ⓒ Ⓓ Ⓔ

The machine can make 10 copies in 4 seconds. Therefore, in one minute (which is 60 seconds) the machine can make 15 times that many copies, which is 15(10) = 150 copies. Thus, in 6 minutes the machine can make

$$6(150) = 900 \text{ copies.}$$

The answer is A

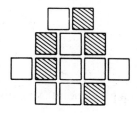

17. The figure above is made up of shaded and unshaded squares of the same size. What is the ratio of the number of shaded squares to the total number of shaded and unshaded squares?

(A) $\dfrac{13}{5}$ (B) $\dfrac{8}{5}$ (C) $\dfrac{5}{8}$ (D) $\dfrac{1}{2}$ (E) $\dfrac{5}{13}$

Ⓐ Ⓑ Ⓒ Ⓓ Ⓔ

There are 5 shaded squares and 8 unshaded squares. Therefore, the ratio of the number of shaded squares to the total number of shaded and unshaded squares is

$$\frac{5}{5+8} = \frac{5}{13}.$$

The answer is E

18. If $a = 2$, $b = 4$, and $c = 5$, then $\dfrac{a+b}{c} - \dfrac{c}{a+b} =$

(A) 1

(B) $\dfrac{11}{30}$

(C) 0

(D) $-\dfrac{11}{30}$

(E) −1

Ⓐ Ⓑ Ⓒ Ⓓ Ⓔ

Substituting the values for a, b, and c, we get:

$$\frac{a+b}{c} - \frac{c}{a+b} = \frac{2+4}{5} - \frac{5}{2+4}$$

$$= \frac{6}{5} - \frac{5}{6}$$

$$= \frac{36}{30} - \frac{25}{30}$$

$$= \frac{11}{30}$$

The answer is B

19. In the xy-plane, which of the following points is the greatest distance from the origin?

   (A) (0, 3)
   (B) (1, 3)
   (C) (2, 1)
   (D) (2, 3)
   (E) (3, 0)

Ⓐ Ⓑ Ⓒ Ⓓ Ⓔ

In terms of the coordinates of a given point (x,y), distance d from the origin is given by the formula:

$$d = \sqrt{x^2 + y^2}$$

Checking each option:

   (A)   For $(0,3)$ $d = \sqrt{0^2 + 3^2} = \sqrt{9}$
   (B)   For $(1,3)$ $d = \sqrt{1^2 + 3^2} = \sqrt{10}$
   (C)   For $(2,1)$ $d = \sqrt{2^2 + 1^2} = \sqrt{5}$
   (D)   For $(2,3)$ $d = \sqrt{2^2 + 3^2} = \sqrt{13}$
   (E)   For $(3,0)$ $d = \sqrt{3^2 + 0^2} = \sqrt{9}$

The answer is D

For a different solution, see next page.

Plotting the points on the *xy*-plane would yield the following:

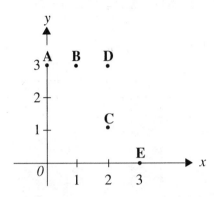

Visually, *C* is closest to *0*; *A* and *E* are tied for next closest at 3 units' distance. *B* and *D* are more than 3 units from *0*, and clearly, *D* is farther away than *B*. Therefore, point (2, 3) is the greatest distance from *0*. No calculations are necessary.

20. If $\frac{y}{x} = -1$, then $y + x =$

    (A) –2   (B) –1   (C) 0   (D) 1   (E) 2

Ⓐ Ⓑ Ⓒ Ⓓ Ⓔ

Multiplying both sides of the equation by *x* gives

$$x(\frac{y}{x}) = x(-1)$$
$$y = -x$$

and adding *x* to both sides of the new equation gives

$$y + x = -x + x$$
$$y + x = 0$$

The answer is C

Questions 21-25 refer to the following graphs.

SALES AND EARNINGS OF COMPANY X

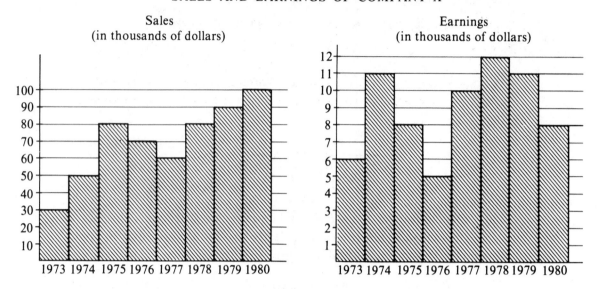

Note: Drawn to scale.

21. For the years 1974 to 1979 inclusive, what was the amount of the greatest increase in sales from one year to the next?

(A) $5,000 **(B) $10,000** **(C) $12,000** **(D) $30,000** **(E) $80,000**

Ⓐ Ⓑ Ⓒ Ⓓ Ⓔ

With reference to the Sales graph, for the years 1974 to 1979 inclusive, the greatest increase from one year to the next was from 1974 ($50,000) to 1975 ($80,000). The amount of the increase was $30,000.

The answer is D

22. For the period from 1973 to 1977 inclusive, what were the average (arithmetic mean) sales per year?

(A) $57,000 **(B) $58,000** **(C) $59,500** **(D) $60,300** **(E) $61,700**

Ⓐ Ⓑ Ⓒ Ⓓ Ⓔ

With reference to the Sales graph, the sales from 1973 to 1977 inclusive were:

1973	:	$ 30,000
1974	:	50,000
1975	:	80,000
1976	:	70,000
1977	:	60,000
Total	:	$290,000

The average per year was $290,000/5 = $58,000.

The answer is B

23. In which of the years from 1974 to 1979 inclusive, did earnings change by the greatest percent over the previous year?

(A) 1974   (B) 1975   (C) 1977   (D) 1978   (E) 1979

Ⓐ Ⓑ Ⓒ Ⓓ Ⓔ

The question asks for the percent change in earnings, which cannot be read directly from the graph. The change in percent for each of the years listed in the options were:

$$1974: \quad \frac{11-6}{6} = 83\%$$

$$1975: \quad \frac{8-11}{11} = -27\%$$

$$1977: \quad \frac{10-5}{5} = 100\%$$

$$1978: \quad \frac{12-10}{10} = 20\%$$

$$1979: \quad \frac{11-12}{12} = -8\%$$

Note that a careful look at the graph before doing any calculations — noticing visually that the bar for 1977 shows the greatest proportional increase from the previous year — could eliminate the need for any calculating.

The answer is C

24. If at the end of 1973 Company *X* sold 30,000 shares of common stock for 35 times Company *X*'s earnings for the year, what was the price of a share of common stock at that time?

(A) $ 7.00
(B) $10.00
(C) $17.50
(D) $35.00
(E) $70.00

Ⓐ Ⓑ Ⓒ Ⓓ Ⓔ

The Earnings graph shows that Company *X* earned $6,000 in 1973; so the 30,000 shares of common stock sold for

$$35(\$6,000) = \$210,000.$$

Therefore, the price per share was

$$\$210,000 / 30,000 = \$7.00$$

The answer is A

25. If Company *X* considered a good year to be any year in which earnings were at least 20 percent of sales, how many of the years shown were good years?

(A) None   (B) One   (C) Two   (D) Three   (E) Four

Ⓐ Ⓑ Ⓒ Ⓓ Ⓔ

Compare 20% of each sales figure to the corresponding earnings figure.

$$1973 : 0.20(30) = 6, \text{ compared to } 6 \text{ (yes)}$$
$$1974 : 0.20(50) = 10, \text{ compared to } 11 \text{ (yes)}$$
$$1975 : 0.20(80) = 16, \text{ compared to } 8 \text{ (no)}$$
$$1976 : 0.20(70) = 14, \text{ compared to } 5 \text{ (no)}$$
$$1977 : 0.20(60) = 12, \text{ compared to } 10 \text{ (no)}$$
$$1978 : 0.20(80) = 16, \text{ compared to } 12 \text{ (no)}$$
$$1979 : 0.20(90) = 18, \text{ compared to } 11 \text{ (no)}$$
$$1980 : 0.20(100) = 20, \text{ compared to } 8 \text{ (no)}$$

The comparisons show that 1973 and 1974 were the only "good" years.

The answer is C

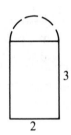

26. A rectangular window with dimensions 2 meters by 3 meters is to be enlarged by cutting out a semicircular region in the wall as shown above. What is the area, in square meters, of this semicircular region?

(A) $\dfrac{\pi}{4}$ (B) $\dfrac{\pi}{2}$ (C) π (D) 2π (E) 4π

Ⓐ Ⓑ Ⓒ Ⓓ Ⓔ

The diameter of the semicircular region is 2; so its radius is 1. The area of the semicircular region is equal to $\dfrac{1}{2}$ the area of a circle whose radius is 1, or

$$\left(\dfrac{1}{2}\right)[\pi(1)^2] = \dfrac{\pi}{2}.$$

The answer is B

27. $\dfrac{10^2(10^8 + 10^8)}{10^4} =$

(A) $2(10^4)$ (B) $2(10^6)$ (C) 10^8 (D) $2(10^8)$ (E) 10^{10}

Ⓐ Ⓑ Ⓒ Ⓓ Ⓔ

$$\frac{10^2(10^8+10^8)}{10^4} = \frac{10^2(2\cdot 10^8)}{10^4}$$

$$= \frac{2\cdot 10^{10}}{10^4} \quad \text{(adding exponents)}$$

$$= 2\cdot 10^6 \quad \text{(subtracting exponents)}$$

The answer is B

For a different solution, see below:

$$\frac{10^2(10^8+10^8)}{10^4} = \frac{10^2(10^8)+10^2(10^8)}{10^4} \quad \text{(using the distributive property)}$$

$$= \frac{10^{10}+10^{10}}{10^4} \quad \text{(adding exponents)}$$

$$= \frac{2\cdot 10^{10}}{10^4}$$

$$= 2\cdot 10^6$$

The answer is B

28. Worker *W* produces *n* units in 5 hours. Workers *V* and *W*, working independently but at the same time, produce *n* units in 2 hours. How long would it take *V* alone to produce *n* units?

(A) **1 hr 26 min**

(B) **1 hr 53 min**

(C) **2 hr 30 min**

(D) **3 hr 20 min**

(E) **3 hr 30 min**

Ⓐ   Ⓑ   Ⓒ   Ⓓ   Ⓔ

Working alone, *W* produces *n* units in 5 hours or $\dfrac{n}{5}$ units in 1 hour, or

$$2\cdot \frac{n}{5} = \frac{2n}{5} \text{ units in 2 hours.}$$

Since *W* and *V* together can produce *n* units in 2 hours, it follows that *V* can produce

$$n - \frac{2n}{5} = \frac{3n}{5} \text{ units in 2 hours.}$$

Therefore, *V* needs to work $\dfrac{5}{3}$ times 2 hours to produce *n* units (because

$\left(\dfrac{5}{3}\right)\left(\dfrac{3n}{5}\right) = n$). So *V* must work

$$\frac{5}{3} \cdot 2 = \frac{10}{3} = 3\frac{1}{3} \text{ hours}$$
$$= 3 \text{ hours } 20 \text{ minutes.}$$

The answer is D

For a different solution, see below.

This problem can be solved as a straightforward work problem:

W can do the job in 5 hours or $\frac{1}{5}$ of the job in 1 hour. V can do the job in x hours or $\frac{1}{x}$ of the job in 1 hour. And since W and V can do the job together in 2 hours, they can do $\frac{1}{2}$ the job in 1 hour.

Hence: $\frac{1}{5} + \frac{1}{x} = \frac{1}{2}$

Multiplying both sides of the equation by $10x$ gives

$$2x + 10 = 5x$$
$$10 = 3x$$
$$3\frac{1}{3} = x$$

The answer is D

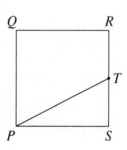

29. **In square *PQRS* above, *T* is the midpoint of side *RS*. If *PT* $= 8\sqrt{5}$, what is the length of a side of the square?**

(A) 16 (B) $6\sqrt{5}$ (C) $4\sqrt{5}$ (D) 8 (E) $2\sqrt{6}$

Ⓐ Ⓑ Ⓒ Ⓓ Ⓔ

110

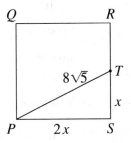

Since $PQRS$ is a square, $PS = RS$. Since T is the midpoint of RS, it follows that PS is twice as long as TS (see lengths labeled x and $2x$ in the figure above). Using the Pythagorean Theorem:

$$(8\sqrt{5})^2 = x^2 + (2x)^2$$
$$64(5) = x^2 + 4x^2$$
$$320 = 5x^2$$
$$64 = x^2$$
$$8 = x$$

The length of the side of the square is $2x = (2)(8) = 16$.

The answer is A

30. If $q \neq 0$ and $k = \dfrac{qr}{2} - s$, then what is r in terms of k, q, and s?

(A) $\dfrac{2k+s}{q}$

(B) $\dfrac{2sk}{q}$

(C) $\dfrac{2(k-s)}{q}$

(D) $\dfrac{2k+sq}{q}$

(E) $\dfrac{2(k+s)}{q}$

Ⓐ Ⓑ Ⓒ Ⓓ Ⓔ

Multiplying both sides of the equation by 2 gives:

$$2k = qr - 2s$$
$$2k + 2s = qr$$
$$\frac{2k+2s}{q} = r$$
$$\frac{2(k+s)}{q} = r$$

The answer is E

SECTION 2

38 Questions

<u>Directions:</u> Each sentence below has one or two blanks, each blank indicating that something has been omitted. Beneath the sentence are five lettered words or sets of words. Choose the word or set of words for each blank that <u>best</u> fits the meaning of the sentence as a whole.

1. **Hydrogen is the ------- element of the universe in that it provides the building blocks from which the other elements are produced.**

   **(A) steadiest   (B) expendable   (C) lightest
   (D) final   (E) fundamental**

   Ⓐ Ⓑ Ⓒ Ⓓ Ⓔ

The phrase "in that" tells you that the last part of the sentence explains the first part. Therefore, the statement that "it (hydrogen) provides the building blocks from which the other elements are produced" explains what kind of element hydrogen is.

(A) is not the answer. The statement that hydrogen provides building blocks suggests that it may be steady, but there is no evidence in the sentence that it is the "steadiest" element of the universe.

(B) is not the answer. An element that provides the building blocks for other elements is far from "expendable," that is, it cannot be readily replaced or done without.

(C) is not the answer. There is no evidence in the sentence to suggest that hydrogen is the "lightest" element. Furthermore, the fact that hydrogen provides building blocks is not an explanation of its weight.

(D) is not the answer. There is no information in the sentence to explain how an element could be "final."

* (E) is the answer. An element that "provides the building blocks from which the other elements are produced" can be properly described as "fundamental," which means "serving as a basis."

2. **Few of us take the pains to study our cherished convictions; indeed, we almost have a natural ------- doing so.**

   **(A) aptitude for   (B) repugnance to   (C) interest in
   (D) ignorance of   (E) reaction after**

   Ⓐ Ⓑ Ⓒ Ⓓ Ⓔ

The first part of the sentence says that people are not likely to take the pains to study their cherished convictions. The word "indeed" indicates that the second part of the sentence will amplify the message in the first part. In this case, the second part of the sentence also explains the reason why people do not take the pains to study their cherished convictions.

112

(A) is not the answer. Having a natural "aptitude for" taking the pains to study cherished beliefs does not explain the failure to do so.

* (B) is the answer. People's having a "repugnance to" taking the pains to study their cherished beliefs explains in strong terms why they do not do so.

(C) is not the answer. To have an "interest in" taking the pains to study cherished convictions does not explain the failure to do so.

(D) is not the answer. One cannot have "ignorance of" taking the pains to study one's own beliefs.

(E) is not the answer. A person's having a "reaction after" taking the pains to study cherished convictions could explain why few people take the pains to study their convictions. But the sentence does not provide information that would support this inference: a natural reaction is not necessarily an aversive experience.

3. **It is his dubious distinction to have proved what nobody would think of denying, that Romero at the age of sixty-four writes with all the characteristics of -------.**

   (A) maturity (B) fiction (C) inventiveness (D) art (E) brilliance

   Ⓐ Ⓑ Ⓒ Ⓓ Ⓔ

The phrase "what nobody would think of denying" indicates that the second part of the sentence will state the obvious.

* (A) is the answer. It is obvious that a person at the age of sixty-four is likely to write with all the characteristics of "maturity."

(B) is not the answer. The word "fiction" applies to what Romero might have written, not to the way Romero writes.

(C) is not the answer. The information in the sentence does not make it obvious that Romero's writing is characterized by "inventiveness."

(D) is not the answer. The information in the sentence does not make it obvious that Romero's writing is characterized by "art."

(E) is not the answer. The information in the sentence does not make it obvious that Romero's writing is characterized by "brilliance."

4. **The primary criterion for ------- a school is its recent performance: critics are ------- to extend credit for earlier victories.**

   (A) evaluating. . prone
   (B) investigating. .hesitant
   (C) judging. .reluctant
   (D) improving. .eager
   (E) administering. .persuaded

   Ⓐ Ⓑ Ⓒ Ⓓ Ⓔ

A criterion is a standard that is used by critics to assess worth, in this case, the worth of a school. Therefore, the first missing word has to do with assessing a school's performance. The word that fills the second blank is determined by the opposition between "earlier victories" and "recent performance."

(A) is not the answer. The statement that critics are "prone" to extend credit for earlier victories is not consistent with the idea that recent performance is the critics' primary criterion for "evaluating" a school.

(B) is not the answer. "Investigating" refers to the observation or study of a school, and does not necessarily convey the idea of assessment that is implied by "extend credit."

* (C) is the answer. The critics' use of recent performance as the criterion for "judging" a school is consistent with their being "reluctant" to credit earlier victories.

(D) is not the answer. "Improving" has to do with taking actions rather than with assessing worth.

(E) is not the answer. Critics who would make recent performance the primary criterion for "administering" a school would be unlikely, as a consequence, to be "persuaded" to extend credit for earlier victories.

5. **Number theory is rich in problems of an especially ------- sort: they are tantalizingly simple to state but ------- difficult to solve.**

   (A) **cryptic. .deceptively**
   (B) **spurious. .equally**
   (C) **abstruse. .ostensibly**
   (D) **elegant. .rarely**
   (E) **vexing. .notoriously**

Ⓐ Ⓑ Ⓒ Ⓓ Ⓔ

The colon (:) between the two parts of the sentence indicates that the second part of the sentence will elaborate on the first part. The first missing word will describe succinctly the sort of problem described in the second part. The second missing word must help to clarify the opposition that the word "but" has established between "simple" and "difficult" in the second part of the sentence.

(A) is not the answer. "Cryptic" problems are problems that are stated in a way that is difficult to understand. The second part of the sentence suggests the opposite.

(B) is not the answer. The word "tantalizingly," which parallels the second missing word in the structure of the sentence, does not establish a comparison so that "equally," which implies comparison, can be correct. Problems that are "spurious" are not by definition simple to state but difficult to solve. A "spurious" problem is a false problem.

(C) is not the answer. Although the problems of number theory may be especially "abstruse," or difficult to comprehend, "abstruse" does not describe a problem that is "tantalizingly simple to state."

(D) is not the answer. The word "rarely" does not establish opposition between "simple" and "difficult."

* (E) is the answer. Problems that are tantalizingly simple to state but "notoriously" difficult to solve can indeed be described succinctly as "vexing," or causing distress.

114

6. In failing to see that the justice's pronouncement merely ------- previous decisions rather than actually establishing a precedent, the novice law clerk ------- the scope of the justice's judgment.

   (A) synthesized. .limited
   (B) overturned. .misunderstood
   (C) endorsed. .nullified
   (D) qualified. .overemphasized
   (E) recapitulated. .defined

         Ⓐ   Ⓑ   Ⓒ   Ⓓ   Ⓔ

The word "merely" indicates that the justice's pronouncement did something less than establish a precedent. The first missing word will explain how the pronouncement was related to previous decisions, and the missing word must be chosen in light of our knowledge that the pronouncement did less than establish a precedent. The novice failed to notice that the pronouncement did not establish a precedent. The second missing word must explain in what way the novice, as a result of that failure, incorrectly interpreted the scope of the judgment.

    (A) is not the answer. The novice's failure to notice that the pronouncement did not establish a precedent would not have led him or her to limit its scope.

    (B) is not the answer. To have "overturned" previous decisions would have established a precedent.

    (C) is not the answer. Scope is a characteristic of the judgment itself, and cannot be "nullified" by the novice's misinterpretation.

   * (D) is the answer. If the pronouncement "qualified" previous decisions, it did less than establish something new. The novice did not see this, and so "overemphasized" the scope of the judgment.

    (E) is not the answer. The word "defined" does not describe an incorrect estimate of the judgment's scope.

7. When theories formerly considered to be ------- in their scientific objectivity are found instead to reflect a consistent observational and evaluative bias, then the presumed neutrality of science gives way to the recognition that categories of knowledge are human -------.

   (A) disinterested. .constructions
   (B) callous. .errors
   (C) verifiable. .prejudices
   (D) convincing. .imperatives
   (E) unassailable. .fantasies

         Ⓐ   Ⓑ   Ⓒ   Ⓓ   Ⓔ

The first missing word should describe the scientific objectivity of theories in a way that is the opposite of consistent bias. The second missing word must describe the categories of knowledge as products of human endeavor rather than of the neutrality of science.

* (A) is the answer. Theories that are "disinterested" are clearly not biased. Human "constructions" are not products of scientific neutrality.

(B) is not the answer. Being "callous" is not the opposite of being biased.

(C) is not the answer. A theory that is "verifiable" is not necessarily unbiased. Categories of knowledge can reflect human "prejudices"; they cannot actually be "prejudices."

(D) is not the answer. "Convincing" could fit reasonably into the first blank. However, although categories of knowledge can reflect human "imperatives," they cannot actually be "imperatives."

(E) is not the answer. "Unassailable" could fit reasonably into the first blank. However, the fact that theories are not absolutely objective does not justify describing categories of knowledge as "fantasies," a term that suggests that they have no basis in reality at all.

Directions: In each of the following questions, a related pair of words or phrases is followed by five lettered pairs of words or phrases. Select the lettered pair that best expresses a relationship similar to that expressed in the original pair.

8. CHOIR:SINGER ::

(A) election:voter
(B) anthology:poet
(C) cast:actor
(D) orchestra:composer
(E) convention:speaker

Ⓐ Ⓑ Ⓒ Ⓓ Ⓔ

A "choir" is a group of people that is composed of more than one "singer." Therefore, a rationale for this analogy might be "X (a choir) is a group of people that is composed of more than one Y (singer)."

(A) is not the answer. More than one "voter" participates in an election, but the "election" is not itself a group of people.

(B) is not the answer. An "anthology" is composed of works, not of persons. The "poet" or poets author the works.

* (C) is the answer. The "cast" (of a play) is a group of people that is made up of more than one "actor."

(D) is not the answer. An "orchestra" is a group of people that is composed of more than one musician. It is not a group of composers.

(E) is not the answer. A "convention" may have more than one "speaker," but it is not necessarily made up of speakers.

9. GLARING:BRIGHT ::

(A) iridescent:colorful
(B) perceptible:visible
(C) discordant:harmonious
(D) peppery:salty
(E) deafening:loud

Ⓐ Ⓑ Ⓒ Ⓓ Ⓔ

116

One meaning of "glaring" is uncomfortably "bright." A rationale for this analogy could be "Something described as X is so strongly Y as to be uncomfortable for people to perceive."

(A) is not the answer. "Iridescent" means producing a play of colors and does not imply strength of color.

(B) is not the answer. To be "visible" is to be "perceptible" in a particular way. No difference in strength is implied.

(C) is not the answer. "Discordant" and "harmonious" are opposites and so cannot be related to one another in the way described in the rationale.

(D) is not the answer. "Peppery" does not mean strongly "salty."

* (E) is the answer. Something properly described as "deafening" is so "loud" that it is uncomfortable for people to perceive it.

10. MAVERICK:CONFORMITY ::

(A) renegade:ambition
(B) extrovert:reserve
(C) reprobate:humility
(D) zealot:loyalty
(E) strategist:decisiveness

Ⓐ Ⓑ Ⓒ Ⓓ Ⓔ

A "maverick," by definition, is a person who does not conform with his or her group. A rationale for this analogy could be "An X is one who, by definition, does not display Y."

(A) is not the answer. A "renegade" is not necessarily characterized by lack of "ambition."

* (B) is the answer. An "extrovert" is defined as a person who does not display "reserve" (restraint or caution).

(C) is not the answer. A "reprobate" is a person who is morally abandoned or depraved. Although it seems likely that a true reprobate's actions are not characterized by "humility," this lack is not an essential element of the definition of a "reprobate."

(D) is not the answer. A "zealot" is a person whose actions are likely to be characterized by greater-than-usual "loyalty."

(E) is not the answer. A "strategist" is not by definition a person who displays a lack of "decisiveness."

11. SLITHER:SNAKE :: (A) perch:eagle (B) bask:lizard
(C) waddle:duck (D) circle:hawk (E) croak:frog

Ⓐ Ⓑ Ⓒ Ⓓ Ⓔ

In order to go forward, a "snake" will "slither." A possible rationale for this analogy is "In order to go forward, animal Y will X." An alternative rationale is "To X is a characteristic way for animal Y to move forward."

(A) is not the answer. An "eagle" may "perch," but to "perch" does not imply forward movement.

(B) is not the answer. A "lizard" may "bask," but to "bask" does not imply forward movement.

* (C) is the answer. In order to go forward, a "duck" will "waddle." To "waddle" is a characteristic way for a "duck" to go forward.

(D) is not the answer. "Circle" describes the path of forward motion, not the characteristic physical motion by which the "hawk" moves forward.

(E) is not the answer. A "frog" can "croak," but to "croak" is not a way of moving forward.

12. COUNTENANCE:TOLERATION ::

**(A) defer:ignorance   (B) renounce:mistrust   (C) encroach:jealousy
(D) demur:objection   (E) reject:disappointment**

Ⓐ Ⓑ Ⓒ Ⓓ Ⓔ

To "countenance" can mean to approve or make a show of "toleration." Therefore, a rationale for this analogy could be "To X is to show Y." You can tell that "countenance" is used as a verb, not as a noun, because "defer," the first word in choice (A), can be used only as a verb and not as a noun.

(A) is not the answer. To "defer" does not clearly mean to express "ignorance." To "defer" could show "ignorance" in certain contexts, but there is not enough information in the analogy to allow this conclusion.

(B) is not the answer. To "renounce" could indicate "mistrust," but more information would be needed before one could draw this conclusion. "Mistrust" is not an essential element in the definition of renunciation.

(C) is not the answer. To "encroach" could be said to cause "jealousy," not to show it.

* (D) is the answer. To "demur" means to express or to show an "objection."

(E) is not the answer. To "reject" could be a way of showing "disappointment," but more information would be needed to confirm this conclusion. Rejection is not an essential element in the definition of "disappointment."

13. PROCTOR:SUPERVISE ::

(A) prophet:rule
(B) profiteer:consume
(C) profligate:demand
(D) prodigal:squander
(E) prodigy:wonder

Ⓐ Ⓑ Ⓒ Ⓓ Ⓔ

A "proctor" is by definition one who is to "supervise." A rationale for this analogy could be "An X is one who, by definition, Ys, that is supervise(s)." You can tell that "proctor" is used as a noun, not as a verb, because "prophet," the first word in choice (A), can be used only as a noun, not as a verb.

118

(A) is not the answer. A "prophet" does not by definition "rule."

(B) is not the answer. A "profiteer" may "consume," but to "consume" is not a part of the definition of a "profiteer."

(C) is not the answer. A "profligate" (one who is wildly extravagant) is likely to "demand," but demanding is not a defining characteristic of a "profligate."

* (D) is the answer. By definition, a "prodigal," one who is recklessly extravagant, "squander(s)," or spends wastefully.

(E) is not the answer. A "prodigy" may cause wonder, but to "wonder" is not a defining characteristic of a "prodigy."

14. REDOLENT:SMELL ::

   (A) **curious:knowledge**
   (B) **lucid:sight**
   (C) **torpid:motion**
   (D) **ephemeral:touch**
   (E) **piquant:taste**

Something "redolent" stimulates the sense of "smell." You can tell that "smell" is used as a noun, not as a verb, because "knowledge," the second word in option (A), can be used only as a noun, not as a verb. A rationale for this analogy could be "Something described as X stimulates sense Y."

(A) is not the answer. Something "curious" might stimulate one to acquire "knowledge," but "knowledge" itself cannot be stimulated.

(B) is not the answer. "Lucid" means intelligible, clear, or understandable. Something "lucid" does not necessarily stimulate one's sense of "sight."

(C) is not the answer. "Torpid" means having lost "motion."

(D) is not the answer. Something "ephemeral" lasts for only a short time. No conclusions can be drawn about its ability to stimulate the sense of "touch."

* (E) is the answer. Something described as "piquant" stimulates the sense of "taste."

15. TORQUE:ROTATION ::

   (A) **centrifuge:axis**
   (B) **osmosis:membrane**
   (C) **tension:elongation**
   (D) **elasticity:variation**
   (E) **gas:propulsion**

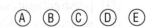

Broadly speaking, "torque" is a force that produces "rotation." The rationale for this analogy could be "X is the name of a force that produces reaction Y."

(A) is not the answer. An "axis" is not a reaction and cannot be produced by a "centrifuge."

(B) is not the answer. A "membrane" is not a reaction and cannot be produced by "osmosis."

* (C) is the answer. One meaning of "tension" is a force causing or tending to cause extension or "elongation." "Elongation" is one way something reacts to the application of "tension."

(D) is not the answer. "Elasticity" is not a force, but a characteristic of a material.

(E) is not the answer. Although "gas" could produce a force that could cause "propulsion," "gas" is not itself a force.

16. SUBSIDY:SUPPORT ::

(A) **assistance:endowment**
(B) **funds:fellowship**
(C) **credit:payment**
(D) **debt:obligation**
(E) **loan:note**

Ⓐ Ⓑ Ⓒ Ⓓ Ⓔ

A "subsidy" is a form of "support," in particular, financial support. A rationale for this analogy could be "X is a kind of Y."

(A) is not the answer. An "endowment" is a form of financial "assistance," but "assistance" is not a kind of "endowment."

(B) is not the answer. "Funds" could be used to provide a "fellowship" (a stipend), but "funds" are not a kind of "fellowship."

(C) is not the answer. "Credit" can be used in place of "payment"; it is not a kind of "payment."

* (D) is the answer. A "debt" is a kind of "obligation," often a financial one.

(E) is not the answer. A "note" is an acknowledgment of a "loan," but it is not itself a kind of "loan."

Directions: Each passage in this group is followed by questions based on its content. After reading a passage, choose the best answer to each question. Answer all questions following a passage on the basis of what is stated or implied in that passage.

Questions 17-20

By the time the American colonists took up arms against Great Britain in order to secure their independence, the institution of Black slavery was deeply entrenched. But the contradiction inherent in this situation was, for many, a source of constant embarrassment. "It always appeared a most iniquitous scheme to me," Abigail Adams wrote her husband in 1774, "to fight ourselves for what we are daily robbing and plundering from those who have as good a right to freedom as we have."

Many Americans besides Abigail Adams were struck by the inconsistency of their stand during the War of Independence, and they were not averse to making moves to emancipate the slaves. Quakers and other religious groups organized antislavery societies, while numerous individuals manumitted their slaves. In fact, within several years of the end of the War of Independence, most of the Eastern states had made provisions for the gradual emancipation of slaves.

17. Which of the following best states the central idea of the passage?

  (A) The War of Independence produced among many Black Americans a heightened consciousness of the inequities in American society.

  (B) The War of Independence strengthened the bonds of slavery of many Black Americans while intensifying their desire to be free.

  (C) The War of Independence exposed to many Americans the contradiction of slavery in a country seeking its freedom and resulted in efforts to resolve that contradiction.

  (D) The War of Independence provoked strong criticisms by many Americans of the institution of slavery, but produced little substantive action against it.

  (E) The War of Independence renewed the efforts of many American groups toward achieving Black emancipation.

Ⓐ Ⓑ © Ⓓ Ⓔ

The question asks for the central idea of the passage. The answer should state completely and accurately the main point of the passage.

(A) is not the answer. Although it is likely that this statement is true, the passage does not specifically discuss the reactions of Black Americans to the War of Independence.

(B) is not the answer. The passage does not specifically discuss the reactions of Black Americans to the fight for independence, and it mentions ways in which the bonds of slavery were weakened, rather than strengthened.

*(C) is the answer. The first paragraph of the passage discusses "the contradiction inherent in this situation," and the second paragraph describes steps that were taken to resolve the contradiction.

(D) is not the answer. Although the War of Independence did, according to the passage, provoke strong criticisms of slavery, the second paragraph describes substantive action that was taken against slavery.

(E) is not the answer. Although the War of Independence inspired efforts toward "achieving Black emancipation," there is no indication in the passage that these were renewed efforts.

18. The passage contains information that would support which of the following statements about the colonies before the War of Independence?

  (A) They contained organized antislavery societies.
  (B) They allowed individuals to own slaves.
  (C) They prohibited religious groups from political action.
  (D) They were inconsistent in their legal definitions of slave status.
  (E) They encouraged abolitionist societies to expand their influence.

Ⓐ Ⓑ © Ⓓ Ⓔ

The question asks you to identify a statement that is not necessarily explicit in the passage but that is suggested by the information given there. It is important to note that the question asks about the colonies **before** the War of Independence, whereas most of the passage is concerned with the colonies during and after the war.

(A) is not the answer. Although the colonies may have contained organized antislavery societies before the War of Independence, there is no indication of this in the passage.

* (B) is the answer. The first sentence states that by the time the War of Independence began "the institution of Black slavery was deeply entrenched." The second paragraph states that during the war "numerous individuals manumitted their slaves." Together, these statements imply that individuals in the colonies were allowed to own slaves before the War of Independence.

(C) is not the answer. There is no suggestion in the passage that religious groups were prohibited from taking political action.

(D) is not the answer. The passage does not discuss definitions of slave status at all.

(E) is not the answer. There is no indication in the passage of the attitude of the colonies toward the abolitionist societies.

19. **According to the passage, the War of Independence was embarrassing to some Americans for which of the following reasons?**

   I. **It involved a struggle for many of the same liberties that Americans were denying to others.**

  II. **It involved a struggle for independence from the very nation that had founded the colonies.**

 III. **It involved a struggle based on inconsistencies in the participants' conceptions of freedom.**

  (A) I only
  (B) II only
  (C) I and II only
  (D) I and III only
  (E) I, II, and III

(A) (B) (C) (D) (E)

The question asks specifically why the War of Independence was embarrassing to some Americans. Lines 3 and 4 in the passage state that "the contradiction inherent in this situation was, for many, a source of constant embarrassment."

I is an answer. It states the "contradiction inherent in" the colonists' situation: the colonies were fighting for their own rights while denying these same rights to others. The contradiction is stated in the words of Abigail Adams at the end of the first paragraph.

II is not an answer. It correctly describes an aspect of the War of Independence, but this aspect of the situation is not discussed in the passage.

III is not an answer. It describes an aspect of the War of Independence that is not discussed in the passage. Whereas the passage suggests that those who participated in the war may have had conceptions of freedom that contained inconsistencies — they believed that freedom was important for themselves, but not for slaves — there is no indication that the war involved a struggle based on such inconsistencies.

* (A) is the answer. **I** answers the question posed. **II** and **III** do not.

(B) is not the answer. **II** does not answer the question posed.

(C) is not the answer. **I** answers the question posed, but **II** does not.

(D) is not the answer. **I** answers the question posed, but **III** does not.

(E) is not the answer. **I** answers the question posed, but **II** and **III** do not.

20. Which of the following statements regarding American society in the years immediately following the War of Independence is best supported by the passage?

(A) **The unexpected successes of the antislavery societies led to their gradual demise in the Eastern states.**

(B) **Some of the newly independent American states had begun to make progress toward abolishing slavery.**

(C) **Americans like Abigail Adams became disillusioned with the slow progress of emancipation and gradually abandoned the cause.**

(D) **Emancipated slaves gradually were accepted in the Eastern states as equal members of American society.**

(E) **The abolition of slavery in many Eastern states was the result of close cooperation between religious groups and free Blacks.**

Ⓐ Ⓑ Ⓒ Ⓓ Ⓔ

In contrast to question 18, this question asks about American society **after** the War of Independence. The words "best supported" suggest that the answer to the question may not be directly stated in the passage.

(A) is not the answer. The passage states only that antislavery societies were organized and that steps toward emancipation were taken. There is no indication of the success or the eventual fate of the societies.

* (B) is the answer. The last sentence indicates that "gradual emancipation," a step toward the abolition of slavery, was being accomplished.

(C) is not the answer. The passage does not include information that would allow one to draw conclusions about the postwar attitudes of "Americans like Abigail Adams."

(D) is not the answer. The passage states that provisions were made for gradual emancipation, but there is no information about the acceptance of the emancipated slaves in American society.

(E) is not the answer. There is no discussion in the passage of what role free Blacks played in abolishing slavery.

Questions 21-27

The evolution of sex ratios has produced, in most plants and animals with separate sexes, approximately equal numbers of males and females. Why should this be so? Two main kinds of answers have been offered. One is couched in terms of advantage to population. It is argued that the sex ratio will evolve so as to maximize the number of meetings between individuals of the opposite sex. This is essentially a "group selection" argument. The other, and in my view correct, type of answer was first put forward by Fisher in 1930. This "genetic" argument starts from the assumption that genes can influence the relative numbers of male and female offspring produced by an individual carrying the genes. That sex ratio will be favored which maximizes the number of descendants an individual will have and hence the number of gene copies transmitted. Suppose that the population consisted mostly of females: then an individual who produced sons only would have more grandchildren. In contrast, if the population consisted mostly of males, it would pay to have daughters. If, however, the population consisted of equal numbers of males and females, sons and daughters would be equally valuable. Thus a one-to-one sex ratio is the only stable ratio; it is an "evolutionarily stable strategy." Although Fisher wrote before the mathematical theory of games had been developed, his theory incorporates the essential feature of a game — that the best strategy to adopt depends on what others are doing.

Since Fisher's time, it has been realized that genes can sometimes influence the chromosome or gamete in which they find themselves so that the gamete will be more likely to participate in fertilization. If such a gene occurs on a sex-determining (X or Y) chromosome, then highly aberrant sex ratios can occur. But more immediately relevant to game theory are the sex ratios in certain parasitic wasp species that have a large excess of females. In these species, fertilized eggs develop into females and unfertilized eggs into males. A female stores sperm and can determine the sex of each egg she lays by fertilizing it or leaving it unfertilized. By Fisher's argument, it should still pay a female to produce equal numbers of sons and daughters. Hamilton, noting that the eggs develop within their host — the larva of another insect — and that the newly emerged adult wasps mate immediately and disperse, offered a remarkably cogent analysis. Since only one female usually lays eggs in a given larva, it would pay her to produce one male only, because this one male could fertilize all his sisters on emergence. Like Fisher, Hamilton looked for an evolutionarily stable strategy, but he went a step further in *recognizing* that he was looking for a strategy.

21. **The author suggests that the work of Fisher and Hamilton was similar in that both scientists**

    (A) **conducted their research at approximately the same time**

    (B) **sought to manipulate the sex ratios of some of the animals they studied**

    (C) **sought an explanation of why certain sex ratios exist and remain stable**

    (D) **studied game theory, thereby providing important groundwork for the later development of strategy theory**

    (E) **studied reproduction in the same animal species**

(A) (B) (C) (D) (E)

This question asks you to compare the work of two scientists, Fisher and Hamilton. Fisher's work is discussed in the first paragraph and is mentioned again in the second paragraph. Hamilton's work is discussed in the last half of the second paragraph.

(A) is not the answer. According to the first paragraph, Fisher put forth his explanation in 1930. The first few words in the second paragraph, "Since Fisher's time," indicate that the research described in this paragraph took place after that described in the first paragraph.

(B) is not the answer. There is no information in the passage to suggest that either Fisher or Hamilton actually tried to change or influence (manipulate) the sex ratios of animals.

* (C) is the answer. In the first paragraph, the author describes Fisher's "genetic" explanation of the evolution of sex ratios and of the reasons for their stability. In the second paragraph, the author indicates that Hamilton also investigated sex ratios — those of parasitic wasps — and sought to explain why the ratios are "evolutionarily stable."

(D) is not the answer. According to the passage, "Fisher wrote before the mathematical theory of games had been developed." Therefore, he, at least, could not have studied game theory.

(E) is not the answer. There is no information in the passage to suggest exactly which animal species Fisher studied.

22. It can be inferred from the passage that the author considers Fisher's work to be

(A) fallacious and unprofessional
(B) definitive and thorough
(C) inaccurate but popular, compared with Hamilton's work
(D) admirable, but not as up-to-date as Hamilton's work
(E) accurate, but trivial compared with Hamilton's work

Ⓐ Ⓑ Ⓒ Ⓓ Ⓔ

This question asks you to infer from the passage the author's opinion of the work of Fisher.

(A) is not the answer. The author states in the first paragraph that, in his view, the "genetic" argument put forth by Fisher is correct, not "fallacious."

(B) is not the answer. Although Fisher's argument is correct in the author's view, Hamilton "went a step further." Therefore, Fisher's work cannot be described as "definitive."

(C) is not the answer. In the first paragraph, the author states that, in his view, the "genetic" argument first put forth by Fisher is correct, not "inaccurate." No mention is made of the relative popularity of the theories.

* (D) is the answer. The author's statement that Fisher's "genetic" argument was correct and his description of Fisher's work as incorporating features of game theory before the theory had been developed suggest that the author thinks Fisher's work is "admirable." However, because Hamilton took advantage of later developments, his work is more "up-to-date."

(E) is not the answer. There is no indication in the passage that the author believes Fisher's work to be "trivial." Rather, the author suggests that Fisher's work was important and advanced for its time.

23. The passage contains information that would answer which of the following questions about wasps?

    I. How many eggs does the female wasp usually lay in a single host larva?

    II. Can some species of wasp determine sex ratios among their offspring?

    III. What is the approximate sex ratio among the offspring of parasitic wasps?

    (A) I only   (B) II only   (C) III only   (D) I and II only

     (E) II and III only

Ⓐ Ⓑ Ⓒ Ⓓ Ⓔ

This question asks you to determine whether the passage contains sufficient information to answer one or more questions about wasps. The way the question is posed indicates that the information required may or may not be directly stated in the passage.

I cannot be answered. **I** asks "how many" eggs a female wasp lays. There is no information in the passage to suggest either a specific or a general number of eggs.

II can be answered. According to the passage, "A female (wasp) . . . can determine the sex of each egg she lays . . ." This implies that she can therefore determine the sex ratio among her offspring.

III cannot be answered. **III** asks for an "approximate sex ratio among the offspring of parasitic wasps." The passage states that some species of wasp have a "large excess of females," but there is nothing to indicate what the ratio is among parasitic wasps in general.

    (A) is not the answer. **I** cannot be answered.

  * (B) is the answer. **II** can be answered; **I** and **III** cannot.

    (C) is not the answer. **III** cannot be answered.

    (D) is not the answer. **II** can be answered, but **I** cannot.

    (E) is not the answer. **II** can be answered, but **III** cannot.

24. It can be inferred that the author discusses the genetic theory in greater detail than the group selection theory primarily because he believes that the genetic theory is more

    (A) complicated   (B) accurate   (C) popular   (D) comprehensive

    (E) accessible

Ⓐ Ⓑ Ⓒ Ⓓ Ⓔ

This question asks what characteristic of the genetic theory accounts for its being discussed in greater detail than the group selection theory.

    (A) is not the answer. There is no information in the passage to indicate whether one of the theories is more "complicated" than the other.

  * (B) is the answer. In the first paragraph, the author mentions the "group selection" theory. He then describes the "genetic" argument as "The other, and in my view correct, type of answer." Clearly, then, the author believes that the genetic argument is more "accurate" than the group selection theory.

(C) is not the answer. There is no indication in the passage of the "popularity" of either theory.

(D) is not the answer. There is no discussion in the passage of how "comprehensive" either theory is.

(E) is not the answer. There is no discussion in the passage of how "accessible" either theory is.

25. According to the passage, successful game strategy depends on

    (A) the ability to adjust one's behavior in light of the behavior of others
    (B) one's awareness that there is safety in numbers
    (C) the degree of stability one can create in one's immediate environment
    (D) the accuracy with which one can predict future events
    (E) the success one achieves in conserving and storing one's resources

Ⓐ Ⓑ Ⓒ Ⓓ Ⓔ

The question asks you to identify the element in game strategy on which success depends.

    * (A) is the answer. At the end of the first paragraph, the author states that "the essential feature of a game (is) that the best strategy to adopt depends on what others are doing." Choice (A) paraphrases the statement in the passage.

(B) is not the answer. There is no indication in the passage that successful game strategy depends on awareness of safety in numbers.

(C) is not the answer. There is no indication in the passage that successful game strategy depends on the degree of stability one can create.

(D) is not the answer. There is no indication in the passage that successful game strategy depends on accurately predicting future events.

(E) is not the answer. There is no indication in the passage that successful game strategy depends on success in saving resources.

26. It can be inferred from the passage that the mathematical theory of games has been

    (A) developed by scientists with an interest in genetics
    (B) adopted by Hamilton in his research
    (C) helpful in explaining how genes can sometimes influence gametes
    (D) based on animal studies conducted prior to 1930
    (E) useful in explaining some biological phenomena

Ⓐ Ⓑ Ⓒ Ⓓ Ⓔ

This question asks about the mathematical theory of games that is mentioned in the passage. Since the answer "can be inferred," it is clear that the answer is not explicitly stated in the passage. You must put together pieces of information in the passage in order to answer.

(A) is not the answer. There is no information in the passage to suggest that geneticists developed game theory, although there is a suggestion that game theory is applicable to the work of geneticists.

(B) is not the answer. Hamilton may have applied principles of game theory in his work, but there is no indication in the passage that he went so far as to adopt game theory, or even that he was aware of it as a theory.

(C) is not the answer. The passage gives no indication that game theory can explain how the influence of genes on gametes is exerted.

(D) is not the answer. There is no indication in the passage that game theory was based on animal studies.

* (E) is the answer. The author mentions that Fisher's "genetic" argument, an argument explaining biological phenomena, incorporates a feature of game theory. Hamilton's study of sex ratios (a biological phenomenon) in wasps is discussed in relation to game theory. Therefore, it can be inferred that the author finds game theory useful in explaining biological phenomena.

27. Which of the following is NOT true of the species of parasitic wasps discussed in the passage?

(A) Adult female wasps are capable of storing sperm.

(B) Female wasps lay their eggs in the larvae of other insects.

(C) The adult female wasp can be fertilized by a male that was hatched in the same larva as herself.

(D) So few male wasps are produced that extinction is almost certain.

(E) Male wasps do not emerge from their hosts until they reach sexual maturity.

Ⓐ Ⓑ Ⓒ Ⓓ Ⓔ

This question asks you to identify a statement that is NOT true of the species of wasps discussed in the passage.

(A) is not the answer because, according to the passage, female wasps are indeed capable of storing sperm.

(B) is not the answer because, according to the passage, female wasps do lay their eggs in the larvae of other insects.

(C) is not the answer because the statement is true. The fact that "one male could fertilize all his sisters on emergence" implies that a female can be fertilized by a male hatched in the same larva as herself.

* (D) is the answer because this statement is NOT true. The fact that the wasp species mentioned continue to produce males, though relatively few males, indicates that this strategy does not lead to extinction of the species.

(E) is not the answer because, according to the passage, "the newly emerged adult wasps mate immediately and disperse." The fact that the wasps mate immediately implies that they do not emerge from their hosts until they are sexually mature.

Directions: Each question below consists of a word printed in capital letters, followed by five lettered words or phrases. Choose the lettered word or phrase that is most nearly opposite in meaning to the word in capital letters.

Since some of the questions require you to distinguish fine shades of meaning, be sure to consider all the choices before deciding which one is best.

128

28. COMMOTION: (A) desirability (B) likability (C) propensity (D) changeability (E) tranquillity

A general definition of "commotion" is noisy confusion; agitation. "Commotion" implies a flurry of activity and excitement.

(A) is not the answer. "Desirability" means attractiveness. There is no implication of activity or lack of activity in its definition.

(B) is not the answer. "Likability" means ability to inspire regard or liking. There is no implication of activity or lack of activity in its definition.

(C) is not the answer. A "propensity" is a natural inclination. It has more to do with feelings than with actions.

(D) is not the answer. "Changeability" means alterability, or ability to change. Acitivity, rather than its opposite, is implied.

* (E) is the answer. "Tranquillity" means freedom from agitation.

29. INDETERMINATE: (A) qualified (B) definite (C) stubborn (D) effective (E) committed

"Indeterminate" means not definitely or precisely determined or fixed.

(A) is not the answer. "Qualified" may mean limited or modified. It implies a limitation but does not specifically imply a clear determination.

* (B) is the answer. "Definite," which means having distinct or certain limits (boundaries), is the opposite of "indeterminate."

(C) is not the answer. "Stubborn," which means obstinate or unyielding, implies intractability or determination.

(D) is not the answer. "Effective" means producing or capable of producing a result; it does not necessarily imply a clear or precise determination.

(E) is not the answer. "Committed" means pledged or assigned to a particular course of action. Its opposite is more nearly "undecided," a characteristic of persons rather than of situations.

30. DIVERGE: (A) relay (B) bypass (C) enclose (D) work quickly (E) come together

ⒶⒷⒸⒹⒺ

To "diverge" can mean to become different, or to go in different directions, or to draw apart.

(A) is not the answer. To "relay" means to pass along in stages. (Even though "relay" can be used either as a noun or as a verb, you can tell that here it is used as a verb because "diverge" can be used only as a verb and not as a noun.)

(B) is not the answer. To "bypass" means to go around.

(C) is not the answer. To "enclose" means to surround.

(D) is not the answer. To "work quickly" does not mean the opposite of to draw apart.

* (E) is the answer. To "come together" is the opposite of "to draw apart."

31. FLIPPANT: (A) evenly distributed (B) well coordinated (C) inflexible (D) sane (E) earnest

ⒶⒷⒸⒹⒺ

"Flippant" means lacking proper respect or seriousness.

(A) is not the answer. "Evenly distributed" describes a physical characteristic rather than an aspect of character, like "flippant."

(B) is not the answer. Being "well coordinated" has nothing to do with seriousness or the lack of it.

(C) is not the answer. "Inflexible" means rigid or unyielding; it does not suggest lack of seriousness or respect.

(D) is not the answer. One who is "sane" may or may not be "flippant."

* (E) is the answer. To be "earnest" means to be grave or serious.

32. NEXUS: (A) disconnected components (B) tangled threads (C) lost direction (D) unseen obstacle (E) damaged parts

Ⓐ Ⓑ Ⓒ Ⓓ Ⓔ

A "nexus" is a connection or link or a connected group or series.

* (A) is the answer. The opposite of a connected group is "disconnected components."

(B) is not the answer. "Tangled threads" are connected entities. A "nexus" could be formed from threads or other components.

(C) is not the answer. "Lost direction" could lead to disconnection, but it is not the opposite of a connection.

(D) is not the answer. An "unseen obstacle" is an invisible barrier.

(E) is not the answer. "Damaged parts" are not necessarily connected or unconnected.

33. LEVY: (A) reconsider (B) relinquish (C) repatriate (D) revitalize (E) rescind

Ⓐ Ⓑ Ⓒ Ⓓ Ⓔ

To "levy" means to impose or collect by legal authority.

(A) is not the answer. To "reconsider" means to consider again with a view to making a change.

(B) is not the answer. To "relinquish" means to withdraw from or let go of.

(C) is not the answer. To "repatriate" means to return to a country of origin.

(D) is not the answer. To "revitalize" means to give new life or vigor to.

* (E) is the answer. To "rescind" means to take back or make void. It is often used in referring to a legal action, as is "levy."

34. ANOMALOUS: (A) porous (B) viscous (C) essential (D) normal (E) elemental

Ⓐ Ⓑ Ⓒ Ⓓ Ⓔ

"Anomalous" means deviating from the normal or not in keeping with the expected.

(A) is not the answer. "Porous" means having pores or permeable by liquids.

(B) is not the answer. "Viscous" means sticky or gummy.

(C) is not the answer. "Essential" means necessary or indispensible.

* (D) is the answer. "Normal" means natural, usual, or expected.

(E) is not the answer. "Elemental" means basic or essential rather than usual.

35. GROUSE: **(A) rejoice** **(B) rekindle** **(C) restore** **(D) reject**
   (E) reflect

Ⓐ Ⓑ Ⓒ Ⓓ Ⓔ

To "grouse" means to complain or grumble. You can tell that "grouse" is used as a verb, and not as a noun, because "rejoice" in choice (A) can be used only as a verb and not as a noun.

   * (A) is the answer. To "rejoice" means to show delight.

   (B) is not the answer. To "rekindle" means to once again arouse or set fire to.

   (C) is not the answer. To "restore" means to return to a former state or to renew.

   (D) is not the answer. To "reject" means to refuse or decline.

   (E) is not the answer. To "reflect" means to think quietly.

36. GIST:
   (A) tangential point
   (B) tentative explanation
   (C) faulty assumption
   (D) flawed argument
   (E) meaningless distinction

Ⓐ Ⓑ Ⓒ Ⓓ Ⓔ

The "gist" (of an argument, for instance) is the main point.

   * (A) is the answer. A "tangential point" is a point not related to the main one.

   (B) is not the answer. A "tentative explanation" is an explanation that is uncertain or not final. There is no reason to suppose that a "tentative explanation" does not address the main point.

   (C) is not the answer. A "faulty assumption" is an incorrect supposition. There is no reason to suppose that a "faulty assumption" is unrelated to the main point.

   (D) is not the answer. A "flawed argument" is not itself the opposite of the main point. An argument can have a "gist" despite its flaw.

   (E) is not the answer. A "meaningless distinction" may be part of an argument, but it is not by definition the opposite of the main point.

37. EFFRONTERY: **(A) decorum** **(B) candor** **(C) resolution**
   (D) perplexity **(E) mediation**

Ⓐ Ⓑ Ⓒ Ⓓ Ⓔ

"Effrontery" means an act of crass discourtesy; insolence (a haughty attitude or an insulting act); or shameless boldness.

   * (A) is the answer. "Decorum" refers to acts that are conducted with regard for propriety (accepted social standards). A person who observed "decorum" would not commit an act of "effrontery."

   (B) is not the answer. "Candor" means forthright honesty.

   (C) is not the answer. "Resolution" has many meanings, among them reducing to a simpler form, and firmness of resolve. None is the opposite of "effrontery."

(D) is not the answer. "Perplexity" means bewilderment. It is a state of mind, whereas "effrontery" refers to a way of acting.

(E) is not the answer. "Mediation" refers to a means of promoting reconciliation or compromise. This effort might be undermined by a show of "effrontery," but "mediation" is not the opposite of "effrontery."

38. LIMPID: **(A) rampant** **(B) vapid** **(C) turbid** **(D) rigid** **(E) resilient**

Ⓐ Ⓑ Ⓒ Ⓓ Ⓔ

"Limpid" means transparent or clear. These meanings apply whether the word is used literally or figuratively.

(A) is not the answer. "Rampant" means widespread or unrestrained.

(B) is not the answer. "Vapid" means uninteresting or lacking in liveliness.

* (C) is the answer. "Turbid" means confused (unclear) or opaque (not transparent). It may be used literally (as in describing water filled with sediment) or figuratively (as in describing difficult prose).

(D) is not the answer. "Rigid" means inflexible or unyielding.

(E) is not the answer. "Resilient" means elastic or capable of bouncing back.

SECTION 3
25 Questions

<u>Directions:</u> Each question or group of questions is based on a passage or set of conditions. In answering some of the questions, it may be useful to draw a rough diagram. For each question, select the best answer choice given.

<u>Questions 1-7</u>

A certain code uses only the letters K, L, M, N, and O. Words in the code are written from left to right. Code words are only those words that conform to the following conditions:

> The minimum length for code words is two letters, not necessarily different from each other.
> K cannot be the first letter in a word.
> L must occur more than once in a word, if it occurs at all.
> M cannot be the last letter in a word, nor the next-to-the-last letter.
> N must occur in a word if K occurs in the word.
> O cannot be the last letter in a word unless L occurs in the word.

1. Which of the following letters could be placed after O in L O to form a code word exactly three letters long?

(A) K (B) L (C) M (D) N (E) O

Ⓐ Ⓑ Ⓒ Ⓓ Ⓔ

Since L must occur more than once in a word, if it occurs at all, a three-letter code word beginning LO must have L as its third letter. Therefore, (B) is the correct answer.

2. If the only kinds of letters that are available are K, L, and M, then the total number of different code words, each exactly two letters long, that it is possible to make is

(A) 1
(B) 3
(C) 6
(D) 9
(E) 12

Ⓐ Ⓑ Ⓒ Ⓓ Ⓔ

Since N must occur in a word if K occurs in the word, but N is not available, K cannot be used. M cannot be used in any two-letter code word since M cannot be the last letter in a word, nor the next-to-last letter. L can be used, but only if it is used twice. Thus, the only two-letter code word that can be made under the stated conditions is LL, and the correct answer is (A).

3. Which of the following is a code word?

(A) K L L N
(B) L O M L
(C) M L L O
(D) N M K O
(E) O N K M

Ⓐ Ⓑ Ⓒ Ⓓ Ⓔ

(A) is incorrect because K appears as the first letter.
(B) is incorrect because M appears as the next-to-last letter.
(C) is the correct answer because it violates none of the conditions.
(D) is incorrect because O appears last, but L does not occur.
(E) is incorrect because M appears as the last letter.

4. What is the total number of different code words exactly three identical letters long that it is possible to make?

(A) 1 (B) 2 (C) 3 (D) 4 (E) 5

Ⓐ Ⓑ Ⓒ Ⓓ Ⓔ

KKK   is impossible: it has K as the first letter and does not include N.
LLL   is possible: no rules prohibit it.
MMM is impossible: it has M both as the last and next-to-last letter.
NNN   is possible: no rules prohibit it.
OOO   is impossible: it has O as the last letter but does not include L.

The correct answer is therefore (B).

5. The code word M M L L O K N can be turned into another code word by carrying out any one of the following changes EXCEPT

(A) replacing every L with an N
(B) replacing the first M with an O
(C) replacing the N with an O
(D) moving the O to the immediate right of the N
(E) moving the second L to the immediate left of the K

Ⓐ Ⓑ Ⓒ Ⓓ Ⓔ

The change that cannot be carried out is (C), for if the N were replaced with an O, the resulting sequence MMLLOKO would violate the condition that N must occur in a word if K occurs in the word. The changes described in (A), (B), (D), and (E), when carried out, each result in sequences that conform to all the conditions on code words.

6. Which of the following is not a code word but could be turned into one by changing the order of the letters within the word?

(A) K L M N O
(B) L L L K N
(C) M K N O N
(D) N K L M L
(E) O M M L L

Ⓐ Ⓑ Ⓒ Ⓓ Ⓔ

(A) cannot be a code word in any order because it contains a single L. (B), (C), and (E) are all acceptable code words as they stand, so they do not satisfy the first part of the question under consideration.

(D) is not a code word as it stands, but only because it has M as the next-to-last letter. Any shift of M to the left will place M in an acceptable position, and a code word will result from this kind of change of order. Therefore, (D) is the correct answer.

7. Which of the following could be turned into a code word by replacing the "X" with a letter used in the code?

(A) M K X N O
(B) M X K M N
(C) X M M K O
(D) X M O L K
(E) X O K L L

Ⓐ Ⓑ Ⓒ Ⓓ Ⓔ

(E) is a sequence that could be turned into a code word by replacing the X with the letter N. This makes (E) the correct answer.

For explanations of the other answer choices, see below:

(A), (C): If O is to be the last letter of a code word, L must occur in that word, too. An L can be introduced by replacing the X with the letter L. But L, if it occurs at all, must occur more than once. Since there are no further X's, no further L's can be created, and thus no code word can be made by means of replacements for X.

(B): M is the next-to-last letter. This fact will not change regardless of how X is replaced. Therefore, no code word can result from any such replacement.

(D): Since K is present and N is not, the replacement of X by N appears necessary if a code word is to be made. Since a single L is present, the replacement of X by L appears necessary. But since X cannot be replaced by both N and L at the same time, no code word can be made by replacing X.

Questions 8-9

"On the whole," Ms. Dennis remarked, "engineering students are lazier now than they used to be. I know because fewer and fewer of my students regularly do the work they are assigned."

8. **The conclusion drawn above depends on which of the following assumptions?**

   (A) Engineering students are working less because, in a booming market, they are spending more and more time investigating different job opportunities.
   (B) Whether or not students do the work they are assigned is a good indication of how lazy they are.
   (C) Engineering students should work harder than students in less demanding fields.
   (D) Ms. Dennis' students are doing less work because Ms. Dennis is not as effective a teacher as she once was.
   (E) Laziness is something most people do not outgrow.

   Ⓐ Ⓑ Ⓒ Ⓓ Ⓔ

The conclusion that engineering students are lazier now than they used to be does not follow from the stated observation that fewer and fewer of Ms. Dennis' students regularly do the work they are assigned. In fact, the conclusion is not in any way supported by the reported observation unless failure to do the assigned work suggests laziness. That latter proposition must therefore be one of the tacit assumptions underlying the conclusion. (B) best expresses this assumption and is thus the correct answer.

For explanations of the other answer choices, see below:

(A): Ms. Dennis concludes that her students are lazy on the basis of what she sees as a consequence of that laziness. (A) suggests a cause of that laziness. But Ms. Dennis does not have to make any assumptions about the causes of that laziness in order to draw her conclusion.

(C): This comparison between the work demands on engineering students and those on other students is irrelevant to the question of whether the work habits of engineering students have changed over time.

(D): If Ms. Dennis believed that the reason for her own students' decreasing performance was her own declining effectiveness, she would not think of her students as exemplifying trends among engineering students in general.

(E): Since there is no reason to think that the engineering students Ms. Dennis is referring to now are significantly different in maturity from the engineering students she had in the past, it is irrelevant whether or not she believes laziness is usually outgrown.

9. **Which of the following identifies a flaw in Ms. Dennis' reasoning?**

   (A) Plenty of people besides engineering students do not work as hard as they should.
   (B) Ms. Dennis does not consider the excuses her students may have for being lazy.
   (C) The argument does not propose any constructive solutions to the problem it identifies.
   (D) The argument assumes that Ms. Dennis' students are representative of engineering students in general.

(E) Ms. Dennis does not seem sympathetic to the problems of her students.

Ⓐ Ⓑ Ⓒ Ⓓ Ⓔ

Since the constantly decreasing work output of Ms. Dennis' students could stem from causes specific to those students, Ms. Dennis is not logically justified in extending her judgment about her own students to engineering students in general. (D) is a concise statement of the logically flawed assumption Ms. Dennis must be making in so extending her judgment. (D) is thus the correct answer.

For explanations of the other answer choices, see below:

(A): Whether or not other groups resemble engineering students has no bearing on whether or not certain conclusions about engineering students follow logically from certain observations about some engineering students. Thus, Ms. Dennis' disregard of people who are not engineering students is not a flaw in her reasoning.

(B): Any excuses offered for laziness do not alter it, though they might help us understand it. Ms. Dennis is only concerned with establishing that the laziness of engineering students is a fact; she does not inquire into possible explanations. It is not a flaw of her reasoning as it stands that it addresses the particular concerns it addresses.

(C): Ms. Dennis' reasoning is involved in reaching a conclusion on the basis of certain evidence. It does not go beyond that. (C) concerns itself with matters beyond the ones Ms. Dennis reasons about, and can thus not be a flaw in her reasoning.

(E): The logical merits or flaws of an argument are independent of the emotional attitudes of the person making the argument. Since (E) describes an emotional attitude, it cannot identify a reasoning flaw.

Ⓐ Ⓑ Ⓒ Ⓓ Ⓔ

10. **Popular culture in the United States has become Europeanized to an extent unimaginable twenty-five years ago. Not many people then drank wine with meals, and no one drank imported mineral water. No idea would have been more astonishing than that Americans would pay to watch soccer games. Such thoughts arise because of a report that the American Association of State Highway and Transportation Officials has just adopted a proposal to develop the country's first comprehensive interstate system of routes for bicycles.**

    Which of the following inferences is best supported by the passage?

    (A) **Long-distance bicycle routes are used in Europe.**
    (B) **Drinking imported mineral water is a greater luxury than drinking imported wine.**
    (C) **United States culture has benefited from exposure to foreign ideas.**
    (D) **Most Europeans make regular use of bicycles.**
    (E) **The influence of the United States on European culture has assumed unprecedented proportions in the last twenty-five years.**

    Ⓐ Ⓑ Ⓒ Ⓓ Ⓔ

When the author learns that an interstate system of bicycle routes is being planned, case after case of European customs becoming accepted in the United States comes to his or her mind. This mental association would be a natural one if the system of bicycle routes is itself yet another case of a European phenomenon being brought to the United States. This in turn presupposes that long-distance bicycle routes are indeed a European phenomenon, an idea expressed by (A), the correct answer.

For explanations of the other answer choices, see below:

(B): The passage does not support any inference that the European practices in question are luxuries, let alone which of them are more or less of a luxury than the others.

(C): The passage is completely neutral on whether "Europeanization" has been beneficial, detrimental, or neither.

(D): The passage can be taken to suggest that bicycles are indeed used fairly widely in Europe, but nothing supports the inference that the majority of Europeans are regular users of bicycles.

(E): The passage is concerned solely with the influence of Europe on popular culture in the United States and not at all with any influence going the other way.

Questions 11-16

Six knights — P, Q, R, S, T, and U — assemble for a long journey in two traveling parties. For security, each traveling party consists of at least two knights. The two parties travel by separate routes, northern and southern. After one month, the routes of the northern and southern groups converge for a brief time and at that point the knights can, if they wish, rearrange their traveling parties before continuing, again in two parties along separate northern and southern routes. Throughout the entire trip, the composition of traveling parties must be in accord with the following conditions:

P and R are deadly enemies and, although they may meet briefly, can never travel together.
P must travel in the same party with S.
Q cannot travel by the southern route.
U cannot change routes.

11. **If one of the two parties of knights consists of P and U and two other knights and travels by the southern route, the other members of this party besides P and U must be**

    (A) Q and S
    (B) Q and T
    (C) R and S
    (D) R and T
    (E) S and T

    Ⓐ Ⓑ Ⓒ Ⓓ Ⓔ

Since P is traveling by the southern route, R cannot be. Q cannot travel by the southern route in any event. That leaves S and T to be the travel companions of P and U. The correct answer is, therefore, (E).

12. **If each of the two parties of knights consists of exactly three members, which of the following is NOT a possible traveling party and route?**

    (A) P, S, Q by the northern route
    (B) P, S, T by the northern route
    (C) P, S, T by the southern route
    (D) P, S, U by the southern route
    (E) Q, R, T by the northern route

    Ⓐ Ⓑ Ⓒ Ⓓ Ⓔ

If P, S, and T were to travel by the northern route, the party traveling by the southern route would have to be Q, R, and U. This is impossible since Q cannot travel by the southern route. So, P, S, and T cannot be traveling by the northern route. The correct answer is (B).

13. **If one of the two parties of knights consists of U and two other knights and travels by the northern route, the other members of this party besides U must be**

    (A) P and S
    (B) P and T
    (C) Q and R
    (D) Q and T
    (E) R and T

    Ⓐ Ⓑ Ⓒ Ⓓ Ⓔ

Since Q cannot travel by the southern route, Q must be one of U's travel companions by the northern route. The third member of the party can be neither P nor S since those two must travel together. So they must travel by the southern route. But if P travels by the southern route, R must travel by the northern route. It follows that Q and R must be U's travel companions, and the correct answer is (C).

14. **If each of the two parties of knights consists of exactly three members, S and U are members of different parties, and R travels by the northern route, then T must travel by the**

    (A) southern route with P and S
    (B) southern route with Q and R
    (C) southern route with R and U
    (D) northern route with Q and R
    (E) northern route with R and U

    Ⓐ Ⓑ Ⓒ Ⓓ Ⓔ

If R travels by the northern route, P must travel by the southern route. That means that S must also travel by the southern route, and U by the northern route. Q must travel by the northern route in any case. That leaves T to join P and S on the southern route. (A) is the correct answer.

15. If, when the two parties of knights encounter one another after a month, exactly one knight changes from one traveling party to the other traveling party, that knight must be

(A) P   (B) Q   (C) R   (D) S   (E) T

Ⓐ Ⓑ Ⓒ Ⓓ Ⓔ

If exactly one knight changes from one traveling party to the other, that knight can be neither P nor S because neither of the two could change parties without the other doing so as well. But if P stays put, so must R, since P and R cannot end up traveling in the same party. Q cannot change parties since Q must stay on the northern route. U cannot ever change parties. (E) is thus the correct answer.

16. If one of the changes after a month's traveling is that T changes from a party of two knights traveling by the southern route to a party of four knights traveling by the northern route, then all of the following must be true EXCEPT:

(A) **During the first month, U was traveling by the southern route.**
(B) **During the first month, P was traveling by the northern route.**
(C) **During the first month, R was traveling with T.**
(D) **After the first month, R travels with T.**
(E) **After the first month, S travels by the southern route.**

Ⓐ Ⓑ Ⓒ Ⓓ Ⓔ

If T started in a party of two knights traveling by the southern route, R must have been his companion (since P, who always travels with S, could not have been). Consequently, P, Q, S, and U must have been the party of four that started out on the northern route. (A) is thus seen to be a false statement, which makes it the correct answer to this question. (B) and (C) are readily seen from the above to be true statements.

For explanations of the other answer choices, see below:
    (D) and (E): If T is to be one of four traveling by the northern route after the first month, at least one of the four traveling by the northern route during the first month must change parties. Neither Q nor U can change parties. So it must be either P or S; but if it is either of them, it must be both. In sum, after the first month, P and S must change to the southern route, and as a consequence, not just T but also R must change to the northern route.

Questions 17-19

A particular auto race involved eight cars — S, T, U, V, W, X, Y, and Z. At the end of every lap, an accurate record was made of the position of the cars, from first (position 1) to last (position 8). For each of the records the following statements are true:

No two cars occupy the same position.

S is in some position ahead of Z.

There is exactly one car between T and X, regardless of whether T or X is ahead of the other.

U is in the position immediately ahead of Y.

Both V and Y are in positions ahead of S.

W is in first position.

17. **Which of the following could be noted on one of the records as the positions of the cars from position 1 through position 8?**

   (A) W, U, S, Y, V, T, Z, X
   (B) W, U, Y, S, T, V, Z, X
   (C) W, U, Y, V, S, T, Z, X
   (D) W, U, Y, Z, V, T, S, X
   (E) W, V, S, U, Y, T, Z, X

   Ⓐ   Ⓑ   Ⓒ   Ⓓ   Ⓔ

(A), (B), and (E) can be eliminated because, according to these options, S is ahead of either V, or Y, or both. (Other reasons for eliminating them can also be found). (D) can be eliminated because it lists Z as being ahead of S. (C) is an order of cars that might appear on the record, and (C) is thus the correct answer.

18. **If on one of the records Y and X are in positions 4 and 5, respectively, which of the following must be true of that record?**

   (A) S is in position 2.
   (B) S is in position 7.
   (C) T is in position 3.
   (D) V is in position 3.
   (E) Z is in position 8.

   Ⓐ   Ⓑ   Ⓒ   Ⓓ   Ⓔ

If Y is fourth, U must be third. That means that T must come after X, in position 7. S must come after Y but before Z: the only way this could be true in these circumstances is for S to be sixth and for Z to be eighth. The only answer choice that correctly states one of these inferences is (E).

19. **If on one of the records V is in some position behind T, which car must be in position 7 on that record?**

   (A) S   (B) T   (C) V   (D) X   (E) Z

   Ⓐ   Ⓑ   Ⓒ   Ⓓ   Ⓔ

If V is somewhere behind T, then S must be behind both V and T. S must also be behind Y, and thus also behind U. Clearly, S must be behind W as well. S must also be behind X even if X is itself behind T, for S could not be directly behind T since S must be behind V, which is to be behind T. This makes six cars ahead of S. There is one car, Z, that must be behind S. So S must be in position 7, and (A) is the correct answer.

An airline company is offering a particular group of people two package tours involving eight European cities — London, Madrid, Naples, Oslo, Paris, Rome, Stockholm, and Trieste. While half the group goes on tour number one to visit five of the cities, the other half will go on tour number two to visit the other three cities. The group must select the cities to be included in each tour. The selection must conform to the following restrictions:

Madrid cannot be in the same tour as Oslo.

Naples must be in the same tour as Rome.

If tour number one includes Paris, it must also include London.

If tour number two includes Stockholm, it cannot include Madrid.

20. If tour number two includes Rome, which of the following CANNOT be true?

(A) London is in tour number one.
(B) Oslo is in tour number one.
(C) Trieste is in tour number one.
(D) Madrid is in tour number two.
(E) Stockholm is in tour number two.

Tour number two includes a total of three cities. Since Rome is one of the three, then Naples must be, too. Further, since Madrid and Oslo cannot both be in tour number one, one of them must be the third city that completes the tour-two package. Consequently, Stockholm cannot be in tour number two. (E) is thus the correct answer.

21. If tour number two includes Paris, which of the following must be true?

(A) London is in tour number one.
(B) Naples is in tour number one.
(C) London is in tour number two.
(D) Oslo is in tour number two.
(E) Trieste is in tour number two.

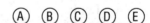

Since Madrid and Oslo cannot both be in tour number one, one of them must be in tour number two along with Paris. Since Naples must be in the same tour as Rome, and since there is only one spot left to fill in tour number two, neither Naples nor Rome can be in tour number two; rather, they must both be in tour number one. (B) correctly states a part of this inference, which makes (B) the correct answer. All other answer choices could be, but do not have to be, true.

22. **If tour number one includes Paris and tour number two includes Madrid, which of the following must also be included in tour number two?**

(A) **London**
(B) **Oslo**
(C) **Rome**
(D) **Stockholm**
(E) **Trieste**

Ⓐ Ⓑ Ⓒ Ⓓ Ⓔ

If tour number one includes Paris, it also includes London. Tour number one also includes Oslo, since Madrid is in tour number two. Tour number one must also include Stockholm since Stockholm could not be in tour number two together with Madrid. At this point, tour number one is known to include at least: London, Oslo, Paris, and Stockholm. Since Naples must be in the same tour as Rome, and since there is only one spot left to fill in tour number one, neither Naples nor Rome can be in tour number one; rather, they must both be in tour number two. Therefore, (C) is the correct answer.

23. **In the 1980 United States census, marital status was described under one of five categories: single, now married (but not separated), separated, divorced, widowed. In the category "separated," including both those who were legally separated and those who were estranged and living apart from their spouses, one million more women than men were counted.**

Which of the following, if true, provide(s) or contribute(s) to an explanation for this result?

I. **There are more women of marriageable age than men of marriageable age in the United States.**
II. **More of the separated men than separated women in the United States could not be found by the census takers during the census.**
III. **Many more separated men than separated women left the United States for residence in another country.**

(A) **I only**
(B) **II only**
(C) **III only**
(D) **I and II only**
(E) **II and III only**

Ⓐ Ⓑ Ⓒ Ⓓ Ⓔ

Proposition I is completely irrelevant to the particular imbalance: the imbalance concerns people who married each other and who are now separated. There ought to be as many men as women in this category. What proposition I suggests is a different imbalance: one among people of marriageable age who do not marry. Proposition II, on the other hand, does help explain the imbalance, as does proposition III: in both cases, a reason is given for why census takers did not count as many separated men as they did separated women. Therefore (E), "II and III only," is the correct answer.

24. **In recent years shrimp harvests of commercial fishermen in the South Atlantic have declined dramatically in total weight. The decline is due primarily to competition from a growing number of recreational fishermen, who are able to net young shrimp in the estuaries where they mature.**

    Which of the following regulatory actions would be most likely to help increase the shrimp harvests of commercial fishermen?

    (A) **Requiring commercial fishermen to fish in estuaries**
    (B) **Limiting the total number of excursions per season for commercial fishermen**
    (C) **Requiring recreational fishermen to use large-mesh nets in their fishing**
    (D) **Putting an upper limit on the size of the shrimp recreational fishermen are allowed to catch**
    (E) **Allowing recreational fishermen to move out of estuaries into the South Atlantic**

    Ⓐ Ⓑ Ⓒ Ⓓ Ⓔ

If recreational fishermen were required to use large-mesh nets in their fishing, fewer young shrimp would be trapped in those nets (assuming, of course, that young, immature shrimp are smaller than mature shrimp and that by "large-mesh nets" is meant nets with spaces big enough for young shrimp to pass through them). Thus, there is a strong likelihood that such a requirement will help increase commercial shrimp harvests. This makes (C) the best, and thus the correct, answer.

For explanations of the other answer choices, see below:

(A): This requirement is most unlikely to bring relief; if anything, it will exacerbate the problem if commercial fishermen, too, start netting young shrimp.

(B): This requirement would presumably make sense if the problem were caused by commercial fishermen catching too many mature shrimp. But the passage clearly indicates that the main problem is that too many young shrimp are netted before they reach maturity.

(D): Since the problem lies mainly in the numbers of immature, and thus presumably small, shrimp that recreational fishermen catch, preventing those fishermen from catching large shrimp above a certain size is unlikely to provide a solution.

(E): Nothing in the passage suggests that recreational fishermen are not already free to move into the open ocean if they own ocean-going craft. And if they are not already free to move into the open ocean, there is still nothing to suggest that they are interested in doing so in large enough numbers to relieve the overfishing of young shrimp in estuaries.

25. **The 38 corporations that filed United States income tax returns showing a net income of more than $100 million accounted for 53 percent of the total taxable income from foreign sources reported on all tax returns. Sixty percent of the total taxable income from foreign sources came from the 200 returns reporting income from 10 or more countries.**

   If the statements above are true, which of the following must also be true?

   (A) **Most of the total taxable income earned by corporations with net income above $100 million was earned from foreign sources.**

   (B) **Wealthy individuals with large personal incomes reported 47 percent of the total taxable income from foreign sources.**

   (C) **Income from foreign sources amounted to between 53 and 60 percent of all reported taxable income.**

   (D) **Some of the corporations with net income above $100 million reported income from 10 or more countries.**

   (E) **Most of the tax returns showing income from 10 or more countries reported net income of more than $100 million.**

Ⓐ Ⓑ Ⓒ Ⓓ Ⓔ

If 38 tax returns in one category account for 53 percent of the total taxable income from foreign sources, and if 200 tax returns in another category account for 60 percent of the same amount, then the two categories must overlap to some extent. Only if the two percentages, added together, amounted to 100 percent or less is there not necessarily any overlap. Here, the two percentages add up to 113 percent. The answer choice that expresses an overlap between the category of corporations with a net income of above $100 million and that of corporations with income from 10 or more countries is (D).

For explanations of the other answer choices, see below:

   (A): While corporations with net incomes of above $100 million account for more than half of the total taxable income from foreign sources, we cannot tell from the information given what proportion of their own total incomes from all sources is derived from incomes from foreign sources.

   (B): All we can infer is that 47 percent was reported by taxpayers other than corporations with net incomes above $100 million. These taxpayers could be other corporations with somewhat lower incomes.

   (C): The figures of 53 and 60 percent refer to percentages of total taxable income from foreign sources. Neither these nor any other figures in the passage refer to or imply any percentages of all reported taxable income.

   (E): Since there are only 38 corporations with reported net incomes of more than $100 million, but 200 taxpayers with income from 10 or more countries, at the very most somewhat less than 20 percent of those 200 taxpayers could report net incomes of more than $100 million.

SECTION 5
30 Questions

Numbers: All numbers used are real numbers.

Figures: Position of points, angles, regions, etc., can be assumed to be in the order shown; and angle measures can be assumed to be positive.

Lines shown as straight can be assumed to be straight.

Figures can be assumed to lie in a plane unless otherwise indicated.

Figures that accompany questions are intended to provide information useful in answering the questions. However, unless a note states that a figure is drawn to scale, you should solve these problems NOT by estimating sizes by sight or by measurement, but by using your knowledge of mathematics (see Example 2 below).

Directions: Each of the Questions 1-15 consists of two quantities, one in Column A and one in Column B. You are to compare the two quantities and choose

A   if the quantity in Column A is greater;
B   if the quantity in Column B is greater;
C   if the two quantities are equal;
D   if the relationship cannot be determined from the information given.

Note: Since there are only four choices, NEVER MARK (E).

Common
Information: In a question, information concerning one or both of the quantities to be compared is centered above the two columns. A symbol that appears in both columns represents the same thing in Column A as it does in Column B.

	Column A	Column B	Sample Answers
Example 1:	2×6	$2 + 6$	● Ⓑ Ⓒ Ⓓ Ⓔ

Examples 2-4 refer to $\triangle PQR$.

	Column A	Column B	Sample Answers
Example 2:	PN	NQ	Ⓐ Ⓑ Ⓒ ● Ⓔ

(since equal measures cannot be assumed, even though PN and NQ appear equal)

Example 3:	x	y	Ⓐ ● Ⓒ Ⓓ Ⓔ

(since N is between P and Q)

Example 4:	$w + z$	180	Ⓐ Ⓑ ● Ⓓ Ⓔ

(since PQ is a straight line)

146

A   if the quantity in Column A is greater;

B   if the quantity in Column B is greater;

C   if the two quantities are equal;

D   if the relationship cannot be determined from the information given.

Column A   **Column B**

$x = 9$ and $y = 3$

1. $x^2 - 9$ $81 - y^2$

                                              Ⓐ Ⓑ Ⓒ Ⓓ Ⓔ

Since $x = 9$, $x^2 - 9 = 81 - 9$

Since $y = 3$, $81 - y^2 = 81 - 9$

The answer is C

2.   26,003 $2(10^4) + 6(10^3) + 3(10)$

                                              Ⓐ Ⓑ Ⓒ Ⓓ Ⓔ

$2(10^4) = 20,000$

$6(10^3) = 6,000$

$\underline{3(10^1) = 30}$

Sum $= 26,030$, which is greater than 26,003.

The answer is B

A size S soup can is 10 centimeters high and
a size T soup can is 12.5 centimeters high.

3. The height of a stack   **62.5 centimeters**
   of cans if each can is
   size S except the can
   on the bottom of the
   stack, which is size T

                                                Ⓐ Ⓑ Ⓒ Ⓓ Ⓔ

Since the number of size S soup cans is not known, the height of the stack of cans could be smaller, equal to, or greater than 62.5 centimeters.

The answer is D

A if the quantity in Column A is greater;
B if the quantity in Column B is greater;
C if the two quantities are equal;
D if the relationship cannot be determined from the information given.

	Column A	**Column B**
4.	$\dfrac{5}{6}+1$	$\dfrac{10}{3}-1$

Ⓐ Ⓑ Ⓒ Ⓓ Ⓔ

$$\frac{5}{6}+1=1\frac{5}{6}$$

$$\frac{10}{3}-1=3\frac{1}{3}-1=2\frac{1}{3}$$

The answer is B

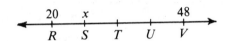

On the number line above, x is the number that corresponds to point S and $RS = ST = TU = UV$.

5.	x	**24**

Ⓐ Ⓑ Ⓒ Ⓓ Ⓔ

The distance from R to V is divided into 4 equal segments. Since R and V are 28 units apart, R and S must be 28/4, or 7, units apart. Therefore, $x = 20 + 7 = 27$.

The answer is A

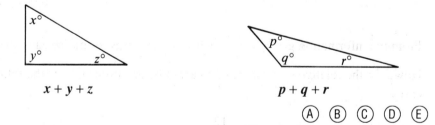

6.	$x + y + z$	$p + q + r$

Ⓐ Ⓑ Ⓒ Ⓓ Ⓔ

For every triangle in a plane, the sum of its angle measures is 180°. Therefore, $x + y + z = p + q + r = 180$.

The answer is C

7.	$-2 - (-4)$	$-1 + (-5)$

Ⓐ Ⓑ Ⓒ Ⓓ Ⓔ

$-2 - (-4) = -2 + 4 = 2$

$-1 + (-5) = -1 - 5 = -6$

The answer is A

148

Column A	**Column B**

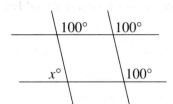

8. x **100**

Ⓐ Ⓑ Ⓒ Ⓓ Ⓔ

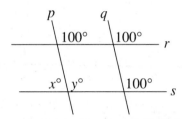

In the figure, lines r and s are parallel because the corresponding angles formed by transversal q have equal measures (both 100°). Thus, $y = 100$, and since $x + y = 180$, it follows that $x = 80$.

The answer is B

$$r > \frac{s}{3} > 0$$

9. r s

Ⓐ Ⓑ Ⓒ Ⓓ Ⓔ

From the information given, $r > \frac{s}{3}$, where r and s must be positive numbers.

However, the relative sizes of r and s cannot be determined. Note the following cases:

If $r = 10$ and $s = 12$, then $10 > \frac{12}{3}$. (true)

If $r = 10$ and $s = 10$, then $10 > \frac{10}{3}$. (true)

If $r = 10$ and $s = 8$, then $10 > \frac{8}{3}$. (true)

Therefore, s can be less than, equal to, or greater than r.

The answer is D

149

A if the quantity in Column A is greater;

B if the quantity in Column B is greater;

C if the two quantities are equal;

D if the relationship cannot be determined from the information given.

<u>Column A</u>   <u>Column B</u>

In a certain school, 75 students are enrolled in English, 85 students are enrolled in mathematics, and 60 students are enrolled in both.

10. **The ratio of the number of students enrolled in both English and mathematics to the number of students enrolled in English**

$\dfrac{3}{5}$

Ⓐ Ⓑ Ⓒ Ⓓ Ⓔ

$$\text{Ratio} = \frac{\text{number in both courses}}{\text{number in English}}$$

$$= \frac{60}{75}$$

$$= \frac{4}{5}$$

The answer is A

$$3x - y = 10$$

11. $\dfrac{6x - 2y}{3}$ $\dfrac{19}{3}$

Ⓐ Ⓑ Ⓒ Ⓓ Ⓔ

Multiplying both sides of the equation $3x - y = 10$ by 2 gives

$$6x - 2y = 20.$$

Therefore, $\dfrac{6x - 2y}{3} = \dfrac{20}{3}$,

which is greater than $\dfrac{19}{3}$.

The answer is A

Column A	Column B

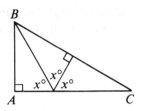

$$\angle ABC = y°$$

12. x y

Ⓐ Ⓑ Ⓒ Ⓓ Ⓔ

From the figure, it is clear that $3x = 180$, or $x = 60$. Thus, the three small triangles and $\triangle ABC$ are all 30-60-90 triangles. Angle ABC, which has measure $y°$, is therefore composed of two 30° angles, which means that $y = 60$.

The answer is C

13. The average of three numbers, the greatest of which is 78

The average of three numbers, the greatest of which is 3

Ⓐ Ⓑ Ⓒ Ⓓ Ⓔ

If only positive numbers were allowed, the Column A average would definitely be greater than the Column B average. However, since nonpositive numbers can be used, the Column A average could be smaller than (or equal to) the Column B average. For example, if the numbers were

   –78, 0, 78 for Column A and

    1, 2, 3 for Column B, then

the average for Column A would be $\dfrac{0}{3} = 0$, and

the average for Column B would be $\dfrac{6}{3} = 2$.

The answer is D

A if the quantity in Column A is greater;
B if the quantity in Column B is greater;
C if the two quantities are equal;
D if the relationship cannot be determined from the information given.

<u>Column A</u>   <u>Column B</u>

The total cost of renting a boat was originally to be shared equally by 8 people. If the number of people is increased by 4, the cost per person will be $1 less.

14. **The total cost of**   **$25**
     renting the boat

Ⓐ Ⓑ Ⓒ Ⓓ Ⓔ

If x = the original cost per person, then the total cost for 8 people is $(8)(x)$. After the increase of 4 people, the total cost can be represented by $(12)(x-1)$. Equating them we get:

$$12(x-1) = 8x$$
$$12x - 12 = 8x$$
$$4x = 12$$
$$x = 3$$

Therefore, the total cost is $8(3) = \$24$, which is smaller than $25.

The answer is B

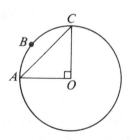

O is the center of the circle.
The area of $\triangle ACO$ is 2.

15. **The length of arc** π
     ABC

Ⓐ Ⓑ Ⓒ Ⓓ Ⓔ

Since the base and height of triangle ACO are both equal to the radius r, the area of triangle ACO is

$$(\frac{1}{2})(r)(r) = 2$$

which means that $r = 2$.

The circumference of the circle is $2\pi r = (2\pi)(2) = 4\pi$. Therefore, arc ABC, which is $\frac{1}{4}$ of the circumference, has length equal to $\left(\frac{1}{4}\right)(4\pi) = \pi$.

The answer is C

Directions: Each of the Questions 16-30 has five answer choices. For each of these questions, select the best of the answer choices given.

16. **A supervisor was paid for her travel expenses at the rate of $0.20 per mile. If she received $14.40, for how many miles was she paid?**

    (A) 28.8 (B) 36 (C) 57.6 (D) 72 (E) 144

    Ⓐ Ⓑ Ⓒ Ⓓ Ⓔ

If x is the number of miles for which the supervisor was paid, then

$$(0.20)(x) = 14.40$$
$$x = 14.40 / 0.20$$
$$x = 72$$

The answer is D

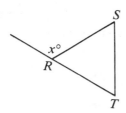

17. **If $RS = ST = TR$ in the figure above, what is the value of x ?**

    (A) 60 (B) 90 (C) 120 (D) 135 (E) 180

    Ⓐ Ⓑ Ⓒ Ⓓ Ⓔ

Since triangle RST is equilateral, each of its angles measures $60°$. Therefore,

$$x + 60 = 180$$
$$x = 120$$

The answer is C

18. **How many layers of gold leaf, each 0.00001 inch thick, would be required to cover an object with a coating of gold leaf 0.1 inch thick?**

    (A) 100,000
    (B)   10,000
    (C)   1,000
    (D)   100
    (E)   10

    Ⓐ Ⓑ Ⓒ Ⓓ Ⓔ

If x is the number of layers needed, then

$$(x)(0.00001) = 0.1$$
$$x = \frac{0.1}{0.00001}$$
$$x = 10,000$$

The answer is B

19. If $y = 8x + 12$ and $x = z + 2$, what is y in terms of z ?

(A) $z + 14$ (B) $8z - 4$ (C) $8z + 10$ (D) $8z + 14$ (E) $8z + 28$

Ⓐ Ⓑ Ⓒ Ⓓ Ⓔ

To get y in terms of z, we can substitute $z + 2$ for x in the first equation:

$$y = 8(z + 2) + 12$$
$$= 8z + 16 + 12$$
$$= 8z + 28$$

The answer is E

20. If a, b, and c are three consecutive integers and if
$a > b > c$, then $(a - b)(a - c)(b - c) =$

(A) 2
(B) 1
(C) 0
(D) −1
(E) −2

Ⓐ Ⓑ Ⓒ Ⓓ Ⓔ

Since a, b, and c are consecutive integers, $a > b > c$,

a is one unit greater than b, or $a - b = 1$,

a is two units greater than c, or $a - c = 2$,

b is one unit greater than c, or $b - c = 1$.

Therefore, $(a - b)(a - c)(b - c) = (1)(2)(1) = 2$.

The answer is A

Questions 21-25 refer to the following data.

AVERAGE COSTS TO OPERATE THREE TYPES OF CARS
OVER A FOUR-YEAR PERIOD
(based on 15,000 miles per year)

	Standard Car	Compact Car	Subcompact Car
Purchase Price	$8,000	$5,600	$4,800
Interest	2,112	1,479	1,267
Insurance	2,000	2,000	2,000
Maintenance/Tires	1,120	1,080	920
Fuel*/Oil	6,429	4,500	3,000
Subtotal	19,661	14,659	11,987
Resale Value	−2,000	−1,400	−1,200
Total cost to Operate the Car	$17,661	$13,259	$10,787

AVERAGE ANNUAL SAVINGS* THROUGH CAR-POOLING TO WORK
RATHER THAN DRIVING ALONE

Type of Car	Annual Cost Driving to Work Alone	Annual Savings Per Person			
		2-person Car Pool	3-person Car Pool	4-person Car Pool	5-person Car Pool
Standard	$2,491	$1,146	$1,544	$1,719	$1,843
Compact	1,870	860	1,159	1,290	1,384
Subcompact	1,521	700	943	1,050	1,126

155

AVERAGE DAILY COST* IF VAN-POOLING TO WORK

Round-Trip Miles	Van Pool Cost per Passenger
20	$1.45
25	1.54
30	1.63
40	1.81
50	1.99
60	2.17

* Based on $1.50 per gallon for fuel

21. What is the difference between the average purchase prices of a standard car and a compact car?

(A) $600   (B) $2,400   (C) $2,800   (D) $3,200   (E) $4,400

Ⓐ Ⓑ Ⓒ Ⓓ Ⓔ

The Average Costs table shows that:

The average purchase price of a standard car = $8,000.

The average purchase price of a compact car = $5,600.

Therefore, the difference is 8,000 – 5,600 = $2,400.

The answer is B

22. Over the four-year period, the average cost for insurance on a compact car is approximately what percent of the average total cost to operate a compact car?

(A) 11%
(B) 13%
(C) 15%
(D) 17%
(E) 19%

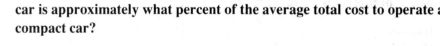

Ⓐ Ⓑ Ⓒ Ⓓ Ⓔ

From the Average Daily Cost table:

The average cost of insurance on a compact car = $2,000.

The average total cost to operate a compact car = $13,259.

Therefore,

$$\frac{2,000}{13,259} = 0.15084$$

$$= \text{approximately } 15\%$$

The answer is C

23. **The average daily cost per passenger in a van pool traveling 50 miles round trip to work is approximately what percent greater than the average daily cost per passenger in a van pool traveling 40 miles round trip to work?**

   (A) 8%
   (B) 10%
   (C) 12%
   (D) 13%
   (E) 18%

   Ⓐ Ⓑ Ⓒ Ⓓ Ⓔ

For the Average Daily Cost table:

For a 50-mile round trip, the average daily cost per passenger is $1.99.

For a 40-mile round trip, the average daily cost per passenger is $1.81.

Therefore, calculating the percent increase from $1.81 to $1.99, we get:

$$\frac{1.99 - 1.81}{1.81} = \frac{0.18}{1.81}$$

$$= \text{approximately } 10\%$$

The answer is B

24. **If the cost of oil is negligible, what is the mileage (average miles per gallon of fuel) of a compact car?**

   (A) 13
   (B) 18
   (C) 20
   (D) 25
   (E) 28

   Ⓐ Ⓑ Ⓒ Ⓓ Ⓔ

From the Average Costs table, the average cost for fuel/oil for a compact car is $4,500, based on 15,000 miles driven per year. At $1.50 per gallon (see footnote on table), the compact uses 4,500/1.50 = 3,000 gallons of fuel in four years.

In four years, the compact travels 4(15,000) = 60,000 miles. Therefore, the mileage (average miles per gallon of fuel) is

$$60,000/3,000 = 20 \text{ mpg.}$$

The answer is C

25. **If 2 people, who would otherwise be driving alone in subcompact cars, drive in a 2-person car pool using subcompact cars, what is the total of their average annual costs of transportation to work?**

   (A) $821   (B) $1,400   (C) $1,521   (D) $1,642   (E) $2,342

   Ⓐ Ⓑ Ⓒ Ⓓ Ⓔ

From the Average Annual Savings table, the average annual cost per person driving to work alone in a subcompact is $1,521. If two people were driving separately in subcompacts, their total expense would be 2 ($1,521), or $3,042. Since they are each saving $700 by driving in a two-person car pool, they are saving a total of $1,400.

Therefore, their total cost is

$$\$3,042 - \$1,400 = \$1,642.$$

The answer is D

26. **Which of the following equations can be used to find the value of x if 7 less than $5x$ is 5 more than the product of 3 and x?**

   (A) $5x - 7 = 5 + 3x$
   (B) $5x - 7 = 5 + (3 + x)$
   (C) $7 - 5x = 5 + 3x$
   (D) $7 - 5x = (5 + 3)x$
   (E) $7 - 5x + 5 = 3x$

   Ⓐ Ⓑ Ⓒ Ⓓ Ⓔ

"7 less than $5x$" is expressed as "$5x - 7$" and "5 more than the product of 3 and x" is expressed as "$3x + 5$." Therefore, we can write

$$5x - 7 = 3x + 5,$$

which is equivalent to

$$5x - 7 = 5 + 3x.$$

The answer is A

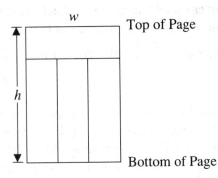

27. **The figure above shows the dimensions of a page that has been divided into four rectangular advertising spaces of equal area. What is the height, in terms of h, of one of the advertising spaces at the bottom of the page?**

(A) $\frac{1}{4}h$ (B) $\frac{1}{3}h$ (C) $\frac{1}{2}h$ (D) $\frac{2}{3}h$ (E) $\frac{3}{4}h$

Ⓐ Ⓑ Ⓒ Ⓓ Ⓔ

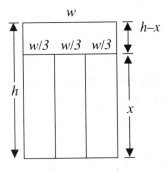

Let x represent the height we are looking for. The area of the rectangular region at the top is $w(h - x)$. The area of each of the other rectangular regions is $(\frac{w}{3})x$. Since all four regions have equal area:

$$\left(\frac{w}{3}\right)x = w(h - x)$$

Multiplying each side by $\frac{3}{w}$,

$$x = 3h - 3x$$
$$4x = 3h$$
$$x = \frac{3h}{4}$$

The answer is E

28. The ratio of $\left(\dfrac{1}{2}\right)^3$ to $\left(\dfrac{1}{2}\right)^4$ is

(A) $\dfrac{2}{1}$　(B) $\dfrac{3}{2}$　(C) $\dfrac{3}{4}$　(D) $\dfrac{1}{2}$　(E) $\dfrac{1}{4}$

Ⓐ　Ⓑ　Ⓒ　Ⓓ　Ⓔ

The ratio of $\left(\dfrac{1}{2}\right)^3$ to $\left(\dfrac{1}{2}\right)^4$ is $\dfrac{\left(\dfrac{1}{2}\right)^3}{\left(\dfrac{1}{2}\right)^4} = \dfrac{1}{\left(\dfrac{1}{2}\right)^1} = \dfrac{1}{\dfrac{1}{2}} = \dfrac{2}{1}$.

The answer is A

29. $\left(1 - \dfrac{x}{x+1}\right) - \dfrac{1-x}{x+1} =$

(A) 0

(B) 1

(C) $\dfrac{1}{x+1}$

(D) $\dfrac{x}{x+1}$

(E) $\dfrac{-2x}{x+1}$

Ⓐ　Ⓑ　Ⓒ　Ⓓ　Ⓔ

We can express 1 as $\dfrac{x+1}{x+1}$.

Therefore, the expression is:

$$\dfrac{x+1}{x+1} - \dfrac{x}{x+1} - \dfrac{1-x}{x+1} = \dfrac{x+1-x-1+x}{x+1} = \dfrac{x}{x+1}.$$

The answer is D

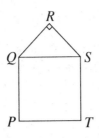

30. The area of square _PQST_ in the figure above is 100. If _QR = RS_, what is the perimeter of △ _QRS_?

(A) $5\sqrt{2}+10$ (B) 20 (C) $10\sqrt{2}+10$ (D) 30 (E) $20\sqrt{2}+10$

Ⓐ Ⓑ Ⓒ Ⓓ Ⓔ

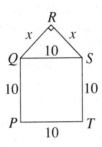

Since _PQST_ is a square with area 100, each of its sides is equal to 10. Since _QRS_ is a right triangle, with _QR = RS = x_, we can apply the Pythagorean Theorem:

$$x^2 + x^2 = 10^2$$
$$2x^2 = 100$$
$$x^2 = 50$$
$$x = \sqrt{50} = 5\sqrt{2}$$

Therefore, the perimeter of _QRS_ is $2(5\sqrt{2})+10$, or $10\sqrt{2}+10$.

The answer is C

SECTION 6
38 Questions

<u>Directions:</u> Each sentence below has one or two blanks, each blank indicating that something has been omitted. Beneath the sentence are five lettered words or sets of words. Choose the word or set of words for each blank that <u>best</u> fits the meaning of the sentence as a whole.

1. **Although the minuet appeared simple, its ------- steps had to be studied very carefully before they could be gracefully ------- in public.**

   (A) progressive. .revealed
   (B) intricate. .executed
   (C) rudimentary. . allowed
   (D) minute. .discussed
   (E) entertaining. .stylized

   Ⓐ Ⓑ Ⓒ Ⓓ Ⓔ

The words "Although the minuet appeared simple" clearly indicate that the minuet was not simple. The first missing word describes the steps that made up the minuet, and the structure of the sentence requires that this word contrast with the minuet's simple appearance. The second missing word is what could be gracefully done in public only after careful study of the minuet's steps. That the minuet is a dance and that the activity called for is done gracefully suggest public performance of the minuet.

(A) is not the answer. It is possible that the minuet's steps were "progressive," but "progressive" does not contrast clearly with the minuet's apparent simplicity. "Revealed" suggests that the steps had not previously been seen. There is no evidence of this in the sentence.

* (B) is the answer. That the minuet's steps were "intricate," or not simple, is suggested by the initial clause of the sentence. "Executed" means performed.

(C) is not the answer. There is no indication in the sentence that the steps of the minuet were "rudimentary," or that anyone restricted their public performance, as "allowed" suggests.

(D) is not the answer. There is no indication in the sentence that the steps of the minuet were "minute" (very small). It is unlikely that the steps were "discussed" in public.

(E) is not the answer. "Entertaining" does not contrast clearly with "simple." To be "stylized" means to be made to conform to a conventional pattern. It is performance of stylized steps, rather than their stylizing, that is done in public.

2. **The results of the experiments performed by Elizabeth Hazen and Rachel Brown were ------- not only because these results challenged old assumptions but also because they called the ------- methodology into question.**

   (A) provocative. .prevailing
   (B) predictable. .contemporary
   (C) inconclusive. .traditional
   (D) intriguing. .projected
   (E) specious. .original

   Ⓐ Ⓑ Ⓒ Ⓓ Ⓔ

The first missing word describes the results of experiments performed by Hazen and Brown. That Hazen's and Brown's results challenged old assumptions suggests that the results were not like previous results. The second missing word describes a methodology that these new results call into question.

   * (A) is the answer. It is likely that results that challenge old assumptions are "provocative" (stimulating, likely to stir up controversy). Novel results may call "prevailing" (currently accepted) methods into question, and this, like the challenging of old assumptions, is likely to be "provocative."

   (B) is not the answer. Results that are "predictable" are not likely to challenge old assumptions, nor is there any reason to believe that such results call "contemporary" methodology into question.

   (C) is not the answer. Results cannot be called "inconclusive" simply because they challenge old assumptions or because they call "traditional" methodology into question.

   (D) is not the answer. Results may be "intriguing" because they challenge old assumptions, but there is no reason to suppose that a "projected" methodology (one planned for the future) would be called into question.

   (E) is not the answer. There is no reason to suppose that results that challenge old assumptions or call "original" methodologies into question are "specious," that is, that they have the appearance of truth even though they are not true.

3. **Despite the ------- of many of their colleagues, some scholars have begun to emphasize "pop culture" as a key for ------- the myths, hopes, and fears of contemporary society.**

   (A) antipathy. .entangling
   (B) discernment. .evaluating
   (C) pedantry. .reinstating
   (D) skepticism. .deciphering
   (E) enthusiasm. .symbolizing

   Ⓐ Ⓑ Ⓒ Ⓓ Ⓔ

The first missing word expresses the attitude of some scholars' colleagues toward emphasis on pop culture. "Despite" suggests opposition on the part of the colleagues to the scholars' emphasis. The second missing word describes something that a key (here, an aid to interpretation or identification) could do to the myths, hopes, and fears of contemporary society.

163

(A) is not the answer. "Antipathy" expresses opposition on the part of the colleagues, but the kind of key mentioned in the sentence would be used for clarifying rather than for "entangling" myths, hopes, and fears.

(B) is not the answer. A key cannot be a standard used for "evaluating" myths, hopes, and fears. "Discernment" does not describe a disapproving attitude that colleagues could have.

(C) is not the answer. Colleagues' "pedantry" could explain their opposition, but "pedantry" does not necessarily indicate opposition. There is no reason to suppose that myths, hopes, and fears need "reinstating" or that a key could be used to reinstate them.

* (D) is the answer. "Skepticism" suggests opposition on the part of the colleagues. The kind of key mentioned in the sentence could be used for "deciphering."

(E) is not the answer. "Enthusiasm" does not suggest opposition on the part of the colleagues. A key is used for unlocking or interpreting rather than for "symbolizing."

4. **In the seventeenth century, direct flouting of a generally accepted system of values was regarded as -------, even as a sign of madness.**

   **(A) adventurous   (B) frivolous   (C) willful   (D) impermissible
   (E) irrational**

   Ⓐ Ⓑ Ⓒ Ⓓ Ⓔ

The word "even" suggests that the second part of the sentence will state the idea of the first part in stronger terms. Therefore, the missing word is related to the word "madness." It is likely that the missing word will describe what might be seen as a mild form of madness.

(A) is not the answer. Flouting generally accepted values can be seen as "adventurous," but adventurousness does not suggest a form of madness.

(B) is not the answer. Flouting generally accepted values can be seen as "frivolous," but frivolousness does not suggest a form of madness.

(C) is not the answer. Flouting generally accepted values can be seen as "willful," but willfulness does not suggest a form of madness. Though willfulness may result in flouting, willfulness suggests that one has control over one's actions, whereas madness suggests lack of control.

(D) is not the answer. Flouting generally accepted values might be regarded as "impermissible" at any time. However, "even as a sign of madness" suggests that, in the seventeenth century, flouting accepted values was taken very seriously. Therefore, a word that suggests a mild form of madness, rather than just unacceptability, would be a better choice.

* (E) is the answer. Flouting generally accepted values can be seen as "irrational," and irrationality can be seen as an element in (or a mild form of) madness.

5. **Queen Elizabeth I has quite correctly been called a ------- of the arts, because many young artists received her patronage.**

   (A) connoisseur   (B) critic   (C) friend   (D) scourge   (E) judge

   Ⓐ Ⓑ Ⓒ Ⓓ Ⓔ

The word "because" indicates that the missing word is defined by the words "many young artists received her patronage." The most obvious choice to fill this blank would be patron or supporter. However, neither patron nor supporter is among the choices.

(A) is not the answer. A "connoisseur" understands and is competent to judge. A "connoisseur" does not necessarily support the arts.

(B) is not the answer. A "critic" judges, but does not necessarily support, the arts.

*(C) is the answer. In the context of a sentence about patronage, a friend is defined as one who favors or promotes.

(D) is not the answer. A "scourge" is one who criticizes or inflicts punishment, not one who provides support.

(E) is not the answer. A "judge" is qualified to give an authoritative opinion but is not necessarily supportive.

6. **Because outlaws were denied ------- under medieval law, anyone could raise a hand against them with legal ------.**

   (A) **propriety. .authority**
   (B) **protection. .impunity**
   (C) **collusion. .consent**
   (D) **rights. .collaboration**
   (E) **provisions. .validity**

   Ⓐ Ⓑ Ⓒ Ⓓ Ⓔ

The sentence states that "anyone could raise a hand against (medieval outlaws)." The phrase "with legal _____" suggests that to do so was sanctioned in some way. Thus, the second missing word should indicate the legal acceptability of acting against outlaws. The word "because" indicates that the first missing word will tell what element denied to outlaws made acting against them legally acceptable.

(A) is not the answer. "Propriety" means properness, or a standard of social acceptability for conduct. Denying outlaws a standard of social conduct would not have permitted others to legally attack them. "Propriety" is not bestowed by law as "under medieval law" suggests.

*(B) is the answer. To deny outlaws "protection" under the law would permit others to attack them with legal "impunity" (freedom from punishment).

(C) is not the answer. "Collusion" (secret agreement or cooperation for fraudulent or deceitful purposes) is accomplished by the outlaws themselves. It can be punished but cannot be denied them by the law.

(D) is not the answer. To deny the outlaws their "rights" does not imply direct "collaboration" (or cooperation) between the law and those who raised a hand against them.

(E) is not the answer. Under the law, "provisions" are ways of providing for something. However, lack of "provisions" alone does not indicate specifically why anyone could raise a hand against the outlaws. It cannot be assumed that the lack of "provisions" gave legal "validity," or sanction, to attacks on outlaws.

7. Rather than enhancing a country's security, the successful development of nuclear weapons could serve at first to increase that country's -------.

(A) boldness (B) influence (C) responsibility
(D) moderation (E) vulnerability

Ⓐ Ⓑ Ⓒ Ⓓ Ⓔ

The words "Rather than" tell you that the second part of the sentence will express an idea that is the opposite of "enhancing a country's security." An increase in the characteristic expressed by the missing word is the opposite of enhancing security. Such an increase will lessen security.

(A) is not the answer. An increase in "boldness" is not the opposite of an enhancement of security.

(B) is not the answer. A country's "influence" may increase with the development of nuclear weapons, but this increase is not the opposite of an enhancement of the country's security.

(C) is not the answer. An increase in "responsibility" is likely to follow from a country's development of nuclear weapons, but this increase is not the opposite of an enhancement of the country's security.

(D) is not the answer. An increase in "moderation" is not the opposite of an enhancement of security. In addition, "moderation" is not a quality that is generally said to increase.

* (E) is the answer. An increase in a country's "vulnerability" is the opposite of an enhancement of its security.

Directions: In each of the following questions, a related pair of words or phrases is followed by five lettered pairs of words or phrases. Select the lettered pair that best expresses a relationship similar to that expressed in the original pair.

8. WATER:SWIM :: (A) grass:grow (B) knot:tie
(C) plan:implement (D) flood:damage (E) snow:ski

Ⓐ Ⓑ Ⓒ Ⓓ Ⓔ

"Water" is a medium in which one can "swim." A rationale for this analogy is "X (water) is a medium in which people often Y (swim)."

(A) is not the answer. "Grass" itself can "grow," but "grass" is not a medium in which one can "grow."

(B) is not the answer. One can "tie" a "knot," but a "knot" is not a medium in which one can "tie."

(C) is not the answer. One can "implement" a "plan," but a "plan" is not a medium in which one can "implement."

(D) is not the answer. "Damage" is done by a "flood," but a "flood" is the agent that does "damage" rather than the medium in which "damage" is done.

* (E) is the answer. "Snow" is a medium in which people can and often do "ski."

9. TILE:MOSAIC :: (A) wood:totem (B) stitch:sampler
(C) ink:scroll (D) pedestal:column (E) tapestry:rug

Ⓐ Ⓑ Ⓒ Ⓓ Ⓔ

A "tile" is a basic unit of which a "mosaic" is composed. A rationale for this analogy could be "An X is a small unit, many of which are used to make up the design in a Y."

(A) is not the answer. A "totem" could be made of "wood," but "wood" is not one of many small units.

* (B) is the answer. A "stitch" is one of many small units that make up the design of a "sampler."

(C) is not the answer. A design on a "scroll" may be made in "ink," but "ink" is not a unit.

(D) is not the answer. A "pedestal" may be in the form of a "column," or it may be part of a "column," but many pedestals are not used to make up a "column."

(E) is not the answer. A "tapestry" is not a unit in a "rug."

10. SCHOOL:FISH ::   (A) posse:crowd   (B) arrow:feathers   (C) union:labor   (D) flock:birds   (E) stock:cattle

Ⓐ Ⓑ Ⓒ Ⓓ Ⓔ

A "school" is a group of "fish" that swim together. A rationale for this analogy could be "An X is a natural group of many Y (where Y represents some kind of animal)."

(A) is not the answer. A "posse" is a group of people. A "crowd" is also a group of people; the word "crowd" does not fit into the rationale given above.

(B) is not the answer. An "arrow" may have "feathers" on it, but "arrow" is not a name for a group of "feathers."

(C) is not the answer. A "union" could not be called a group of "labor," although it could be a group of laborers.

* (D) is the answer. "Flock" is a name for a natural group of many "birds."

(E) is not the answer. "Cattle" may be classified as "stock." However, "stock" does not refer specifically to cattle, but may include any kind of animal that is raised for use. In addition, "stock" does not refer to a natural group of "cattle."

11. CASTIGATION:DISAPPROVAL ::

(A) grief:indignation

(B) hostility:intention

(C) hope:insight

(D) innocence:patience

(E) blasphemy:irreverence

Ⓐ Ⓑ Ⓒ Ⓓ Ⓔ

"Castigation" means punishment, severe criticism, or reproof. Therefore, since "castigation" is a way of expressing "disapproval," a rationale for this analogy could be "X is always a strong expression of Y."

(A) is not the answer. "Grief" is an emotion. It is not an expression of "indignation."

(B) is not the answer. "Hostility" is not a strong expression of "intention."

(C) is not the answer. "Hope" is not a strong expression of "insight."

(D) is not the answer. "Innocence" is not a strong expression of "patience."

* (E) is the answer. "Blasphemy" is defined as a strong expression of "irreverence."

12. REDOUBTABLE:AWE ::

(A) tart:pungency
(B) tacit:solitude
(C) despicable:contempt
(D) engrossing:obliviousness
(E) venerable:renown

Ⓐ Ⓑ Ⓒ Ⓓ Ⓔ

"Redoubtable" means formidable, or worthy of awe or reverence. Therefore, a rationale for this analogy could be "Something properly described as X is capable of inspiring Y."

(A) is not the answer. Something described as "tart" cannot be said to inspire "pungency."

(B) is not the answer. "Tacit" refers to something that is implied without being expressed. To be "tacit" does not inspire "solitude."

* (C) is the answer. "Despicable" means contemptible, or capable of inspiring "contempt."

(D) is not the answer. Something "engrossing" takes up one's attention completely. Even though being engrossed could lead one to be oblivious of everything except that which engrosses, to be "engrossing" cannot be said to lead to unqualified "obliviousness," since one is not oblivious of that which engrosses.

(E) is not the answer. Something that is "venerable" (worthy of respect) may be "renowned," but renown is a characteristic of the venerated object, and not a feeling inspired in another.

13. ACCELERATE:SPEED ::

(A) assess:value
(B) elaborate:quality
(C) disperse:strength
(D) prolong:duration
(E) enumerate:quantity

Ⓐ Ⓑ Ⓒ Ⓓ Ⓔ

To "accelerate" means to increase in "speed" or to increase the "speed" of something. A rationale for this analogy could be "To X means to increase Y."

(A) is not the answer. To "assess" means to judge "value" rather than to increase it.

(B) is not the answer. To "elaborate" means to develop in detail, or to become more complex. No increase in "quality" is implied.

(C) is not the answer. To "disperse" means to scatter or break up. Dispersion may in some cases imply weakening; there is, however, no necessary connection between dispersion and strengthening or weakening.

* (D) is the answer. To "prolong" means to extend or lengthen in time. "Duration" means time during which something exists. To "proiong" means to increase "duration."

(E) is not the answer. To "enumerate" means to count or list, rather than to increase "quantity."

14. COMPLAIN:CARP ::   (A) supply:donate   (B) argue:debate   (C) grumble:accuse   (D) drink:guzzle   (E) pacify:intervene

Ⓐ Ⓑ Ⓒ Ⓓ Ⓔ

To "carp" means to whine, to find fault, or to "complain" habitually. One rationale for this analogy could be "To Y means to X in a particular way." A more specific rationale might be "To Y is to X constantly in a way that is unpleasant to others." Or, "Y is a term that adds disparaging connotations to the meaning of X."

(A) is not the answer. To "donate" is one way to "supply," but to "donate" has positive rather than negative connotations. Although this pair of words fits the more general rationale given above, it does not fit the more specific ones.

(B) is not the answer. To "debate" is a way of arguing, but the word "debate" does not imply habitual or unpleasant argument, nor does it imply disparagement.

(C) is not the answer. To "accuse" is not a way to "grumble" (to mutter discontentedly).

* (D) is the answer. To "guzzle" means to "drink" greedily.

(E) is not the answer. One may "intervene" in order to "pacify," but to "intervene" is not a specific way to "pacify."

15. FILIGREE:WIRE ::   (A) embroidery:knot   (B) bead:string   (C) lace:thread   (D) fringe:yarn   (E) rope:strand

Ⓐ Ⓑ Ⓒ Ⓓ Ⓔ

"Filigree" refers specifically to ornamental openwork (work intended to have open spaces as part of its design) made of "wire." A rationale for this analogy could be "X is openwork made of Y."

(A) is not the answer. "Embroidery" may include decorative knots, but a "knot" is not the substance of which "embroidery" is made.

(B) is not the answer. A "bead" is strung on a "string," not made of "string."

* (C) is the answer. "Lace" is openwork made of "thread."

(D) is not the answer. A "fringe" may be made of "yarn," but "fringe" does not imply openwork design.

(E) is not the answer. A "rope" is made of strands, but it is not ornamental openwork.

16. SKIRMISH:INSIGNIFICANCE ::

(A) revolution:democracy
(B) duel:formality
(C) feud:impartiality
(D) bout:sparring
(E) crusade:remoteness

Ⓐ Ⓑ Ⓒ Ⓓ Ⓔ

A "skirmish" is a minor fight in a war; it is relatively insignificant. Therefore, a rationale for this analogy could be "X is characterized by relative Y compared to others in its class." In this case, a "skirmish" is characterized by relative "insignificance" compared to other kinds of battles or fights.

(A) is not the answer. A "revolution" may be fought for "democracy," but it is not necessarily characterized by "democracy."

*(B) is the answer. A "duel" is a fight that is conducted according to certain rules and is therefore characterized by relative "formality," compared with other kinds of two-person fights.

(C) is not the answer. A "feud" is a fight that is carried on because of a lack of "impartiality."

(D) is not the answer. A "bout" may include "sparring," but "sparring" is not a characteristic that a "bout" could have in relative degrees.

(E) is not the answer. A "crusade" is a remedial enterprise undertaken with zeal and enthusiasm. Although the Crusades that took place in the Middle Ages were undertaken far from the native lands of the Crusaders, there is nothing in the definition of "crusade" to suggest "remoteness," either in terms of distance or in terms of emotional attitude.

Directions: Each passage in this group is followed by questions based on its content. After reading a passage, choose the best answer to each question. Answer all questions following a passage on the basis of what is <u>stated</u> or <u>implied</u> in that passage.

Questions 17-24

Thomas Hardy's impulses as a writer, all of which he indulged in his novels, were numerous and divergent, and they did not always work together in harmony. Hardy was to some degree interested in exploring his characters' psychologies, though impelled less by curiosity than by
(5) sympathy. Occasionally he felt the impulse to comedy (in all its detached coldness) as well as the impulse to farce, but he was more often inclined to see tragedy and record it. He was also inclined to literary realism in the several senses of that phrase. He wanted to describe ordinary human beings; he wanted to speculate on their dilemmas rationally (and, unfortu-

(10) nately, even schematically); and he wanted to record precisely the material
universe. Finally, he wanted to be more than a realist. He wanted to
transcend what he considered to be the banality of solely recording things
exactly and to express as well his awareness of the occult and the strange.
In his novels these various impulses were sacrificed to each other
(15) inevitably and often. Inevitably, because Hardy did not care in the way
that novelists such as Flaubert or James cared, and therefore took paths of
least resistance. Thus, one impulse often surrendered to a fresher one and,
unfortunately, instead of exacting a compromise, simply disappeared. A
desire to throw over reality a light that never was might give way abruptly
(20) to the desire on the part of what we might consider a novelist-scientist to
record exactly and concretely the structure and texture of a flower. In this
instance, the new impulse was at least an energetic one, and thus its
indulgence did not result in a relaxed style. But on other occasions Hardy
abandoned a perilous, risky, and highly energizing impulse in favor of
(25) what was for him the fatally relaxing impulse to classify and schematize
abstractly. When a relaxing impulse was indulged, the style — that sure
index of an author's literary worth — was certain to become verbose.
Hardy's weakness derived from his apparent inability to control the
comings and goings of these divergent impulses and from his unwilling-
(30) ness to cultivate and sustain the energetic and risky ones. He submitted to
first one and then another, and the spirit blew where it listed; hence the
unevenness of any one of his novels. His most controlled novel, *Under the
Greenwood Tree,* prominently exhibits two different but reconcilable
impulses — a desire to be a realist-historian and a desire to be a psycholo-
(35) gist of love — but the slight interlockings of plot are not enough to bind
the two completely together. Thus even this book splits into two distinct
parts.

17. **Which of the following is the most appropriate title for the passage,
based on its content?**

   (A) *Under the Greenwood Tree:* **Hardy's Ambiguous Triumph**
   (B) **The Real and the Strange: The Novelist's Shifting Realms**
   (C) **Energy *Versus* Repose: The Role of Ordinary People in Hardy's
         Fiction**
   (D) **Hardy's Novelistic Impulses: The Problem of Control**
   (E) **Divergent Impulses: The Issue of Unity in the Novel**

Ⓐ Ⓑ Ⓒ Ⓓ Ⓔ

This question asks you to choose an appropriate title for the passage, taking into
account the content of the passage. That is, it is how well a title expresses (summarizes) the content of the passage that will determine appropriateness, and not
characteristics of the title itself, such as its originality or its elegance.

   (A) is not the answer. It is conceivable that *Under the Greenwood Tree* might
be called Hardy's ambiguous triumph, but the novel is mentioned only at the end
of the passage to illustrate Hardy's problems with divergent impulses. Therefore,
the novel itself is not a major element in the content of the passage.

(B) is not the answer. Although the passage suggests that the real and the strange were realms of interest to Hardy, the passage focuses primarily on Hardy's numerous and divergent impulses, rather than on two areas (realms) of interest to him.

(C) is not the answer. The role of ordinary people in Hardy's fiction is mentioned but not discussed in the passage. In addition, there is no indication in the passage that energy and repose in Hardy's fiction are related only to his treatment of ordinary people.

* (D) is the answer. The passage focuses on the difficulty that Hardy had in controlling his creative impulses as he wrote novels.

(E) is not the answer. Divergent impulses are discussed in the passage, but the issue of unity in the novel in general is not discussed.

18. The passage suggests that the author would be most likely to agree with which of the following statements about literary realism?

(A) Literary realism is most concerned with the exploration of the internal lives of ordinary human beings.

(B) The term "literary realism" is susceptible to more than a single definition.

(C) Literary realism and an interest in psychology are likely to be at odds in a novelist's work.

(D) "Literary realism" is the term most often used by critics in describing the method of Hardy's novels.

(E) A propensity toward literary realism is a less interesting novelistic impulse than is an interest in the occult and the strange.

Ⓐ Ⓑ Ⓒ Ⓓ Ⓔ

The question asks you to infer the beliefs of the author of the passage concerning literary realism. Hardy's impulse toward literary realism is discussed in the first paragraph.

(A) is not the answer. The author mentions the desire to "describe ordinary human beings" as part of Hardy's impulse toward literary realism, but there is no indication that the author believes that literary realism is most concerned with this.

* (B) is the answer. The author's discussion of "the several senses" of literary realism in the first paragraph indicates that he believes the phrase to be susceptible to several definitions.

(C) is not the answer. The author indicates that the impulse toward literary realism and the impulse toward exploring characters' psychology were sometimes at odds in Hardy's work. However, the passage does not generalize the idea to other novelists, nor is there any indication that this conflict is a common one.

(D) is not the answer. There is no indication in the passage that most critics describe Hardy's method as literary realism.

(E) is not the answer. There is no indication in the passage of the author's opinion of how interesting different literary impulses might be.

19. The author of the passage considers a writer's style to be

    (A) a reliable means by which to measure the writer's literary merit

    (B) most apparent in those parts of the writer's work that are not realistic

    (C) problematic when the writer attempts to follow perilous or risky impulses

    (D) shaped primarily by the writer's desire to classify and schematize

    (E) the most accurate index of the writer's literary reputation

Ⓐ Ⓑ Ⓒ Ⓓ Ⓔ

This question asks you to identify a belief of the author's concerning literary style in general. The question does not say whether the information is stated in the passage, or must be inferred.

  * (A) is the answer. This option paraphrases the words in lines 26-27, "style — that sure index of an author's literary worth."

  (B) is not the answer. There is no indication in the passage that, in general, a writer's style is less apparent when his or her work is realistic.

  (C) is not the answer. The author discusses Hardy's perilous or risky impulses, but makes no statement about problems that such impulses might cause for writers in general.

  (D) is not the answer. The author mentions that Hardy sometimes was inclined to classify and schematize, but there is no indication in the passage that any writer's style is shaped primarily by the desire to do so.

  (E) is not the answer. Style is mentioned as an index of a writer's literary worth, not as an index of reputation.

20. Which of the following words could best be substituted for "relaxed" (line 23) without substantially changing the author's meaning?

    (A) informal

    (B) confined

    (C) risky

    (D) wordy

    (E) metaphoric

Ⓐ Ⓑ Ⓒ Ⓓ Ⓔ

The question refers you to line 23 so that you can determine how a particular word with several possible meanings is used in context. The substitution of the correct option should not change the meaning of the passage.

  (A) is not the answer, although one might expect that a "relaxed" style is also an "informal" style. There is no indication that Hardy's "relaxed" style was informal. The "relaxing impulse" described in lines 25-26 led to schematizing and classifying activities that do not suggest informality.

  (B) is not the answer. There is no indication that Hardy's relaxed style was "confined" (kept within limits). Indeed, a "confined" style would not be described as a "relaxed" style.

  (C) is not the answer. The author uses the word "risky" to characterize the impulses that led Hardy into the opposite of a relaxed style.

* (D) is the answer. Lines 21-23 indicate that the indulgence of an energetic impulse did not lead to a relaxed style. This implies that indulgence of the opposite of an energetic impulse — a relaxing impulse — did lead to a relaxed style. Lines 26-27 state that indulgence of the relaxing impulse, which led Hardy into a relaxed style, also led him to become "verbose" (wordy). Thus, in the context of the passage, a relaxed style is a wordy style.

(E) is not the answer. There is no indication in the passage that Hardy's relaxed style included use of metaphor.

21. **The passage supplies information to suggest that its author would be most likely to agree with which of the following statements about the novelists Flaubert and James?**

    (A) **They indulged more impulses in their novels than did Hardy in his novels.**

    (B) **They have elicited a greater degree of favorable response from most literary critics than has Hardy.**

    (C) **In the writing of their novels, they often took pains to effect a compromise among their various novelistic impulses.**

    (D) **Regarding novelistic construction, they cared more about the opinions of other novelists than about the opinions of ordinary readers.**

    (E) **They wrote novels in which the impulse toward realism and the impulse away from realism were evident in equal measure.**

    Ⓐ Ⓑ Ⓒ Ⓓ Ⓔ

This question asks you to infer the author's beliefs concerning Flaubert and James, whose names are mentioned in line 16.

(A) is not the answer. There is no mention in the passage of the particular impulses Flaubert and James indulged in their novels; thus, no comparison of numbers of impulses can be made. The passage suggests that Flaubert and James indulged fewer impulses than did Hardy, rather than more.

(B) is not the answer. There is no mention in the passage of the response of literary critics to the work of Flaubert and James.

* (C) is the answer. In lines 14-18, the author contrasts Hardy's approach to writing with the approaches of Flaubert and James. The word "therefore" in line 16 indicates that Hardy acted as he did because of his lack of care. "Thus" in line 17 indicates that his lack of care led to an inability to resolve conflicts among his impulses. In contrast, Flaubert and James cared more, and this implies that they took the trouble to effect compromises among their impulses.

(D) is not the answer. The statement that Flaubert and James "cared" (line 16) refers to their desire to effect compromise among their impulses; there is no suggestion that either of them sought to impress other novelists.

(E) is not the answer. There is no indication in the passage of the kinds of impulses that characterized the work of Flaubert and James.

22. Which of the following statements best describes the organization of lines 17 to 26 of the passage ("Thus . . . abstractly")?

(A) The author makes a disapproving observation and then presents two cases, one of which leads to a qualification of his disapproval and the other of which does not.

(B) The author draws a conclusion from a previous statement, explains his conclusion in detail, and then gives a series of examples that have the effect of resolving an inconsistency.

(C) The author concedes a point and then makes a counterargument, using an extended comparison and contrast that qualifies his original concession.

(D) The author makes a judgment, points out an exception to his judgment, and then contradicts his original assertion.

(E) The author summarizes and explains an argument and then advances a brief history of opposing arguments.

Ⓐ Ⓑ Ⓒ Ⓓ Ⓔ

This question asks you to identify a description of the organization of a given part of the passage.

* (A) is the answer. The author makes the disapproving observation that some of Hardy's impulses "unfortunately, . . . simply disappeared." The first case, described in lines 18-21, elicits qualified disapproval — "the new impulse was at least an energetic one." The second, described in lines 23-26, leads to unqualified disapproval, as the author describes Hardy's "fatally relaxing impulse."

(B) is not the answer. In lines 17-18, the author is not drawing a conclusion so much as illustrating the previous statement. The examples the author provides do not resolve an inconsistency.

(C) is not the answer. The author neither concedes a point nor makes a counterargument.

(D) is not the answer. Lines 17-18 could be said to make a judgment. However, the example in lines 23-26 supports rather than contradicts the author's assertion in lines 17-18.

(E) is not the answer. Lines 17-18 provide an illustration rather than a summary of an argument; no history of opposing arguments is given.

23. Which of the following statements about the use of comedy in Hardy's novels is best supported by the passage?

(A) Hardy's use of comedy in his novels tended to weaken his literary style.

(B) Hardy's use of comedy in his novels was inspired by his natural sympathy.

(C) Comedy appeared less frequently in Hardy's novels than did tragedy.

(D) Comedy played an important role in Hardy's novels though that comedy was usually in the form of farce.

(E) Comedy played a secondary role in Hardy's more controlled novels only.

Ⓐ Ⓑ Ⓒ Ⓓ Ⓔ

The use of comedy in Hardy's novels is discussed only in lines 5-7. This question asks you to choose a statement about comedy that is supported by the passage.

(A) is not the answer. There is no discussion in the passage of the relationship between Hardy's use of comedy and his literary style.

(B) is not the answer. The parenthetical phrase "in all its detached coldness" indicates that the use of comedy cannot be inspired by natural sympathy.

* (C) is the answer. According to lines 5-7, Hardy occasionally felt the impulse to comedy, but "he was more often inclined to see tragedy and record it."

(D) is not the answer. There is no indication in lines 5-7, the portion of the passage in which the author distinguishes the impulse to comedy from the impulse to farce, that comedy was particularly important in Hardy's novels or that his use of comedy inclined toward farce.

(E) is not the answer. The passage states only that Hardy sometimes felt an impulse to comedy. There is no clear indication of the exact role played by comedy in any of Hardy's novels.

24. **The author implies which of the following about *Under the Greenwood Tree* in relation to Hardy's other novels?**

    (A) It is Hardy's most thorough investigation of the psychology of love.
    (B) Although it is his most controlled novel, it does not exhibit any harsh or risky impulses.
    (C) It, more than his other novels, reveals Hardy as a realist interested in the history of ordinary human beings.
    (D) In it Hardy's novelistic impulses are managed somewhat better than in his other novels.
    (E) Its plot, like the plots of all of Hardy's other novels, splits into two distinct parts.

    Ⓐ Ⓑ Ⓒ Ⓓ Ⓔ

This question asks you to compare *Under the Greenwood Tree* with other novels discussed in the passage. The word "implies" indicates that the answer is not directly stated in the passage. You may have to use information from different parts of the passage to answer the question.

(A) is not the answer. According to lines 32-35, Hardy wished to be a psychologist of love in *Under the Greenwood Tree*, but there is no information to suggest that it was his "most thorough investigation of the psychology of love."

(B) is not the answer. Lines 32-33 indicate that *Under the Greenwood Tree* is Hardy's most controlled novel. However, there is no indication of the author's opinion of the harshness or riskiness of the impulses exhibited in *Under the Greenwood Tree*.

(C) is not the answer. According to lines 32-35, Hardy wished to be a realist-historian in *Under the Greenwood Tree*, but there is no indication that he succeeded in this novel more than in other works.

* (D) is the answer. Lines 28-32 indicate that Hardy was unable to control his divergent impulses in any of his novels. Lines 32-33 state that *Under the Greenwood Tree* was Hardy's most controlled novel. If these pieces of information are put together, it can be inferred that, in *Under the Greenwood Tree*, Hardy's impulses are managed or controlled somewhat better than in his other novels.

176

(E) is not the answer. The last sentence of the passage indicates that *Under the Greenwood Tree* splits into two parts, but there is no indication that Hardy's other novels are so split.

Questions 25-27

Upwards of a billion stars in our galaxy have burnt up their internal energy sources, and so can no longer produce the heat a star needs to oppose the inward force of gravity. These stars, of more than a few solar masses, evolve, in general, much more rapidly than does a star like the Sun. Moreover, it is just these more massive stars whose collapse does not halt at intermediate stages (that is, as white dwarfs or neutron stars). Instead, the collapse continues until a singularity (an infinitely dense concentration of matter) is reached.

It would be wonderful to observe a singularity and obtain direct evidence of the undoubtedly bizarre phenomena that occur near one. Unfortunately in most cases a distant observer cannot see the singularity; outgoing light rays are dragged back by gravity so forcefully that even if they could start out within a few kilometers of the singularity, they would end up in the singularity itself.

25. The author's primary purpose in the passage is to

    (A) describe the formation and nature of singularities
    (B) explain why large numbers of stars become singularities
    (C) compare the characteristics of singularities with those of stars
    (D) explain what happens during the stages of a singularity's formation
    (E) imply that singularities could be more easily studied if observers could get closer to them

                  Ⓐ Ⓑ Ⓒ Ⓓ Ⓔ

This question asks you to identify the author's main purpose in the passage.

  * (A) is the answer. The author describes, in a general way, the formation and some of the characteristics of singularities.

  (B) is not the answer. The passage gives hints as to why stars become singularities, but the primary purpose is not to explain why large numbers do so.

  (C) is not the answer. The author describes singularities and mentions some characteristics of stars. However, singularities, rather than comparisons of singularities with stars, are the subject of the passage.

  (D) is not the answer. The passage mentions but does not explain what happens during the stages of a singularity's formation.

  (E) is not the answer. The author states that it is unfortunate that a distant observer cannot see a singularity. However, the passage presents no clear evidence that being closer to singularities would permit observers to study them more easily. The difficulties of observing singularities, in any case, are not the primary focus of the passage.

26. The passage suggests which of the following about the Sun?

    I.   The Sun could evolve to a stage of collapse that is less dense than a singularity.

   II.   In the Sun, the inward force of gravity is balanced by the generation of heat.

  III.   The Sun emits more observable light than does a white dwarf or a neutron star.

  (A) I only
  (B) III only
  (C) I and II only
  (D) II and III only
  (E) I, II, and III

Ⓐ Ⓑ Ⓒ Ⓓ Ⓔ

This question asks you to identify one or more statements about the Sun that are suggested by the passage.

I is an answer. That "more massive stars" do not halt at intermediate stages implies that less massive stars like the Sun could achieve a less dense state.

II is an answer. The passage makes it clear that the Sun is not one of the stars that no longer has the heat it needs to oppose the inward force of gravity.

III is not an answer. There is no information in the passage about the amount of observable light emitted by stars other than singularities.

  (A) is not the answer. The passage suggests **I**, but **II** is also suggested.

  (B) is not the answer. **III** is not suggested in the passage.

* (C) is the answer. **I** and **II** are suggested in the passage; **III** is not.

  (D) is not the answer. **II** is suggested in the passage, but **III** is not.

  (E) is not the answer. **I** and **II** are suggested in the passage, but **III** is not.

27. Which of the following sentences would most probably follow the last sentence of the passage?

  (A) Thus, a physicist interested in studying phenomena near singularities would necessarily hope to find a singularity with a measurable gravitational field.

  (B) Accordingly, physicists to date have been unable to observe directly any singularity.

  (C) It is specifically this startling phenomenon that has allowed us to codify the scant information currently available about singularities.

  (D) Moreover, the existence of this extraordinary phenomenon is implied in the extensive reports of several physicists.

  (E) Although unanticipated, phenomena such as these are consistent with the structure of a singularity.

Ⓐ Ⓑ Ⓒ Ⓓ Ⓔ

This question asks you to use the information that is in the passage to choose the most logical and coherent continuation of the passage.

(A) is not the answer. If light rays are dragged into the singularity by gravity, then the gravitational field of any singularity must be not only measurable but also very strong. This option implies that some singularities do not have measurable gravitational fields. Therefore, the option does not follow from the information in the passage as "Thus" implies.

* (B) is the answer. This sentence states explicitly the conclusion that can be drawn from the second paragraph of the passage.

(C) is not the answer. The "startling phenomenon" mentioned in this option is a phenomenon that hinders scientists' efforts to learn about singularities; therefore, there is no indication that the phenomenon aids in codification of the information available.

(D) is not the answer. It is possible that existence of the phenomenon described is implied in the extensive reports of several physicists. However, since the existence of singularities is assumed in the passage, this sentence is not a logical continuation of the passage.

(E) is not the answer. There is no information in the passage to suggest that these phenomena are unanticipated or to tie the phenomena to the structure of a singularity. (E) does not follow clearly from the information in the passage, and thus is not a logical continuation.

Directions: Each question below consists of a word printed in capital letters, followed by five lettered words or phrases. Choose the lettered word or phrase that is most nearly opposite in meaning to the word in capital letters.

Since some of the questions require you to distinguish fine shades of meaning, be sure to consider all the choices before deciding which one is best.

28. STABILIZE: (A) penetrate (B) minimize (C) fluctuate (D) analyze (E) isolate

Ⓐ Ⓑ Ⓒ Ⓓ Ⓔ

One meaning of to "stabilize" is to make steady or to become steady.

(A) is not the answer. To "penetrate" means to pass into or through. One might "penetrate" something in order to "stabilize" it, but the two words are not opposite in meaning.

(B) is not the answer. To "minimize" means to belittle or to reduce to a minimum.

* (C) is the answer. To "fluctuate" means to shift back and forth uncertainly. It implies constant, irregular changes that are the opposite of steadiness.

(D) is not the answer. To "analyze" means to study by separating or distinguishing component parts; analysis is not directly related to steadiness.

(E) is not the answer. To "isolate" means to set apart rather than to make unsteady.

29. RENOVATE: (A) design to specifications (B) keep hidden (C) cause to decay (D) duplicate (E) complicate

Ⓐ Ⓑ Ⓒ Ⓓ Ⓔ

To "renovate" means to restore or renew. It is often used in the context of restoration of such material artifacts as buildings.

(A) is not the answer. To "design to specifications" could be a part of renovation, but it is not the opposite of "renovate."

(B) is not the answer. To "keep hidden" is the opposite of to reveal rather than of to "renovate."

* (C) is the answer. To "cause to decay" means to cause to fall into ruin, whereas to "renovate" implies a rebuilding or renewal.

(D) is not the answer. To "duplicate" means to make a copy or counterpart rather than to operate on an original.

(E) is not the answer. To "complicate" means to make less simple.

30. PROFUSE: (A) sequential (B) shoddy (C) scant (D) surly (E) supreme

Ⓐ Ⓑ Ⓒ Ⓓ Ⓔ

"Profuse" means liberal, extravagant, or abundant.

(A) is not the answer. "Sequential" means consecutive or following in sequence. It does not imply a lack of extravagance or abundance.

(B) is not the answer. A lack of profusion (of money, for instance) could lead to shoddiness, but "shoddy" describes the appearance or quality of something, whereas "profuse" implies quantity.

* (C) is the answer. "Scant" means barely sufficient, lacking in amplitude or quantity.

(D) is not the answer. "Surly" can mean rude or sullen, and it describes persons rather than quantities.

(E) is not the answer. "Supreme" means highest, and does not necessarily imply quantity.

31. ANCHOR: (A) unwind (B) unbend (C) disjoin (D) disrupt (E) dislodge

Ⓐ Ⓑ Ⓒ Ⓓ Ⓔ

To "anchor" means to secure or hold in place. You can tell that "anchor" is used as a verb, not as a noun, because "unwind" in choice (A) can be used only as a verb and not as a noun.

(A) is not the answer. To "unwind" means to relax or to uncoil. One might "unwind" the rope holding an anchor, but "unwind" does not itself mean the opposite of "anchor."

(B) is not the answer. To "unbend" can mean to untie, a step that is at one remove from pulling up an anchor.

(C) is not the answer. To "disjoin" means to detach or separate. It does not imply setting free.

(D) is not the answer. To "disrupt" means to break apart or to throw into disorder. It does not mean the opposite of holding securely.

* (E) is the answer. To "dislodge" means to force out of a secure resting place.

32. REFUTE: (A) reveal (B) associate (C) recognize (D) understand (E) prove

Ⓐ Ⓑ Ⓒ Ⓓ Ⓔ

To "refute" means to provide evidence against. Refuting entails logical disproving of a claim or argument.

(A) is not the answer. To "reveal" means to make known. Revelation may uncover evidence, but to "reveal" does not imply intent to prove.

(B) is not the answer. To "associate" can mean to connect one thing with another, but no intent to prove or disprove anything is implied.

(C) is not the answer. To "recognize" can mean to admit or acknowledge, but it does not imply that evidence is provided.

(D) is not the answer. To "understand" does not imply intent to prove or to disprove.

* (E) is the answer. To "prove" means to provide evidence of the truth of something.

33. NADIR:

(A) immobile object
(B) uniform measurement
(C) extreme distance
(D) topmost point
(E) regular phenomenon

Ⓐ Ⓑ Ⓒ Ⓓ Ⓔ

"Nadir" means the lowest point.

(A) is not the answer. An "immobile object" is something that does not move. Its position is not implied.

(B) is not the answer. "Uniform measurement" implies that an activity has been performed, and does not imply anything about position in space.

(C) is not the answer. "Extreme distance" could be in any direction from any specified point. Since nothing is known about the reference point from which "extreme distance" is to be judged, an "extreme distance" is not necessarily the opposite of the lowest point.

* (D) is the answer. The "topmost point" is the highest point.

(E) is not the answer. A "regular phenomenon" is an occurrence rather than a position in space.

34. APPROBATION: (A) disinclination (B) stagnation (C) condemnation (D) false allegation (E) immediate repulsion

Ⓐ Ⓑ Ⓒ Ⓓ Ⓔ

"Approbation" means praise or formal approval. It is an expression of a positive human feeling or judgment.

(A) is not the answer. A "disinclination" is not a strongly negative feeling, whereas "approbation" is a strongly positive feeling.

(B) is not the answer. "Stagnation" means dullness or inactivity; it is a characteristic rather than an expression of feeling.

* (C) is the answer. "Condemnation" is an expression of strong disapproval.

(D) is not the answer. A "false allegation" is an unsupported claim.

(E) is not the answer. Repulsion can be a feeling of aversion or an expression of aversion, but immediacy is not an element in the definition of "approbation." Therefore, "immediate repulsion" is not the most exact opposite of "approbation."

35. FATUOUSNESS: (A) sensibleness (B) courage (C) obedience (D) aloofness (E) forcefulness

Ⓐ Ⓑ Ⓒ Ⓓ Ⓔ

"Fatuousness" means foolishness or silliness. It implies a lack of awareness of reality.

* (A) is the answer. "Sensibleness" means having good sense, being reasonable. It implies awareness, cognizance.

(B) is not the answer. To have "courage" implies much more than awareness. It suggests a willingness to act or endure in the face of danger.

(C) is not the answer. One who is fatuous may or may not be characterized by "obedience."

(D) is not the answer. "Aloofness" means distance or reserve.

(E) is not the answer. "Forcefulness" means vigorousness. It does not imply awareness.

36. TIMOROUS: (A) consummate (B) faithful (C) intrepid (D) antagonistic (E) impulsive

Ⓐ Ⓑ Ⓒ Ⓓ Ⓔ

To be "timorous" means to be fearful, particularly to lack independence and decisiveness.

(A) is not the answer. "Consummate" means skilled, or of the highest excellence. Its application is much more general than that of "timorous."

(B) is not the answer. To be "faithful" implies keeping promises or adhering to principles. It might be difficult for the "timorous" to do this, but "faithful" does not mean the opposite of "timorous."

* (C) is the answer. "Intrepid" means fearless and implies independence and decisiveness.

(D) is not the answer. To be "antagonistic" means to oppose rather than to be fearless.

(E) is not the answer. To be "impulsive" means to act in an unpremeditated way. A "timorous" person may or may not be "impulsive."

37. SEMINAL:

(A) withholding peripheral information
(B) promoting spirited exchange
(C) suggesting contradictory hypotheses
(D) displaying cultural biases
(E) hampering further development

Ⓐ Ⓑ Ⓒ Ⓓ Ⓔ

"Seminal" means original, or containing the seeds of future growth or work. To be "seminal" means to be a source.

(A) is not the answer. The opposite of "withholding peripheral information" could be providing peripheral information or providing essential information.

(B) is not the answer. "Promoting spirited exchange" is more likely to be characteristic of a "seminal" act than to be an opposite of "seminal."

(C) is not the answer. "Suggesting contradictory hypotheses" may or may not promote future growth, depending on the situation.

(D) is not the answer. "Displaying cultural biases" may not promote future growth, but it is not the opposite of promoting future growth.

* (E) is the answer. "Hampering further development" is the opposite of promoting future growth or work.

38. DISINGENUOUSNESS:

(A) coherent thought
(B) polite conversation
(C) acquisitiveness
(D) guilelessness
(E) contentiousness

Ⓐ Ⓑ Ⓒ Ⓓ Ⓔ

To be disingenuous means to lack candor, or to scheme while appearing to be honest. The opposite of "disingenuousness" would be candor or genuine innocence.

(A) is not the answer. "Coherent thought" means clear thinking rather than candor.

(B) is not the answer. "Polite conversation" may have an element of honesty or openness, but it is not the opposite of "disingenuousness."

(C) is not the answer. A person might use "disingenuousness" to satisfy "acquisitiveness" (a strong desire to possess things), but "acquisitiveness" is not the opposite of "disingenuousness."

* (D) is the answer. "Guilelessness" means innocence or artlessness.

(E) is not the answer. "Contentiousness" means a tendency to be argumentative, and does not imply candor or lack of candor.

SECTION 7
25 Questions

<u>Directions:</u> Each question or group of questions is based on a passage or set of conditions. In answering some of the questions, it may be useful to draw a rough diagram. For each question, select the best answer choice given.

<u>Questions 1-4</u>

Six products — U, V, W, X, Y, and Z — are to be placed in the display window of a vending machine with six compartments, numbered 1 through 6 from left to right. The products must be placed in the window, one product in each compartment, according to the following conditions:

U cannot be immediately to the left or immediately to the right of V.
W must be immediately to the left of X.
Z cannot be in compartment 6.

1. **Which of the following products CANNOT be placed in compartment 1 ?**

    (A) U   (B) V   (C) W   (D) X   (E) Z

    Ⓐ Ⓑ Ⓒ Ⓓ Ⓔ

Since compartment 1 is the leftmost compartment, and since X must have W immediately to its left, X cannot be placed in compartment 1. The correct answer is (D).

2. **If X is placed in compartment 3, W must be placed in compartment**

    (A) 1   (B) 2   (C) 4   (D) 5   (E) 6

    Ⓐ Ⓑ Ⓒ Ⓓ Ⓔ

Since W must be immediately to the left of X, and since compartment 2 is immediately to the left of compartment 3, W must be placed in compartment 2. (B) is the correct answer.

3. **If U is placed in compartment 5, which of the following products must be placed in compartment 6?**

    (A) V   (B) W   (C) X   (D) Y   (E) Z

    Ⓐ Ⓑ Ⓒ Ⓓ Ⓔ

The product in compartment 6 must be Y since all other possibilities can be eliminated. It cannot be V because V cannot be next to U. It cannot be W since W must have X to its right, and 6 is the rightmost compartment. It cannot be X since X has to have W, not U, immediately to its left. And it cannot be Z, by virtue of an express condition. So (D) is the correct answer.

4. **If Z is placed in compartment 3, immediately to the right of X, which of the following products must be placed in compartment 5 ?**
    (A) U   (B) V   (C) W   (D) X   (E) Y

    Ⓐ Ⓑ Ⓒ Ⓓ Ⓔ

184

If Z is in compartment 3, and X in 2, then W must be in 1. That leaves U, V, and Y for compartments 4 through 6. Neither U nor V can be in 5, because if one of them were in 5, the other would be in either 4 or 6 — that is, next to it. So the only product left for placement in compartment 5 is Y, which makes (E) the correct answer.

5. **Athletic director: "Members of our sports teams included, for the fall season, 80 football players and 40 cross-country runners; for the winter season, 20 wrestlers and 40 swimmers; for the spring season, 50 track-team members and 20 lacrosse players. Each team athlete participates in his or her sport five days a week for the whole three-month season, and no athlete is on two teams during any one season. Therefore, adding these figures, we find that our team sports program serves 250 different individual athletes."**

   In drawing the conclusion above, the athletic director fails to consider the relevant possibility that

   (A) athletes can be on more than one team in a single season

   (B) athletes can be on teams in more than one season

   (C) some of the team sports require a larger number of athletes on the team than do others

   (D) more athletes participate in team sports during one season than during another

   (E) an athlete might not participate in every one of the practice sessions and athletic contests in his or her sport

   Ⓐ Ⓑ Ⓒ Ⓓ Ⓔ

The athletic director has clearly added up the 120 athletes active in the fall, the 60 athletes active in the winter, and the 70 athletes active in the spring. But while we know that the total number of athletes for each season is composed of different individuals, there is nothing in the rules cited that would prevent athletes from being active in two or in all three seasons. So, the sum of 250 may include athletes that have been counted twice or three times. This is the possibility that has not been considered. (B) is thus the correct answer.

For explanations of the other answer choices, see below:

   (A) is incorrect. The athletic director has specifically ruled this out as a possibility.

   (C) is incorrect. This possibility is reflected adequately in the different numbers of athletes active in each sport. No oversight seems likely here.

   (D) is incorrect. Not only does the athletic director not overlook this, he or she has the figures to prove it.

   (E) is incorrect. The athletic director could say that the program has served an athlete even if that athlete has not participated to the fullest extent possible.

6. As soon as any part of a person's conduct affects prejudicially the interests of others, society has jurisdiction over it, and the question of whether the general welfare will or will not be promoted by interfering with it becomes open to discussion. If a person's conduct does not affect prejudicially the interests of others, it should not come under the jurisdiction of society in the first place.

The author in the passage above argues that

(A) society is independent of the actions of individuals

(B) the general welfare of a society is promoted when a person's conduct benefits others

(C) conduct that does not infringe on the interests of others should not be under the jurisdiction of society

(D) interference with the actions of individuals does not enhance the general welfare

(E) in general, the interests of persons are mutually exclusive

(C) is a close paraphrase of the final sentence of the passage. Therefore, (C) is the correct answer.

For explanations of the other answer choices, see below:

(A) is incorrect. If an individual's actions had no power to affect society, then interference with those actions could have no such power either. But the passage suggests that interference may have such power. Therefore, the passage does not suggest that society is independent of the actions of individuals.

(B) is incorrect. The author may believe (B), or some version of it, but nothing at all is said or implied about conduct that benefits others.

(D) is incorrect. If the author believed (D), then the author would not talk about the possible effects of such interference as a sensible topic for discussion.

(E) is incorrect. The passage does not state or imply anything about how common or how rare it is for the satisfaction of one person's interests to preclude the satisfaction of another's.

7. Therapists find that treatment of those people who seek help because they are unable to stop smoking or overeating is rarely successful. From these experiences, therapists have concluded that such habits are intractable, and success in breaking them is rare.

As surveys show, millions of people have dropped the habit of smoking, and many people have successfully managed a substantial weight loss.

If all the statements above are correct, an explanation of their apparent contradiction is provided by the hypothesis that

(A) there have been some successes in therapy, and those successes were counted in the surveys

(B) it is easier to stop smoking than it is to stop overeating

(C) it is easy to break the habits of smoking and overeating by exercising willpower

(D) the group of people selected for the survey did not include those who failed to break their habits even after therapy

(E) those who succeed in curing themselves do not go for treatment and so are not included in the therapists' data

Ⓐ Ⓑ Ⓒ Ⓓ Ⓔ

If, as (E) suggests, the very people who would lead the therapists to view such habits as more tractable do not come for treatment, it is quite understandable why therapists persist in their pessimistic view. At the same time, (E) is consistent with the survey results. Therefore, (E) is the correct answer.

For explanations of the other answer choices, see below:

(A) is incorrect. Even assuming that (A) is true, no light is shed on why successes should be so rare in therapy, and yet, if the surveys are to be believed, so common overall.

(B) is incorrect. Since the comparative strength of habits is not an issue in the therapists' findings or the surveys, it could not have anything to do with the apparent contradiction; consequently, information about it could not help resolve that contradiction.

(C) is incorrect. If (C) were true, the survey results would appear rather unremarkable, but the therapists' findings would be baffling. The apparent contradiction would not be diminished but underscored.

(D) is incorrect. The survey results as reported focus on the numbers of people who have successfully fought a habit, not on the proportion of those who tried to break their habits who succeeded. (D) pertains only to the latter and so is essentially irrelevant.

Questions 8-11

Seven people — Tomás, Nadine, Pavel, Marta, Rachel, Fred, and Kurt — are planning to travel down a river on two rafts. The group will be assigned to the rafts according to the following conditions:

Tomás must be assigned to the same raft as Rachel.
Fred cannot be on the same raft as Pavel unless Marta is also on that raft.
The maximum number of persons on each raft is four.
Neither Nadine nor Pavel can be assigned to the same raft as Kurt.

8. If Fred is assigned to the same raft as Nadine, which of the following must be true?

(A) Kurt is assigned to the other raft.
(B) Marta is assigned to the other raft.
(C) Pavel is assigned to the other raft.
(D) Rachel is assigned to the same raft as Fred and Nadine.
(E) Tomás is assigned to the same raft as Fred and Nadine.

Ⓐ Ⓑ Ⓒ Ⓓ Ⓔ

By assumption, Fred is assigned to the same raft as Nadine. Since Nadine cannot be on a raft with Kurt, Kurt must be on the other raft. Hence, (A) is the correct answer. Pavel, who also cannot be on the raft with Kurt, must therefore be on the raft carrying Fred and Nadine. But if Pavel is to be on a raft with Fred, Marta must be on that raft, too. This gives Fred, Marta, Nadine, and Pavel (= the maximum of four persons) for the one raft and Kurt, Rachel, and Tomás for the other raft. (B) through (E) can thus all be seen to be incorrect.

9. **If Rachel is assigned to the same raft as Pavel, which of the following must be true?**

   (A) **Kurt is assigned to the same raft as Rachel and Pavel.**
   (B) **Nadine is assigned to the same raft as Kurt.**
   (C) **Nadine is assigned to the raft other than the one to which Pavel is assigned.**
   (D) **Rachel and Pavel are assigned to the raft carrying four people.**
   (E) **Tomás is assigned to the raft other than the one to which Pavel is assigned.**

   Ⓐ Ⓑ Ⓒ Ⓓ Ⓔ

If Rachel is on the same raft as Pavel, Tomás must be on the same raft as Pavel, too. Nadine must be on that raft as well, because Nadine and Pavel must always be together on the raft that does not carry Kurt. These results show (D) to be the correct answer, and they also show (A), (B), (C), and (E) all to be false.

10. **If Kurt is assigned to the same raft as Marta, which of the following must be true?**

    (A) **Fred is assigned to the same raft as Nadine.**
    (B) **Fred is assigned to the same raft as Tomás.**
    (C) **Nadine is assigned to the same raft as Pavel.**
    (D) **Nadine is assigned to the same raft as Kurt and Marta.**
    (E) **Rachel is assigned to the same raft as Kurt and Marta.**

    Ⓐ Ⓑ Ⓒ Ⓓ Ⓔ

Nadine and Pavel must be on a raft other than the one Kurt is on. Specifically, then, Nadine and Pavel must be on a raft together. So (C) is the correct answer.

For explanations of the other answer choices, see below:

(A) is incorrect. Nadine and Pavel are on a raft other than the one Kurt and Marta are on. This means that Fred cannot be on Nadine's and Pavel's raft since Fred and Pavel could be on a raft together only if Marta were on that raft, too.

(B) and (E) are incorrect. Check (A) to see that Fred, Kurt, and Marta must be together on one raft. Tomás and Rachel must be together on one raft. That raft cannot be the one carrying Fred, Kurt, and Marta, because a raft can carry at most four persons. So (E) is false. Furthermore, Fred and Tomás cannot be on a raft together, and (B) is seen to be false.

(D) is incorrect. This must be false since Nadine cannot be on the same raft as Kurt.

11. If Rachel is assigned to the same raft as Fred, which of the following is a complete and accurate list of the people who must then be assigned to the other raft?

(A) Fred, Pavel
(B) Kurt, Tomás
(C) Marta, Tomás
(D) Kurt, Marta, Nadine
(E) Marta, Nadine, Pavel

Ⓐ Ⓑ Ⓒ Ⓓ Ⓔ

The raft Rachel is on must also be the one Tomás is on. Thus, at least Fred, Rachel, and Tomás are on this raft. Pavel cannot also be on it since this would put Fred and Pavel together on a raft that does not carry Marta (no more than four people can be on a raft). So Pavel must be on the other raft. This means that Kurt must be the fourth person on the first raft, since Pavel and Kurt cannot be on a raft together. That leaves Nadine and Marta to share Pavel's raft. Thus, the correct answer is (E).

<u>Questions 12-15</u>

Central Bank is open from Monday through Friday each week. Each day that the bank is open, one bank officer is assigned as AM loan officer and a different bank officer is assigned as PM loan officer. The bank has five officers — Reynolds, Short, Torrez, Underwood, and Vance. The assignment of loan officers is always made in accordance with the following conditions:

Each officer must be assigned as loan officer at least once each week.
An officer is <u>never</u> assigned as a loan officer consecutive days in the same week.
Torrez is <u>never</u> assigned as the AM loan officer.
Vance is always assigned as the PM loan officer on Monday and Wednesday, and has no other assignments.
Underwood is <u>never</u> assigned to be a loan officer on the same day that Short is assigned to be a loan officer.

12. Which of the following is an acceptable assignment of loan officers for a single week?

		<u>Monday</u>	<u>Tuesday</u>	<u>Wednesday</u>	<u>Thursday</u>	<u>Friday</u>
(A)	AM	Underwood	Short	Reynolds	Torrez	Short
	PM	Vance	Torrez	Vance	Underwood	Torrez
(B)	AM	Short	Short	Reynolds	Torrez	Reynolds
	PM	Vance	Torrez	Vance	Short	Torrez
(C)	AM	Short	Torrez	Short	Reynolds	Short
	PM	Reynolds	Vance	Vance	Torrez	Underwood
(D)	AM	Underwood	Short	Reynolds	Short	Reynolds
	PM	Vance	Torrez	Vance	Torrez	Underwood
(E)	AM	Underwood	Torrez	Underwood	Reynolds	Underwood
	PM	Vance	Reynolds	Short	Torrez	Vance

Ⓐ Ⓑ Ⓒ Ⓓ Ⓔ

(A) and (B) can be eliminated because they list Torrez as the AM loan officer on Thursday. (C) and (E) can be eliminated because they show Torrez as the AM officer on Tuesday. (Other reasons for eliminating answer choices (A), (B), (C), and (E) can also be found.) Answer choice (D) shows an acceptable schedule, so (D) is the correct answer.

13. **What is the maximum number of times that Torrez could be assigned as loan officer in a single week?**

    (A) 1   (B) 2   (C) 3   (D) 4   (E) 5

    Ⓐ Ⓑ Ⓒ Ⓓ Ⓔ

Since Torrez can only be assigned as the PM loan officer, and since Vance is always assigned as the PM loan officer on Monday and Wednesday, Torrez might be assigned as loan officer on Tuesday, Thursday, and Friday. But since an officer is never assigned as a loan officer on consecutive days in the same week, Torrez could not be assigned as a loan officer on both Thursday and Friday of a single week. But nothing stops Torrez from being assigned as a loan officer on two days of a week (either Tuesday and Thursday or Tuesday and Friday), so (B) is the correct answer.

14. **In a week in which Underwood is assigned as PM loan officer on Tuesday, which of the following must be true?**

    (A) Underwood is assigned as the PM loan officer on Thursday.
    (B) Reynolds is assigned as the AM loan officer on Friday.
    (C) Reynolds is assigned as the AM loan officer on Tuesday.
    (D) Short is assigned as the AM loan officer on Thursday.
    (E) Underwood is assigned as the AM loan officer on Friday.

    Ⓐ Ⓑ Ⓒ Ⓓ Ⓔ

The AM loan officer on Tuesday cannot be Short because Underwood and Short cannot be assigned to be the two loan officers scheduled for one day. It cannot be Torrez because Torrez is never assigned as the AM loan officer. It can be neither Underwood (he is the PM loan officer) nor Vance (he is only assigned Monday and Wednesday afternoons). So, it must be Reynolds, and (C) is the correct answer.

See below for an explanation of why none of the other answer choices is correct.

(A), (B), (D), and (E) are incorrect. Consider the following possible assignment:

	M	T	W	Th	F
AM	S	R	S	U	S
PM	V	U	V	T	R

(R, S, T, U, and V are the officers' initials). Here, Underwood is the PM loan officer on Tuesday, and none of the conditions for assignments has been violated. None of the answer choices (A), (B), (D), and (E) correctly describes any part of this assignment, so each of them has been shown to be false in at least one possible case.

15. In a week in which Torrez' only assignment as a loan officer is on Friday, which of the following must be true?

(A) Reynolds is assigned as a loan officer on Tuesday.
(B) Reynolds is assigned as a loan officer on Wednesday.
(C) Reynolds is assigned as a loan officer on Friday.
(D) Underwood is assigned as a loan officer on Thursday.
(E) Underwood is assigned as a loan officer on Friday.

Ⓐ Ⓑ Ⓒ Ⓓ Ⓔ

If Torrez' only assignment is as loan officer on Friday, then Torrez can specifically not be loan officer on either Tuesday or Thursday. Vance can also not be loan officer on either of these two days. Short and Underwood cannot be loan officers together on any given day, so also on Tuesday and Thursday, at most one of them can be assigned as the loan officer. This means that on both of those days Reynolds has to be the second loan officer assigned. (A) correctly represents part of this inference and is, therefore, the correct answer.

For explanations of the other answer choices, see below.

(B) and (C) are incorrect. Since Reynolds must be assigned as loan officer on Tuesday and on Thursday, Reynolds cannot be assigned on Monday, Wednesday (answer choice (B)), or Friday (answer choice (C)), since any of these assignments would result in assignments for at least two consecutive days.

(D) and (E) are incorrect. Between them, Reynolds, Torrez, and Vance account for exactly one shift as loan officers on each day of the week. This means that the other shift on each of those days must be covered by either Underwood or Short. Since an officer is never assigned on consecutive days, Underwood could serve Monday, Wednesday, and Friday while Short served Tuesday and Thursday, or their roles could be reversed. Thus, there is some assignment where (D) is not true and some assignment where (E) is not true.

Questions 16-22

Five patients — L, M, N, O, and P — must be scheduled to undergo physical therapy treatments within a seven-day period beginning on the first day of a month and ending on the seventh day of the same month. Exactly one patient can be treated per day. The schedule must accommodate the following conditions:

L is to receive exactly two treatments; the second treatment must be scheduled for the fourth day after the day of the first treatment.
M is to receive exactly one treatment.
N is to receive exactly one treatment, which must be scheduled for either the day before or the day after the day of L's first treatment.
O is to receive exactly one treatment, which must be scheduled for a day anytime before the day of L's second treatment.
P is to receive exactly one treatment, which must be scheduled for the third day after the day of M's treatment.

16. Any of the five patients could be scheduled for the first day of the month EXCEPT

(A) L (B) M (C) N (D) O (E) P

Ⓐ Ⓑ Ⓒ Ⓓ Ⓔ

Since P's only treatment must be scheduled for the third day after the day of M's treatment, P's treatment cannot be scheduled for the first day of the seven-day period. The correct answer is, therefore, (E).

17. Which of the following is a possible schedule, including the open day for which no patient is scheduled, from the first day through the seventh day of the month?

(A) L, M, N, O, L, P, open day
(B) M, L, N, P, open day, L, O
(C) N, L, M, O, P, L, open day
(D) N, L, O, M, open day, L, P
(E) Open day, L, M, O, L, N, P

Ⓐ Ⓑ Ⓒ Ⓓ Ⓔ

(A) can be eliminated because N's treatment is not scheduled for the day before or the day after L's first treatment. (B) can be eliminated because O's treatment does not come before L's second treatment. (C) can be eliminated because P's treatment comes on the second, and not on the third, day after the day of M's treatment. (E) can be eliminated because L's second treatment comes on the third, and not on the fourth, day after L's first treatment. (D) is the correct answer because (D) meets all of the conditions.

18. The day of M's treatment must be no more than how many days after L's first treatment?

(A) 1 (B) 2 (C) 3 (D) 4 (E) 5

Ⓐ Ⓑ Ⓒ Ⓓ Ⓔ

In order to allow for P's treatment, M can be scheduled for no later day than the fourth. L's first treatment can be as early as the first day. M's treatment can, therefore, be as many as three days after L's first treatment, which makes (C) the correct answer.

19. N could be scheduled for any of the following days EXCEPT the

(A) first (B) second (C) third (D) fourth (E) fifth

Ⓐ Ⓑ Ⓒ Ⓓ Ⓔ

N cannot be scheduled for the fifth day. If he or she were, L's first treatment would have to be scheduled for the fourth day, which would make it impossible to schedule L's second treatment. The correct answer is (E).

20. If M is to be scheduled for the first day of the month, which of the following pairs of patients CANNOT be scheduled for consecutive days?

   (A) **L and P**
   (B) **M and L**
   (C) **M and N**
   (D) **N and O**
   (E) **N and P**

Ⓐ   Ⓑ   Ⓒ   Ⓓ   Ⓔ

M's treatment on the first means P's treatment on the fourth. Since L's first treatment must come before the fourth and N's treatment cannot come on the fourth, N's treatment must also come before the fourth. This means that N's treatment will either be on the second or on the third day, flanked by L's first treatment and either M's or P's treatment. In none of these circumstances will N's treatment be either on the day before or on the day after O's. Therefore, the correct answer is (D).

For a detailed explanation of the complete solution, see below:

(A) and (C) are incorrect.	Days:	1st	2nd	3rd	4th	5th	6th	7th
M on the first is given, and P on the fourth follows.		M			P			
Now try L on the third.		M		L	P			
This means L again on the seventh.		M		L	P			L
It also means N must be on the second.		M	N	L	P			L
O is either on the fifth		M	N	L	P	O	—	L
or on the sixth.		M	N	L	P	—	O	L

(B) and (E) are incorrect.	Days:	1st	2nd	3rd	4th	5th	6th	7th
Given: M on the first.		M						
This means P on the fourth.		M			P			

L's first treatment must be either the second or third if L's second treatment is to be filled in.

		1st	2nd	3rd	4th	5th	6th	7th
So try L on the second.		M	L		P			
This means L again on the sixth, and also N on the third.		M	L	N	P		L	
Now O must be on the fifth (before L's second turn).		M	L	N	P	O	L	
The open day is the seventh.		M	L	N	P	O	L	—

21. If no patient is to be scheduled for the first of the month, which of the following could be true?

(A) M is scheduled for the day before the day of L's first treatment.
(B) N is scheduled for the day before the day of L's first treatment.
(C) O is scheduled for the day before the day of L's first treatment.
(D) P is scheduled for the day before the day of L's second treatment.
(E) P is scheduled for the day after the day of O's treatment.

Ⓐ Ⓑ Ⓒ Ⓓ Ⓔ

L's first treatment will be on either the second or the third day of the month. The only way to schedule all treatments if L's first treatment is on the second is in the order L, N, M, O, L, P. The only way to schedule all treatments if L's first treatment is on the third is in the order M, L, N, P, O, L. It follows that (A) could be true (provided L's first treatment is on the third), but that none of (B) through (E) could be true.

For a detailed explanation of the complete solution, see below:

(B) through (E) are incorrect.

Days:	1st	2nd	3rd	4th	5th	6th	7th

Given: No patients on the first.

	—						

This leaves only the second or third for L's first treatment if L's second treatment is to be filled in.
So try L on the second.

	—	L					

This means N on the third,
and also L again on the sixth.

	—	L	N			L	

Now, M will fit nowhere but the
fourth, with P on the seventh.

	—	L	N	M		L	P

Which leaves the fifth for O.

	—	L	N	M	O	L	P

(B) through (E) are incorrect.

Days:	1st	2nd	3rd	4th	5th	6th	7th

Given: No patients on the first.

	—						

Now try L on the third.

	—		L				

This means L again on the seventh.

	—		L				L

Now, M will fit nowhere but the
second, with P on the fifth.

	—	M	L		P		L

N must be next to L's first turn.

	—	M	L	N	P		L

Which leaves the sixth for O.

	—	M	L	N	P	O	L

194

22. If N is scheduled for the day before the day of L's first treatment, the days for which M's treatment can be scheduled include the

  (A) first day and second day
  (B) first day and fourth day
  (C) second day and third day
  (D) second day and fourth day
  (E) third day and fourth day

Ⓐ Ⓑ Ⓒ Ⓓ Ⓔ

If N and L are scheduled for days one and two, M must be scheduled for the fourth day. M can never be scheduled for later than the fourth day nor can M be scheduled for the third day in these circumstances because M's scheduling then would require P's treatment on the sixth day while the scheduling of L's first treatment would require L's second treatment on the sixth day. If N and L are scheduled for days two and three, M must be scheduled for the first day. M could not be scheduled for the fourth day because of the resulting scheduling conflict between P's treatment and L's second treatment. In sum, M can be scheduled for the first or the fourth day, so (B) is the correct answer.

23. The Supreme Court is no longer able to keep pace with the tremendous number of cases it agrees to decide. The Court schedules and hears 160 hours of oral argument each year, and 108 hours of next year's term will be taken up by cases left over from this year. Certainly the Court cannot be asked to increase its already burdensome hours. The most reasonable long-range solution to this problem is to allow the Court to decide many cases without hearing oral argument; in this way the Court might eventually increase dramatically the number of cases it decides each year.

Which of the following, if true, could best be used to argue against the feasibility of the solution suggested above?

  (A) The time the Court spends hearing oral argument is only a small part of the total time it spends deciding a case.
  (B) The Court cannot legitimately avoid hearing oral argument in any case left over from last year.
  (C) Most authorities agree that 160 hours of oral argument is the maximum number that the Court can handle per year.
  (D) Even now the Court decides a small number of cases without hearing oral argument.
  (E) In many cases, the delay of a hearing for a full year can be extremely expensive to the parties involved.

Ⓐ Ⓑ Ⓒ Ⓓ Ⓔ

The passage suggests that the number of cases heard by the Supreme Court each year might eventually be increased dramatically if the Supreme Court were allowed to decide many cases without the customary oral argument. If (A) is true, however, then the number of cases decided by the Supreme Court is primarily determined by time other than the time spent hearing oral argument. Thus, the time spent hearing oral argument does not constitute a significant bottleneck. So (A) could be used rather well to argue against the proposal made in the passage.

For explanations of the other answer choices, see below:

(B) is incorrect. This argues not against the feasibility of the proposed solution; it merely warns that the benefits from it would be delayed. The fact that, in view of (B), there would probably not be any significant immediate relief from the burdens of hearing oral argument is irrelevant: the passage expressly concerns itself with finding a long-range solution.

(C) is incorrect. The thrust of the proposal is to make the 160 hours available for hearing oral argument go farther. The person making the proposal accepts the 160 hours as an upper limit. Thus, this statement supports rather than argues against the proposed solution.

(D) is incorrect. From a knowledge of (D) no further conclusions regarding the proposal follow. (D) is simply part of the current state of affairs that the proposal is designed to improve.

(E) is incorrect. The concern of (E), cost to the parties involved, plays no part whatever in the argument developed in the passage; the passage is concerned solely with time-related limitations on the number of cases the Supreme Court is able to decide.

24. **That social institutions influence the formation of character has become a generally accepted proposition. This doctrine views individuals as but compliant recipients of social influence: personalities are entirely the products of society, and at any point in life an individual's personality can be changed by management of the social world. Crime is said to exist only because society has in some ways failed in its responsibility to give every person the resources to lead a productive life. However, whereas it is true that extreme poverty forces some people to steal, it is obvious that some persons will commit crimes no matter how well society treats them.**

Which of the following is implied by the "doctrine" (line 2) described in the passage above?

(A) **Social institutions may reflect personality as much as they shape it.**
(B) **Social influence on personality is most strongly felt by the affluent.**
(C) **The concentration of wealth in the hands of a privileged few accounts for the existence of crime.**
(D) **Bringing about social reform is the most likely means of curtailing crime.**
(E) **Less severe punishment of crime would be likely to result in more crime.**

Ⓐ Ⓑ Ⓒ Ⓓ Ⓔ

The "doctrine" ascribes crime to a failure of society to give every person the resources to lead a productive life. (D) is therefore implicit in this doctrine: if society is suitably reformed (so as to make such failure less common), crime should also become less prevalent.

For explanations of the other answer choices, see below:

(A) is incorrect. The passage is confined entirely to influences that social institutions have on character and personality. Nothing at all is said or implied about what shapes social institutions or what they reflect.

(B) is incorrect. The doctrine as it is described in the passage does not make any distinctions as to what groups are more or less strongly under social influence on personality. Moreover, the doctrine as described seems to view material well-being itself as being influenced by society, and not as an independently given category.

(C) is incorrect. Since the concentration of wealth in the hands of a privileged few is not necessarily incompatible with every person having the resources to lead a productive life, (C) cannot be said to be implied by the doctrine as described.

(E) is incorrect. The doctrine takes no position on the effect, if any, that the severity of punishment of crime has on the number of crimes committed. The doctrine purports only to explain the existence of crime, so (E) is not implied by it.

25. **The sense of delayed gratification, of working now for later pleasure, has helped shape the economic behavior of our society. However, that sense is no longer nurtured as consistently in our children as it once was. For example, it used to take a bit of patience to put together the toys that children got in cereal boxes; now the toys come from the boxes whole.**

    Which of the following is an assumption of the passage above?

    (A) **The toys in cereal boxes have changed partly because the economic conditions of our society have improved.**
    (B) **The influence of promotion gimmicks on the economic behavior of our society has increased over the years.**
    (C) **The toys that used to come in cereal boxes were put together by the same children who played with them.**
    (D) **Part of the pleasure of any toy lies in putting the toy together before playing with it.**
    (E) **Today's children do not expect a single toy to provide pleasure for a long period of time.**

    Ⓐ Ⓑ Ⓒ Ⓓ Ⓔ

The phrases "delayed gratification" and "working now for later pleasure" clearly refer to somebody's effort or sacrifice at an earlier time which is designed to yield, for that same person, pleasure at a later time. If toy components packed in cereal boxes are to provide this experience for children, then (C) has to be true. Therefore, (C) is the correct answer.

For explanations of the other answer choices, see below:

(A) is incorrect. The passage indicates nothing about the reasons for the change from packing components to packing complete toys.

(B) is incorrect. (B) may or may not be true as far as the passage goes. The passage suggests only that the influence of promotion gimmicks has changed in character, not necessarily that it has increased.

(D) is incorrect. The passage strongly suggests that the pleasure comes after the effort or the work involved, not that it accompanies the effort or work. So while (D) may be true, there is no indication that it is an assumption that the author of the passage makes.

(E) is incorrect. The references to passage of time found in the passage ("delayed" in line 1; "now . . . later" in line 1; "patience" in line 4) concern the time from receipt of unassembled toys to completion of assembly. The passage neither says nor presumes anything about the length of time for which pleasure from a given toy will persist.

NO TEST MATERIAL ON THIS PAGE

NO TEST MATERIAL ON THIS PAGE

THE GRADUATE RECORD EXAMINATIONS
GENERAL TEST

You will have 3 hours and 30 minutes in which to work on this test, which consists of seven sections. During the time allowed for one section, you may work only on that section. The time allowed for each section is 30 minutes.

Your score will be based on the number of questions for which you select the best answer choice given. No deduction will be made for a question for which you do not select the best answer choice given. Therefore, you are advised to answer all questions.

You are advised to work as rapidly as you can without losing accuracy. Do not spend too much time on questions that are too difficult for you. Go on to the other questions and come back to the difficult ones later.

There are several different types of questions; you will find special directions for each type in the test itself. Be sure you understand the directions before attempting to answer any questions.

For each question several answer choices (lettered A-E or A-D) are given from which you are to select the ONE best answer. YOU MUST INDICATE ALL OF YOUR ANSWERS ON THE SEPARATE ANSWER SHEET. No credit will be given for anything written in this examination book, but to work out your answers you may write in the book as much as you wish. After you have decided which of the suggested answers is best, blacken the corresponding space on the answer sheet. Be sure to:

- Use a soft black lead pencil (No. 2 or HB).

- Mark only one answer to each question. No credit will be given for multiple answers.

- Mark your answer in the row with the same number as the number of the question you are answering.

- Carefully and completely blacken the space corresponding to the answer you select for each question. Fill the space with a dark mark so that you cannot see the letter inside the space. Light or partial marks may not be read by the scoring machine. See the example of proper and improper answer marks below.

- Erase all stray marks. If you change an answer, be sure that you completely erase the old answer before marking your new answer. Incomplete erasures may be read as intended answers.

Example:

What city is the capital of France?

(A) Rome
(B) Paris
(C) London
(D) Cairo
(E) Oslo

Sample Answer

Ⓐ ● Ⓒ Ⓓ Ⓔ   BEST ANSWER PROPERLY MARKED

Ⓐ Ⓧ Ⓒ Ⓓ Ⓔ
Ⓐ ⓐ Ⓒ Ⓓ Ⓔ
Ⓐ ⓑ Ⓒ Ⓓ Ⓔ   IMPROPER MARKS
Ⓐ ⓑ Ⓒ Ⓓ Ⓔ

Do not be concerned that the answer sheet provides spaces for more answers than there are questions in the test. Some or all of the passages for this test have been adapted from published material to provide the examinee with significant problems for analysis and evaluation. To make the passages suitable for testing purposes, the style, content, or point of view of the original may have been altered in some cases. The ideas contained in the passages do not necessarily represent the opinions of the Graduate Record Examinations Board or Educational Testing Service.

CLOSE YOUR TEST BOOK AND WAIT FOR FURTHER INSTRUCTIONS FROM THE SUPERVISOR.

I

NOTE: To ensure the prompt and accurate processing of test results, your cooperation in following these directions is needed. The procedures that follow have been kept to the minimum necessary. They will take a few minutes to complete, but it is essential that you fill in all blanks exactly as directed.

GENERAL TEST

A. Print and sign your full name in this box:

PRINT: _____
         (LAST)   (FIRST)   (MIDDLE)

SIGN: _____

B. Your answer sheet contains areas which will be used to ensure accurate reporting of your test results. It is essential that you fill in these areas exactly as explained below.

⬚1 YOUR NAME, MAILING ADDRESS, AND TEST CENTER: Place your answer sheet so that the heading "Graduate Record Examinations—General Test" is at the top. In box 1 below that heading print your name. Enter your current mailing address. Print the name of the city, state or province, and country in which the test center is located, and the center number.

⬚2 YOUR NAME: Print all the information requested in the boxes at the top of the columns (first four letters of your last name, your first initial, and middle initial), and then blacken fully the appropriate space beneath each entry.

⬚3 DATE OF BIRTH: Blacken the space beside the month in which you were born. Then enter the day of the month on which you were born in the boxes at the top of the columns. Blacken the appropriate space beneath each entry. Be sure to treat zeros like any other digit, and to add a zero before any single digit; for example 03, not 3. (Your year of birth is not required on the answer sheet.)

⬚4 SEX: Blacken the appropriate space.

⬚5 REGISTRATION NUMBER: Copy your registration number from your admission ticket into the boxes at the top of the columns and then blacken the appropriate space beneath each entry. Check your admission ticket again to make certain that you have copied your registration number accurately.

⬚6 TITLE CODE: Copy the numbers shown below and blacken the appropriate spaces beneath each entry as shown. When you have completed item 6, check to be sure it is identical to the illustration below.

⬚7 CERTIFICATION STATEMENT: In the boxed area, please write (do not print) the following statement: I certify that I am the person whose name appears on this answer sheet. I also agree not to disclose the contents of the test I am taking today to anyone. Sign and date where indicated.

⬚8 FORM CODE: Copy _GR86-1_ in the box.

⬚9 TEST BOOK SERIAL NUMBER: Copy the serial number of your test book in the box. It is printed in red at the upper right on the front cover of your test book.

C. WHEN YOU HAVE FINISHED THESE INSTRUCTIONS, PLEASE TURN YOUR ANSWER SHEET OVER AND SIGN YOUR NAME IN THE BOX EXACTLY AS YOU DID FOR ITEM ⬚7.

When you have finished, wait for further instructions from the supervisor. DO NOT OPEN YOUR TEST BOOK UNTIL YOU ARE TOLD TO DO SO.

VERBAL ABILITY						QUANTITATIVE ABILITY						ANALYTICAL ABILITY					
Section II			Section VI			Section I			Section V			Section III			Section VII		
Number	Answer	P+	Number	Answer	P+	Number	Answer	P+	Number	Answer	P+	Number	Answer	P+	Number	Answer	P+
1	E	89	1	B	80	1	C	84	1	C	89	1	B	82	1	D	68
2	B	66	2	A	69	2	B	87	2	B	90	2	A	75	2	B	92
3	A	52	3	D	76	3	A	90	3	D	88	3	C	89	3	D	85
4	C	58	4	E	67	4	C	75	4	B	90	4	B	31	4	E	74
5	E	51	5	C	64	5	C	76	5	A	81	5	C	47	5	B	76
6	D	45	6	B	59	6	B	69	6	C	83	6	D	58	6	C	88
7	A	10	7	E	66	7	D	65	7	A	85	7	E	46	7	E	68
8	C	82	8	E	96	8	C	53	8	B	71	8	B	88	8	A	82
9	E	80	9	B	41	9	A	69	9	D	61	9	D	86	9	D	69
10	B	61	10	D	87	10	C	53	10	A	77	10	A	53	10	C	63
11	C	82	11	E	67	11	D	34	11	A	56	11	E	76	11	E	70
12	D	36	12	C	38	12	B	59	12	C	42	12	B	42	12	D	80
13	D	35	13	D	53	13	A	42	13	D	42	13	C	51	13	B	33
14	E	48	14	D	33	14	A	36	14	B	49	14	A	56	14	C	31
15	C	46	15	C	37	15	D	33	15	C	31	15	E	76	15	A	16
16	D	23	16	B	25	16	A	88	16	D	96	16	A	26	16	E	49
17	C	89	17	D	70	17	E	86	17	C	82	17	C	75	17	D	52
18	B	77	18	B	44	18	B	82	18	B	77	18	E	28	18	C	34
19	A	21	19	A	36	19	D	83	19	E	71	19	A	35	19	E	33
20	B	69	20	D	19	20	C	75	20	A	69	20	E	20	20	D	23
21	C	80	21	C	71	21	D	94	21	B	92	21	B	23	21	A	20
22	D	62	22	A	30	22	B	80	22	C	57	22	C	41	22	B	31
23	B	43	23	C	66	23	C	66	23	B	51	23	E	21	23	A	50
24	B	64	24	D	47	24	A	48	24	C	34	24	C	37	24	D	31
25	A	59	25	A	49	25	C	44	25	D	28	25	D	24	25	C	30
26	E	42	26	C	33	26	B	52	26	A	62						
27	D	66	27	B	60	27	B	50	27	E	62						
28	E	86	28	C	94	28	D	30	28	A	51						
29	B	82	29	C	85	29	A	26	29	D	46						
30	E	81	30	C	72	30	E	44	30	C	47						
31	E	51	31	E	79												
32	A	44	32	E	59												
33	E	52	33	D	43												
34	D	49	34	C	45												
35	A	46	35	A	41												
36	A	27	36	C	34												
37	A	28	37	E	27												
38	C	23	38	D	24												

*Estimated P+ for the group of examinees who took the GRE General Test in a recent three-year period.

SCORE CONVERSIONS AND PERCENTS BELOW* for GRE GENERAL TEST, GR86-1

Raw Score	Scaled Scores and Percents Below						Raw Score	Scaled Scores and Percents Below					
	Verbal	%	Quantitative	%	Analytical	%		Verbal	%	Quantitative	%	Analytical	%
72-76	800	99					35	410	32	500	38	660	86
71	790	99					34	400	29	490	35	640	83
70	780	99					33	390	27	470	31	630	81
69	770	99					32	380	25	460	28	610	78
68	750	98					31	370	22	450	26	590	73
67	740	98					30	360	20	430	22	570	68
66	730	97					29	360	20	420	20	560	65
65	720	96					28	350	18	410	18	540	60
64	700	95					27	340	16	390	15	520	54
63	690	94					26	330	14	380	13	510	51
62	680	93					25	320	12	370	12	490	46
61	670	92					24	310	11	350	9	470	39
60	660	91	800	99			23	300	10	340	8	450	34
59	650	89	800	99			22	290	8	330	7	440	30
58	630	86	800	99			21	280	7	320	6	420	26
57	620	85	790	99			20	270	5	300	5	400	21
56	610	83	770	97			19	260	4	290	4	390	19
55	600	81	760	95			18	250	4	280	3	370	15
54	590	80	750	94			17	240	3	260	2	350	11
53	580	78	730	91			16	230	2	250	2	330	8
52	570	76	720	89			15	220	1	240	1	320	7
51	560	73	710	87			14	210	1	220	1	300	4
50	550	71	690	83	800	99	13	200	0	210	1	280	3
49	540	68	680	81	800	99	12	200		200	0	270	2
48	530	65	670	79	800	99	11	200		200		250	1
47	520	63	650	74	800	99	10	200		200		230	1
46	510	60	640	73	800	99	9	200		200		210	0
45	500	57	630	70	800	99	0-8	200		200		200	0
44	490	55	620	67	800	99							
43	480	52	600	64	800	99							
42	470	49	590	61	780	98							
41	460	46	580	58	760	97							
40	450	43	560	53	750	97							
39	440	40	550	51	730	95							
38	430	37	540	48	710	93							
37	420	35	520	43	690	91							
36	410	32	510	41	680	90							

*Percent scoring below the given scaled score, based on the performance of the 785,276 examinees who took the General Test between October 1, 1981, and September 30, 1984.

THE GRADUATE RECORD EXAMINATIONS

General Test

*Do not break the seal
until you are told to do so.*

*The contents of this test are confidential.
Disclosure or reproduction of any portion
of it is prohibited.*

THIS TEST BOOK MUST NOT BE TAKEN FROM THE ROOM.

SECTION 1
Time — 30 minutes
38 Questions

Directions: Each sentence below has one or two blanks, each blank indicating that something has been omitted. Beneath the sentence are five lettered words or sets of words. Choose the word or set of words for each blank that best fits the meaning of the sentence as a whole.

1. Psychology has slowly evolved into an ------- scientific discipline that now functions autonomously with the same privileges and responsibilities as other sciences.

   (A) independent   (B) unusual
   (C) outmoded   (D) uncontrolled
   (E) inactive

2. A major goal of law, to deter potential criminals by punishing wrongdoers, is not served when the penalty is so seldom invoked that it ------- to be a ------- threat.

   (A) tends. .serious
   (B) appears. .real
   (C) ceases. .credible
   (D) fails. .deceptive
   (E) seems. .coercive

3. When people are happy, they tend to give ------- interpretations of events they witness: the eye of the beholder is ------- by the emotions of the beholder.

   (A) charitable. .colored
   (B) elaborate. .disquieted
   (C) conscientious. .deceived
   (D) vague. .sharpened
   (E) coherent. .confused

4. Even those who disagreed with Carmen's views rarely faulted her for expressing them, for the positions she took were as ------- as they were controversial.

   (A) complicated   (B) political
   (C) subjective   (D) commonplace
   (E) thoughtful

5. New research on technology and public policy focuses on how seemingly ------- design features, generally overlooked in most analyses of public works projects or industrial machinery, actually ------- social choices of profound significance.

   (A) insignificant. .mask
   (B) inexpensive. .produce
   (C) innovative. .represent
   (D) ingenious. .permit
   (E) inopportune. .hasten

6. Paradoxically, Robinson's excessive denials of the worth of early works of science fiction suggest that she has become quite ------- them.

   (A) reflective about   (B) enamored of
   (C) skeptical of   (D) encouraged by
   (E) offended by

7. Cézanne's delicate watercolor sketches often served as ------- of a subject, a way of gathering fuller knowledge before the artist's final engagement of the subject in an oil painting.

   (A) an abstraction
   (B) an enhancement
   (C) a synthesis
   (D) a reconnaissance
   (E) a transcription

GO ON TO THE NEXT PAGE.

Directions: In each of the following questions, a related pair of words or phrases is followed by five lettered pairs of words or phrases. Select the lettered pair that best expresses a relationship similar to that expressed in the original pair.

8. HAMMER : CARPENTER ::
   (A) brick : mason   (B) road : driver
   (C) kitchen : cook   (D) letter : secretary
   (E) knife : butcher

9. EMBRACE : AFFECTION ::
   (A) jeer : sullenness
   (B) glower : ridicule
   (C) frown : displeasure
   (D) cooperation : respect
   (E) flattery : love

10. PLUMMET : FALL ::   (A) radiate : glow
    (B) converge : attract   (C) flounder : move
    (D) swerve : turn   (E) flow : ebb

11. GRAZING : FORAGERS ::
    (A) skipping : readers
    (B) strolling : prisoners
    (C) weeding : gardeners
    (D) stalking : hunters
    (E) resting : pickers

12. TEXT : EXTEMPORIZE ::
    (A) score : improvise
    (B) style : decorate
    (C) exhibit : demonstrate
    (D) diagram : realize
    (E) sketch : outline

13. PERTINENT : RELEVANCE ::
    (A) insistent : rudeness
    (B) benevolent : perfection
    (C) redundant : superfluity
    (D) prevalent : universality
    (E) aberrant : uniqueness

14. ASSERT : BELABOR ::
    (A) tend : fuss   (B) refine : temper
    (C) describe : demean   (D) resemble : portray
    (E) contaminate : purge

15. TRANSGRESSION : MORALITY ::
    (A) mistake : probity   (B) invitation : hospitality
    (C) gift : generosity   (D) presumption : propriety
    (E) misconception : curiosity

16. BLOWHARD : BOASTFUL ::
    (A) cynic : perspicacious
    (B) highbrow : grandiloquent
    (C) exhibitionist : embarrassed
    (D) misanthrope : affected
    (E) toady : obsequious

GO ON TO THE NEXT PAGE.

207

Directions: Each passage in this group is followed by questions based on its content. After reading a passage, choose the best answer to each question. Answer all questions following a passage on the basis of what is <u>stated</u> or <u>implied</u> in that passage.

Ragtime is a musical form that synthesizes folk melodies and musical techniques into a brief quadrille-like structure, designed to be played—exactly as
Line
(5) written—on the piano. A strong analogy exists between European composers like Ralph Vaughan Williams, Edvard Grieg, and Anton Dvořák who combined folk tunes and their own original materials in larger compositions and the pioneer ragtime composers in the United States. Composers like Scott Joplin and James Scott
(10) were in a sense collectors or musicologists, collecting dance and folk music in Black communities and consciously shaping it into brief suites or anthologies called piano rags.

It has sometimes been charged that ragtime is
(15) mechanical. For instance, Wilfred Mellers comments, "rags were transferred to the pianola roll and, even if not played by a machine, should be played <u>like</u> a machine, with meticulous precision." However, there is no reason to assume that ragtime is inherently mechan
(20) ical simply because commercial manufacturers applied a mechanical recording method to ragtime, the only way to record pianos at that date. Ragtime's is not a mechanical precision, and it is not precision limited to the style of performance. It arises from ragtime's following a well-
(25) defined form and obeying simple rules within that form.

The classic formula for the piano rag disposes three to five themes in sixteen-bar strains, often organized with repeats. The rag opens with a bright, memorable strain or theme, followed by a similar theme, leading to
(30) a trio of marked lyrical character, with the structure concluded by a lyrical strain that parallels the rhythmic developments of the earlier themes. The aim of the structure is to rise from one theme to another in a stair-step manner, ending on a note of triumph or exhilaration.
(35) Typically, each strain is divided into two 8-bar segments that are essentially alike, so the rhythmic-melodic unit of ragtime is only eight bars of 2/4 measure. Therefore, themes must be brief with clear, sharp melodic figures. Not concerned with development of musical themes, the
(40) ragtime composer instead sets a theme down intact, in finished form, and links it to various related themes. Tension in ragtime compositions arises from a polarity between two basic ingredients: a continuous bass— called by jazz musicians a boom-chick bass—in the
(45) pianist's left hand, and its melodic, syncopated counterpart in the right hand.

Ragtime remains distinct from jazz both as an instrumental style and as a genre. Ragtime style stresses a pattern of repeated rhythms, not the constant inventions
(50) and variations of jazz. As a genre, ragtime requires strict attention to structure, not inventiveness or virtuosity. It exists as a tradition, a set of conventions, a body of written scores, separate from the individual players associated with it. In this sense ragtime is more akin to folk music of the nineteenth century than to jazz.

17. Which of the following best describes the main purpose of the passage?

(A) To contrast ragtime music and jazz
(B) To acknowledge and counter significant adverse criticisms of ragtime music
(C) To define ragtime music as an art form and describe its structural characteristics
(D) To review the history of ragtime music and analyze ragtime's effect on listeners
(E) To explore the similarities between ragtime music and certain European musical compositions

18. According to the passage, each of the following is a characteristic of ragtime compositions that follow the classic ragtime formula EXCEPT

(A) syncopation
(B) well-defined melodic figures
(C) rising rhythmic-melodic intensity
(D) full development of musical themes
(E) a bass line distinct from the melodic line

GO ON TO THE NEXT PAGE.

19. According to the passage, Ralph Vaughan Williams, Anton Dvořák, and Scott Joplin are similar in that they all

    (A) conducted research into musicological history
    (B) wrote original compositions based on folk tunes
    (C) collected and recorded abbreviated piano suites
    (D) created intricate sonata-like musical structures
    (E) explored the relations between Black music and continental folk music

20. The author rejects the argument that ragtime is a mechanical music because that argument

    (A) overlooks the precision required of the ragtime player
    (B) does not accurately describe the sound of ragtime pianola music
    (C) confuses the means of recording and the essential character of the music
    (D) exaggerates the influence of the performance style of professional ragtime players on the reputation of the genre
    (E) improperly identifies commercial ragtime music with the subtler classic ragtime style

21. It can be inferred that the author of the passage believes that the most important feature of ragtime music is its

    (A) commercial success
    (B) formal structure
    (C) emotional range
    (D) improvisational opportunities
    (E) role as a forerunner of jazz

22. It can be inferred from the passage that the essential nature of ragtime has been obscured by commentaries based on

    (A) the way ragtime music was first recorded
    (B) interpretations of ragtime by jazz musicians
    (C) the dance fashions that were contemporary with ragtime
    (D) early reviewers' accounts of characteristic structure
    (E) the musical sources used by Scott Joplin and James Scott

23. Which of the following is most nearly analogous in source and artistic character to a ragtime composition as described in the passage?

    (A) Symphonic music derived from complex jazz motifs
    (B) An experimental novel based on well-known cartoon characters
    (C) A dramatic production in which actors invent scenes and improvise lines
    (D) A ballet whose disciplined choreography is based on folk-dance steps
    (E) A painting whose abstract shapes evoke familiar objects in a natural landscape

GO ON TO THE NEXT PAGE.

Echolocating bats emit sounds in patterns—characteristic of each species—that contain both frequency-modulated (FM) and constant-frequency (CF)
Line signals. The broadband FM signals and the narrowband
(5) CF signals travel out to a target, reflect from it, and return to the hunting bat. In this process of transmission and reflection, the sounds are changed, and the changes in the echoes enable the bat to perceive features of the target.

(10) The FM signals report information about target characteristics that modify the timing and the fine frequency structure, or spectrum, of echoes—for example, the target's size, shape, texture, surface structure, and direction in space. Because of their narrow bandwidth, CF
(15) signals portray only the target's presence and, in the case of some bat species, its motion relative to the bat's. Responding to changes in the CF echo's frequency, bats of some species correct in flight for the direction and velocity of their moving prey.

24. According to the passage, the information provided to the bat by CF echoes differs from that provided by FM echoes in which of the following ways?

    (A) Only CF echoes alert the bat to moving targets.
    (B) Only CF echoes identify the range of widely spaced targets.
    (C) Only CF echoes report the target's presence to the bat.
    (D) In some species, CF echoes enable the bat to judge whether it is closing in on its target.
    (E) In some species, CF echoes enable the bat to discriminate the size of its target and the direction in which the target is moving.

25. According to the passage, the configuration of the target is reported to the echolocating bat by changes in the

    (A) echo spectrum of CF signals
    (B) echo spectrum of FM signals
    (C) direction and velocity of the FM echoes
    (D) delay between transmission and reflection of the CF signals
    (E) relative frequencies of the FM and the CF echoes

26. The author presents the information concerning bat sonar in a manner that could be best described as

    (A) argumentative   (B) commendatory
    (C) critical   (D) disbelieving   (E) objective

27. Which of the following best describes the organization of the passage?

    (A) A fact is stated, a process is outlined, and specific details of the process are described.
    (B) A fact is stated, and examples suggesting that a distinction needs correction are considered.
    (C) A fact is stated, a theory is presented to explain that fact, and additional facts are introduced to validate the theory.
    (D) A fact is stated, and two theories are compared in light of their explanations of this fact.
    (E) A fact is stated, a process is described, and examples of still another process are illustrated in detail.

GO ON TO THE NEXT PAGE.

Directions: Each question below consists of a word printed in capital letters, followed by five lettered words or phrases. Choose the lettered word or phrase that is most nearly opposite in meaning to the word in capital letters.

Since some of the questions require you to distinguish fine shades of meaning, be sure to consider all the choices before deciding which one is best.

28. CONSTRAIN: (A) release   (B) sever
    (C) abandon   (D) unload   (E) agree

29. SQUAT: (A) dim and dark   (B) tall and thin
    (C) misty and vague   (D) sharp and shrill
    (E) flat and narrow

30. OPAQUENESS: (A) opalescence   (B) clarity
    (C) density   (D) magnetism   (E) latency

31. COMELINESS:
    (A) disagreement
    (B) humiliation
    (C) ambition
    (D) unattractiveness
    (E) shortsightedness

32. PROFUNDITY: (A) speciousness
    (B) solicitude   (C) succinctness
    (D) superficiality   (E) solidarity

33. BURGEON: (A) subside   (B) esteem
    (C) placate   (D) tempt   (E) wean

34. SINEWY: (A) new   (B) weak
    (C) corrupt   (D) subtle   (E) substantial

35. EXHAUSTIVE: (A) incomplete   (B) energetic
    (C) strong   (D) indecisive   (E) conserving

36. PINE: (A) fall apart   (B) become invigorated
    (C) become enraged   (D) move ahead
    (E) stand firm

37. OBSTINACY: (A) persuasiveness
    (B) tractability   (C) antipathy
    (D) neutrality   (E) magnanimity

38. EXACT: (A) deny   (B) judge   (C) deprive
    (D) forgive   (E) establish

STOP

IF YOU FINISH BEFORE TIME IS CALLED, YOU MAY CHECK YOUR WORK ON THIS SECTION ONLY. DO NOT TURN TO ANY OTHER SECTION IN THE TEST.

SECTION 2

Time—30 minutes

30 Questions

Numbers: All numbers used are real numbers.

Figures: Position of points, angles, regions, etc. can be assumed to be in the order shown; and angle measures can be assumed to be positive.

Lines shown as straight can be assumed to be straight.

Figures can be assumed to lie in a plane unless otherwise indicated.

Figures that accompany questions are intended to provide information useful in answering the questions. However, unless a note states that a figure is drawn to scale, you should solve these problems NOT by estimating sizes by sight or by measurement, but by using your knowledge of mathematics (see Example 2 below).

Directions: Each of the Questions 1-15 consists of two quantities, one in Column A and one in Column B. You are to compare the two quantities and choose

A if the quantity in Column A is greater;
B if the quantity in Column B is greater;
C if the two quantities are equal;
D if the relationship cannot be determined from the information given.

Note: Since there are only four choices, NEVER MARK (E).

Common
Information: In a question, information concerning one or both of the quantities to be compared is centered above the two columns. A symbol that appears in both columns represents the same thing in Column A as it does in Column B.

	Column A	Column B	Sample Answers
Example 1:	2×6	$2 + 6$	● Ⓑ Ⓒ Ⓓ Ⓔ

Examples 2-4 refer to $\triangle PQR$.

Example 2:	PN	NQ	Ⓐ Ⓑ Ⓒ ● Ⓔ

(since equal measures cannot be assumed, even though PN and NQ appear equal)

Example 3:	x	y	Ⓐ ● Ⓒ Ⓓ Ⓔ

(since N is between P and Q)

Example 4:	$w + z$	180	Ⓐ Ⓑ ● Ⓓ Ⓔ

(since PQ is a straight line)

GO ON TO THE NEXT PAGE.

A if the quantity in Column A is greater;
B if the quantity in Column B is greater;
C if the two quantities are equal;
D if the relationship cannot be determined from the information given.

Column A	Column B

1. The average (arithmetic mean) of 15, 16, and 180

   The average (arithmetic mean) of 57, 58, and 60

$$x + 3 = 23$$
$$24 - y = 3$$

2. x

   y

---

12 is $\frac{2}{3}$ of n.

3. $2n$

   16

---

4. $11 + (-12) + 13 + (-14)$

   $2(-1)$

---

5. The cost per gram of carrots if 3 cans of carrots cost $0.90

   The cost per gram of onions if 5 cans of onions cost $1.50

---

6. $8 + \left(6 \cdot \dfrac{1}{14}\right)$

   $8 + \dfrac{3}{7}$

---

7. $\dfrac{6}{7}$

   $\dfrac{5}{6}$

$$r > 0$$

8. The area of a square region with side r

   The area of a circular region with radius r

Column A	Column B

$$\frac{1}{x} = 3$$

9. x

   1

10. y

    120

A certain car gets 24 miles per gallon of gasoline for city driving, which is 60 percent of the number of miles per gallon of gasoline the car gets for highway driving.

11. The number of gallons of gasoline used to drive this car 30 miles in the city

    The number of gallons of gasoline used to drive this car 45 miles on the highway

12. $x + y$

    z

GO ON TO THE NEXT PAGE.

213

A   if the quantity in Column A is greater;
B   if the quantity in Column B is greater;
C   if the two quantities are equal;
D   if the relationship cannot be determined from the information given.

Column A   Column B

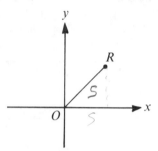

R is a point in the rectangular coordinate system and $OR = 5$.

13. The x-coordinate of   5
     point R

$$x > 0$$
$$n > 0$$

14. $\dfrac{x^n}{x^{n+1}}$ $\dfrac{x^{n+1}}{x^n}$

x^{-1} x

$\dfrac{1}{x^4}$ $\times$

Column A   Column B

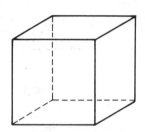

The volume of the cube is x cubic meters and the surface area is x square meters.

15. The length of an edge   6 meters

GO ON TO THE NEXT PAGE.

$x \cdot x \cdot x = x^3$

x^3 $V = a^3$
             $A = 6a^2$

$6x^2$

Directions: Each of the Questions 16-30 has five answer choices. For each of these questions, select the best of the answer choices given.

16. $\dfrac{(12)(27) - (27)(5)}{12 - 5} =$

27 (12-5)

(A) 0   (B) 1   (C) $\dfrac{60}{7}$ (D) 27   (E) 189

7	8	9	10	11
16	15	14	13	12
17	18	19	20	21
26	25	24	23	22
27	28	29	30	31

17. The figure above consists of 25 squares. If the figure were folded along the dotted diagonal to form a flat triangle, then 26 minus the number in the square that would coincide with the square containing 26 would be

26

(A) 13   (B) 14   (C) 15   (D) 16   (E) 17

18. If $D = (S - W)T$ and $D \ne 0,$ then $S =$

(A) $W - \dfrac{T}{D}$ $\dfrac{D}{T} + \omega$

(B) $\dfrac{D}{T} + W$

(C) $DT - W$

(D) $DT + W$

(E) $D + WT$

19. The selling price of a certain book is $12.00. For each copy of the book sold, the author receives $2.40. What percent of the selling price does the author receive?

(A) 20%   (B) 5%   (C) 2%

(D) 0.5%   (E) 0.2%

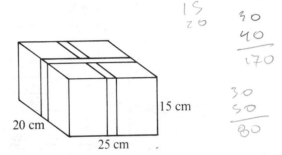

15 cm

20 cm

25 cm

20. The rectangular box shown above has been wrapped with two tapes, each going once around the box without overlap and running parallel to the edges of the box. How many centimeters of tape were used on the box?

(A) 70   (B) 80   (C) 120   (D) 140   (E) 150

GO ON TO THE NEXT PAGE.

12 — 100
24 — x

240 / 12

240 | 12 / 20

Questions 21-25 refer to the following graph.

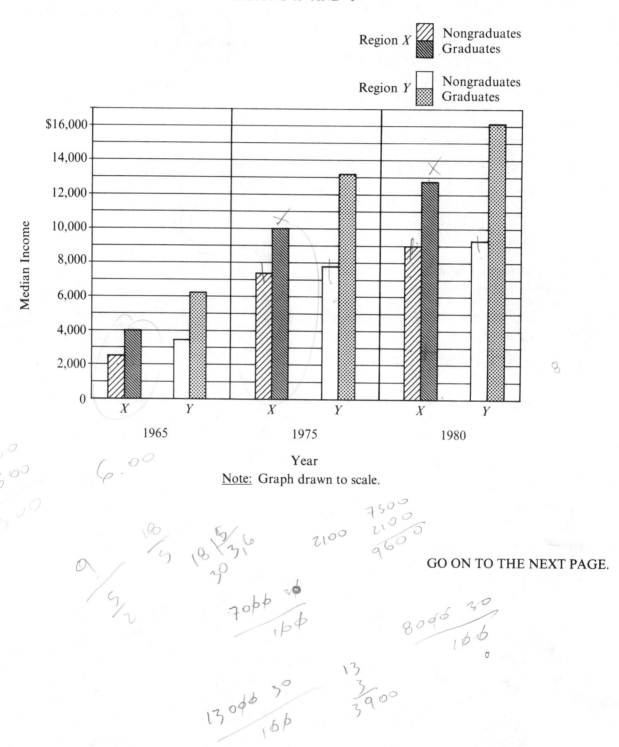

MEDIAN INCOME OF
COLLEGE GRADUATES *VS.* NONGRADUATES
IN REGIONS *X* AND *Y*

Note: Graph drawn to scale.

GO ON TO THE NEXT PAGE.

216

21. The median income of graduates in Region X in 1980 was most nearly equal to the median income of

    (A) graduates in Region X in 1975
    (B) graduates in Region Y in 1975
    (C) graduates in Region Y in 1980
    (D) nongraduates in Region X in 1980
    (E) nongraduates in Region Y in 1980

22. For nongraduates in Region X, the median income in 1980 was approximately how many times as great as it was in 1965 ?

    (A) 2   (B) 2.5   (C) 3   (D) 3.5   (E) 5

23. Of the following 1980 median-income ratios, the greatest was the ratio of the median incomes of

    (A) graduates in Region Y to graduates in Region X
    (B) nongraduates in Region Y to nongraduates in Region X
    (C) graduates in Region Y to nongraduates in Region Y
    (D) graduates in Region X to nongraduates in Region X
    (E) graduates in Region X to nongraduates in Region Y

24. From 1965 to 1975 in Region X, the increase in the median income of graduates was how much more than that of nongraduates?

    (A) $5,000
    (B) $3,000
    (C) $2,500
    (D) $2,000
    (E) $1,000

25. For how many of the four categories given did the median income increase by at least 30 percent from 1975 to 1980 ?

    (A) None
    (B) One
    (C) Two
    (D) Three
    (E) Four

GO ON TO THE NEXT PAGE.

$$\frac{16}{13} \qquad \frac{9}{}$$

$$\frac{16}{9}$$

26. Which of the following indicates all x such that $x^2 < x$?

    (A) $-1 < x < 0$
    (B) $-1 < x < 1$
    (C) $0 < x < 1$
    (D) $x < 0$
    (E) $x > 1$

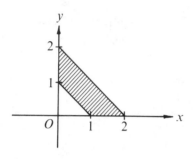

27. In the rectangular coordinate system above, the area of the shaded region is

    (A) $1\frac{1}{2}$ (B) 2 (C) $2\frac{1}{2}$ (D) 3 (E) 4

28. Which of the following equals $x + xy + (x + xy)y$?

    (A) $x(1 + y)^2$
    (B) $x(2 + y + y^2)$
    (C) $2x(1 + y) + y$
    (D) $2xy(1 + y)$
    (E) $x^2(1 + y^2)y$

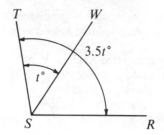

29. If $t = 40$, what is the degree measure of $\angle WSR$?

    (A) 140 (B) 120 (C) 110 (D) 100 (E) 80

30. What is the distance between two points on a number line if the coordinates of the points are $4 + \sqrt{5}$ and $2 - \sqrt{5}$?

    (A) $2 - 2\sqrt{5}$
    (B) $2 + 2\sqrt{5}$
    (C) $6 + 2\sqrt{5}$
    (D) 2
    (E) 6

STOP

IF YOU FINISH BEFORE TIME IS CALLED, YOU MAY CHECK YOUR WORK ON THIS SECTION ONLY.
DO NOT TURN TO ANY OTHER SECTION IN THE TEST.

SECTION 3

Time—30 minutes

25 Questions

Directions: Each question or group of questions is based on a passage or set of conditions. In answering some of the questions, it may be useful to draw a rough diagram. For each question, select the best answer choice given.

Questions 1-6

A team of art historians has the task of determining approximately when certain recently discovered illustrated manuscripts, each the work of a different artist, were created. The art historians consult a chemist who will test for the presence of six pigments on the manuscripts. It is known when these pigments were first manufactured and when, in some cases, they stopped being manufactured and used, as listed below:

Pigment 1: introduced A.D. 1100; stopped being used A.D. 1300.
Pigment 2: introduced A.D. 1250.
Pigment 3: introduced A.D. 1300.
Pigment 4: introduced A.D. 1000; stopped being used A.D. 1250.
Pigment 5: introduced A.D. 1200; stopped being used A.D. 1400.
Pigment 6: introduced A.D. 1350.

1. Which of the following pigments could NOT have been used together in the creation of a manuscript?

(A) 1 and 5
(B) 1 and 6
(C) 2 and 3
(D) 2 and 5
(E) 2 and 6

2. A manuscript illustrated with pigments 1 and 2 must have been created between

(A) A.D. 1050 and A.D. 1100
(B) A.D. 1100 and A.D. 1150
(C) A.D. 1150 and A.D. 1200
(D) A.D. 1200 and A.D. 1250
(E) A.D. 1250 and A.D. 1300

3. The earliest possible date of creation of a manuscript that is illustrated with pigments 1 and 4 is

(A) A.D. 1000
(B) A.D. 1050
(C) A.D. 1100
(D) A.D. 1150
(E) A.D. 1200

4. The team could determine to within a fifty-year period the date of creation of a manuscript that was created with which of the following combinations of pigments?

(A) 2 and 3
(B) 2 and 5
(C) 2 and 6
(D) 3 and 5
(E) 5 and 6

5. How many of the other five pigments could have been used in the creation of a manuscript illustrated with pigment 6 ?

(A) One
(B) Two
(C) Three
(D) Four
(E) Five

6. No further tests are performed on a certain manuscript after two of the pigments are identified, because no additional information in regard to dating would be gained. Which of the following could be the two identified pigments?

(A) 1 and 4
(B) 2 and 3
(C) 2 and 6
(D) 3 and 5
(E) 5 and 6

GO ON TO THE NEXT PAGE.

7. In a study of more than 8,000 people using ten beaches on two of the Great Lakes, ecologists from the University of Toronto determined that the rate of respiratory and gastrointestinal illness among people who had been swimming was 69.6 per 1,000, whereas the respiratory and gastrointestinal illness rate among those who had not been swimming was only 29.5 per 1,000.

Which of the following conclusions can be most properly drawn from the data above?

(A) People tend to underestimate the risks of swimming in these lakes.
(B) Respiratory and gastrointestinal illnesses occur at a higher rate as a result of swimming in either of these lakes than they do as a result of swimming in any other lake.
(C) Illnesses of kinds other than respiratory and gastrointestinal are not likely to be associated with swimming in either of these lakes.
(D) The association between swimming in these lakes and respiratory and gastrointestinal illness is some evidence for a causal relationship between them.
(E) A large percentage of the people who swim in these lakes are immune to the diseases that swimming may cause.

8. The story of Robinson Crusoe's adventures on an uninhabited island is no longer as popular as it once was, nor does it inspire modern versions in popular fiction. This change in the reading public's taste has occurred because it is no longer easy to believe that undiscovered, uninhabited islands still exist.

The author's reasoning about the decreased popularity of Robinson Crusoe-like adventures in popular fiction is based on which of the following assumptions?

(A) Readers of popular fiction no longer wish to exchange their current lives for lives freed from the demands made on them by other people.
(B) Readers of popular fiction prefer settings that they can readily accept as plausible contemporary settings.
(C) The most satisfying type of popular fiction is that which enables the reader to participate vicariously in another person's adventures.
(D) As a result of media coverage, more people are acquainted with foreign locales today than at any time in the past.
(E) Readers of popular fiction are found among people with diverse interests, with the result that no single type of fiction appeals to all.

9. Substances suspected of causing cancer, if carefully administered to experimental animals in quantities in which those substances are ordinarily present in the environment, are virtually guaranteed not to produce cancer at rates significantly above the chance level. The most economical procedure for obtaining informative data is to administer vastly increased amounts of the substance being tested.

The 'economical procedure' described above will not be an effective one if which of the following is true?

(A) Cancer data on experimental animals yield accurate estimates of the risk of cancer for human beings.
(B) Experimental animals will often develop cancer in response to receiving excessive quantities of a substance, regardless of the specific properties of the substance.
(C) When more of a possibly cancer-causing substance is administered to experimental animals, fewer animals are needed for significant data to be obtained.
(D) Among experimental animals, the chance level for many types of cancer is virtually zero.
(E) Substances will often be tested in amounts greater than necessary to obtain informative data.

GO ON TO THE NEXT PAGE.

Questions 10-16

An observatory is setting up a schedule for schoolchildren to view a returning comet. Five school classes—K, L, N, O, and P—will each view the comet exactly once during the four nights, Monday through Thursday, of its maximum brightness. Excellent viewing conditions are predicted for all four nights. The scheduling is subject to the following constraints:

At most two classes can view the comet on any given night.

Class K cannot view the comet on the same night that Class N does.

Class L must view the comet on a night prior to the night when Class P views the comet.

Class O must view the comet on the same night that Class P does.

10. Which of the following is a possible schedule for viewing the comet?

	Monday	Tuesday	Wednesday	Thursday
(A)	N	K, L	O, P	---
(B)	L, N	---	K, O, P	---
(C)	L	K, N	---	O, P
(D)	K	O, P	L	N
(E)	K	L, N	O	P

11. If Class L views the comet on Wednesday, which of the following must be true?

(A) Class K views the comet on Monday.
(B) Class K views the comet on Wednesday.
(C) Class N views the comet on Tuesday.
(D) Class O views the comet on Thursday.
(E) Class P views the comet on Monday.

12. If Class O can view the comet neither on Wednesday nor on Thursday, which of the following must be true?

(A) Class K views the comet on Monday.
(B) Class L views the comet on Monday.
(C) Class L views the comet on Tuesday.
(D) Class N views the comet on Wednesday.
(E) Class N views the comet on Thursday.

13. If Class N views the comet on Thursday, which of the following could be true?

(A) Class P views the comet on Tuesday.
(B) Class O views the comet on Thursday.
(C) Class L views the comet on Thursday.
(D) Class L views the comet on Wednesday.
(E) Class K views the comet on Thursday.

14. Which of the following must be true of any viewing schedule?

(A) Class K views the comet on a night prior to the night Class O views it.
(B) Class N views the comet on a night prior to the night Class P views it.
(C) There is at most one night when no class views the comet.
(D) There is exactly one night when no class views the comet.
(E) At least one class views the comet on each of the four nights.

15. Each of the following could be true EXCEPT:

(A) Class L views the comet on Monday.
(B) Class N views the comet on Wednesday.
(C) Class O views the comet on Tuesday.
(D) Class L and Class N view the comet on Tuesday.
(E) Class N and Class P view the comet on Thursday.

16. If classes K, L, and N have each been scheduled for a different night, which of the following must be true?

(A) One of the three views the comet on Monday.
(B) One of the three views the comet on Thursday.
(C) Class K views the comet on a night prior to the night when Class N views it.
(D) Class L views the comet on a night prior to the night when Class K views it.
(E) Class N views the comet on a night prior to the night when Class O views it.

GO ON TO THE NEXT PAGE.

Questions 17-22

A certain dance involves three couples: L1 and P1, L2 and P2, L3 and P3. Each couple consists of a leader (the L's) and a partner (the P's). The dance begins with the following original configuration:

The L's are in a line: L1 L2 L3
The P's are facing their
    respective L's   P1 P2 P3

The dance consists of any one of a variety of sequences of moves. The four possible moves—two of them exchanges and two of them findings—are listed below. No dancers except those listed in a move description change position during that move.

Exchanges:

There is an immediate exchange (IE), in which L1 takes whatever place L2 currently occupies; L2 takes whatever place L3 currently occupies; L3 takes whatever place L1 currently occupies.
There is a remote exchange (RE), in which L1 and L3 exchange their current places.

Findings:

There is "find your leader" (FL), in which P's move so as to be opposite to the L's they faced at the beginning of the dance.
There is "find your partner" (FP), in which L's move so as to be opposite to the P's they faced at the beginning of the dance.

Two consecutive exchanges cannot be immediately followed by a third exchange.
If, in a configuration, each leader faces his or her original partner, the next move cannot be a finding.

17. Which of the following is an admissible initial sequence of moves?

   (A) FL, RE, IE, FL, FP
   (B) RE, IE, IE, FP, RE
   (C) IE, FL, IE, FL, FL
   (D) RE, FL, IE, RE, IE
   (E) RE, IE, FL, IE, RE

18. If the first move in the dance is RE, followed by FL, which of the following will be the configuration after those two moves?

   (A) L1 L2 L3
       P1 P2 P3

   (B) L2 L1 L3
       P1 P2 P3

   (C) L3 L2 L1
       P3 P2 P1

   (D) L1 L3 L2
       P1 P2 P3

   (E) L3 L1 L2
       P1 P2 P3

19. If the configuration is L2 L1 L3, which of the
                             P2 P1 P3
following lines of leaders is possible after exactly one additional move?

   (A) L1 L2 L3
   (B) L2 L1 L3
   (C) L2 L3 L1
   (D) L3 L1 L2
   (E) L3 L2 L1

20. If, starting from the original configuration, the dancers have performed exactly two moves, both exchanges, but of different types, which of the following could be the resulting configuration?

   (A) L3 L1 L2
       P1 P2 P3

   (B) L1 L3 L2
       P1 P3 P2

   (C) L3 L2 L1
       P1 P2 P3

   (D) L1 L3 L2
       P1 P2 P3

   (E) L3 L2 L1
       P3 P2 P1

21. If the dancers start from the original configuration, which of the following moves or sequences of moves will result in a configuration of L2 L1 L3 ?
                                          P2 P1 P3

   (A) RE
   (B) IE
   (C) RE, IE
   (D) IE, FL
   (E) RE, IE, FL

22. If the dance begins with IE followed by FL, which of the following moves or sequences of moves will result in the dancers' returning to the original configuration?

   (A) RE
   (B) IE
   (C) IE, IE
   (D) RE, FL
   (E) IE, IE, FL

GO ON TO THE NEXT PAGE.

Questions 23-24

How does a building contractor most readily prove compliance with the building codes governing new construction? By using those established technologies that the authors of the codes had in mind when setting specifications. This, unfortunately, means that there will never be any significant technological innovation within the industry.

23. The argument above depends on the assumption that, in choosing the technologies to use in new construction, building contractors

(A) are always more concerned to avoid difficulties in proving compliance with the relevant codes than to be innovative
(B) are always concerned to exceed the official specifications by a wide margin in order to forestall challenges
(C) pay little or no attention to the total construction costs entailed by different technologies
(D) consult directly with the authors of the relevant codes in order to avoid using an unproven technology
(E) are able to foresee any changes the relevant codes may undergo before the completion of a new project

24. Which of the following, if true, casts the most serious doubt on the conclusion above?

(A) Among the authors of codes governing new construction are people who were formerly building contractors.
(B) The authors of codes governing new construction are under pressure to set rigorous specifications.
(C) What are now regarded as established technologies were once so innovative that the authors of the codes then applicable could not have foreseen them.
(D) Noncompliance with the codes governing new construction can prove extremely costly to the building contractor in charge of the project.
(E) The established technologies of one country's building industry can be very different from those of another's.

GO ON TO THE NEXT PAGE.

223

25. X: When a rare but serious industrial accident occurs, people respond by believing that such accidents are becoming more frequent. This belief is irrational. After all, being dealt four aces in a hand of poker, a rare event, hardly increases one's chances of being dealt four aces in a future hand.

Y: To the contrary, the belief is rational because it results in people's sensing a danger to themselves not previously sensed and taking precautionary actions to prevent similar accidents in the future.

Y's attempt to counter X's claim is best described by which of the following?

(A) It questions the aptness of the analogy drawn by X.
(B) It makes apparent X's failure to consider how people vary in their responses to a serious accident.
(C) It shifts the basis for judging rationality to considerations of utility.
(D) It offers an alternative explanation of why people form incorrect beliefs.
(E) It challenges X's assumption that the occurrence of a single event is sufficient to change a belief.

STOP

IF YOU FINISH BEFORE TIME IS CALLED, YOU MAY CHECK YOUR WORK ON THIS SECTION ONLY.
DO NOT TURN TO ANY OTHER SECTION IN THE TEST.

SECTION 4
Time—30 minutes

25 Questions

Directions: Each question or group of questions is based on a passage or set of conditions. In answering some of the questions, it may be useful to draw a rough diagram. For each question, select the best answer choice given.

Questions 1-4

A manager who has exactly four projects—F, G, H, and I—to undertake in a given month has made the following determinations:

F has priority over G.
H has priority over I.
If one project has priority over another, the project with priority must be started earlier than the other one.

1. Given only the determinations above, each of the following is a possible sequence in which the four projects could be started EXCEPT

(A) F, G, H, I
(B) F, H, G, I
(C) F, H, I, G
(D) H, F, I, G
(E) H, G, F, I

2. If each of the projects takes equally long to complete, it must be true that

(A) F is completed before H is completed
(B) F is completed before I is completed
(C) G is completed before H is completed
(D) H is completed before G is completed
(E) H is completed before I is completed

3. There would be exactly one order in which the four projects would have to be started if it were determined that

(A) F has priority over H
(B) F has priority over I
(C) H has priority over G
(D) I has priority over F
(E) I has priority over G

4. Which of the following pairs of additional determinations would NOT conflict with the priorities initially determined?

(A) F has priority over H, and I has priority over F.
(B) F has priority over I, and H has priority over G.
(C) G has priority over H, and H has priority over F.
(D) G has priority over H, and I has priority over F.
(E) G has priority over I, and I has priority over F.

5. Employee Complaint: There are not enough parking spaces in the employee parking lot to accommodate all the people who work here.

Employer's Response: There is no truth to the complaint. No one who gets to work on time has trouble finding a parking space. Only if you are late to work are you unlikely to be able to find a space.

Which of the following, if true, gives the reason why the employer's response fails to address the substance of the issue raised in the complaint?

(A) Each employee does not drive his or her own car to work.
(B) The employer is not obligated to provide parking spaces for all employees.
(C) On days when all employees arrived at work on time, there would be insufficient parking spaces.
(D) On days when a large number of employees were late to work, many of the latecomers would be able to find parking spaces.
(E) The number of employees who come to work each day is not always the same.

GO ON TO THE NEXT PAGE.

225

6. A novel by the deceased author Virginia Woolf that, in its manuscript form, was 48 chapters long and contained 200,000 words is being edited and reduced to 30 chapters and 70,000 words. Every word in the book will be Woolf's own, and the chapters will appear in the order in which she wrote them. The published result will therefore be an authentic Virginia Woolf novel.

The claim that the new work is an authentic Virginia Woolf novel will be most damaged if which of the following is true?

(A) A portion of the manuscript material that editors omitted from the published novel is almost identical to material that Virginia Woolf published in a nonfiction book during her lifetime.

(B) Critics have argued that Virginia Woolf's writing style in the period during which she wrote this manuscript sometimes lacks conciseness.

(C) An authentic novel is characterized by its author's decisions about what should be included in it and what sort of emphasis should be given to what is included.

(D) An authentic novel contains dialogue, characterization, and narrative structures that are recognizably like those found in the author's other major writings, if such writings exist.

(E) Not many of the novels that Virginia Woolf published during her lifetime contain as few as 70,000 words.

7. I. Neither Carol nor Eric will travel by air.
    II. Neither Carol nor Eric will travel to Burgundia.

Statement II must be true if both Statement I and which of the following statements are true?

(A) Immigration officials do not allow travelers without valid visas to enter Burgundia.

(B) The cost of travel to Burgundia other than by air is almost prohibitive.

(C) Until recently, Burgundia was closed to foreign visitors.

(D) It is equally possible to reach Burgundia by commercial as by private airplane.

(E) It is impossible to reach Burgundia except by air.

GO ON TO THE NEXT PAGE.

Questions 8-12

A playwright is creating a play with a cast of exactly seven: four female characters—Penelope, Tanya, Vanessa, and Zelda—and three male characters—Marlon, Rex, and Sterling. The playwright has decided that, during each scene of act one, there will always be a balance of characters according to gender, with either one woman and one man, or two women and two men on stage. The playwright will also observe the following restrictions in act one:

At most four characters can be on stage during any one scene.

Characters who are on stage at the start of a scene cannot leave during that scene, and no new characters can enter the stage during that scene.

No character can be on stage for two or more consecutive scenes.

Rex cannot be on stage at the same time as Sterling.

If either Vanessa or Marlon is on stage, the other must be on stage at the same time.

Tanya and Sterling must be on stage during scene 1.

8. If four characters are on stage during scene 1, which of the following must be included among them?

(A) Penelope and Marlon
(B) Penelope and Rex
(C) Vanessa and Marlon
(D) Vanessa and Rex
(E) Zelda and Marlon

9. If four characters are on stage during scene 1, which of the following must be one of the characters on stage during scene 2?

(A) Penelope   (B) Rex   (C) Sterling
(D) Tanya   (E) Zelda

10. If Tanya and Vanessa are both on stage during scene 4, each of the following could be on stage during scene 5 EXCEPT

(A) Marlon   (B) Penelope   (C) Rex
(D) Sterling   (E) Zelda

11. Which of the following is the minimum number of scenes the playwright must write for act one if each of the seven characters is to be on stage in at least one scene during act one?

(A) Two   (B) Three   (C) Four
(D) Five   (E) Six

12. If each of act one's first three scenes has only two characters in it and no character is on stage for the second time until scene 4, which of the following can be on stage for the first time in scene 4 of act one?

(A) Marlon   (B) Rex   (C) Sterling
(D) Vanessa   (E) Zelda

GO ON TO THE NEXT PAGE.

Questions 13-16

The owner of a computer store is planning a window display of five products. Three are to be hardware items selected from K, L, M, N, and O, and two are to be software manuals selected from R, S, T, and U. The display items are to be selected according to the following conditions:

If K is displayed, U must be displayed.
M cannot be displayed unless both L and R are also displayed.
If N is displayed, O must be displayed, and if O is displayed, N must be displayed.
If S is displayed, neither T nor U can be displayed.

13. Which of the following is an acceptable display?

(A) K, L, M, R, U
(B) K, M, N, O, R
(C) L, M, O, R, S
(D) M, N, O, T, U
(E) N, O, R, S, T

14. If K and T are the first two display items to be selected, how many acceptable groups of items are there that would complete the display?

(A) 1
(B) 2
(C) 3
(D) 4
(E) 5

15. If T and U are displayed, which of the following must also be displayed?

(A) K
(B) L
(C) M
(D) N
(E) R

16. If N and O are not displayed, all of the following must be displayed EXCEPT

(A) K
(B) M
(C) R
(D) T
(E) U

GO ON TO THE NEXT PAGE.

228

Questions 17-22

Historians have established that a particular copy of a rare jazz recording was sold each year on New Year's Day for seven consecutive years, starting in 1931 and ending in 1937. Each person who bought that copy of the record owned it only during that period and owned it for exactly a year. The seven owners of that copy of the record during this period were Javitz, Kallers, Luria, Mapp, Nakamura, Oster, and Pugh. The following are all the additional facts the historians have discovered about the ownership of that copy of the record during the period 1931-1937:

> Luria sold it to Oster.
> Pugh sold it to Mapp.
> Javitz owned it before Oster owned it.
> Nakamura owned it before Luria owned it.

17. Which of the following could be true of that copy of the jazz record during the period 1931-1937?

(A) Javitz sold it to Oster.
(B) Luria sold it to Mapp.
(C) Nakamura sold it to Luria.
(D) Oster sold it to Nakamura.
(E) Pugh sold it to Luria.

18. Which of the following must be true of that copy of the jazz record during the period 1931-1937?

(A) Javitz owned it before Luria owned it.
(B) Luria owned it before Pugh owned it.
(C) Mapp owned it before Pugh owned it.
(D) Nakamura owned it before Mapp owned it.
(E) Pugh owned it before Nakamura owned it.

19. Which of the following could have sold that copy of the jazz record to Javitz on New Year's Day, 1932?

(A) Luria   (B) Mapp   (C) Nakamura
(D) Oster   (E) Pugh

20. Which of the following must have owned that copy of the jazz record before New Year's Day, 1936?

(A) Javitz   (B) Kallers   (C) Luria
(D) Mapp   (E) Pugh

21. If Kallers owned that copy of the jazz record during 1933 and sold it to Luria on New Year's Day in 1934, Mapp must have bought it on New Year's Day in which of the following years?

(A) 1931   (B) 1932   (C) 1935
(D) 1936   (E) 1937

22. If Oster owned that copy of the jazz record during 1937, any one of the following could have owned it during 1935 EXCEPT

(A) Javitz   (B) Kallers   (C) Mapp
(D) Nakamura   (E) Pugh

GO ON TO THE NEXT PAGE.

229

23. A dog hears higher pitches than a human hears; a cat has a greater capacity to see in dim light than a human normally has; a platypus picks up weak electric signals to which a human is normally insensitive.

Which of the following conclusions can be properly drawn from the statements above?

(A) Most animals have sensory capacities superior to those demonstrated by humans.
(B) Some animals have sensory capacities that are different from those of humans.
(C) During evolution the eyes and ears of human beings were modified to make human sense perception less acute.
(D) Researchers should not be surprised to find that all the sensory capacities of platypuses are greater than any of those demonstrated by humans.
(E) Any human who can see in dim light does so less well than any cat.

24. In the early 1970's, when art reached its current high levels of popularity and value, a rash of thefts of works by great artists occurred in major art museums around the world. But, after 1975, sophisticated new security systems were installed in every major museum. As a consequence, important thefts in major museums declined markedly.

Which of the following, if true, is strongest if offered as part of the evidence to show that improved security systems were responsible for the decline in thefts of important works from major museums?

(A) The typical art work stolen during both the 1970's and the 1980's was a small piece that could be concealed on the person of the thief.
(B) Premiums paid by major museums to insure their most important works of art increased considerably between 1975 and 1985.
(C) The prices paid to art thieves for stolen works were lower during the 1980's than the prices paid to art thieves for comparable works during the 1970's.
(D) Thefts from private collections and smaller galleries of works by great artists increased sharply starting in the late 1970's.
(E) Art thefts in Europe, which has the largest number of works by great artists, outnumbered art thefts in the United States during the 1980's.

25. The government's recent policy of reducing payments to hospitals and physicians will, in the long run, actually cost the public more. Every dollar saved by initially providing lower-quality services eventually leads to several dollars spent in caring for subsequent complications.

Which of the following best serves as an assumption that would make the argument above logically correct?

(A) The government is more concerned about limiting its costs than about the well-being of its citizens.
(B) The government will be unwilling to pay for the complications that arise from providing inadequate health care.
(C) The government believes that the provision of lower-quality services need not result in an increase in complications.
(D) Hospitals and physicians will respond to reduced payments by reducing the quality of care they give.
(E) Hospitals and physicians are paid too much money for the services they provide to the public.

STOP

IF YOU FINISH BEFORE TIME IS CALLED, YOU MAY CHECK YOUR WORK ON THIS SECTION ONLY.
DO NOT TURN TO ANY OTHER SECTION IN THE TEST.

SECTION 5

Time — 30 minutes

30 Questions

Numbers: All numbers used are real numbers.

Figures: Position of points, angles, regions, etc. can be assumed to be in the order shown; and angle measures can be assumed to be positive.

Lines shown as straight can be assumed to be straight.

Figures can be assumed to lie in a plane unless otherwise indicated.

Figures that accompany questions are intended to provide information useful in answering the questions. However, unless a note states that a figure is drawn to scale, you should solve these problems NOT by estimating sizes by sight or by measurement, but by using your knowledge of mathematics (see Example 2 below).

Directions: Each of the Questions 1-15 consists of two quantities, one in Column A and one in Column B. You are to compare the two quantities and choose

        A if the quantity in Column A is greater;
        B if the quantity in Column B is greater;
        C if the two quantities are equal;
        D if the relationship cannot be determined from the information given.

Note: Since there are only four choices, NEVER MARK (E).

Common
Information: In a question, information concerning one or both of the quantities to be compared is centered above the two columns. A symbol that appears in both columns represents the same thing in Column A as it does in Column B.

Column A	Column B	Sample Answers

Example 1: 2×6 $2 + 6$ ● Ⓑ Ⓒ Ⓓ Ⓔ

Examples 2-4 refer to $\triangle PQR$.

Example 2: PN NQ Ⓐ Ⓑ Ⓒ ● Ⓔ

(since equal measures cannot be assumed, even though PN and NQ appear equal)

Example 3: x y Ⓐ ● Ⓒ Ⓓ Ⓔ

(since N is between P and Q)

Example 4: $w + z$ 180 Ⓐ Ⓑ ● Ⓓ Ⓔ

(since PQ is a straight line)

GO ON TO THE NEXT PAGE.

A　if the quantity in Column A is greater;
B　if the quantity in Column B is greater;
C　if the two quantities are equal;
D　if the relationship cannot be determined from the information given.

Column A	Column B
1.　$(7 \times 20) + (7 \times 4)$	$(7 \times 25) - 1$

$$\frac{4}{1.2} = \frac{n}{0.9}$$

Column A	Column B
2.　　n	3.7
3.　　$\frac{2}{3} + \frac{2}{3}$	$\left(\frac{2}{3}\right)\left(\frac{2}{3}\right)$

$$x = y$$
$$y = z$$

Column A	Column B
4.　　$x + 1$	$z - 1$

If checks of $455 and x dollars are deducted from a checking account that has a balance of $800, then $305 of the balance will be left.

Column A	Column B
5.　　x	45

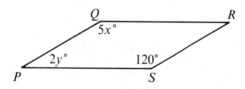

PQRS is a parallelogram.

Column A	Column B
6.　　x	y

$n > 0$

Column A	Column B
7.　　$\dfrac{n^2 + 2}{n}$	$n + \dfrac{1}{n}$　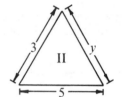

The perimeter of triangle I equals the perimeter of triangle II.

Column A	Column B
8.　　x	y
9.　The number of minutes in y weeks	The number of hours in $60y$ weeks

GO ON TO THE NEXT PAGE.

232

A   if the quantity in Column A is greater;
B   if the quantity in Column B is greater;
C   if the two quantities are equal;
D   if the relationship cannot be determined from the information given.

Column A	Column B

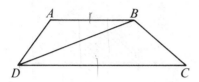

$AB \parallel DC$ and $DC > AB$.

10. $\dfrac{\text{Area of triangular region } ABD}{\text{Area of triangular region } DBC}$ $\dfrac{1}{2}$

11. The ratio of the circumference to the diameter of a circle that has radius 6   The ratio of the circumference to the diameter of a circle that has radius 6.5

12. 8^6 4^9

Column A	Column B

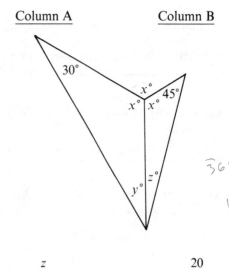

13. z 20

14. $\dfrac{x^m}{x^3}$ $x^{\frac{m}{3}}$

15. The greatest prime factor of $\left(2^4\right)^2 - 1$ 17

GO ON TO THE NEXT PAGE

Directions: Each of the Questions 16-30 has five answer choices. For each of these questions, select the best of the answer choices given.

16. A certain writer noted that, on the average, 3 pages of a manuscript were equivalent to 1 page of the published book. If the writer has a 302-page manuscript, about how many pages will the published book have?

    (A) 100   (B) 150   (C) 300   (D) 600   (E) 900

17. If $x - y = 0$, then xy must equal which of the following?

    (A) 0   (B) 1   (C) x (D) x^2 (E) x^2y

18. If $\dfrac{13}{-4} - \dfrac{7}{7} = n$, then n is

    (A) greater than 3
    (B) between 2 and 3
    (C) between 1 and 2
    (D) between 0 and 1
    (E) less than 0

19. In the repeating decimal 0.0157901579···, the 29th digit to the right of the decimal point is

    (A) 0   (B) 1   (C) 5   (D) 7   (E) 9

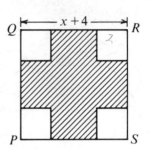

20. In the figure above, square $PQRS$ has side of length $x + 4$ and each of the four smaller squares has side of length 2. If the area of the shaded region is 48, what is the value of x?

    (A) 1   (B) 4   (C) $4\sqrt{2}$ (D) 8   (E) 12

GO ON TO THE NEXT PAGE.

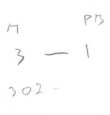

234

Questions 21-25 refer to the following table.

UNITED STATES POPULATION

(official census 1890-1980)

Year	Population (in millions)	10-year Increase (in millions)	Year	Population (in millions)	10-year Increase (in millions)
1890	62.9		1940	131.7	8.9
1900	76.0	13.1	1950	150.7	19.0
1910	92.0	16.0	1960	179.3	28.6
1920	105.7	13.7	1970	203.2	23.9
1930	122.8	17.1	1980	223.9	20.7

21. By how many million did the United States population increase from 1920 to 1950 ?

    (A) 5.3   (B) 19.0   (C) 45.0
    (D) 74.7   (E) 87.8

22. During which of the following 10-year intervals was the United States population increase the least in actual number?

    (A) 1890-1900
    (B) 1900-1910
    (C) 1920-1930
    (D) 1930-1940
    (E) 1940-1950

23. By approximately what percent did the population of the United States increase from 1900 to 1980 ?

    (A)   1.6%
    (B)   2.56%
    (C)   17%
    (D)   116%
    (E)   195%

24. In which of the following years will the United States population first reach 260 million?

    (A) 1990   (B) 1995   (C) 2000   (D) 2005

    (E) It cannot be determined from the information given.

25. If the percent increase in population from 1910 to 1920 had been approximately the same as the percent increase from 1900 to 1910, the 10-year increase, in millions, from 1910 to 1920, would have been approximately

    (A)   3
    (B)   6
    (C)   16
    (D)   19
    (E)   29

GO ON TO THE NEXT PAGE.

26. The Acme Rent-a-Car agency charges $10.00 per day and $0.10 per mile to rent a car. The Super Rent-a-Car agency charges $20.00 per day and $0.05 per mile to rent a car. If a car is rented for 1 day, at how many miles would the rental charges of the two agencies be equal?

(A)　50
(B)　100
(C)　150
(D)　175
(E)　200

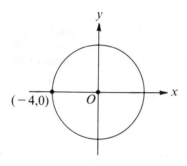

27. If O is the center of the circle above, what is the circumference of the circle?

(A) 4π　(B) 8π　(C) 16π　(D) 32π　(E) 64π

$$10 + 0.1x = 20 + 0.05x$$

$$0.05x = 10$$

$$\frac{10 \times 100}{5}$$

28. If $r = \frac{1}{3}(r + R)$, then what is r in terms of R?

(A) $\frac{1}{3}R$

(B) $\frac{1}{2}R$

(C) $R + 2$

(D) $2R$

(E) $3R$

$$3r = r + R$$
$$2r = R$$

29. If the average (arithmetic mean) of 5, 9, k, and m is 12, what is the average of $k + 7$ and $m - 3$?

(A)　14
(B)　17
(C)　19
(D)　21
(E)　38

30. The length of rectangular field X is 2 kilometers greater than the side of square field Y, and the width of field X is 2 kilometers less than the side of field Y. If y^2 is the area of field Y in square kilometers, which of the following gives the area, in square kilometers, of field X?

(A) $y^2 - 4$
(B) $y^2 - 2$
(C) y^2
(D) $y^2 + 2$
(E) $y^2 + 4$

$$\frac{k + 4 + m}{2} =$$

$$\frac{14 + k + m}{4} = 12$$
$$\quad 48$$
$$\quad \frac{14}{34}$$

STOP

IF YOU FINISH BEFORE TIME IS CALLED, YOU MAY CHECK YOUR WORK ON THIS SECTION ONLY.
DO NOT TURN TO ANY OTHER SECTION IN THE TEST.

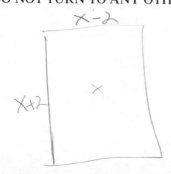

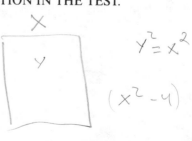

236

SECTION 7

Time—30 minutes

38 Questions

Directions: Each sentence below has one or two blanks, each blank indicating that something has been omitted. Beneath the sentence are five lettered words or sets of words. Choose the word or set of words for each blank that best fits the meaning of the sentence as a whole.

1. Though it would be ------- to expect Barnard to have worked out all of the limitations of his experiment, he must be ------- for his neglect of quantitative analysis.

   (A) unjust..pardoned
   (B) impudent..dismissed
   (C) unrealistic..criticized
   (D) pointless..examined
   (E) inexcusable..recognized

2. The hierarchy of medical occupations is in many ways a ------- system; its strata remain ------- and the practitioners in them have very little vertical mobility.

   (A) health..skilled
   (B) delivery..basic
   (C) regimental..flexible
   (D) training..inferior
   (E) caste..intact

3. Noting the murder victim's flaccid musculature and pearlike figure, she deduced that the unfortunate fellow had earned his living in some ------- occupation.

   (A) treacherous
   (B) prestigious
   (C) ill-paying
   (D) illegitimate
   (E) sedentary

4. In Germany her startling powers as a novelist are widely -------, but she is almost unknown in the English-speaking world because of the difficulties of ------- her eccentric prose.

   (A) ignored..editing
   (B) admired..translating
   (C) espoused..revealing
   (D) obscured..comprehending
   (E) dispersed..transcribing

5. Liberty is not easy, but far better to be an ------- fox, hungry and threatened on its hill, than a ------- canary, safe and secure in its cage.

   (A) unfriendly..fragile
   (B) aging..young
   (C) angry..content
   (D) imperious..lethargic
   (E) unfettered..well-fed

6. Remelting old metal cans rather than making primary aluminum from bauxite ore shipped from overseas saves producers millions of dollars in ------- and production costs.

   (A) distribution
   (B) salvage
   (C) storage
   (D) procurement
   (E) research

7. Johnson never ------- to ignore the standards of decent conduct mandated by company policy if ------- compliance with instructions from his superiors enabled him to do so, whatever the effects on his subordinates.

   (A) deigned..tacit
   (B) attempted..halfhearted
   (C) intended..direct
   (D) scrupled..literal
   (E) wished..feigned

GO ON TO THE NEXT PAGE.

237

Directions: In each of the following questions, a related pair of words or phrases is followed by five lettered pairs of words or phrases. Select the lettered pair that best expresses a relationship similar to that expressed in the original pair.

8. SHOULDER : ROADWAY ::
    (A) margin : page   (B) cord : weaving
    (C) socket : bulb   (D) curtain : scenery
    (E) handle : pitcher

9. TADPOLE : FROG ::   (A) worm : beetle
    (B) caterpillar : butterfly   (C) carrion : vulture
    (D) calf : horse   (E) drone : honeybee

10. CIRCUMFERENCE : CIRCLE ::
    (A) degree : angle
    (B) area : cube
    (C) perimeter : rectangle
    (D) height : cylinder
    (E) arc : ellipse

11. HEDONIST : PLEASURE ::
    (A) humanist : pride
    (B) ascetic : tolerance
    (C) stoic : sacrifice
    (D) recluse : privacy
    (E) idealist : compromise

12. NONCONFORMIST : NORM ::
    (A) pessimist : rule   (B) extremist : conviction
    (C) criminal : motive   (D) deviant : dogma
    (E) heretic : orthodoxy

13. INVEST : CAPITAL ::   (A) gamble : stake
    (B) tax : income   (C) play : sport
    (D) race : record   (E) create : product

14. PREEN : SELF-SATISFACTION ::
    (A) fume : anger
    (B) inhibit : spontaneity
    (C) regret : guilt
    (D) resent : cooperation
    (E) brood : resolution

15. DIGRESSIVE : STATEMENT ::
    (A) connotative : definition
    (B) slanderous : slur
    (C) tangential : presupposition
    (D) biased : opinion
    (E) circuitous : route

16. CHICANERY : CLEVER ::
    (A) expertise : knowledgeable
    (B) certainty : doubtful
    (C) gullibility : skeptical
    (D) machination : heedless
    (E) tactlessness : truthful

GO ON TO THE NEXT PAGE.

Directions: Each passage in this group is followed by questions based on its content. After reading a passage, choose the best answer to each question. Answer all questions following a passage on the basis of what is <u>stated</u> or <u>implied</u> in that passage.

The social sciences are less likely than other intellectual enterprises to get credit for their accomplishments. Arguably, this is so because the theories and conceptual constructs of the social sciences are especially accessible: human intelligence apprehends truths about human affairs with particular facility. And the discoveries of the social sciences, once isolated and labeled, are quickly absorbed into conventional wisdom, whereupon they lose their distinctiveness as scientific advances.

Line
(5)

(10)
This underappreciation of the social sciences contrasts oddly with what many see as their overutilization. Game theory is pressed into service in studies of shifting international alliances. Evaluation research is called upon to demonstrate successes or failures of social programs. Models from economics and demography become the definitive tools for examining the financial base of social security. Yet this rush into practical applications is itself quite understandable: public policy must continually be made, and policymakers rightly feel that even tentative findings and untested theories are better guides to decision-making than no findings and no theories at all.

(15)

(20)

17. The author is primarily concerned with

(A) advocating a more modest view, and less widespread utilization, of the social sciences
(B) analyzing the mechanisms for translating discoveries into applications in the social sciences
(C) dissolving the air of paradox inherent in human beings studying themselves
(D) explaining a peculiar dilemma that the social sciences are in
(E) maintaining a strict separation between pure and applied social science

18. Which of the following is a social science discipline that the author mentions as being possibly overutilized?

(A) Conventional theories of social change
(B) Game theory
(C) Decision-making theory
(D) Economic theories of international alliances
(E) Systems analysis

19. It can be inferred from the passage that, when speaking of the "overutilization" (line 11) of the social sciences, the author is referring to the

(A) premature practical application of social science advances
(B) habitual reliance on the social sciences even where common sense would serve equally well
(C) practice of bringing a greater variety of social science disciplines to bear on a problem than the nature of the problem warrants
(D) use of social science constructs by people who do not fully understand them
(E) tendency on the part of social scientists to recast everyday truths in social science jargon

20. The author confronts the claim that the social sciences are being overutilized with

(A) proof that overextensions of social science results are self-correcting
(B) evidence that some public policy is made without any recourse to social science findings or theories
(C) a long list of social science applications that are perfectly appropriate and extremely fruitful
(D) the argument that overutilization is by and large the exception rather than the rule
(E) the observation that this practice represents the lesser of two evils under existing circumstances

GO ON TO THE NEXT PAGE.

The term "Ice Age" may give a wrong impression. The epoch that geologists know as the Pleistocene and that spanned the 1.5 to 2.0 million years prior to the current geologic epoch was not one long continuous
(5) glaciation, but a period of oscillating climate with ice advances punctuated by times of interglacial climate not very different from the climate experienced now. Ice sheets that derived from an ice cap centered on northern Scandinavia reached southward to Central Europe. And
(10) beyond the margins of the ice sheets, climatic oscillations affected most of the rest of the world; for example, in the deserts, periods of wetter conditions (pluvials) contrasted with drier, interpluvial periods. Although the time involved is so short, about 0.04 percent of the total
(15) age of the Earth, the amount of attention devoted to the Pleistocene has been incredibly large, probably because of its immediacy, and because the epoch largely coincides with the appearance on Earth of humans and their immediate ancestors.

(20) There is no reliable way of dating much of the Ice Age. Geological dates are usually obtained by using the rates of decay of various radioactive elements found in minerals. Some of these rates are suitable for very old rocks but involve increasing errors when used for young
(25) rocks; others are suitable for very young rocks and errors increase rapidly in older rocks. Most of the Ice Age spans a period of time for which no element has an appropriate decay rate.

Nevertheless, researchers of the Pleistocene epoch
(30) have developed all sorts of more or less fanciful model schemes of how they would have arranged the Ice Age had they been in charge of events. For example, an early classification of Alpine glaciation suggested the existence there of four glaciations, named the Günz, Mindel, Riss,
(35) and Würm. This succession was based primarily on a series of deposits and events not directly related to glacial and interglacial periods, rather than on the more usual modern method of studying biological remains found in interglacial beds themselves interstratified
(40) within glacial deposits. Yet this succession was forced willy-nilly onto the glaciated parts of Northern Europe, where there are partial successions of true glacial ground moraines and interglacial deposits, with hopes of ultimately piecing them together to provide a complete
(45) Pleistocene succession. Eradication of the Alpine nomenclature is still proving a Herculean task.

There is no conclusive evidence about the relative length, complexity, and temperatures of the various glacial and interglacial periods. We do not know
(50) whether we live in a postglacial period or an interglacial period. The chill truth seems to be that we are already past the optimum climate of postglacial time. Studies of certain fossil distributions and of the pollen of certain temperate plants suggest decreases of a degree or two in
(55) both summer and winter temperatures and, therefore, that we may be in the declining climatic phase leading to glaciation and extinction.

21. In the passage, the author is primarily concerned with

(A) searching for an accurate method of dating the Pleistocene epoch
(B) discussing problems involved in providing an accurate picture of the Pleistocene epoch
(C) declaring opposition to the use of the term "Ice Age" for the Pleistocene epoch
(D) criticizing fanciful schemes about what happened in the Pleistocene epoch
(E) refuting the idea that there is no way to tell if we are now living in an Ice Age

22. The "wrong impression" (line 1) to which the author refers is the idea that the

(A) climate of the Pleistocene epoch was not very different from the climate we are now experiencing
(B) climate of the Pleistocene epoch was composed of periods of violent storms
(C) Pleistocene epoch consisted of very wet, cold periods mixed with very dry, hot periods
(D) Pleistocene epoch comprised one period of continuous glaciation during which Northern Europe was covered with ice sheets
(E) Pleistocene epoch had no long periods during which much of the Earth was covered by ice

GO ON TO THE NEXT PAGE.

23. According to the passage, one of the reasons for the deficiencies of the "early classification of Alpine glaciation" (lines 32-33) is that it was

(A) derived from evidence that was only tangentially related to times of actual glaciation
(B) based primarily on fossil remains rather than on actual living organisms
(C) an abstract, imaginative scheme of how the period might have been structured
(D) based on unmethodical examinations of randomly chosen glacial biological remains
(E) derived from evidence that had been haphazardly gathered from glacial deposits and inaccurately evaluated

24. Which of the following does the passage imply about the "early classification of Alpine glaciation" (lines 32-33)?

(A) It should not have been applied as widely as it was.
(B) It represents the best possible scientific practice, given the tools available at the time.
(C) It was a valuable tool, in its time, for measuring the length of the four periods of glaciation.
(D) It could be useful, but only as a general guide to the events of the Pleistocene epoch.
(E) It does not shed any light on the methods used at the time for investigating periods of glaciation.

25. It can be inferred from the passage that an important result of producing an accurate chronology of events of the Pleistocene epoch would be a

(A) clearer idea of the origin of the Earth
(B) clearer picture of the Earth during the time that humans developed
(C) clearer understanding of the reasons for the existence of deserts
(D) more detailed understanding of how radioactive dating of minerals works
(E) firmer understanding of how the northern polar ice cap developed

26. The author refers to deserts primarily in order to

(A) illustrate the idea that an interglacial climate is marked by oscillations of wet and dry periods
(B) illustrate the idea that what happened in the deserts during the Ice Age had far-reaching effects even on the ice sheets of Central and Northern Europe
(C) illustrate the idea that the effects of the Ice Age's climatic variations extended beyond the areas of ice
(D) support the view that during the Ice Age sheets of ice covered some of the deserts of the world
(E) support the view that we are probably living in a postglacial period

27. The author would regard the idea that we are living in an interglacial period as

(A) unimportant
(B) unscientific
(C) self-evident
(D) plausible
(E) absurd

GO ON TO THE NEXT PAGE.

241

Directions: Each question below consists of a word printed in capital letters, followed by five lettered words or phrases. Choose the lettered word or phrase that is most nearly opposite in meaning to the word in capital letters.

Since some of the questions require you to distinguish fine shades of meaning, be sure to consider all the choices before deciding which one is best.

28. INSTINCT: (A) hallucination (B) reservation (C) irrational fear (D) learned response (E) unobtainable desire

29. SENSATION:
(A) sketchy account
(B) recurring phenomenon
(C) unfinished story
(D) unnoticed event
(E) well-received effort

30. TRANQUILLITY: (A) leniency (B) virtue (C) pandemonium (D) morbidity (E) eclecticism

31. PLASTICITY: (A) purity (B) solidity (C) rigidity (D) sternness (E) massiveness

32. RIFT: (A) bondage (B) capitulation (C) fidelity (D) consistency (E) reconciliation

33. DESICCATE: (A) lactate (B) hydrate (C) make appetizing (D) allow to putrify (E) start to accelerate

34. ERUDITION: (A) boorishness (B) prescience (C) ignorance (D) wealth (E) simplicity

35. AFFABLE: (A) sentimental (B) disobedient (C) irascible (D) equivocal (E) underhanded

36. APOCRYPHAL: (A) authenticated (B) annotated (C) famous (D) restored (E) sophisticated

37. RECALCITRANT: (A) trustworthy (B) expectant (C) extravagant (D) capable (E) amenable

38. HALCYON: (A) future (B) healthy (C) inane (D) extraordinary (E) miserable

STOP

IF YOU FINISH BEFORE TIME IS CALLED, YOU MAY CHECK YOUR WORK ON THIS SECTION ONLY.
DO NOT TURN TO ANY OTHER SECTION IN THE TEST.

NO TEST MATERIAL ON THIS PAGE

NO TEST MATERIAL ON THIS PAGE

THE GRADUATE RECORD EXAMINATIONS
GENERAL TEST

You will have 3 hours and 30 minutes in which to work on this test, which consists of seven sections. During the time allowed for one section, you may work only on that section. The time allowed for each section is 30 minutes.

Each of your scores will be determined by the number of questions for which you select the best answer from the choices given. Questions for which you mark no answer or more than one answer are not counted in scoring. Nothing is subtracted from a score if you answer a question incorrectly. Therefore, to maximize your scores, it is better for you to guess at an answer than not to respond at all.

You are advised to work as rapidly as you can without losing accuracy. Do not spend too much time on questions that are too difficult for you. Go on to the other questions and come back to the difficult ones later.

There are several different types of questions; you will find special directions for each type in the test itself. Be sure you understand the directions before attempting to answer any questions.

For each question several answer choices (lettered A-E or A-D) are given from which you are to select the ONE best answer. YOU MUST INDICATE ALL YOUR ANSWERS ON THE SEPARATE ANSWER SHEET. No credit will be given for anything written in this examination book, but to work out your answers you may write in the book as much as you wish. After you have decided which of the suggested answers is best, fill in completely the corresponding space on the answer sheet. Be sure to:

- Use a soft black lead pencil (No. 2 or HB).

- Mark only one answer to each question. No credit will be given for multiple answers.

- Mark your answer in the row with the same number as the number of the question you are answering.

- Carefully and completely fill in the space corresponding to the answer you select for each question. Fill the space with a dark mark so that you cannot see the letter inside the space. Light or partial marks may not be read by the scoring machine. See the example of proper and improper answer marks below.

- Erase all stray marks. If you change an answer, be sure that you completely erase the old answer before marking your new answer. Incomplete erasures may be read as intended answers.

Example:

What city is the capital of France?

(A) Rome
(B) Paris
(C) London
(D) Cairo
(E) Oslo

Sample Answer

Ⓐ ● Ⓒ Ⓓ Ⓔ   **BEST ANSWER PROPERLY MARKED**

Ⓐ Ⓧ Ⓒ Ⓓ Ⓔ
Ⓐ Ⓑ Ⓒ Ⓓ Ⓔ
Ⓐ Ⓑ Ⓒ Ⓓ Ⓔ   **IMPROPER MARKS**
Ⓐ Ⓑ Ⓒ Ⓓ Ⓔ

Do not be concerned that the answer sheet provides spaces for more answers than there are questions in the test. Some or all of the passages for this test have been adapted from published material to provide the examinee with significant problems for analysis and evaluation. To make the passages suitable for testing purposes, the style, content, or point of view of the original may have been altered in some cases. The ideas contained in the passages do not necessarily represent the opinions of the Graduate Record Examinations Board or Educational Testing Service.

CLOSE YOUR TEST BOOK AND WAIT FOR FURTHER INSTRUCTIONS FROM THE SUPERVISOR.

I

NOTE: To ensure the prompt and accurate processing of test results, your cooperation in following these directions is needed. The procedures that follow have been kept to the minimum necessary. They will take a few minutes to complete, but it is essential that you fill in all blanks <u>exactly</u> as directed.

GENERAL TEST

A. Print and sign your full name in this box:

PRINT: _____
         (LAST)   (FIRST)   (MIDDLE)

SIGN: _____

B. Side 1 of your answer sheet contains areas that will be used to ensure accurate reporting of your test results. It is essential that you carefully enter the requested information.

[1] through [5] YOUR NAME, DATE OF BIRTH, SOCIAL SECURITY NUMBER, REGISTRATION NUMBER, and ADDRESS: <u>Print</u> all the information requested in the boxes and then fill in completely the appropriate oval beneath each entry.

- For date of birth, be sure to enter a zero before a single digit (e.g., if you were born on the third day of the month, you would enter "03" for the day). Use the last two digits of the year of your birth (for 1966, enter 66).

- Copy the registration number from your admission ticket.

[6] TITLE CODE: Copy the numbers shown below and fill in completely the appropriate spaces beneath each entry as shown. When you have completed item 6, check to be sure it is identical to the illustration below.

[7] TEST NAME: Copy   *General*   in the box.

FORM CODE: Copy   *GR 90 – 14*   in the box.

[8] TEST BOOK SERIAL NUMBER: Copy the serial number of your test book in the box. It is printed in red at the upper right on the front cover of your test book.

[9] <u>Print</u> the requested information and enter the test center number in the boxes.

[10] CERTIFICATION STATEMENT: In the boxed area, <u>WRITE</u> (do not print) the following statement: "I certify that I am the person whose name appears on this answer sheet. I also agree not to disclose the contents of the test I am taking today to anyone." Sign and date where indicated.

When you have finished, wait for further instructions from the supervisor. DO NOT OPEN YOUR TEST BOOK UNTIL YOU ARE TOLD TO DO SO.

Answer Key and Percentages* of Examinees Answering Each Question Correctly

VERBAL ABILITY

Section 1			Section 7		
Number	Answer	P+	Number	Answer	P+
1	A	97	1	C	88
2	C	83	2	E	84
3	A	74	3	E	76
4	E	51	4	B	95
5	A	43	5	E	58
6	B	41	6	D	67
7	D	26	7	D	9
8	E	92	8	A	92
9	C	80	9	B	89
10	D	50	10	C	83
11	D	56	11	D	62
12	A	33	12	E	55
13	C	43	13	A	48
14	A	41	14	A	43
15	D	28	15	E	34
16	E	20	16	E	21
17	C	83	17	D	68
18	D	65	18	B	77
19	B	81	19	A	39
20	C	64	20	E	53
21	B	76	21	B	67
22	A	56	22	D	31
23	D	68	23	A	37
24	D	39	24	A	44
25	B	66	25	B	59
26	E	74	26	C	44
27	A	60	27	D	70
28	A	88	28	D	86
29	B	84	29	D	80
30	B	72	30	C	85
31	D	57	31	C	66
32	D	50	32	E	49
33	A	42	33	B	54
34	B	34	34	C	42
35	A	39	35	C	46
36	B	32	36	A	39
37	B	37	37	E	37
38	D	28	38	E	26

QUANTITATIVE ABILITY

Section 2			Section 5		
Number	Answer	P+	Number	Answer	P+
1	A	90	1	B	86
2	B	91	2	B	83
3	A	79	3	A	87
4	C	85	4	A	80
5	D	74	5	B	82
6	C	83	6	B	63
7	A	80	7	A	81
8	B	65	8	A	67
9	B	79	9	C	66
10	A	69	10	D	70
11	A	57	11	C	49
12	D	59	12	C	35
13	B	54	13	B	49
14	D	25	14	D	41
15	C	16	15	C	26
16	D	79	16	A	95
17	D	79	17	D	69
18	B	74	18	B	80
19	A	84	19	D	87
20	E	72	20	B	60
21	B	91	21	C	91
22	D	65	22	D	74
23	C	71	23	E	62
24	E	61	24	E	71
25	A	44	25	D	33
26	C	53	26	E	60
27	A	56	27	B	60
28	A	52	28	B	52
29	D	52	29	C	48
30	B	49	30	A	45

ANALYTICAL ABILITY

Section 3			Section 4		
Number	Answer	P+	Number	Answer	P+
1	B	87	1	E	88
2	E	89	2	E	83
3	C	81	3	D	51
4	E	60	4	B	77
5	C	74	5	C	80
6	E	29	6	C	82
7	D	87	7	E	92
8	B	75	8	C	90
9	B	56	9	B	74
10	A	92	10	A	57
11	D	80	11	B	54
12	B	81	12	E	61
13	A	69	13	A	92
14	C	65	14	A	33
15	E	75	15	D	15
16	A	58	16	D	55
17	E	34	17	C	76
18	C	61	18	A	67
19	C	41	19	C	62
20	D	33	20	A	41
21	E	31	21	E	45
22	E	28	22	E	34
23	A	65	23	B	62
24	C	53	24	D	45
25	C	38	25	D	45

*Estimated P+ for the group of examinees who took the GRE General Test in a recent three-year period.

SCORE CONVERSIONS AND PERCENTS BELOW*
FOR GRE GENERAL TEST, Form GR90-14 ONLY

Raw Score	Scaled Scores and Percents Below						Raw Score	Scaled Scores and Percents Below					
	Verbal Score	% Below	Quantitative Score	% Below	Analytical Score	% Below		Verbal Score	% Below	Quantitative Score	% Below	Analytical Score	% Below
73-76	800	99					39	440	38	550	48	640	79
72	790	99					38	430	36	540	45	630	76
71	770	99					37	420	33	530	42	610	72
70	760	99					36	410	30	520	40	600	69
69	750	98					35	400	26	510	37	590	67
68	730	97					34	390	24	500	35	570	61
67	720	96					33	390	24	490	32	560	58
66	710	95					32	380	22	470	28	540	52
65	700	95					31	370	20	460	26	530	49
64	680	93					30	360	16	450	24	510	43
63	670	92					29	350	14	440	22	500	40
62	660	90					28	350	14	430	20	480	35
61	650	89					27	340	12	420	18	470	32
60	640	87	800	97			26	330	10	410	16	450	27
59	630	85	800	97			25	320	9	400	14	440	24
58	620	84	800	97			24	310	7	380	12	420	20
57	600	80	780	94			23	310	7	370	10	410	18
56	590	78	760	92			22	300	6	360	9	390	15
55	580	76	750	89			21	290	5	350	7	380	13
54	570	74	730	86			20	280	4	340	6	360	10
53	560	72	720	84			19	270	3	320	5	350	9
52	550	69	700	80			18	260	2	310	4	340	7
51	540	67	690	78			17	250	1	300	3	320	6
	530	64	670	74	800	99	16	240	1	290	2	310	4
	530	64	660	72	800	99	15	230	1	270	2	300	4
	520	61	650	70	800	99	14	220	0	260	1	290	3
	510	59	640	68	770	97	13	210	0	240	1	280	2
	500	56	620	63	750	96	12	200	0	230	0	270	2
	490	54	610	61	730	94	11	200	0	210	0	250	1
44	480	51	600	59	720	92	10	200	0	200	0	240	1
43	470	48	590	57	700	90	9	200	0	200	0	230	1
42	460	44	580	54	690	88	8	200	0	200	0	220	0
41	450	41	570	51	670	85	7	200	0	200	0	210	0
40	440	38	560	49	660	83	0-6	200	0	200	0	200	0

*Percent scoring below the scaled score is based on the performance of 923,359 examinees who took the General Test between October 1, 1986, and September 30, 1989.

01

THE GRADUATE RECORD EXAMINATIONS

General Test

*Do not break the seal
until you are told to do so.*

*The contents of this test are confidential.
Disclosure or reproduction of any portion
of it is prohibited.*

THIS TEST BOOK MUST NOT BE TAKEN FROM THE ROOM.

SECTION 1

Time—30 minutes

25 Questions

Directions: Each question or group of questions is based on a passage or set of conditions. In answering some of the questions, it may be useful to draw a rough diagram. For each question, select the best answer choice given.

Questions 1-6

A personnel officer is scheduling a single interview with each of seven individuals: Fay, Gary, Julio, Mary, Nicholas, Pilar, and Teresa. Each interview is to be 30 minutes in length, and the interviews are to be scheduled back-to-back, starting at 9 a.m., according to the following conditions:

Gary's interview must be scheduled to begin at either 9 a.m. or 10:30 a.m.
Pilar's interview must be scheduled either as the next interview after Gary's interview or as the next interview after Nicholas' interview.
Nicholas' interview must be scheduled to occur sometime after Mary's interview and sometime before Fay's interview.
Julio's interview must be scheduled to begin exactly one hour after Teresa's interview is scheduled to begin.

1. Which of the following is an acceptable schedule for the seven people?

	9 a.m.	9:30 a.m.	10 a.m.	10:30 a.m.	11 a.m.	11:30 a.m.	12 noon
(A)	Gary	Nicholas	Pilar	Mary	Teresa	Fay	Julio
(B)	Gary	Pilar	Teresa	Mary	Julio	Nicholas	Fay
(C)	Mary	Gary	Pilar	Teresa	Nicholas	Julio	Fay
(D)	Mary	Teresa	Julio	Gary	Nicholas	Pilar	Fay
(E)	Teresa	Pilar	Julio	Gary	Mary	Nicholas	Fay

2. Which of the following people can be scheduled for the interview that begins at 9 a.m.?

(A) Fay
(B) Julio
(C) Mary
(D) Nicholas
(E) Pilar

3. The earliest time that Julio's interview can be scheduled to begin is

(A) 9:30 a.m.
(B) 10 a.m.
(C) 10:30 a.m.
(D) 11 a.m.
(E) 11:30 a.m.

4. If Nicholas' interview is scheduled to begin at 9:30 a.m., who must be scheduled for the interview that begins at 11 a.m.?

(A) Fay
(B) Julio
(C) Mary
(D) Pilar
(E) Teresa

5. If the interview schedule shows Teresa's interview as the next after Pilar's and Pilar's interview as the next after Nicholas', how long after Gary's interview is scheduled to begin must Julio's interview be scheduled to begin?

(A) 30 minutes
(B) 1 hour
(C) 90 minutes
(D) 2 hours
(E) 3 hours

6. If Teresa is scheduled for the interview that begins at 9 a.m., Fay's interview must be scheduled to begin at

(A) 9:30 a.m.
(B) 10:30 a.m.
(C) 11 a.m.
(D) 11:30 a.m.
(E) 12 noon

GO ON TO THE NEXT PAGE.

7. Wearing either a lap seat belt or a shoulder-and-lap seat belt protects passengers from the major types of injuries incurred in head-on automobile collisions. In such collisions, however, passengers wearing lap seat belts alone frequently suffer internal injuries caused by the seat belt itself. Such injuries do not occur when shoulder-and-lap seat belts are worn.

Which of the following conclusions about passengers involved in head-on automobile collisions is best supported by the statements above?

(A) No type of seat belt provides passengers with adequate protection from injury.
(B) The injuries that passengers most frequently incur are internal injuries.
(C) Head-on automobile collisions cause more injuries to passengers than any other kind of automobile accident does.
(D) It is safer for passengers to wear a shoulder-and-lap seat belt than to wear a lap seat belt alone.
(E) It is safer for passengers to wear no seat belt than to wear a lap seat belt alone.

8. Nonprescription sunglasses shield the wearer's eyes from damaging ultraviolet sunlight. Squinting, however, provides protection from ultraviolet rays that is at least as good as the protection from nonprescription sunglasses. There is, therefore, no health advantage to be gained by wearing nonprescription sunglasses rather than squinting.

Which of the following, if true, most seriously weakens support for the conclusion above?

(A) Many opticians offer prescription sunglasses that not only screen out ultraviolet sunlight but also provide corrective vision.
(B) Some nonprescription sunglasses provide less protection from ultraviolet sunlight than does squinting.
(C) Squinting strains facial muscles and causes headaches and fatigue.
(D) Many people buy sunglasses because they feel that sunglasses are fashionable.
(E) Some people squint even when they are wearing sunglasses.

9. Studies of workplace safety in construction and manufacturing firms have found that the rate of injuries tends to rise when the firms' work loads increase. Since inexperienced workers are often hired by these firms when work loads increase, the higher rate of injuries is undoubtedly due to a higher accident rate for inexperienced workers.

Which of the following statements, if true, would most weaken the conclusion drawn above?

(A) Many of the inexperienced workers hired when the firms' work loads increase are hired only for temporary positions.
(B) The studies of workplace safety were focused only on injuries that resulted in lost work-days.
(C) There is a much higher rate of injury in construction firms than in manufacturing firms.
(D) The accident rate for experienced workers tends to increase whenever the firms' work loads increase.
(E) Firms that hire inexperienced workers for potentially dangerous jobs are required to provide them with training.

GO ON TO THE NEXT PAGE.

Questions 10-14

A researcher is experimenting with varying arrangements of exactly six units that are electrical conductors—G, J, K, M, P, and S—in a loop containing eight positions, each capable of containing one conductor. In each arrangement, each conductor is at one of the eight positions and two positions are empty. In devising arrangements, the researcher must obey the following restrictions:

G must be directly adjacent to J.
P must be directly adjacent to S.
M must be directly adjacent to S on one side and to an empty position on the other.

A signal can be transferred from one conductor directly to another when the two conductors are directly adjacent to each other, and only then. A signal can be transferred either way around the loop, from one conductor to another, until it reaches an empty position. A signal cannot be transferred across an empty position.

10. If a signal can be transferred, either directly or indirectly, from J to K, it must be true that a signal can be transferred, either directly or indirectly, from

(A) G to K
(B) G to M
(C) J to M
(D) J to P
(E) J to S

11. If K is directly adjacent to P, any of the following could be true EXCEPT:

(A) G is directly adjacent to K.
(B) J is directly adjacent to K.
(C) J is directly adjacent to P.
(D) G is directly adjacent to an empty position.
(E) J is directly adjacent to an empty position.

12. If P is directly adjacent to an empty position, which of the following is the greatest number of conductors, including starting and ending conductors, that can be used in the transfer of a single signal?

(A) Two
(B) Three
(C) Four
(D) Five
(E) Six

13. If there is one conductor that is directly adjacent to both of the empty positions, that conductor must be

(A) J
(B) K
(C) M
(D) P
(E) S

14. If a signal can be transferred from G to S, any of the following conductors could be directly adjacent to an empty position EXCEPT

(A) G
(B) J
(C) K
(D) M
(E) P

GO ON TO THE NEXT PAGE.

252

Questions 15-18

Researchers know that exactly six prehistoric iron-working sites—Q, R, S, T, V, and X—existed in the Windham area. Recently, the researchers have discovered three objects—1, 2, and 3—that they know must have been made by ironworkers in the Windham area. The researchers would like now to determine the specific site at which each object was made. The objects are different enough in composition and style to leave no doubt that each was made at a different site. In addition, the researchers have established the following:

If any of the objects was made at Q, none of them was made at T.
If any of the objects was made at R, none of them was made at S.
One of the objects was made at V.
Object 2 was not made at X.
Object 3 was made neither at S nor at X.

15. If Object 1 was made at T, Object 3 could have been made at which of the following?

(A) Q
(B) R
(C) S
(D) T
(E) X

16. Object 1, Object 2, and Object 3, respectively, could have been made at

(A) Q, S, and X
(B) R, X, and V
(C) T, V, and S
(D) V, Q, and T
(E) V, S, and Q

17. If neither Q nor T was a site at which any of the objects was made, which of the following must be true?

(A) Object 1 was made at X.
(B) Object 2 was made at S.
(C) Object 2 was made at V.
(D) Object 3 was made at R.
(E) Object 3 was made at V.

18. The researchers could determine exactly which object was made at which site if they knew that the only three sites at which objects were made were

(A) Q, R, and V
(B) Q, V, and X
(C) R, T, and V
(D) S, T, and V
(E) S, V, and X

GO ON TO THE NEXT PAGE.

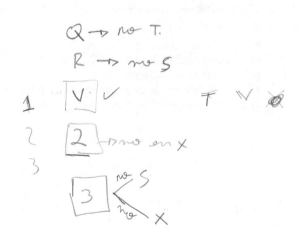

253

Questions 19-22

Seven children—Frank, Joan, Kate, Manuel, Rose, Sam, and Theresa—are eligible to enter a spelling contest. From these seven, two teams must be formed, a red team and a green team, each team consisting of exactly three of the children. No child can be selected for more than one team. Team selection is subject to the following restrictions:

> If Manuel is on the red team, Kate must be selected for the green team.
> If Frank is on the red team, Rose, if selected, must be on the green team.
> Rose cannot be on the same team as Sam.
> Joan cannot be on the same team as Kate.

19. Which of the following can be the three members of the red team?

    (A) Frank, Joan, and Kate
    (B) Frank, Rose, and Theresa
    (C) Joan, Kate, and Theresa
    (D) Kate, Manuel, and Rose
    (E) Manuel, Rose, and Theresa

20. If Manuel and Frank are both on the red team, the green team can consist of which of the following?

    (A) Joan, Kate, and Rose
    (B) Joan, Sam, and Theresa
    (C) Kate, Rose, and Sam
    (D) Kate, Rose, and Theresa
    (E) Rose, Sam, and Theresa

21. If Manuel is on the red team, which of the following, if selected, must also be on the red team?

    (A) Frank
    (B) Joan
    (C) Rose
    (D) Sam
    (E) Theresa

22. If Frank is selected for the red team and Theresa is not selected for either team, then which of the following CANNOT be a member of the green team?

    (A) Joan
    (B) Kate
    (C) Manuel
    (D) Rose
    (E) Sam

GO ON TO THE NEXT PAGE.

254

Questions 23-24

The facts show that the fear of flying in airplanes is not rational. In 1986 alone, there were 46,000 fatalities in highway accidents, but from 1980 to the present an average of only 77 per year in accidents on major domestic airlines. The rate for regional airlines was only slightly higher.

23. If the evidence cited above is accurate, which of the following would be most important to know in order to evaluate the force of that evidence?

    (A) Whether repeated airplane travel allays fear of flying in airplanes
    (B) Whether regional and domestic airlines spend the same average amount of time per aircraft on maintenance
    (C) How many people reported a fear of flying in airplanes that was strong enough to prevent them from traveling by air
    (D) How many people per year have traveled by highway and how many by air since 1980
    (E) How much higher the accident rate has been for regional airlines than for major domestic airlines since 1980

24. Which of the following, if true, would argue most strongly against the conclusion above?

    (A) Since the inventory of spare parts kept at each airport is smaller than in earlier years, planes are often delayed at an airport while parts are flown in from another airport, and then repairs are carefully made and checked.
    (B) Air fatalities from 1980 to the present have been concentrated in the last two years, with the rate rising sharply.
    (C) The number of reports of near collisions in midair in 1986 was less than half those in a typical year of the 1960's, even with double the traffic of the 1960's.
    (D) Many reported near collisions in midair are closer than regulations allow but are nevertheless without actual danger.
    (E) Between 1980 and 1986, safety improvements in the design of automobiles steadily improved their crashworthiness.

25. In 1985 a consumer agency concluded that Xylo brand bicycles are safer to ride than are Zenon brand bicycles. The agency based the conclusion on the ratio of the number of rider injuries to the number of riding hours for each brand of bicycle from 1981 through 1984. Yet for identically designed bicycles manufactured since 1985, the number of rider injuries has been twice as great among riders of Xylos as among riders of Zenons. Therefore, the agency's conclusion would have been different for the period since 1985.

Which of the following is an assumption that, if true, supports the claim that the agency's conclusion would have been different for the period since 1985 ?

    (A) For the period since 1985, the number of riding hours for Zenons totaled at least half the number of riding hours for Xylos.
    (B) Of all the bicycles ridden in the period since 1985, the percentage of Xylos ridden was twice the percentage of Zenons ridden.
    (C) Prior to 1985, Zenon owners were more likely than Xylo owners to report the injuries they sustained while riding their bicycles.
    (D) In 1985 the agency had miscalculated the ratio for Xylos, for Zenons, or for both.
    (E) Soon after the agency had issued its report, consumer demand for Xylos increased more rapidly than did consumer demand for Zenons.

STOP

**IF YOU FINISH BEFORE TIME IS CALLED, YOU MAY CHECK YOUR WORK ON THIS SECTION ONLY.
DO NOT TURN TO ANY OTHER SECTION IN THE TEST.**

SECTION 2
Time—30 minutes
30 Questions

Numbers: All numbers used are real numbers.

Figures: Position of points, angles, regions, etc. can be assumed to be in the order shown; and angle measures can be assumed to be positive.

Lines shown as straight can be assumed to be straight.

Figures can be assumed to lie in a plane unless otherwise indicated.

Figures that accompany questions are intended to provide information useful in answering the questions. However, unless a note states that a figure is drawn to scale, you should solve these problems NOT by estimating sizes by sight or by measurement, but by using your knowledge of mathematics (see Example 2 below).

Directions: Each of the Questions 1-15 consists of two quantities, one in Column A and one in Column B. You are to compare the two quantities and choose

    A if the quantity in Column A is greater;
    B if the quantity in Column B is greater;
    C if the two quantities are equal;
    D if the relationship cannot be determined from the information given.

Note: Since there are only four choices, NEVER MARK (E).

Common
Information: In a question, information concerning one or both of the quantities to be compared is centered above the two columns. A symbol that appears in both columns represents the same thing in Column A as it does in Column B.

	Column A	Column B	Sample Answers
Example 1:	2×6	$2 + 6$	● Ⓑ Ⓒ Ⓓ Ⓔ

Examples 2-4 refer to △ PQR.

	Column A	Column B	Sample Answers
Example 2:	PN	NQ	Ⓐ Ⓑ Ⓒ ● Ⓔ

(since equal measures cannot be assumed, even though PN and NQ appear equal)

	Column A	Column B	Sample Answers
Example 3:	x	y	Ⓐ ● Ⓒ Ⓓ Ⓔ

(since N is between P and Q)

	Column A	Column B	Sample Answers
Example 4:	$w + z$	180	Ⓐ Ⓑ ● Ⓓ Ⓔ

(since PQ is a straight line)

GO ON TO THE NEXT PAGE.

A if the quantity in Column A is greater;
B if the quantity in Column B is greater;
C if the two quantities are equal;
D if the relationship cannot be determined from the information given.

	Column A	Column B
1.	$10.0 + 0.9$	$9(1.0 + 0.09)$

$$r = 30$$
$$r + R = 59$$

	Column A	Column B
2.	r^2	R^2

$$\frac{4}{9} = \frac{7 \times 4}{N \times 9}$$

	Column A	Column B
3.	N	9
4.	$\frac{2}{3} + \frac{1}{2} + \frac{7}{8}$	$\frac{3}{2}$

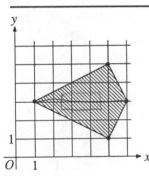

Figure 1   Figure 2

Note: Drawn to scale.

5. The area of the shaded region shown in Figure 1 | The area of the shaded region shown in Figure 2

$$\frac{16 + 12 + 21}{24} = \frac{49}{24}$$

21
12
16

49

Column A | **Column B**

Let the "drop" of a square be defined as the perimeter of the square minus the length of one side.

	Column A	Column B
6.	The drop of a square with area 25	20

	Column A	Column B
7.	A bonus of $450 plus a 9 percent increase in annual salary	A bonus of $500 plus an 8.5 percent increase in annual salary

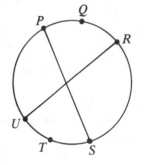

P, Q, R, S, T, and U are points on the circle as shown.

	Column A	Column B
8.	The length of arc PQR	The length of arc STU

$$x > 0$$

	Column A	Column B
9.	The total number of liters of water in x tanks, each containing 20 liters of water, and $2x$ tanks, each containing 35 liters of water	The total number of liters of water in x tanks, each containing 25 liters of water, and $2x$ tanks, each containing 30 liters of water

GO ON TO THE NEXT PAGE.

257

A if the quantity in Column A is greater;
B if the quantity in Column B is greater;
C if the two quantities are equal;
D if the relationship cannot be determined from the information given.

Column A   Column B   Column A   Column B

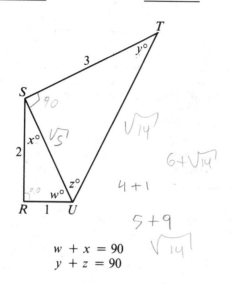

$$(a + b)^2 = 49$$
$$ab = 12$$

13. $a + b$ 7

$$x = 1 - y$$

14. $x^2 + 2xy + y^2$ $x + y$

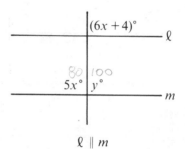

$\ell \parallel m$

$$w + x = 90$$
$$y + z = 90$$

10. The perimeter of $RSTU$ 10   15. y 90

11. $(x - 2)^2$ $(x + 2)^2$

$$(8)(16)(32)(64) = 2^{x+y}$$

12. The average (arithmetic
    mean) of x and y 9

GO ON TO THE NEXT PAGE.

258

Directions: Each of the Questions 16-30 has five answer choices. For each of these questions, select the best of the answer choices given.

16. In a certain class, if there are 35 men and 63 women, then the ratio of men to women is

(A) $\frac{7}{20}$

(B) $\frac{3}{7}$

(C) $\frac{5}{9}$

(D) $\frac{5}{7}$

(E) $\frac{7}{9}$

17. Streets L, M, and N are straight and level, and they intersect to form a triangle. If streets L and M intersect at a 40° angle and if street N is perpendicular to street M, at what acute angle do streets L and N intersect?

(A) 30°
(B) 35°
(C) 40°
(D) 45°
(E) 50°

18. $\left(1 - \frac{1}{2}\right)^2 \left(1 - \frac{1}{3}\right)^2 =$

(A) $\frac{25}{36}$

(B) $\frac{1}{3}$

(C) $\frac{1}{6}$

(D) $\frac{1}{9}$

(E) $\frac{1}{18}$

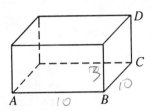

19. The figure above is a rectangular solid with $AB = 10$, $BC = 10$, and $CD = 3$. What is the total surface area of the figure?

(A) 320
(B) 300
(C) 220
(D) 160
(E) 23

20. $6x^2 - 15x - 21 =$

(A) $3(2x + 7)(x - 1)$
(B) $3(2x - 7)(x + 1)$
(C) $3(2x - 1)(x + 7)$
(D) $-9x^2 - 21$
(E) $-9x - 21$

GO ON TO THE NEXT PAGE.

Questions 21-25 refer to the following graphs.

FARMING IN COUNTRY *X*: 1940 TO 1986

Farm Population (in millions)

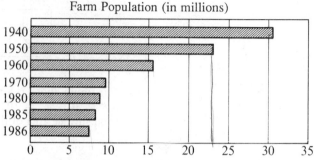

Number of Farms (in millions)

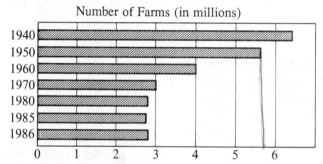

Average Farm Size (in acres)

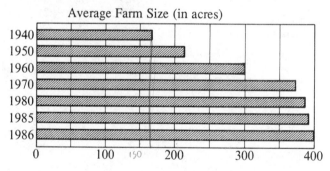

<u>Note</u>: All graphs drawn to scale.

21. Country *X*'s farm population in 1986 was approximately how many million?

(A) 2.5
(B) 5.5
(C) 7.5
(D) 9.0
(E) 10.0

22. The decrease, in millions, in the number of farms from 1950 to 1970 was approximately

(A) 1.6
(B) 2.0
(C) 2.6
(D) 3.0
(E) 3.6

23. To the nearest 10 percent, the decline in farm population in Country *X* between 1950 and 1960 represented what percent of the 1950 farm population?

(A) 10%
(B) 30%
(C) 50%
(D) 60%
(E) 150%

GO ON TO THE NEXT PAGE.

260

24. In Country X, the average farm size in 1940 was approximately what fraction of the average farm size in 1986 ?

    (A) $\frac{1}{4}$

    (B) $\frac{2}{5}$

    (C) $\frac{3}{5}$

    (D) $\frac{2}{3}$

    (E) $\frac{3}{4}$

25. In 1986, Country X had approximately how many million acres of farmland?

    (A) 1,100
    (B)   400
    (C)   140
    (D)   11
    (E)   3

GO ON TO THE NEXT PAGE.

26. If n is the average (arithmetic mean) of the three numbers 6, 9, and k, what is the value of k in terms of n?

    (A) $3n - 15$

    (B) $n - 5$

    (C) $n - 15$

    (D) $\dfrac{n - 15}{3}$

    (E) $\dfrac{n + 15}{3}$

27. Which of the following CANNOT be expressed as the sum of the squares of two integers?

    (A) 13
    (B) 17
    (C) 21
    (D) 29
    (E) 34

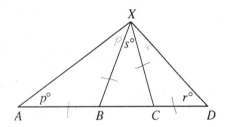

28. If $AB = BX$ and $XC = CD$ in the figure above, what is s in terms of p and r?

    (A) $180 - 2(p + r)$

    (B) $p + r - 90$

    (C) $2(p + r)$

    (D) $p + r$

    (E) $\dfrac{p + r}{2}$

29. Mary has 3 dollars more than Bill has, but 5 dollars less than Jane has. If Mary has x dollars, how many dollars do Jane and Bill have altogether?

    (A) $2x - 8$
    (B) $2x - 5$
    (C) $2x - 2$
    (D) $2x + 2$
    (E) $2x + 8$

30. If n is an integer divisible by 6 but not by 4, then which of the following CANNOT be an integer?

    (A) $\dfrac{n}{2}$

    (B) $\dfrac{n}{3}$

    (C) $\dfrac{n}{6}$

    (D) $\dfrac{n}{10}$

    (E) $\dfrac{n}{12}$

STOP

IF YOU FINISH BEFORE TIME IS CALLED, YOU MAY CHECK YOUR WORK ON THIS SECTION ONLY.
DO NOT TURN TO ANY OTHER SECTION IN THE TEST.

Section 3 starts on page 264.

SECTION 3

Time—30 minutes

37 Questions

Directions: Each sentence below has one or two blanks, each blank indicating that something has been omitted. Beneath the sentence are five lettered words or sets of words. Choose the word or set of words for each blank that best fits the meaning of the sentence as a whole.

1. Although the feeding activities of whales and walruses give the seafloor of the Bering Shelf a devastated appearance, these activities seem to be actually ------- to the area, ------- its productivity.

   (A) destructive. .counterbalancing
   (B) rehabilitative. .diminishing
   (C) beneficial. .enhancing
   (D) detrimental. .redirecting
   (E) superfluous. .encumbering

2. In an age without radio or recordings, an age ------- by print, fiction gained its greatest ascendancy.

   (A) decimated
   (B) denigrated
   (C) dominated
   (D) emphasized
   (E) resurrected

3. Scientists' pristine reputation as devotees of the disinterested pursuit of truth has been ------- by recent evidence that some scientists have deliberately ------- experimental results to further their own careers.

   (A) reinforced. .published
   (B) validated. .suppressed
   (C) exterminated. .replicated
   (D) compromised. .fabricated
   (E) resuscitated. .challenged

4. Although Johnson's and Smith's initial fascination with the fortunes of those jockeying for power in the law firm ------- after a few months, the two paid sufficient attention to determine who their lunch partners should be.

   (A) revived
   (B) emerged
   (C) intensified
   (D) flagged
   (E) persisted

5. A war, even if fought for individual liberty and democratic rights, usually requires that these principles be -------, for they are ------- the regimentation and discipline necessary for military efficiency.

   (A) espoused. .contrary to
   (B) suppressed. .fulfilled through
   (C) suspended. .incompatible with
   (D) followed. .disruptive of
   (E) rejected. .inherent in

6. To test the ------- of borrowing from one field of study to enrich another, simply investigate the extent to which terms from the one may, without forcing, be ------- the other.

   (A) risk. .confused with
   (B) universality. .applied to
   (C) decorum. .illuminated by
   (D) rate. .superseded by
   (E) efficacy. .utilized by

7. The English novelist William Thackeray considered the cult of the criminal so dangerous that he criticized Dickens' *Oliver Twist* for making the characters in the thieves' kitchen so -------.

   (A) threatening
   (B) riveting
   (C) conniving
   (D) fearsome
   (E) irritating

GO ON TO THE NEXT PAGE.

Directions: In each of the following questions, a related pair of words or phrases is followed by five lettered pairs of words or phrases. Select the lettered pair that best expresses a relationship similar to that expressed in the original pair.

8. ANIMAL : CAT ::
   (A) apple : pear
   (B) club : player
   (C) furniture : chair
   (D) landscape : tree
   (E) body : toe

9. CURTAIN : STAGE ::
   (A) footlight : orchestra
   (B) lid : jar
   (C) upholstery : sofa
   (D) veil : face
   (E) screen : film

10. INSOMNIA : SLEEP ::
    (A) dyslexia : read
    (B) hemophilia : bleed
    (C) hyperactivity : move
    (D) paranoia : hallucinate
    (E) malnutrition : eat

11. JEER : DERISION ::
    (A) fidget : restraint
    (B) cower : menace
    (C) slouch : vigilance
    (D) reprimand : censure
    (E) frown : adversity

12. HUMILITY : SUPPLICANT ::
    (A) espionage : felon
    (B) dilettantism : connoisseur
    (C) dogmatism : scholar
    (D) gregariousness : teammate
    (E) resistance : adversary

13. INTEREST : INVEIGLE ::
    (A) evaluate : suggest
    (B) foresee : predict
    (C) plan : scheme
    (D) interpret : examine
    (E) neglect : persecute

14. BARTER : COMMODITIES ::
    (A) arbitrate : disputes
    (B) invade : boundaries
    (C) debate : issues
    (D) correspond : letters
    (E) promote : ranks

15. PARRY : QUESTION ::
    (A) return : affection
    (B) shirk : duty
    (C) confront : dread
    (D) hurl : insult
    (E) surrender : temptation

GO ON TO THE NEXT PAGE.

Directions: Each passage in this group is followed by questions based on its content. After reading a passage, choose the best answer to each question. Answer all questions following a passage on the basis of what is stated or implied in that passage.

(This passage is excerpted from an article that was published in 1981.)

The deep sea typically has a sparse fauna dominated by tiny worms and crustaceans, with an even sparser distribution of larger animals. However, near hydrothermal
Line vents, areas of the ocean where warm water emerges
(5) from subterranean sources, live remarkable densities of
huge clams, blind crabs, and fish.

Most deep-sea faunas rely for food on particulate
matter, ultimately derived from photosynthesis, falling
from above. The food supplies necessary to sustain the
(10) large vent communities, however, must be many times
the ordinary fallout. The first reports describing vent
faunas proposed two possible sources of nutrition: bacterial chemosynthesis, production of food by bacteria
using energy derived from chemical changes, and advec-
(15) tion, the drifting of food materials from surrounding
regions. Later, evidence in support of the idea of intense
local chemosynthesis was accumulated: hydrogen sulfide was found in vent water; many vent-site bacteria
were found to be capable of chemosynthesis; and ex-
(20) tremely large concentrations of bacteria were found in
samples of vent water thought to be pure. This final
observation seemed decisive. If such astonishing concentrations of bacteria were typical of vent outflow, then
food within the vent would dwarf any contribution from
(25) advection. Hence, the widely quoted conclusion was
reached that bacterial chemosynthesis provides the foundation for hydrothermal-vent food chains—an exciting
prospect because no other communities on Earth are
independent of photosynthesis.

(30) There are, however, certain difficulties with this interpretation. For example, some of the large sedentary
organisms associated with vents are also found at ordinary deep-sea temperatures many meters from the
nearest hydrothermal sources. This suggests that bacte-
(35) rial chemosynthesis is not a sufficient source of nutrition
for these creatures. Another difficulty is that similarly
dense populations of large deep-sea animals have been
found in the proximity of "smokers"—vents where
water emerges at temperatures up to 350° C. No bacteria
(40) can survive such heat, and no bacteria were found there.

Unless smokers are consistently located near more hos-
pitable warm-water vents, chemosynthesis can account
for only a fraction of the vent faunas. It is conceivable,
however, that these large, sedentary organisms do in fact
(45) feed on bacteria that grow in warm-water vents, rise in
the vent water, and then rain in peripheral areas to nour-
ish animals living some distance from the warm-water
vents.

Nonetheless, advection is a more likely alternative
(50) food source. Research has demonstrated that advective
flow, which originates near the surface of the ocean
where suspended particulate matter accumulates, trans-
ports some of that matter and water to the vents. Estimates suggest that for every cubic meter of vent dis-
(55) charge, 350 milligrams of particulate organic material
would be advected into the vent area. Thus, for an
average-sized vent, advection could provide more than
30 kilograms of potential food per day. In addition, it is
likely that small live animals in the advected water might
(60) be killed or stunned by thermal and/or chemical shock,
thereby contributing to the food supply of vents.

16. The passage provides information for answering
    which of the following questions?

    (A) What causes warm-water vents to form?
    (B) Do vent faunas consume more than do deep-sea
        faunas of similar size?
    (C) Do bacteria live in the vent water of smokers?
    (D) What role does hydrogen sulfide play in
        chemosynthesis?
    (E) What accounts for the locations of deep-sea
        smokers?

GO ON TO THE NEXT PAGE.

17. The information in the passage suggests that the majority of deep-sea faunas that live in nonvent habitats have which of the following characteristics?

(A) They do not normally feed on particles of food in the water.
(B) They are smaller than many vent faunas.
(C) They are predators.
(D) They derive nutrition from a chemosynthetic food source.
(E) They congregate around a single main food source.

18. The primary purpose of the passage is to

(A) describe a previously unknown natural phenomenon
(B) reconstruct the evolution of a natural phenomenon
(C) establish unequivocally the accuracy of a hypothesis
(D) survey explanations for a natural phenomenon and determine which is best supported by evidence
(E) entertain criticism of the author's research and provide an effective response

19. Which of the following does the author cite as a weakness in the argument that bacterial chemosynthesis provides the foundation for the food chains at deep-sea vents?

(A) Vents are colonized by some of the same animals found in other areas of the ocean floor.
(B) Vent water does not contain sufficient quantities of hydrogen sulfide.
(C) Bacteria cannot produce large quantities of food quickly enough.
(D) Large concentrations of minerals are found in vent water.
(E) Some bacteria found in the vents are incapable of chemosynthesis.

20. Which of the following is information supplied in the passage that would support the statement that the food supplies necessary to sustain vent communities must be many times that of ordinary fallout?

I. Large vent faunas move from vent to vent in search of food.
II. Vent faunas are not able to consume food produced by photosynthesis.
III. Vents are more densely populated than are other deep-sea areas.

(A) I only
(B) III only
(C) I and II only
(D) II and III only
(E) I, II, and III

21. The author refers to "smokers" (line 38) most probably in order to

(A) show how thermal shock can provide food for some vent faunas by stunning small animals
(B) prove that the habitat of most deep-sea animals is limited to warm-water vents
(C) explain how bacteria carry out chemosynthesis
(D) demonstrate how advection compensates for the lack of food sources on the seafloor
(E) present evidence that bacterial chemosynthesis may be an inadequate source of food for some vent faunas

22. Which of the following can be inferred from the passage about the particulate matter that is carried down from the surface of the ocean?

(A) It is the basis of bacterial chemosynthesis in the vents.
(B) It may provide an important source of nutrition for vent faunas.
(C) It may cause the internal temperature of the vents to change significantly.
(D) It is transported as large aggregates of particles.
(E) It contains hydrogen sulfide.

GO ON TO THE NEXT PAGE.

Throughout human history there have been many stringent taboos concerning watching other people eat or eating in the presence of others. There have been
Line attempts to explain these taboos in terms of inappropri-
(5) ate social relationships either between those who are involved and those who are not simultaneously involved in the satisfaction of a bodily need, or between those already satiated and those who appear to be shamelessly gorging. Undoubtedly such elements
(10) exist in the taboos, but there is an additional element with a much more fundamental importance. In pre-historic times, when food was so precious and the on-lookers so hungry, not to offer half of the little food one had was unthinkable, since every glance was a plea
(15) for life. Further, during those times, people existed in nuclear or extended family groups, and the sharing of food was quite literally supporting one's family or, by extension, preserving one's self.

23. If the argument in the passage is valid, taboos against eating in the presence of others who are not also eating would be LEAST likely in a society that

(A) had always had a plentiful supply of food
(B) emphasized the need to share worldly goods
(C) had a nomadic rather than an agricultural way of life
(D) emphasized the value of privacy
(E) discouraged overindulgence

24. The author's hypothesis concerning the origin of taboos against watching other people eat empha-sizes the

(A) general palatability of food
(B) religious significance of food
(C) limited availability of food
(D) various sources of food
(E) nutritional value of food

25. According to the passage, the author believes that past attempts to explain some taboos concerning eating are

(A) unimaginative
(B) implausible
(C) inelegant
(D) incomplete
(E) unclear

26. In developing the main idea of the passage, the author does which of the following?

(A) Downplays earlier attempts to explain the origins of a social prohibition.
(B) Adapts a scientific theory and applies it to a spiritual relationship.
(C) Simplifies a complex biological phenomenon by explaining it in terms of social needs.
(D) Reorganizes a system designed to guide per-sonal behavior.
(E) Codifies earlier, unsystematized conjectures about family life.

GO ON TO THE NEXT PAGE.

268

Directions: Each question below consists of a word printed in capital letters, followed by five lettered words or phrases. Choose the lettered word or phrase that is most nearly <u>opposite</u> in meaning to the word in capital letters.

Since some of the questions require you to distinguish fine shades of meaning, be sure to consider all the choices before deciding which one is best.

27. CONSOLIDATION: (A) instigation
   (B) fragmentation   (C) restriction
   (D) opposition   (E) provocation

28. SECURE: (A) infest   (B) unearth
   (C) impart   (D) implant   (E) unfasten

29. FRACAS: (A) rapture   (B) relic
   (C) novel predicament   (D) peaceful situation
   (E) just reward

30. GRATE: (A) soothe   (B) gather
   (C) acknowledge   (D) forgive   (E) improve

31. HYPERBOLE: (A) equivocation   (B) criticism
   (C) understatement   (D) pessimism
   (E) skepticism

32. INERRANCY: (A) productivity
   (B) generosity   (C) volubility   (D) fallibility
   (E) plausibility

33. STEEP: (A) relax   (B) repulse
   (C) plummet   (D) clarify   (E) parch

34. RECUMBENT: (A) well fortified
   (B) standing up   (C) lacking flexibility
   (D) constricted   (E) alarmed

35. NATTY: (A) sloppy   (B) quiet   (C) loose
   (D) common   (E) difficult

36. EXIGENT: (A) unprepossessing   (B) inquisitive
   (C) devoted   (D) absurd   (E) deferrable

37. PLATITUDE:
   (A) concise formulation
   (B) original observation
   (C) unsubstantiated claim
   (D) relevant concern
   (E) insincere remark

STOP

IF YOU FINISH BEFORE TIME IS CALLED, YOU MAY CHECK YOUR WORK ON THIS SECTION ONLY.
DO NOT TURN TO ANY OTHER SECTION IN THE TEST.

SECTION 4

Time—30 minutes

25 Questions

Directions: Each question or group of questions is based on a passage or set of conditions. In answering some of the questions, it may be useful to draw a rough diagram. For each question, select the best answer choice given.

Questions 1-7

The manager of a commercial printing firm is scheduling exactly six jobs—P, Q, S, T, W, and X—for a particular week, Monday through Saturday. Each job can be completed in one full day, and exactly one job will be scheduled for each day. The jobs must be scheduled according to the following conditions:

P must be printed sometime before S is printed.
T must be printed on the day immediately before or the day immediately after the day on which X is printed.
W must be printed on Thursday.

1. Which of the following is an acceptable schedule of jobs for the week?

	Mon.	Tues.	Wed.	Thurs.	Fri.	Sat.
(A)	P	Q	T	W	X	S
(B)	P	W	S	X	T	Q
(C)	Q	X	T	W	S	P
(D)	T	X	P	W	Q	S
(E)	X	P	T	W	S	Q

2. Any of the following could be printed on Saturday EXCEPT

(A) P
(B) Q
(C) S
(D) T
(E) X

3. If Q is printed on Wednesday, which of the following could be true?

(A) P is printed on Tuesday.
(B) S is printed on Monday.
(C) S is printed on Friday.
(D) T is printed on Monday.
(E) X is printed on Thursday.

4. If X is printed on Monday, which of the following must be true?

(A) P is printed sometime before Q.
(B) P is printed sometime before W.
(C) Q is printed sometime before S.
(D) W is printed sometime before Q.
(E) W is printed sometime before S.

5. If P is printed on Tuesday, which of the following must be true?

(A) Q is printed on Monday.
(B) S is printed on Thursday.
(C) S is printed on Saturday.
(D) T is printed on Wednesday.
(E) X is printed on Saturday.

6. If T is printed on Tuesday, any of the following could be true EXCEPT:

(A) P is printed on Monday.
(B) Q is printed on Saturday.
(C) S is printed on Wednesday.
(D) S is printed on Friday.
(E) X is printed on Wednesday.

7. If Q is printed on Friday, which of the following must be true?

(A) P is printed on Monday.
(B) P is printed on Wednesday.
(C) S is printed on Saturday.
(D) T is printed on Monday.
(E) X is printed on Tuesday.

GO ON TO THE NEXT PAGE.

8. Although the human population around the forest-land in Middlesex County has increased, the amount of forestland has not been reduced. Therefore, the decrease in the county's songbird population cannot be attributed to the growth in the county's human population.

Which of the following, if true, most seriously weakens the conclusion above?

(A) As the human population of Middlesex County has grown, there has been an increase in the number of shopping malls built.
(B) The presence of more garbage cans resulting from the increase in the county's human population ensures the survival of more raccoons, which prey on songbird eggs whenever available.
(C) There has recently been a decrease in the amount of rain-forest land in Central and South America, where songbirds spend the winter months.
(D) Although several species of songbirds are disappearing from Middlesex County, these species are far from being endangered.
(E) The disappearance of songbirds, which eat insects, often results in increased destruction of trees by insects.

9. In October 1987 the United States stock market suffered a major drop in prices. During the weeks after the drop, the volume of stocks traded also dropped sharply to well below what had been the weekly average for the preceding year. However, the volume for the entire year was not appreciably different from the preceding year's volume.

Which of the following, if true, resolves the apparent contradiction presented in the passage above?

(A) Foreign investors usually buy United States stocks only when prices are low.
(B) The number of stock buyers in 1987 remained about the same as it had been the preceding year.
(C) For some portion of 1987, the volume of stocks traded was higher than the average for that year.
(D) The greater the volume of stocks traded in a given year, the lower the average price per share on the United States stock market for that year.
(E) The volume of stocks traded rises and falls in predictable cycles.

10. In a recent year California produced an orange crop equal to only seventy-six percent of Florida's orange crop. However, when citrus crops as a group, including oranges, were compared, the California crop was twenty-three percent greater than Florida's crop for the same year.

If the information above is true, which of the following can properly be concluded about the Florida and California citrus crops in the year mentioned?

(A) Florida's climate was suited only to growing oranges.
(B) Florida produced larger oranges than California did.
(C) California produced more oranges than it did non-orange citrus.
(D) California's proportion of non-orange citrus crops was higher than Florida's.
(E) California had more acreage that could be devoted to agriculture than did Florida.

GO ON TO THE NEXT PAGE.

Questions 11-15

A conference organizer must select exactly three discussants to respond to a paper to be presented by an invited speaker. The three discussants will be selected from seven volunteers, of whom four—Ito, Kemble, López, and Miller—are known to be friendly to the speaker's theoretical point of view. The other three—Shapiro, Thompson, and Ullman—are known to be hostile to the speaker's theoretical point of view. In selecting the three discussants, the conference organizer must observe the following restrictions:

At least one friendly discussant and at least one hostile discussant must be among those selected.
If Ito is selected, Thompson cannot be selected.
If either López or Miller is selected, the other must also be selected.
If either Kemble or Ullman is selected, the other must also be selected.

11. Which of the following could be the group of discussants selected?

   (A) Ito, López, and Miller
   (B) Ito, Shapiro, and Thompson
   (C) Kemble, Shapiro, and Ullman
   (D) López, Shapiro, and Thompson
   (E) Miller, Thompson, and Ullman

12. If Ito is selected as a discussant, which of the following must also be among those selected?

   (A) López
   (B) Miller
   (C) Shapiro
   (D) Thompson
   (E) Ullman

13. Which of the following is a pair of volunteers that can be selected together as discussants?

   (A) Ito and López
   (B) Ito and Shapiro
   (C) Kemble and López
   (D) Miller and Shapiro
   (E) Miller and Ullman

14. The members of the group of discussants would be completely determined if which of the following additional restrictions had to be observed as well?

   (A) Friendly discussants must be in the majority.
   (B) Hostile discussants must be in the majority.
   (C) Neither Ito nor Thompson can be selected.
   (D) Neither Kemble nor Shapiro can be selected.
   (E) Neither López nor Thompson can be selected.

15. The group of discussants selected must include either

   (A) Ito or Shapiro
   (B) Kemble or Shapiro
   (C) Kemble or Thompson
   (D) López or Miller
   (E) López or Ullman

GO ON TO THE NEXT PAGE.

272

Questions 16-18

At a large airport, the airport loop bus travels to Terminal A, Terminal B, and Long-Term Parking. The bus makes four stops at Terminal A—these are called A1, A2, A3, and A4, in that order. Next, the bus makes three stops at Terminal B—B1, B2, and B3, in that order. The bus then stops at Long-Term Parking. From Long-Term Parking the bus proceeds to A1 and repeats the entire loop.

At the same airport, an express monorail travels back and forth between A3 and Long-Term Parking only, and another express monorail travels back and forth between B2 and Long-Term Parking only.

The loop bus and two monorails are the only ways to move among the stops above. All transportation at the airport operates continuously and is available at no charge to all who wish to travel.

16. To travel from Long-Term Parking to A4 making the fewest possible intermediate stops, a person must take the

   (A) loop bus, but neither monorail
   (B) monorail to Terminal A, but neither the loop bus nor the other monorail
   (C) loop bus first and the monorail to Terminal A second
   (D) monorail to Terminal A first and the loop bus second
   (E) monorail to Terminal B first and the loop bus second

17. Which of the following could be the second intermediate stop for a person traveling from A2 to B3 ?

   (A) A3
   (B) B1
   (C) B2
   (D) B3
   (E) Long-Term Parking

18. If all of the following trips are to be made with the fewest possible intermediate stops, the trip that requires use of both a monorail and the loop bus is

   (A) A2 to A3
   (B) A4 to B1
   (C) Long-Term Parking to A2
   (D) Long-Term Parking to A4
   (E) Long-Term Parking to B2

GO ON TO THE NEXT PAGE.

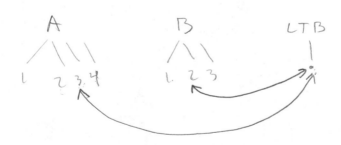

Questions 19-22

A veterinarian is doing an informal study of the growth of exactly seven poodles—Fido, Monet, Pal, Quixote, Rover, Spot, and Tâche—all six-month-old puppies from the same litter. The veterinarian's assistant collected the following comparative data concerning the poodles' heights:

> Rover is taller than Tâche.
> Quixote is taller than Spot.
> Fido is taller than Tâche.
> Pal is taller than Monet, but Tâche is taller than Pal.
> None of the seven poodles is exactly the same height as any other poodle from the litter.

19. Which of the following could be the correct ordering of the poodles from tallest to shortest?

    (A) Fido, Rover, Tâche, Monet, Quixote, Pal, Spot
    (B) Quixote, Spot, Fido, Tâche, Pal, Rover, Monet
    (C) Rover, Fido, Tâche, Pal, Quixote, Monet, Spot
    (D) Rover, Tâche, Quixote, Pal, Spot, Fido, Monet
    (E) Spot, Rover, Fido, Tâche, Pal, Quixote, Monet

20. Which of the following must be true?

    (A) Fido is taller than Pal.
    (B) Fido is taller than Rover.
    (C) Quixote is taller than Pal.
    (D) Spot is taller than Monet.
    (E) Tâche is taller than Spot.

21. If Spot is taller than Tâche, which of the following must be true?

    (A) Quixote is taller than Fido.
    (B) Quixote is taller than Pal.
    (C) Quixote is taller than Rover.
    (D) Rover is taller than Fido.
    (E) Tâche is taller than Quixote.

22. If Tâche is taller than Quixote, any of the following can be true EXCEPT:

    (A) Monet is taller than Quixote.
    (B) Quixote is taller than Pal.
    (C) Quixote is taller than Rover.
    (D) Spot is taller than Monet.
    (E) Spot is taller than Pal.

GO ON TO THE NEXT PAGE.

23. Researchers studying sets of identical twins who were raised apart in dissimilar environments found that in each case the twins were similar in character, medical history, and life experiences. The researchers saw these results as confirmation of the hypothesis that heredity is more important than environment in determining human personalities and life histories.

The existence of which of the following would tend to weaken the support for the hypothesis above most seriously?

(A) A set of identical twins raised together who are shown by appropriate tests to have very similar value systems
(B) A pair of identical twins raised apart who differ markedly with respect to aggressiveness and other personality traits
(C) A younger brother and older sister raised together who have similar personalities and life experiences
(D) A mother and daughter who have the same profession even though they have very different temperaments
(E) A pair of twins raised together who have similar personality traits but different value systems

24. Because the process of freezing food consumes energy, many people keep their electric freezers half-empty, using them only to store commercially frozen foods. Yet freezers that are half-empty often consume more energy than they would if they were kept fully stocked.

Which of the following, if true, contributes most to an explanation of the apparent discrepancy described above?

(A) A given volume of air in a freezer requires much more energy to be maintained at a temperature below freezing than does an identical volume of frozen food.
(B) The more often a freezer's door is opened, the more energy is required to maintain that freezer's normal temperature.
(C) When unfrozen foods are placed in a freezer, the average temperature of a given volume of air inside that freezer rises temporarily.
(D) A person who normally maintains a half-empty freezer can cut energy costs considerably by using a freezer that is 50 percent smaller.
(E) An electric freezer can operate efficiently only if chilled air is free to circulate within the freezing compartment.

25. People often do not make decisions by using the basic economic principle of rationally weighing all possibilities and then making the choice that can be expected to maximize benefits and minimize harm. Routinely, people process information in ways that are irrational in this sense.

Any of the following, if true, would provide evidence in support of the assertions above EXCEPT:

(A) People tend to act on new information, independent of its perceived relative merit, rather than on information they already have.
(B) People prefer a major risk taken voluntarily to a minor one that has been forced on them, even if they know that the voluntarily taken risk is statistically more dangerous.
(C) People tend to take up potentially damaging habits even though they have clear evidence that their own peers as well as experts disapprove of such behavior.
(D) People avoid situations in which they could become involved in accidents involving large numbers of people more than they do situations where single-victim accidents are possible, even though they realize that an accident is more likely in the latter situations than in the former.
(E) People usually give more weight to a physician's opinion about the best treatment for a disease than they do to the opinion of a neighbor if they realize that the neighbor is not an expert in disease treatment.

STOP

IF YOU FINISH BEFORE TIME IS CALLED, YOU MAY CHECK YOUR WORK ON THIS SECTION ONLY.
DO NOT TURN TO ANY OTHER SECTION IN THE TEST.

SECTION 5

Time—30 minutes

38 Questions

Directions: Each sentence below has one or two blanks, each blank indicating that something has been omitted. Beneath the sentence are five lettered words or sets of words. Choose the word or set of words for each blank that best fits the meaning of the sentence as a whole.

1. The discovery that, friction excluded, all bodies fall at the same rate is so simple to state and to grasp that there is a tendency to ------- its significance.

   (A) underrate
   (B) control
   (C) reassess
   (D) praise
   (E) eliminate

2. Their mutual teasing seemed -------, but in fact it ------- a long-standing hostility.

   (A) aimless. .produced
   (B) friendly. .masked
   (C) playful. .contravened
   (D) bitter. .revealed
   (E) clever. .averted

3. Noting that few employees showed any ------- for complying with the corporation's new safety regulations, Peterson was forced to conclude that acceptance of the regulations would be -------, at best.

   (A) aptitude. .unavoidable
   (B) regard. .indeterminate
   (C) respect. .negotiable
   (D) patience. .imminent
   (E) enthusiasm. .grudging

4. It has been argued that politics as -------, whatever its transcendental claims, has always been the systematic organization of common hatreds.

   (A) a theory
   (B) an ideal
   (C) a practice
   (D) a contest
   (E) an enigma

5. In many science fiction films, the opposition of good and evil is portrayed as a ------- between technology, which is -------, and the errant will of a depraved intellectual.

   (A) fusion. .useful
   (B) struggle. .dehumanizing
   (C) parallel. .unfettered
   (D) conflict. .beneficent
   (E) similarity. .malevolent

6. Although scientists claim that the seemingly ------- language of their reports is more precise than the figurative language of fiction, the language of science, like all language, is inherently -------.

   (A) ornamental. .subtle
   (B) unidimensional. .unintelligible
   (C) symbolic. .complex
   (D) literal. .allusive
   (E) subjective. .metaphorical

7. In recent decades the idea that Cézanne influenced Cubism has been caught in the ------- between art historians who credit Braque with its invention and those who ------- Picasso.

   (A) crossfire. .tout
   (B) interplay. .advocate
   (C) paradox. .prefer
   (D) deliberation. .attribute
   (E) tussle. .substitute

GO ON TO THE NEXT PAGE.

Directions: In each of the following questions, a related pair of words or phrases is followed by five lettered pairs of words or phrases. Select the lettered pair that best expresses a relationship similar to that expressed in the original pair.

8. DISGUISE : IDENTIFICATION ::
    (A) equivocation : ambiguity
    (B) facade : decoration
    (C) forgery : wealth
    (D) camouflage : detection
    (E) manipulation : advantage

9. BIRD : FEATHERS ::
    (A) mammal : spine
    (B) hand : fingers
    (C) branch : fruit
    (D) limb : fur
    (E) fish : scales

10. ELBOW : JOINT ::
    (A) cell : tissue
    (B) corpuscle : blood
    (C) muscle : bone
    (D) skull : skeleton
    (E) heart : organ

11. ENDOW : INCOME ::
    (A) emit : signals
    (B) endorse : approval
    (C) enchant : magic
    (D) embark : voyage
    (E) endure : hardships

12. BOMBAST : POMPOUS ::
    (A) prose : economical
    (B) circumlocution : patient
    (C) prattle : succinct
    (D) verbiage : mundane
    (E) tirade : critical

13. CARET : INSERTION ::
    (A) pound : heaviness
    (B) tongs : extraction
    (C) comma : pause
    (D) quotation : agreement
    (E) clip : attachment

14. OPAQUE : LIGHT ::
    (A) inaudible : sound
    (B) unbreakable : plastic
    (C) reflective : mirror
    (D) nonporous : liquid
    (E) viscous : fluid

15. FEARLESS : DAUNT ::
    (A) perplexed : enlighten
    (B) nondescript : neglect
    (C) avaricious : motivate
    (D) impassive : perturb
    (E) tranquil : pacify

16. QUERULOUS : COMPLAIN ::
    (A) humble : fawn
    (B) prodigal : spend
    (C) treacherous : trust
    (D) laconic : talk
    (E) culpable : blame

GO ON TO THE NEXT PAGE.

Directions:　Each passage in this group is followed by questions based on its content. After reading a passage, choose the best answer to each question. Answer all questions following a passage on the basis of what is <u>stated</u> or <u>implied</u> in that passage.

(This passage is from a book published in 1975.)

That Louise Nevelson is believed by many critics to be the greatest twentieth-century sculptor is all the more remarkable because the greatest resistance to
Line women artists has been, until recently, in the field of
(5) sculpture. Since Neolithic times, sculpture has been considered the prerogative of men, partly, perhaps, for purely physical reasons:　it was erroneously assumed that women were not suited for the hard manual labor required in sculpting stone, carving wood, or working in
(10) metal. It has been only during the twentieth century that women sculptors have been recognized as major artists, and it has been in the United States, especially since the decades of the fifties and sixties, that women sculptors have shown the greatest originality and creative power.
(15) Their rise to prominence parallels the development of sculpture itself in the United States:　while there had been a few talented sculptors in the United States before the 1940's, it was only after 1945—when New York was rapidly becoming the art capital of the world—that
(20) major sculpture was produced in the United States. Some of the best was the work of women.

By far the most outstanding of these women is Louise Nevelson, who in the eyes of many critics is the most original female artist alive today. One famous and influ-
(25) ential critic, Hilton Kramer, said of her work, "For myself, I think Ms. Nevelson succeeds where the painters often fail."

Her works have been compared to the Cubist constructions of Picasso, the Surrealistic objects of Miro,
(30) and the Merzbau of Schwitters. Nevelson would be the first to admit that she has been influenced by all of these, as well as by African sculpture, and by Native American and pre-Columbian art, but she has absorbed all these influences and still created a distinctive art that
(35) expresses the urban landscape and the aesthetic sensibility of the twentieth century. Nevelson says, "I have always wanted to show the world that art is everywhere, except that it has to pass through a creative mind."

Using mostly discarded wooden objects like packing
(40) crates, broken pieces of furniture, and abandoned architectural ornaments, all of which she has hoarded for years, she assembles architectural constructions of great beauty and power. Creating very freely with no sketches, she glues and nails objects together, paints them black,
(45) or more rarely white or gold, and places them in boxes. These assemblages, walls, even entire environments create a mysterious, almost awe-inspiring atmosphere. Although she has denied any symbolic or religious intent in her works, their three-dimensional grandeur and even
(50) their titles, such as *Sky Cathedral* and *Night Cathedral*, suggest such connotations. In some ways, her most ambitious works are closer to architecture than to traditional sculpture, but then neither Louise Nevelson nor her art fits into any neat category.

17. The passage focuses primarily on which of the following?

(A) A general tendency in twentieth-century art
(B) The work of a particular artist
(C) The artistic influences on women sculptors
(D) Critical responses to twentieth-century sculpture
(E) Materials used by twentieth-century sculptors

18. Which of the following statements is supported by information given in the passage?

(A) Since 1945 women sculptors in the United States have produced more sculpture than have men sculptors.
(B) Since 1950 sculpture produced in the United States has been the most original and creative sculpture produced anywhere.
(C) From 1900 to 1950 women sculptors in Europe enjoyed more recognition for their work than did women sculptors in the United States.
(D) Prior to 1945 there were many women sculptors whose work was ignored by critics.
(E) Prior to 1945 there was little major sculpture produced by men or women sculptors working in the United States.

19. The author quotes Hilton Kramer in lines 25-27 most probably in order to illustrate which of the following?

(A) The realism of Nevelson's work
(B) The unique qualities of Nevelson's style
(C) The extent of critical approval of Nevelson's work
(D) A distinction between sculpture and painting
(E) A reason for the prominence of women sculptors since the 1950's

GO ON TO THE NEXT PAGE.

20. Which of the following is one way in which Nevelson's art illustrates her theory as it is expressed in lines 36-38 ?

    (A) She sculpts in wood rather than in metal or stone.
    (B) She paints her sculptures and frames them in boxes.
    (C) She makes no preliminary sketches but rather allows the sculpture to develop as she works.
    (D) She puts together pieces of ordinary objects once used for different purposes to make her sculptures.
    (E) She does not deliberately attempt to convey symbolic or religious meanings through her sculpture.

21. It can be inferred from the passage that the author believes which of the following about Nevelson's sculptures?

    (A) They suggest religious and symbolic meanings.
    (B) They do not have qualities characteristic of sculpture.
    (C) They are mysterious and awe-inspiring, but not beautiful.
    (D) They are uniquely American in style and sensibility.
    (E) They show the influence of twentieth-century architecture.

22. The author regards Nevelson's stature in the art world as "remarkable" (line 3) in part because of which of the following?

    (A) Her work is currently overrated.
    (B) Women sculptors have found it especially difficult to be accepted and recognized as major artists.
    (C) Nevelson's sculptures are difficult to understand.
    (D) Many art critics have favored painting over sculpture in writing about developments in the art world.
    (E) Few of the artists prominent in the twentieth century have been sculptors.

23. Which of the following statements about Nevelson's sculptures can be inferred from the passage?

    (A) They are meant for display outdoors.
    (B) They are often painted in several colors.
    (C) They are sometimes very large.
    (D) They are hand carved by Nevelson.
    (E) They are built around a central wooden object.

GO ON TO THE NEXT PAGE.

Volcanic rock that forms as fluid lava chills rapidly is called pillow lava. This rapid chilling occurs when lava erupts directly into water (or beneath ice) or when it
Line flows across a shoreline and into a body of water. While
(5) the term "pillow lava" suggests a definite shape, in fact geologists disagree. Some geologists argue that pillow lava is characterized by discrete, ellipsoidal masses. Others describe pillow lava as a tangled mass of cylindrical, interconnected flow lobes. Much of this controversy
(10) probably results from unwarranted extrapolations of the original configuration of pillow flows from two-dimensional cross sections of eroded pillows in land outcroppings. Virtually any cross section cut through a tangled mass of interconnected flow lobes would give
(15) the appearance of a pile of discrete ellipsoidal masses. Adequate three-dimensional images of intact pillows are essential for defining the true geometry of pillowed flows and thus ascertaining their mode of origin. Indeed, the term "pillow," itself suggestive of discrete masses, is probably a misnomer.

24. Which of the following is a fact presented in the passage?

    (A) The shape of the connections between the separate, sacklike masses in pillow lava is unknown.
    (B) More accurate cross sections of pillow lava would reveal the mode of origin.
    (C) Water or ice is necessary for the formation of pillow lava.
    (D) No three-dimensional examples of intact pillows currently exist.
    (E) The origin of pillow lava is not yet known.

25. In the passage, the author is primarily interested in

    (A) analyzing the source of a scientific controversy
    (B) criticizing some geologists' methodology
    (C) pointing out the flaws in a geological study
    (D) proposing a new theory to explain existing scientific evidence
    (E) describing a physical phenomenon

26. The author of the passage would most probably agree that the geologists mentioned in line 6 ("Some geologists") have made which of the following errors in reasoning?

    I. Generalized unjustifiably from available evidence.
    II. Deliberately ignored existing counterevidence.
    III. Repeatedly failed to take new evidence into account.

    (A) I only   (B) II only   (C) III only
    (D) I and II only   (E) II and III only

27. The author implies that the "controversy" (line 9) might be resolved if

    (A) geologists did not persist in using the term "pillow"
    (B) geologists did not rely on potentially misleading information
    (C) geologists were more willing to confer directly with one another
    (D) two-dimensional cross sections of eroded pillows were available
    (E) existing pillows in land outcroppings were not so badly eroded

GO ON TO THE NEXT PAGE.

Directions: Each question below consists of a word printed in capital letters, followed by five lettered words or phrases. Choose the lettered word or phrase that is most nearly opposite in meaning to the word in capital letters.

Since some of the questions require you to distinguish fine shades of meaning, be sure to consider all the choices before deciding which one is best.

28. PEER:
    (A) a complicated structure
    (B) an insignificant explanation
    (C) a subordinate person
    (D) an inept musician
    (E) an unreliable worker

29. SYNCHRONOUS:
    (A) unusual in appearance
    (B) of a distinct origin
    (C) occurring at different times
    (D) monotonous
    (E) shapeless

30. ALIENATE: (A) reunite   (B) influence
    (C) relieve   (D) match   (E) revitalize

31. PREDESTINE: (A) jumble   (B) doubt
    (C) leave to chance   (D) arrange incorrectly
    (E) defy authority

32. AERATE: (A) generate   (B) create   (C) elevate
    (D) combine water with   (E) remove air from

33. FALLOW: (A) abundant   (B) valuable
    (C) necessary   (D) in use   (E) in demand

34. CORROBORATE: (A) tire   (B) rival
    (C) deny   (D) antagonize   (E) disengage

35. PERUSE: (A) glide along   (B) argue against
    (C) strive for   (D) pick up   (E) glance at

36. SEEMLY: (A) indecorous   (B) inapparent
    (C) disconnected   (D) disingenuous
    (E) deleterious

37. TENUOUS: (A) substantial   (B) obdurate
    (C) permanent   (D) ubiquitous   (E) intelligible

38. GRATUITOUS: (A) thankless   (B) warranted
    (C) trying   (D) discreet   (E) spurious

STOP

IF YOU FINISH BEFORE TIME IS CALLED, YOU MAY CHECK YOUR WORK ON THIS SECTION ONLY.
DO NOT TURN TO ANY OTHER SECTION IN THE TEST.

SECTION 6
Time—30 minutes
30 Questions

Numbers: All numbers used are real numbers.

Figures: Position of points, angles, regions, etc. can be assumed to be in the order shown; and angle measures can be assumed to be positive.

Lines shown as straight can be assumed to be straight.

Figures can be assumed to lie in a plane unless otherwise indicated.

Figures that accompany questions are intended to provide information useful in answering the questions. However, unless a note states that a figure is drawn to scale, you should solve these problems NOT by estimating sizes by sight or by measurement, but by using your knowledge of mathematics (see Example 2 below).

Directions: Each of the Questions 1-15 consists of two quantities, one in Column A and one in Column B. You are to compare the two quantities and choose

A if the quantity in Column A is greater;
B if the quantity in Column B is greater;
C if the two quantities are equal;
D if the relationship cannot be determined from the information given.

Note: Since there are only four choices, NEVER MARK (E).

Common
Information: In a question, information concerning one or both of the quantities to be compared is centered above the two columns. A symbol that appears in both columns represents the same thing in Column A as it does in Column B.

	Column A	Column B	Sample Answers
Example 1:	2×6	$2 + 6$	● Ⓑ Ⓒ Ⓓ Ⓔ

Examples 2-4 refer to $\triangle PQR$.

	Column A	Column B	Sample Answers
Example 2:	PN	NQ	Ⓐ Ⓑ Ⓒ ● Ⓔ

(since equal measures cannot be assumed, even though PN and NQ appear equal)

Example 3:	x	y	Ⓐ ● Ⓒ Ⓓ Ⓔ

(since N is between P and Q)

Example 4:	$w + z$	180	Ⓐ Ⓑ ● Ⓓ Ⓔ

(since PQ is a straight line)

GO ON TO THE NEXT PAGE.

A if the quantity in Column A is greater;
B if the quantity in Column B is greater;
C if the two quantities are equal;
D if the relationship cannot be determined from the information given.

Column A	Column B

1. $\dfrac{3}{7}$ $\dfrac{9}{49}$

2. $2x + 3y = 3x + 2y$

  x y

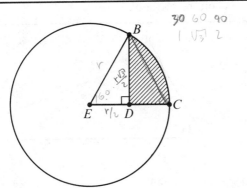

The circle with center E has radius r.

$$ED = \frac{r}{2}$$

3. The area of $\triangle EBD$ | The area of the shaded region

$xy \neq 0$

4. $\dfrac{x - y}{x}$ $\dfrac{x - y}{y}$

5. $\sqrt{21} + \sqrt{15}$ $\sqrt{21 + 15}$

Column A	Column B

$x > y > 0$

6. $y - x$ 0

7. The area of a circular region with circumference 16π | The circumference of a circular region with area 16π

$3 < x < 4$
$y = 5$

8. $\dfrac{x}{y}$ 0.7

A discount of 40 percent of the original selling price of an item reduces the price to $72.

9. The original selling price of the item $120

GO ON TO THE NEXT PAGE.

283

A if the quantity in Column A is greater;
B if the quantity in Column B is greater;
C if the two quantities are equal;
D if the relationship cannot be determined from the information given.

Column A	Column B

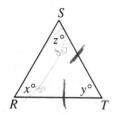

80
80

$$x = z$$

10. RT RS

Item X costs twice as much as item Z, and item Y costs \$3 more than half the cost of item Z.

11. The cost of item X The cost of item Y

For all integers x and y, let $x \star y$ be defined as follows.

$$x \star y = -|x + y|$$

12. $3 \star (-4)$ $3 - 4$

13. 0.4 $\sqrt{0.4}$

$X = 2Z$ 10
$Y = 3 + \dfrac{Z}{2}$ 4

$= -|3 - 4|$

Column A	Column B

A rectangular textbook page measures $8\frac{1}{2}$ inches by 11 inches. The page is partitioned into rectangular spaces each $\frac{1}{12}$ inch by $\frac{1}{8}$ inch.

14. The number of such spaces $17 \times 11 \times 48$
     on the textbook page

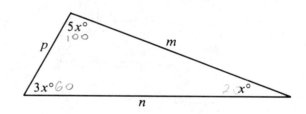

15. n^2 $p^2 + m^2$

$$\frac{11 \times 17}{2}$$

$$\frac{1}{12 \times 8}$$

$$\frac{11 \times \cancel{12} \times 17 \times 18}{\cancel{2}}$$

GO ON TO THE NEXT PAGE.

17/2

$9X = 180$
$X = 20$

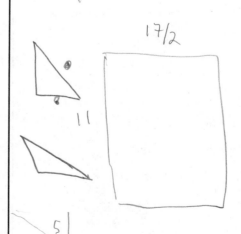

Directions: Each of the Questions 16-30 has five answer choices. For each of these questions, select the best of the answer choices given.

16. If $2x + y = 8$ and $3x = 6$, then $y =$

    (A) 2
    (B) 4
    (C) 6
    (D) 8
    (E) 12

	Number of Lawn Mowers
Monday	752
Tuesday	747
Wednesday	755
Thursday	754
Friday	

750

17. The table above shows the number of lawn mowers produced by Company L each workday last week except Friday. If Company L produced an average (arithmetic mean) of 750 lawn mowers per day for the workweek, how many lawn mowers did it produce on Friday?

    (A) 736
    (B) 739
    (C) 742
    (D) 750
    (E) 758

18. Mario bought equal numbers of 2-cent and 3-cent stamps. If the total cost of the stamps was $1.00, what was the total number of stamps bought?

    (A) 25
    (B) 34
    (C) 40
    (D) 46
    (E) 50

0. X
$2x + 3x = 100$
$2 \times 20 + 3 \times 20 = 100$
20

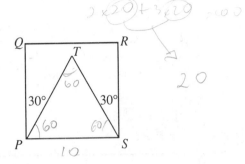

19. In square $PQRS$ above, $\triangle PTS$ has a perimeter of 30. What is the area of square $PQRS$?

    (A) 30
    (B) 50
    (C) 60
    (D) 75
    (E) 100

20. If $r > 0$, then $\sqrt{0.25r^6} =$

    (A) $0.05r^3$
    (B) $0.05r^4$
    (C) $0.05r^5$
    (D) $0.5r^2$
    (E) $0.5r^3$

0.5

747
750
752
754
755

3 8

11

11

GO ON TO THE NEXT PAGE.

285

Questions 21-25 refer to the following data.

PRODUCTION OF PHOTOGRAPHIC EQUIPMENT AND SUPPLIES

World Production 1965-1969
(value in millions of dollars)

Country	1965		1966		1967		1968		1969	
	Value	Percent of Total	Value	Percent of Total	Value	Percent of Total	Value	Percent of Total	Value	Percent of Total
United States ----	2,296	64.5	2,831	67.5	3,138	68.4	3,505	68.4	3,770	67.0
Japan ----------	350	9.8	371	8.9	411	9.0	450	8.8	550	9.8
West Germany---	350	9.8	363	8.7	370	8.1	439	8.6	510	9.1
United Kingdom -	247	7.0	274	6.5	283	6.2	299	5.8	310	5.5
France----------	96	2.7	95	2.3	106	2.3	120	2.4	140	2.5
Belgium --------	95	2.7	104	2.5	107	2.3	115	2.3	130	2.3
Italy ----------	76	2.1	80	1.9	89	2.0	105	2.1	115	2.1
Other countries --	50	1.4	72	1.7	76	1.7	82	1.6	95	1.7
Total -----	3,560	100.0	4,190	100.0	4,580	100.0	5,115	100.0	5,620	100.0

UNITED STATES PRODUCTION

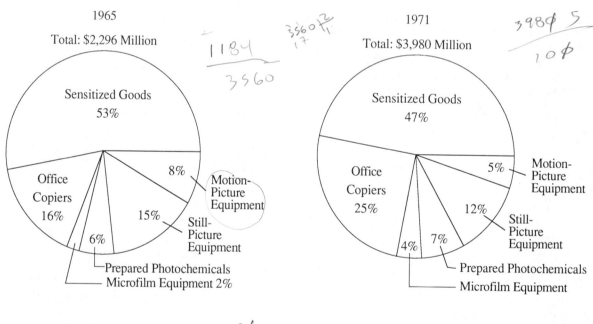

GO ON TO THE NEXT PAGE.

286

21. In 1969 the value of photographic equipment and supplies produced outside the United States was how many million dollars?

    (A)   550
    (B) 1,850
    (C) 5,620
    (D) 7,470
    (E) 11,240

22. What was the value, in millions of dollars, of the motion-picture equipment produced in the United States in 1971 ?

    (A) 184
    (B) 188
    (C) 193
    (D) 199
    (E) 203

23. In 1965 which country's total production of photographic equipment and supplies was nearest in value to the combined production of motion-picture and microfilm equipment in the United States in the same year?

    (A) Italy
    (B) France
    (C) United Kingdom
    (D) West Germany
    (E) Japan

24. In 1965 the value of sensitized goods produced in the United States was approximately what percent of the value of photographic equipment and supplies produced in the world?

    (A) 60%
    (B) 50%
    (C) 45%
    (D) 40%
    (E) 35%

25. From 1968 to 1969, the value of photographic equipment and supplies produced by Japan increased by approximately what percent?

    (A) 22%
    (B) 18%
    (C) 15%
    (D) 12%
    (E) 10%

GO ON TO THE NEXT PAGE.

26. For which of the following sets of numbers is the product of the three numbers less than each member of the set?

    I. $\frac{1}{4}, \frac{2}{3}, \frac{3}{4}$

    II. $-\frac{1}{2}, -1, 4$

    III. $-2, 3, 5$

    (A) I only
    (B) II only
    (C) III only
    (D) I and III
    (E) II and III

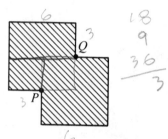

27. The figure above is formed by two overlapping squares, each having sides of 6 centimeters in length. If P and Q are the midpoints of the intersecting sides, what is the area, in square centimeters, of the shaded region?

    (A) 72
    (B) 63
    (C) 60
    (D) 54
    (E) 45

28. If x and y are numbers on the number line above, which of the following statements must be true?

    I. $xy < 0$
    II. $x + y < 0$
    III. $x - y < 0$

    (A) I only
    (B) III only
    (C) I and II only
    (D) I and III only
    (E) I, II, and III

29. If x is an odd negative integer and y is an even positive integer, then xy must be which of the following?

    (A) Odd and positive
    (B) Odd and negative
    (C) Even and positive
    (D) Even and negative
    (E) It cannot be determined from the information given.

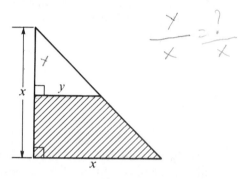

30. Which of the following expresses the area of the shaded region in the figure above?

    (A) $\dfrac{x^2 - y^2}{2}$

    (B) $\dfrac{x^2 + y^2}{2}$

    (C) $x^2 - y^2$

    (D) $\dfrac{x^2 + xy}{4}$

    (E) $\dfrac{x^2 - xy}{4}$

STOP

IF YOU FINISH BEFORE TIME IS CALLED, YOU MAY CHECK YOUR WORK ON THIS SECTION ONLY. DO NOT TURN TO ANY OTHER SECTION IN THE TEST.

NO TEST MATERIAL ON THIS PAGE

NO TEST MATERIAL ON THIS PAGE

THE GRADUATE RECORD EXAMINATIONS
GENERAL TEST

You will have 3 hours and 30 minutes in which to work on this test, which consists of seven sections. During the time allowed for one section, you may work only on that section. The time allowed for each section is 30 minutes.

Each of your scores will be determined by the number of questions for which you select the best answer from the choices given. Questions for which you mark no answer or more than one answer are not counted in scoring. Nothing is subtracted from a score if you answer a question incorrectly. Therefore, to maximize your scores, it is better for you to guess at an answer than not to respond at all.

You are advised to work as rapidly as you can without losing accuracy. Do not spend too much time on questions that are too difficult for you. Go on to the other questions and come back to the difficult ones later.

There are several different types of questions; you will find special directions for each type in the test itself. Be sure you understand the directions before attempting to answer any questions.

For each question several answer choices (lettered A-E or A-D) are given from which you are to select the ONE best answer. YOU MUST INDICATE ALL YOUR ANSWERS ON THE SEPARATE ANSWER SHEET. No credit will be given for anything written in this examination book, but to work out your answers you may write in the book as much as you wish. After you have decided which of the suggested answers is best, fill in completely the corresponding space on the answer sheet. Be sure to:

- Use a soft black lead pencil (No. 2 or HB).

- Mark only one answer to each question. No credit will be given for multiple answers.

- Mark your answer in the row with the same number as the number of the question you are answering.

- Carefully and completely fill in the space corresponding to the answer you select for each question. Fill the space with a dark mark so that you cannot see the letter inside the space. Light or partial marks may not be read by the scoring machine. See the example of proper and improper answer marks below.

- Erase all stray marks. If you change an answer, be sure that you completely erase the old answer before marking your new answer. Incomplete erasures may be read as intended answers.

Example:

What city is the capital of France?

(A) Rome
(B) Paris
(C) London
(D) Cairo
(E) Oslo

Sample Answer

Ⓐ ● Ⓒ Ⓓ Ⓔ

BEST ANSWER
PROPERLY MARKED

Ⓐ Ⓑ Ⓒ Ⓓ Ⓔ
Ⓐ Ⓑ Ⓒ Ⓓ Ⓔ
Ⓐ Ⓑ Ⓒ Ⓓ Ⓔ
Ⓐ Ⓑ Ⓒ Ⓓ Ⓔ

IMPROPER MARKS

Do not be concerned that the answer sheet provides spaces for more answers than there are questions in the test. Some or all of the passages for this test have been adapted from published material to provide the examinee with significant problems for analysis and evaluation. To make the passages suitable for testing purposes, the style, content, or point of view of the original may have been altered in some cases. The ideas contained in the passages do not necessarily represent the opinions of the Graduate Record Examinations Board or Educational Testing Service.

CLOSE YOUR TEST BOOK AND WAIT FOR FURTHER INSTRUCTIONS FROM THE SUPERVISOR.

I

NOTE: To ensure the prompt and accurate processing of test results, your cooperation in following these directions is needed. The procedures that follow have been kept to the minimum necessary. They will take a few minutes to complete, but it is essential that you fill in all blanks exactly as directed.

GENERAL TEST

A. Print and sign your full name in this box:

PRINT: _____
　　　　　　(LAST)　　　　　　　(FIRST)　　　　　　(MIDDLE)

SIGN: _____

B. Side 1 of your answer sheet contains areas that will be used to ensure accurate reporting of your test results. It is essential that you carefully enter the requested information.

[1] through [5] YOUR NAME, DATE OF BIRTH, SOCIAL SECURITY NUMBER, REGISTRATION NUMBER, and ADDRESS: Print all the information requested in the boxes and then fill in completely the appropriate oval beneath each entry.

- For date of birth, be sure to enter a zero before a single digit (e.g., if you were born on the third day of the month, you would enter "03" for the day). Use the last two digits of the year of your birth (for 1966, enter 66).

- Copy the registration number from your admission ticket.

[6] TITLE CODE: Copy the numbers shown below and fill in completely the appropriate spaces beneath each entry as shown. When you have completed item 6, check to be sure it is identical to the illustration below.

```
6. TITLE CODE
 3  4  5  6  7
 ⓪  ⓪  ⓪  ⓪  ⓪
 ①  ①  ①  ①  ①
 ②  ②  ②  ②  ②
 ●  ③  ③  ③  ③
 ④  ●  ④  ④  ④
 ⑤  ⑤  ●  ⑤  ⑤
 ⑥  ⑥  ⑥  ●  ⑥
 ⑦  ⑦  ⑦  ⑦  ●
 ⑧  ⑧  ⑧  ⑧  ⑧
 ⑨  ⑨  ⑨  ⑨  ⑨
```

[7] TEST NAME: Copy _General_ in the box.

FORM CODE: Copy _GR 90-15_ in the box.

[8] TEST BOOK SERIAL NUMBER: Copy the serial number of your test book in the box. It is printed in red at the upper right on the front cover of your test book.

[9] Print the requested information and enter the test center number in the boxes.

[10] CERTIFICATION STATEMENT: In the boxed area, WRITE (do not print) the following statement: "I certify that I am the person whose name appears on this answer sheet. I also agree not to disclose the contents of the test I am taking today to anyone." Sign and date where indicated.

When you have finished, wait for further instructions from the supervisor. DO NOT OPEN YOUR TEST BOOK UNTIL YOU ARE TOLD TO DO SO.

FOR GENERAL TEST, FORM GR90-15 ONLY
Answer Key and Percentages* of Examinees Answering Each Question Correctly

VERBAL ABILITY

Section 3			Section 5		
Number	Answer	P +	Number	Answer	P +
1	C	93	1	A	89
2	C	91	2	B	82
3	D	79	3	E	56
4	D	69	4	C	55
5	C	68	5	D	45
6	E	54	6	D	42
7	B	58	7	A	49
8	C	90	8	D	86
9	D	70	9	E	91
10	A	49	10	E	75
11	D	46	11	B	52
12	E	36	12	E	44
13	C	34	13	C	43
14	D	28	14	D	32
15	B	31	15	D	28
16	C	53	16	B	29
17	B	26	17	B	82
18	D	76	18	E	67
19	A	50	19	C	54
20	B	56	20	D	68
21	E	58	21	A	55
22	B	70	22	B	89
23	A	70	23	C	61
24	C	84	24	C	70
25	D	66	25	A	47
26	A	40	26	A	56
27	B	85	27	B	43
28	E	87	28	C	85
29	D	79	29	C	90
30	A	78	30	A	81
31	C	70	31	C	81
32	D	54	32	E	72
33	E	32	33	D	37
34	B	33	34	C	37
35	A	24	35	E	37
36	E	22	36	A	27
37	B	22	37	A	24
			38	B	18

QUANTITATIVE ABILITY

Section 2			Section 6		
Number	Answer	P +	Number	Answer	P +
1	A	90	1	A	83
2	A	90	2	C	74
3	B	80	3	B	80
4	A	80	4	D	75
5	C	62	5	A	71
6	B	66	6	B	77
7	D	61	7	A	66
8	D	52	8	D	66
9	A	59	9	C	57
10	B	54	10	D	51
11	D	49	11	D	45
12	C	41	12	C	47
13	D	18	13	B	41
14	C	38	14	C	33
15	A	32	15	A	29
16	C	83	16	B	90
17	E	80	17	C	82
18	D	62	18	C	77
19	A	50	19	E	69
20	B	66	20	E	62
21	C	79	21	B	93
22	C	90	22	D	85
23	B	76	23	C	75
24	B	71	24	E	57
25	A	45	25	A	45
26	A	49	26	D	46
27	C	47	27	B	64
28	A	46	28	D	54
29	D	43	29	D	62
30	E	22	30	A	35

ANALYTICAL ABILITY

Section 1			Section 4		
Number	Answer	P +	Number	Answer	P +
1	B	76	1	D	90
2	C	83	2	A	86
3	B	69	3	D	59
4	E	32	4	E	56
5	E	34	5	A	59
6	E	51	6	C	68
7	D	95	7	C	61
8	C	62	8	B	75
9	D	72	9	C	76
10	A	60	10	D	88
11	C	57	11	C	83
12	B	54	12	E	41
13	B	57	13	D	33
14	E	38	14	D	24
15	B	66	15	E	18
16	E	54	16	D	60
17	A	29	17	E	38
18	E	24	18	D	52
19	E	51	19	C	73
20	D	60	20	A	68
21	B	48	21	B	59
22	E	35	22	C	50
23	D	62	23	B	72
24	B	61	24	A	64
25	A	19	25	E	38

*Estimated P+ for the group of examinees who took the GRE General Test in a recent three-year period.

293

SCORE CONVERSIONS AND PERCENTS BELOW*
FOR GRE GENERAL TEST, Form GR90-15 ONLY

Raw Score	Scaled Scores and Percents Below						Raw Score	Scaled Scores and Percents Below					
	Verbal Score	% Below	Quantitative Score	% Below	Analytical Score	% Below		Verbal Score	% Below	Quantitative Score	% Below	Analytical Score	% Below
72-75	800	99					39	440	38	590	57	670	85
71	790	99					38	430	36	580	54	660	83
70	770	99					37	420	33	570	52	650	81
69	760	99					36	410	30	560	49	630	76
68	750	98					35	400	27	550	48	620	74
67	730	97					34	390	24	540	45	610	72
66	720	96					33	380	22	530	42	600	69
65	710	95					32	380	22	510	37	580	64
64	700	95					31	370	20	500	35	570	61
63	680	93					30	360	16	490	32	560	58
62	670	92					29	350	14	480	30	540	52
61	660	90					28	340	12	470	28	530	49
60	650	89	800	97			27	340	12	460	26	520	46
59	640	87	800	97			26	330	10	450	24	500	40
58	630	85	790	96			25	320	9	430	20	490	38
57	610	82	780	94			24	310	7	420	18	470	32
56	600	80	770	93			23	300	6	410	16	460	31
55	590	78	760	92			22	290	5	390	13	440	24
54	580	76	750	89			21	280	4	380	12	420	20
53	570	74	740	88			20	270	3	360	9	410	18
52	560	72	730	86			19	260	2	350	7	390	15
51	550	69	720	84			18	250	1	340	6	380	13
50	540	67	710	82	800	99	17	240	1	320	5	360	10
49	530	64	700	80	800	99	16	230	1	310	4	340	7
48	520	61	690	78	800	99	15	220	0	290	2	330	6
47	510	59	680	77	790	98	14	200	0	270	2	310	4
46	500	56	670	74	770	97	13	200	0	260	1	290	3
45	490	54	660	72	760	96	12	200	0	240	1	280	2
	480	51	640	68	740	95	11	200	0	230	0	260	1
	470	48	630	66	730	94	10	200	0	220	0	250	1
	460	44	620	63	710	91	9	200	0	210	0	240	1
	450	41	610	61	700	90	8	200	0	200	0	220	0
	450	41	600	59	690	88	7	200	0	200	0	210	0
							0-6	200	0	200	0	200	0

*Percent scoring below the scaled score is based on the performance of 923,359 examinees who took the General Test between October 1, 1986, and September 30, 1989.

General Test Average Scores for Seniors and Nonenrolled College Graduates,
Classified by Intended Graduate Major Field Group*
(Based on the performance of seniors and nonenrolled college graduates
tested at any of the five annual international administrations
between October 1, 1984, and September 30, 1987)**

Intended Graduate Major Field Group	Number of Examinees	Verbal Ability	Quantitative Ability	Analytical Ability
HUMANITIES				
Arts	8,887	496	497	534
Languages, Other Humanities	32,620	542	532	556
SOCIAL SCIENCES				
Education	26,266	453	483	511
Behavioral Sciences	63,143	509	526	544
Other Social Sciences	30,139	475	487	514
BIOLOGICAL SCIENCES				
Bioscience	19,922	507	582	570
Health Sciences	33,123	467	505	523
Other Applied Bioscience	10,985	487	554	554
PHYSICAL SCIENCES				
Engineering	35,954	477	677	582
Mathematical Sciences	22,475	487	659	596
Physical Sciences	18,040	518	641	591

*Limited to those who earned their college degree within five years of the test date.
** Note that the data in the table are based on examinees from 1984-1987 instead of 1986-1989. This is due to changes made in 1988 in the classifications of major fields.

GRADUATE RECORD EXAMINATIONS-GENERAL TEST

(Use for GRE Administrations between 10/1/90 and 9/30/91 only.)

SIDE 1

Use only a pencil with a soft, black lead (No. 2 or HB) to complete this answer sheet.
Be sure to fill in completely the space that corresponds to your answer choice.
Completely erase any errors or stray marks.

DO NOT USE INK.

7. TEST NAME:

FORM CODE:

8. TEST BOOK SERIAL NUMBER:

SHADED AREA FOR ETS USE ONLY

6. TITLE CODE

9.
YOUR NAME:
Last Name(Family or Surname)   First Name(Given)   M.I.

MAILING ADDRESS:
(Print)
P.O. Box or Street Address

City

Country

State or Province

Zip or Postal Code

CENTER:
City

Country

State or Province

Center Number

10. CERTIFICATION STATEMENT

SIGNATURE:

DATE: _____ / _____ / _____
        Month   Day   Year

540TF30P250e   I.N.275415   Q1868-07

1. NAME

Omit spaces, apostrophes, Jr., II, etc.

Last Name (Family or Surname) - first 15 letters

First Name (Given) - first 12 letters

M.I.

5. P.O. Box or Street Address first 10 characters

Indicate a space in address by leaving a blank box and filling in the corresponding diamond.

4. REGISTRATION NUMBER

3. SOCIAL SECURITY NUMBER

2. DATE OF BIRTH

Month	Day	Year
Jan.		
Feb.		
Mar.		
Apr.		
May		
June		
July		
Aug.		
Sept.		
Oct.		
Nov.		
Dec.		

SIDE 2

GENERAL TEST

SIGNATURE:

DO NOT SIGN UNTIL AFTER THE BREAK

IF YOU DO NOT WANT THIS ANSWER SHEET TO BE SCORED

If you want to cancel your scores from this administration, complete A and B below. No record of this test will be sent to your designated recipients, and there will be no scores on your GRE record. You will receive confirmation of this cancellation. Once a score is canceled, it cannot be reinstated.

To cancel your scores from this test administration, you must:

A. fill in both ovals here . . . . . ○ – ○

B. sign your name in full below:

BE SURE EACH MARK IS DARK AND COMPLETELY FILLS THE INTENDED SPACE AS ILLUSTRATED HERE: ⬬.
YOU MAY FIND MORE RESPONSE SPACES THAN YOU NEED. IF SO, PLEASE LEAVE THEM BLANK.

SECTION 1	SECTION 2	SECTION 3	SECTION 4	SECTION 5	SECTION 6	SECTION 7
1. Ⓐ Ⓑ Ⓒ Ⓓ Ⓔ	1. Ⓐ Ⓑ Ⓒ Ⓓ Ⓔ	1. Ⓐ Ⓑ Ⓒ Ⓓ Ⓔ	1. Ⓐ Ⓑ Ⓒ Ⓓ Ⓔ	1. Ⓐ Ⓑ Ⓒ Ⓓ Ⓔ	1. Ⓐ Ⓑ Ⓒ Ⓓ Ⓔ	1. Ⓐ Ⓑ Ⓒ Ⓓ Ⓔ
2. Ⓐ Ⓑ Ⓒ Ⓓ Ⓔ	2. Ⓐ Ⓑ Ⓒ Ⓓ Ⓔ	2. Ⓐ Ⓑ Ⓒ Ⓓ Ⓔ	2. Ⓐ Ⓑ Ⓒ Ⓓ Ⓔ	2. Ⓐ Ⓑ Ⓒ Ⓓ Ⓔ	2. Ⓐ Ⓑ Ⓒ Ⓓ Ⓔ	2. Ⓐ Ⓑ Ⓒ Ⓓ Ⓔ
3. Ⓐ Ⓑ Ⓒ Ⓓ Ⓔ	3. Ⓐ Ⓑ Ⓒ Ⓓ Ⓔ	3. Ⓐ Ⓑ Ⓒ Ⓓ Ⓔ	3. Ⓐ Ⓑ Ⓒ Ⓓ Ⓔ	3. Ⓐ Ⓑ Ⓒ Ⓓ Ⓔ	3. Ⓐ Ⓑ Ⓒ Ⓓ Ⓔ	3. Ⓐ Ⓑ Ⓒ Ⓓ Ⓔ
4. Ⓐ Ⓑ Ⓒ Ⓓ Ⓔ	4. Ⓐ Ⓑ Ⓒ Ⓓ Ⓔ	4. Ⓐ Ⓑ Ⓒ Ⓓ Ⓔ	4. Ⓐ Ⓑ Ⓒ Ⓓ Ⓔ	4. Ⓐ Ⓑ Ⓒ Ⓓ Ⓔ	4. Ⓐ Ⓑ Ⓒ Ⓓ Ⓔ	4. Ⓐ Ⓑ Ⓒ Ⓓ Ⓔ
5. Ⓐ Ⓑ Ⓒ Ⓓ Ⓔ	5. Ⓐ Ⓑ Ⓒ Ⓓ Ⓔ	5. Ⓐ Ⓑ Ⓒ Ⓓ Ⓔ	5. Ⓐ Ⓑ Ⓒ Ⓓ Ⓔ	5. Ⓐ Ⓑ Ⓒ Ⓓ Ⓔ	5. Ⓐ Ⓑ Ⓒ Ⓓ Ⓔ	5. Ⓐ Ⓑ Ⓒ Ⓓ Ⓔ
6. Ⓐ Ⓑ Ⓒ Ⓓ Ⓔ	6. Ⓐ Ⓑ Ⓒ Ⓓ Ⓔ	6. Ⓐ Ⓑ Ⓒ Ⓓ Ⓔ	6. Ⓐ Ⓑ Ⓒ Ⓓ Ⓔ	6. Ⓐ Ⓑ Ⓒ Ⓓ Ⓔ	6. Ⓐ Ⓑ Ⓒ Ⓓ Ⓔ	6. Ⓐ Ⓑ Ⓒ Ⓓ Ⓔ
7. Ⓐ Ⓑ Ⓒ Ⓓ Ⓔ	7. Ⓐ Ⓑ Ⓒ Ⓓ Ⓔ	7. Ⓐ Ⓑ Ⓒ Ⓓ Ⓔ	7. Ⓐ Ⓑ Ⓒ Ⓓ Ⓔ	7. Ⓐ Ⓑ Ⓒ Ⓓ Ⓔ	7. Ⓐ Ⓑ Ⓒ Ⓓ Ⓔ	7. Ⓐ Ⓑ Ⓒ Ⓓ Ⓔ
8. Ⓐ Ⓑ Ⓒ Ⓓ Ⓔ	8. Ⓐ Ⓑ Ⓒ Ⓓ Ⓔ	8. Ⓐ Ⓑ Ⓒ Ⓓ Ⓔ	8. Ⓐ Ⓑ Ⓒ Ⓓ Ⓔ	8. Ⓐ Ⓑ Ⓒ Ⓓ Ⓔ	8. Ⓐ Ⓑ Ⓒ Ⓓ Ⓔ	8. Ⓐ Ⓑ Ⓒ Ⓓ Ⓔ
9. Ⓐ Ⓑ Ⓒ Ⓓ Ⓔ	9. Ⓐ Ⓑ Ⓒ Ⓓ Ⓔ	9. Ⓐ Ⓑ Ⓒ Ⓓ Ⓔ	9. Ⓐ Ⓑ Ⓒ Ⓓ Ⓔ	9. Ⓐ Ⓑ Ⓒ Ⓓ Ⓔ	9. Ⓐ Ⓑ Ⓒ Ⓓ Ⓔ	9. Ⓐ Ⓑ Ⓒ Ⓓ Ⓔ
10. Ⓐ Ⓑ Ⓒ Ⓓ Ⓔ	10. Ⓐ Ⓑ Ⓒ Ⓓ Ⓔ	10. Ⓐ Ⓑ Ⓒ Ⓓ Ⓔ	10. Ⓐ Ⓑ Ⓒ Ⓓ Ⓔ	10. Ⓐ Ⓑ Ⓒ Ⓓ Ⓔ	10. Ⓐ Ⓑ Ⓒ Ⓓ Ⓔ	10. Ⓐ Ⓑ Ⓒ Ⓓ Ⓔ
11. Ⓐ Ⓑ Ⓒ Ⓓ Ⓔ	11. Ⓐ Ⓑ Ⓒ Ⓓ Ⓔ	11. Ⓐ Ⓑ Ⓒ Ⓓ Ⓔ	11. Ⓐ Ⓑ Ⓒ Ⓓ Ⓔ	11. Ⓐ Ⓑ Ⓒ Ⓓ Ⓔ	11. Ⓐ Ⓑ Ⓒ Ⓓ Ⓔ	11. Ⓐ Ⓑ Ⓒ Ⓓ Ⓔ
12. Ⓐ Ⓑ Ⓒ Ⓓ Ⓔ	12. Ⓐ Ⓑ Ⓒ Ⓓ Ⓔ	12. Ⓐ Ⓑ Ⓒ Ⓓ Ⓔ	12. Ⓐ Ⓑ Ⓒ Ⓓ Ⓔ	12. Ⓐ Ⓑ Ⓒ Ⓓ Ⓔ	12. Ⓐ Ⓑ Ⓒ Ⓓ Ⓔ	12. Ⓐ Ⓑ Ⓒ Ⓓ Ⓔ
13. Ⓐ Ⓑ Ⓒ Ⓓ Ⓔ	13. Ⓐ Ⓑ Ⓒ Ⓓ Ⓔ	13. Ⓐ Ⓑ Ⓒ Ⓓ Ⓔ	13. Ⓐ Ⓑ Ⓒ Ⓓ Ⓔ	13. Ⓐ Ⓑ Ⓒ Ⓓ Ⓔ	13. Ⓐ Ⓑ Ⓒ Ⓓ Ⓔ	13. Ⓐ Ⓑ Ⓒ Ⓓ Ⓔ
14. Ⓐ Ⓑ Ⓒ Ⓓ Ⓔ	14. Ⓐ Ⓑ Ⓒ Ⓓ Ⓔ	14. Ⓐ Ⓑ Ⓒ Ⓓ Ⓔ	14. Ⓐ Ⓑ Ⓒ Ⓓ Ⓔ	14. Ⓐ Ⓑ Ⓒ Ⓓ Ⓔ	14. Ⓐ Ⓑ Ⓒ Ⓓ Ⓔ	14. Ⓐ Ⓑ Ⓒ Ⓓ Ⓔ
15. Ⓐ Ⓑ Ⓒ Ⓓ Ⓔ	15. Ⓐ Ⓑ Ⓒ Ⓓ Ⓔ	15. Ⓐ Ⓑ Ⓒ Ⓓ Ⓔ	15. Ⓐ Ⓑ Ⓒ Ⓓ Ⓔ	15. Ⓐ Ⓑ Ⓒ Ⓓ Ⓔ	15. Ⓐ Ⓑ Ⓒ Ⓓ Ⓔ	15. Ⓐ Ⓑ Ⓒ Ⓓ Ⓔ
16. Ⓐ Ⓑ Ⓒ Ⓓ Ⓔ	16. Ⓐ Ⓑ Ⓒ Ⓓ Ⓔ	16. Ⓐ Ⓑ Ⓒ Ⓓ Ⓔ	16. Ⓐ Ⓑ Ⓒ Ⓓ Ⓔ	16. Ⓐ Ⓑ Ⓒ Ⓓ Ⓔ	16. Ⓐ Ⓑ Ⓒ Ⓓ Ⓔ	16. Ⓐ Ⓑ Ⓒ Ⓓ Ⓔ
17. Ⓐ Ⓑ Ⓒ Ⓓ Ⓔ	17. Ⓐ Ⓑ Ⓒ Ⓓ Ⓔ	17. Ⓐ Ⓑ Ⓒ Ⓓ Ⓔ	17. Ⓐ Ⓑ Ⓒ Ⓓ Ⓔ	17. Ⓐ Ⓑ Ⓒ Ⓓ Ⓔ	17. Ⓐ Ⓑ Ⓒ Ⓓ Ⓔ	17. Ⓐ Ⓑ Ⓒ Ⓓ Ⓔ
18. Ⓐ Ⓑ Ⓒ Ⓓ Ⓔ	18. Ⓐ Ⓑ Ⓒ Ⓓ Ⓔ	18. Ⓐ Ⓑ Ⓒ Ⓓ Ⓔ	18. Ⓐ Ⓑ Ⓒ Ⓓ Ⓔ	18. Ⓐ Ⓑ Ⓒ Ⓓ Ⓔ	18. Ⓐ Ⓑ Ⓒ Ⓓ Ⓔ	18. Ⓐ Ⓑ Ⓒ Ⓓ Ⓔ
19. Ⓐ Ⓑ Ⓒ Ⓓ Ⓔ	19. Ⓐ Ⓑ Ⓒ Ⓓ Ⓔ	19. Ⓐ Ⓑ Ⓒ Ⓓ Ⓔ	19. Ⓐ Ⓑ Ⓒ Ⓓ Ⓔ	19. Ⓐ Ⓑ Ⓒ Ⓓ Ⓔ	19. Ⓐ Ⓑ Ⓒ Ⓓ Ⓔ	19. Ⓐ Ⓑ Ⓒ Ⓓ Ⓔ
20. Ⓐ Ⓑ Ⓒ Ⓓ Ⓔ	20. Ⓐ Ⓑ Ⓒ Ⓓ Ⓔ	20. Ⓐ Ⓑ Ⓒ Ⓓ Ⓔ	20. Ⓐ Ⓑ Ⓒ Ⓓ Ⓔ	20. Ⓐ Ⓑ Ⓒ Ⓓ Ⓔ	20. Ⓐ Ⓑ Ⓒ Ⓓ Ⓔ	20. Ⓐ Ⓑ Ⓒ Ⓓ Ⓔ
21. Ⓐ Ⓑ Ⓒ Ⓓ Ⓔ	21. Ⓐ Ⓑ Ⓒ Ⓓ Ⓔ	21. Ⓐ Ⓑ Ⓒ Ⓓ Ⓔ	21. Ⓐ Ⓑ Ⓒ Ⓓ Ⓔ	21. Ⓐ Ⓑ Ⓒ Ⓓ Ⓔ	21. Ⓐ Ⓑ Ⓒ Ⓓ Ⓔ	21. Ⓐ Ⓑ Ⓒ Ⓓ Ⓔ
22. Ⓐ Ⓑ Ⓒ Ⓓ Ⓔ	22. Ⓐ Ⓑ Ⓒ Ⓓ Ⓔ	22. Ⓐ Ⓑ Ⓒ Ⓓ Ⓔ	22. Ⓐ Ⓑ Ⓒ Ⓓ Ⓔ	22. Ⓐ Ⓑ Ⓒ Ⓓ Ⓔ	22. Ⓐ Ⓑ Ⓒ Ⓓ Ⓔ	22. Ⓐ Ⓑ Ⓒ Ⓓ Ⓔ
23. Ⓐ Ⓑ Ⓒ Ⓓ Ⓔ	23. Ⓐ Ⓑ Ⓒ Ⓓ Ⓔ	23. Ⓐ Ⓑ Ⓒ Ⓓ Ⓔ	23. Ⓐ Ⓑ Ⓒ Ⓓ Ⓔ	23. Ⓐ Ⓑ Ⓒ Ⓓ Ⓔ	23. Ⓐ Ⓑ Ⓒ Ⓓ Ⓔ	23. Ⓐ Ⓑ Ⓒ Ⓓ Ⓔ
24. Ⓐ Ⓑ Ⓒ Ⓓ Ⓔ	24. Ⓐ Ⓑ Ⓒ Ⓓ Ⓔ	24. Ⓐ Ⓑ Ⓒ Ⓓ Ⓔ	24. Ⓐ Ⓑ Ⓒ Ⓓ Ⓔ	24. Ⓐ Ⓑ Ⓒ Ⓓ Ⓔ	24. Ⓐ Ⓑ Ⓒ Ⓓ Ⓔ	24. Ⓐ Ⓑ Ⓒ Ⓓ Ⓔ
25. Ⓐ Ⓑ Ⓒ Ⓓ Ⓔ	25. Ⓐ Ⓑ Ⓒ Ⓓ Ⓔ	25. Ⓐ Ⓑ Ⓒ Ⓓ Ⓔ	25. Ⓐ Ⓑ Ⓒ Ⓓ Ⓔ	25. Ⓐ Ⓑ Ⓒ Ⓓ Ⓔ	25. Ⓐ Ⓑ Ⓒ Ⓓ Ⓔ	25. Ⓐ Ⓑ Ⓒ Ⓓ Ⓔ
26. Ⓐ Ⓑ Ⓒ Ⓓ Ⓔ	26. Ⓐ Ⓑ Ⓒ Ⓓ Ⓔ	26. Ⓐ Ⓑ Ⓒ Ⓓ Ⓔ	26. Ⓐ Ⓑ Ⓒ Ⓓ Ⓔ	26. Ⓐ Ⓑ Ⓒ Ⓓ Ⓔ	26. Ⓐ Ⓑ Ⓒ Ⓓ Ⓔ	26. Ⓐ Ⓑ Ⓒ Ⓓ Ⓔ
27. Ⓐ Ⓑ Ⓒ Ⓓ Ⓔ	27. Ⓐ Ⓑ Ⓒ Ⓓ Ⓔ	27. Ⓐ Ⓑ Ⓒ Ⓓ Ⓔ	27. Ⓐ Ⓑ Ⓒ Ⓓ Ⓔ	27. Ⓐ Ⓑ Ⓒ Ⓓ Ⓔ	27. Ⓐ Ⓑ Ⓒ Ⓓ Ⓔ	27. Ⓐ Ⓑ Ⓒ Ⓓ Ⓔ
28. Ⓐ Ⓑ Ⓒ Ⓓ Ⓔ	28. Ⓐ Ⓑ Ⓒ Ⓓ Ⓔ	28. Ⓐ Ⓑ Ⓒ Ⓓ Ⓔ	28. Ⓐ Ⓑ Ⓒ Ⓓ Ⓔ	28. Ⓐ Ⓑ Ⓒ Ⓓ Ⓔ	28. Ⓐ Ⓑ Ⓒ Ⓓ Ⓔ	28. Ⓐ Ⓑ Ⓒ Ⓓ Ⓔ
29. Ⓐ Ⓑ Ⓒ Ⓓ Ⓔ	29. Ⓐ Ⓑ Ⓒ Ⓓ Ⓔ	29. Ⓐ Ⓑ Ⓒ Ⓓ Ⓔ	29. Ⓐ Ⓑ Ⓒ Ⓓ Ⓔ	29. Ⓐ Ⓑ Ⓒ Ⓓ Ⓔ	29. Ⓐ Ⓑ Ⓒ Ⓓ Ⓔ	29. Ⓐ Ⓑ Ⓒ Ⓓ Ⓔ
30. Ⓐ Ⓑ Ⓒ Ⓓ Ⓔ	30. Ⓐ Ⓑ Ⓒ Ⓓ Ⓔ	30. Ⓐ Ⓑ Ⓒ Ⓓ Ⓔ	30. Ⓐ Ⓑ Ⓒ Ⓓ Ⓔ	30. Ⓐ Ⓑ Ⓒ Ⓓ Ⓔ	30. Ⓐ Ⓑ Ⓒ Ⓓ Ⓔ	30. Ⓐ Ⓑ Ⓒ Ⓓ Ⓔ
31. Ⓐ Ⓑ Ⓒ Ⓓ Ⓔ	31. Ⓐ Ⓑ Ⓒ Ⓓ Ⓔ	31. Ⓐ Ⓑ Ⓒ Ⓓ Ⓔ	31. Ⓐ Ⓑ Ⓒ Ⓓ Ⓔ	31. Ⓐ Ⓑ Ⓒ Ⓓ Ⓔ	31. Ⓐ Ⓑ Ⓒ Ⓓ Ⓔ	31. Ⓐ Ⓑ Ⓒ Ⓓ Ⓔ
32. Ⓐ Ⓑ Ⓒ Ⓓ Ⓔ	32. Ⓐ Ⓑ Ⓒ Ⓓ Ⓔ	32. Ⓐ Ⓑ Ⓒ Ⓓ Ⓔ	32. Ⓐ Ⓑ Ⓒ Ⓓ Ⓔ	32. Ⓐ Ⓑ Ⓒ Ⓓ Ⓔ	32. Ⓐ Ⓑ Ⓒ Ⓓ Ⓔ	32. Ⓐ Ⓑ Ⓒ Ⓓ Ⓔ
33. Ⓐ Ⓑ Ⓒ Ⓓ Ⓔ	33. Ⓐ Ⓑ Ⓒ Ⓓ Ⓔ	33. Ⓐ Ⓑ Ⓒ Ⓓ Ⓔ	33. Ⓐ Ⓑ Ⓒ Ⓓ Ⓔ	33. Ⓐ Ⓑ Ⓒ Ⓓ Ⓔ	33. Ⓐ Ⓑ Ⓒ Ⓓ Ⓔ	33. Ⓐ Ⓑ Ⓒ Ⓓ Ⓔ
34. Ⓐ Ⓑ Ⓒ Ⓓ Ⓔ	34. Ⓐ Ⓑ Ⓒ Ⓓ Ⓔ	34. Ⓐ Ⓑ Ⓒ Ⓓ Ⓔ	34. Ⓐ Ⓑ Ⓒ Ⓓ Ⓔ	34. Ⓐ Ⓑ Ⓒ Ⓓ Ⓔ	34. Ⓐ Ⓑ Ⓒ Ⓓ Ⓔ	34. Ⓐ Ⓑ Ⓒ Ⓓ Ⓔ
35. Ⓐ Ⓑ Ⓒ Ⓓ Ⓔ	35. Ⓐ Ⓑ Ⓒ Ⓓ Ⓔ	35. Ⓐ Ⓑ Ⓒ Ⓓ Ⓔ	35. Ⓐ Ⓑ Ⓒ Ⓓ Ⓔ	35. Ⓐ Ⓑ Ⓒ Ⓓ Ⓔ	35. Ⓐ Ⓑ Ⓒ Ⓓ Ⓔ	35. Ⓐ Ⓑ Ⓒ Ⓓ Ⓔ
36. Ⓐ Ⓑ Ⓒ Ⓓ Ⓔ	36. Ⓐ Ⓑ Ⓒ Ⓓ Ⓔ	36. Ⓐ Ⓑ Ⓒ Ⓓ Ⓔ	36. Ⓐ Ⓑ Ⓒ Ⓓ Ⓔ	36. Ⓐ Ⓑ Ⓒ Ⓓ Ⓔ	36. Ⓐ Ⓑ Ⓒ Ⓓ Ⓔ	36. Ⓐ Ⓑ Ⓒ Ⓓ Ⓔ
37. Ⓐ Ⓑ Ⓒ Ⓓ Ⓔ	37. Ⓐ Ⓑ Ⓒ Ⓓ Ⓔ	37. Ⓐ Ⓑ Ⓒ Ⓓ Ⓔ	37. Ⓐ Ⓑ Ⓒ Ⓓ Ⓔ	37. Ⓐ Ⓑ Ⓒ Ⓓ Ⓔ	37. Ⓐ Ⓑ Ⓒ Ⓓ Ⓔ	37. Ⓐ Ⓑ Ⓒ Ⓓ Ⓔ
38. Ⓐ Ⓑ Ⓒ Ⓓ Ⓔ	38. Ⓐ Ⓑ Ⓒ Ⓓ Ⓔ	38. Ⓐ Ⓑ Ⓒ Ⓓ Ⓔ	38. Ⓐ Ⓑ Ⓒ Ⓓ Ⓔ	38. Ⓐ Ⓑ Ⓒ Ⓓ Ⓔ	38. Ⓐ Ⓑ Ⓒ Ⓓ Ⓔ	38. Ⓐ Ⓑ Ⓒ Ⓓ Ⓔ
39. Ⓐ Ⓑ Ⓒ Ⓓ Ⓔ	39. Ⓐ Ⓑ Ⓒ Ⓓ Ⓔ	39. Ⓐ Ⓑ Ⓒ Ⓓ Ⓔ	39. Ⓐ Ⓑ Ⓒ Ⓓ Ⓔ	39. Ⓐ Ⓑ Ⓒ Ⓓ Ⓔ	39. Ⓐ Ⓑ Ⓒ Ⓓ Ⓔ	39. Ⓐ Ⓑ Ⓒ Ⓓ Ⓔ
40. Ⓐ Ⓑ Ⓒ Ⓓ Ⓔ	40. Ⓐ Ⓑ Ⓒ Ⓓ Ⓔ	40. Ⓐ Ⓑ Ⓒ Ⓓ Ⓔ	40. Ⓐ Ⓑ Ⓒ Ⓓ Ⓔ	40. Ⓐ Ⓑ Ⓒ Ⓓ Ⓔ	40. Ⓐ Ⓑ Ⓒ Ⓓ Ⓔ	40. Ⓐ Ⓑ Ⓒ Ⓓ Ⓔ
41. Ⓐ Ⓑ Ⓒ Ⓓ Ⓔ	41. Ⓐ Ⓑ Ⓒ Ⓓ Ⓔ	41. Ⓐ Ⓑ Ⓒ Ⓓ Ⓔ	41. Ⓐ Ⓑ Ⓒ Ⓓ Ⓔ	41. Ⓐ Ⓑ Ⓒ Ⓓ Ⓔ	41. Ⓐ Ⓑ Ⓒ Ⓓ Ⓔ	41. Ⓐ Ⓑ Ⓒ Ⓓ Ⓔ
42. Ⓐ Ⓑ Ⓒ Ⓓ Ⓔ	42. Ⓐ Ⓑ Ⓒ Ⓓ Ⓔ	42. Ⓐ Ⓑ Ⓒ Ⓓ Ⓔ	42. Ⓐ Ⓑ Ⓒ Ⓓ Ⓔ	42. Ⓐ Ⓑ Ⓒ Ⓓ Ⓔ	42. Ⓐ Ⓑ Ⓒ Ⓓ Ⓔ	42. Ⓐ Ⓑ Ⓒ Ⓓ Ⓔ
43. Ⓐ Ⓑ Ⓒ Ⓓ Ⓔ	43. Ⓐ Ⓑ Ⓒ Ⓓ Ⓔ	43. Ⓐ Ⓑ Ⓒ Ⓓ Ⓔ	43. Ⓐ Ⓑ Ⓒ Ⓓ Ⓔ	43. Ⓐ Ⓑ Ⓒ Ⓓ Ⓔ	43. Ⓐ Ⓑ Ⓒ Ⓓ Ⓔ	43. Ⓐ Ⓑ Ⓒ Ⓓ Ⓔ
44. Ⓐ Ⓑ Ⓒ Ⓓ Ⓔ	44. Ⓐ Ⓑ Ⓒ Ⓓ Ⓔ	44. Ⓐ Ⓑ Ⓒ Ⓓ Ⓔ	44. Ⓐ Ⓑ Ⓒ Ⓓ Ⓔ	44. Ⓐ Ⓑ Ⓒ Ⓓ Ⓔ	44. Ⓐ Ⓑ Ⓒ Ⓓ Ⓔ	44. Ⓐ Ⓑ Ⓒ Ⓓ Ⓔ
45. Ⓐ Ⓑ Ⓒ Ⓓ Ⓔ	45. Ⓐ Ⓑ Ⓒ Ⓓ Ⓔ	45. Ⓐ Ⓑ Ⓒ Ⓓ Ⓔ	45. Ⓐ Ⓑ Ⓒ Ⓓ Ⓔ	45. Ⓐ Ⓑ Ⓒ Ⓓ Ⓔ	45. Ⓐ Ⓑ Ⓒ Ⓓ Ⓔ	45. Ⓐ Ⓑ Ⓒ Ⓓ Ⓔ
46. Ⓐ Ⓑ Ⓒ Ⓓ Ⓔ	46. Ⓐ Ⓑ Ⓒ Ⓓ Ⓔ	46. Ⓐ Ⓑ Ⓒ Ⓓ Ⓔ	46. Ⓐ Ⓑ Ⓒ Ⓓ Ⓔ	46. Ⓐ Ⓑ Ⓒ Ⓓ Ⓔ	46. Ⓐ Ⓑ Ⓒ Ⓓ Ⓔ	46. Ⓐ Ⓑ Ⓒ Ⓓ Ⓔ
47. Ⓐ Ⓑ Ⓒ Ⓓ Ⓔ	47. Ⓐ Ⓑ Ⓒ Ⓓ Ⓔ	47. Ⓐ Ⓑ Ⓒ Ⓓ Ⓔ	47. Ⓐ Ⓑ Ⓒ Ⓓ Ⓔ	47. Ⓐ Ⓑ Ⓒ Ⓓ Ⓔ	47. Ⓐ Ⓑ Ⓒ Ⓓ Ⓔ	47. Ⓐ Ⓑ Ⓒ Ⓓ Ⓔ
48. Ⓐ Ⓑ Ⓒ Ⓓ Ⓔ	48. Ⓐ Ⓑ Ⓒ Ⓓ Ⓔ	48. Ⓐ Ⓑ Ⓒ Ⓓ Ⓔ	48. Ⓐ Ⓑ Ⓒ Ⓓ Ⓔ	48. Ⓐ Ⓑ Ⓒ Ⓓ Ⓔ	48. Ⓐ Ⓑ Ⓒ Ⓓ Ⓔ	48. Ⓐ Ⓑ Ⓒ Ⓓ Ⓔ
49. Ⓐ Ⓑ Ⓒ Ⓓ Ⓔ	49. Ⓐ Ⓑ Ⓒ Ⓓ Ⓔ	49. Ⓐ Ⓑ Ⓒ Ⓓ Ⓔ	49. Ⓐ Ⓑ Ⓒ Ⓓ Ⓔ	49. Ⓐ Ⓑ Ⓒ Ⓓ Ⓔ	49. Ⓐ Ⓑ Ⓒ Ⓓ Ⓔ	49. Ⓐ Ⓑ Ⓒ Ⓓ Ⓔ
50. Ⓐ Ⓑ Ⓒ Ⓓ Ⓔ	50. Ⓐ Ⓑ Ⓒ Ⓓ Ⓔ	50. Ⓐ Ⓑ Ⓒ Ⓓ Ⓔ	50. Ⓐ Ⓑ Ⓒ Ⓓ Ⓔ	50. Ⓐ Ⓑ Ⓒ Ⓓ Ⓔ	50. Ⓐ Ⓑ Ⓒ Ⓓ Ⓔ	50. Ⓐ Ⓑ Ⓒ Ⓓ Ⓔ

FOR ETS USE ONLY	V1R	V2R	VTR	VCS	Q1R	Q2R	QTR	QCS	A1R	A2R	ATR	ACS

GRADUATE RECORD EXAMINATIONS-GENERAL TEST

(Use for GRE Administrations between 10/1/90 and 9/30/91 only.)

SIDE 1

Use only a pencil with a soft, black lead (No. 2 or HB) to complete this answer sheet.
Be sure to fill in completely the space that corresponds to your answer choice.
Completely erase any errors or stray marks.

DO NOT USE INK.

1. NAME

Omit spaces, apostrophes, Jr., II, etc.

Last Name (Family or Surname) - first 15 letters

First Name (Given) - first 12 letters

MI

2. DATE OF BIRTH

Month	Day	Year
Jan.		
Feb.		
Mar.		
Apr.		
May		
June		
July		
Aug.		
Sept.		
Oct.		
Nov.		
Dec.		

3. SOCIAL SECURITY NUMBER

4. REGISTRATION NUMBER

5. P.O. Box or Street Address
first 10 characters

Indicate a space in address by leaving a blank box and filling in the corresponding diamond.

6. TITLE CODE

7. TEST NAME:

FORM CODE:

8. TEST BOOK SERIAL NUMBER:

SHADED AREA FOR ETS USE ONLY

9. YOUR NAME:

Last Name(Family or Surname)   First Name(Given)   M.I.

MAILING ADDRESS:
(Print)

P.O. Box or Street Address

City   State or Province

Country   Zip or Postal Code

CENTER:

City   State or Province

Country

Center Number

10. CERTIFICATION STATEMENT

SIGNATURE:

DATE: ___ / ___ / ___
     Month   Day   Year

54OTF30P250e   I.N.275415   Q1868-07

SIGNATURE:

_____

DO NOT SIGN UNTIL AFTER THE BREAK

IF YOU DO NOT WANT THIS ANSWER SHEET TO BE SCORED

If you want to cancel your scores from this administration, complete A and B below. No record of this test will be sent to your designated recipients, and there will be no scores on your GRE record. You will receive confirmation of this cancellation. Once a score is canceled, it cannot be reinstated.

To cancel your scores from this test administration, you must:
A. fill in both ovals here ..... ◯ – ◯
B. sign your name in full below:

BE SURE EACH MARK IS DARK AND COMPLETELY FILLS THE INTENDED SPACE AS ILLUSTRATED HERE: ●.
YOU MAY FIND MORE RESPONSE SPACES THAN YOU NEED. IF SO, PLEASE LEAVE THEM BLANK.

SECTION 1	SECTION 2	SECTION 3	SECTION 4	SECTION 5	SECTION 6	SECTION 7

Each section contains numbered rows 1 through 50, each with answer ovals Ⓐ Ⓑ Ⓒ Ⓓ Ⓔ.

(Section 1, Row 1 shows marked ovals C and E.)

FOR ETS USE ONLY	V1R	V2R	VTR	VCS	Q1R	Q2R	QTR	QCS	A1R	A2R	ATR	ACS

GRADUATE RECORD EXAMINATIONS-GENERAL TEST

SIDE 1

(Use for GRE Administrations between 10/1/90 and 9/30/91 only.)

Use only a pencil with a soft, black lead (No. 2 or HB) to complete this answer sheet.
Be sure to fill in completely the space that corresponds to your answer choice.
Completely erase any errors or stray marks.

DO NOT USE INK.

1. NAME

Omit spaces, apostrophes, Jr., II, etc.

Last Name (Family or Surname) - first 15 letters | First Name (Given) - first 12 letters | MI

2. DATE OF BIRTH

Month	Day	Year
Jan.		
Feb.		
Mar.		
Apr.		
May		
June		
July		
Aug.		
Sept.		
Oct.		
Nov.		
Dec.		

3. SOCIAL SECURITY NUMBER

4. REGISTRATION NUMBER

5. P.O. Box or Street Address first 10 characters

Indicate a space in address by leaving a blank box and filling in the corresponding diamond.

6. TITLE CODE

7. TEST NAME:

FORM CODE:

8. TEST BOOK SERIAL NUMBER:

SHADED AREA FOR ETS USE ONLY

9. YOUR NAME:

Last Name (Family or Surname) | First Name (Given) | M.I.

MAILING ADDRESS:
(Print)

P.O. Box or Street Address

City | State or Province

Country | Zip or Postal Code

CENTER:

City | State or Province

Country | Center Number

10. CERTIFICATION STATEMENT

SIGNATURE:

DATE: _____ / _____ / _____
Month   Day   Year

540TF30P250e   I.N.275415   Q1868-07

SIDE 2

GENERAL TEST

SIGNATURE:

DO NOT SIGN UNTIL AFTER THE BREAK

IF YOU DO NOT WANT THIS ANSWER SHEET TO BE SCORED

If you want to cancel your scores from this administration, complete A and B below. No record of this test will be sent to your designated recipients, and there will be no scores on your GRE record. You will receive confirmation of this cancellation. Once a score is canceled, it cannot be reinstated.

To cancel your scores from this test administration, you must:

A. fill in both ovals here . . . . . ◯ – ◯

B. sign your name in full below:

BE SURE EACH MARK IS DARK AND COMPLETELY FILLS THE INTENDED SPACE AS ILLUSTRATED HERE: ⬬.
YOU MAY FIND MORE RESPONSE SPACES THAN YOU NEED. IF SO, PLEASE LEAVE THEM BLANK.

SECTION 1	SECTION 2	SECTION 3	SECTION 4	SECTION 5	SECTION 6	SECTION 7
1. Ⓐ Ⓑ Ⓒ Ⓓ Ⓔ	1. Ⓐ Ⓑ Ⓒ Ⓓ Ⓔ	1. Ⓐ Ⓑ Ⓒ Ⓓ Ⓔ	1. Ⓐ Ⓑ Ⓒ Ⓓ Ⓔ	1. Ⓐ Ⓑ Ⓒ Ⓓ Ⓔ	1. Ⓐ Ⓑ Ⓒ Ⓓ Ⓔ	1. Ⓐ Ⓑ Ⓒ Ⓓ Ⓔ
2. Ⓐ Ⓑ Ⓒ Ⓓ Ⓔ	2. Ⓐ Ⓑ Ⓒ Ⓓ Ⓔ	2. Ⓐ Ⓑ Ⓒ Ⓓ Ⓔ	2. Ⓐ Ⓑ Ⓒ Ⓓ Ⓔ	2. Ⓐ Ⓑ Ⓒ Ⓓ Ⓔ	2. Ⓐ Ⓑ Ⓒ Ⓓ Ⓔ	2. Ⓐ Ⓑ Ⓒ Ⓓ Ⓔ
3. Ⓐ Ⓑ Ⓒ Ⓓ Ⓔ	3. Ⓐ Ⓑ Ⓒ Ⓓ Ⓔ	3. Ⓐ Ⓑ Ⓒ Ⓓ Ⓔ	3. Ⓐ Ⓑ Ⓒ Ⓓ Ⓔ	3. Ⓐ Ⓑ Ⓒ Ⓓ Ⓔ	3. Ⓐ Ⓑ Ⓒ Ⓓ Ⓔ	3. Ⓐ Ⓑ Ⓒ Ⓓ Ⓔ
4. Ⓐ Ⓑ Ⓒ Ⓓ Ⓔ	4. Ⓐ Ⓑ Ⓒ Ⓓ Ⓔ	4. Ⓐ Ⓑ Ⓒ Ⓓ Ⓔ	4. Ⓐ Ⓑ Ⓒ Ⓓ Ⓔ	4. Ⓐ Ⓑ Ⓒ Ⓓ Ⓔ	4. Ⓐ Ⓑ Ⓒ Ⓓ Ⓔ	4. Ⓐ Ⓑ Ⓒ Ⓓ Ⓔ
5. Ⓐ Ⓑ Ⓒ Ⓓ Ⓔ	5. Ⓐ Ⓑ Ⓒ Ⓓ Ⓔ	5. Ⓐ Ⓑ Ⓒ Ⓓ Ⓔ	5. Ⓐ Ⓑ Ⓒ Ⓓ Ⓔ	5. Ⓐ Ⓑ Ⓒ Ⓓ Ⓔ	5. Ⓐ Ⓑ Ⓒ Ⓓ Ⓔ	5. Ⓐ Ⓑ Ⓒ Ⓓ Ⓔ
6. Ⓐ Ⓑ Ⓒ Ⓓ Ⓔ	6. Ⓐ Ⓑ Ⓒ Ⓓ Ⓔ	6. Ⓐ Ⓑ Ⓒ Ⓓ Ⓔ	6. Ⓐ Ⓑ Ⓒ Ⓓ Ⓔ	6. Ⓐ Ⓑ Ⓒ Ⓓ Ⓔ	6. Ⓐ Ⓑ Ⓒ Ⓓ Ⓔ	6. Ⓐ Ⓑ Ⓒ Ⓓ Ⓔ
7. Ⓐ Ⓑ Ⓒ Ⓓ Ⓔ	7. Ⓐ Ⓑ Ⓒ Ⓓ Ⓔ	7. Ⓐ Ⓑ Ⓒ Ⓓ Ⓔ	7. Ⓐ Ⓑ Ⓒ Ⓓ Ⓔ	7. Ⓐ Ⓑ Ⓒ Ⓓ Ⓔ	7. Ⓐ Ⓑ Ⓒ Ⓓ Ⓔ	7. Ⓐ Ⓑ Ⓒ Ⓓ Ⓔ
8. Ⓐ Ⓑ Ⓒ Ⓓ Ⓔ	8. Ⓐ Ⓑ Ⓒ Ⓓ Ⓔ	8. Ⓐ Ⓑ Ⓒ Ⓓ Ⓔ	8. Ⓐ Ⓑ Ⓒ Ⓓ Ⓔ	8. Ⓐ Ⓑ Ⓒ Ⓓ Ⓔ	8. Ⓐ Ⓑ Ⓒ Ⓓ Ⓔ	8. Ⓐ Ⓑ Ⓒ Ⓓ Ⓔ
9. Ⓐ Ⓑ Ⓒ Ⓓ Ⓔ	9. Ⓐ Ⓑ Ⓒ Ⓓ Ⓔ	9. Ⓐ Ⓑ Ⓒ Ⓓ Ⓔ	9. Ⓐ Ⓑ Ⓒ Ⓓ Ⓔ	9. Ⓐ Ⓑ Ⓒ Ⓓ Ⓔ	9. Ⓐ Ⓑ Ⓒ Ⓓ Ⓔ	9. Ⓐ Ⓑ Ⓒ Ⓓ Ⓔ
10. Ⓐ Ⓑ Ⓒ Ⓓ Ⓔ	10. Ⓐ Ⓑ Ⓒ Ⓓ Ⓔ	10. Ⓐ Ⓑ Ⓒ Ⓓ Ⓔ	10. Ⓐ Ⓑ Ⓒ Ⓓ Ⓔ	10. Ⓐ Ⓑ Ⓒ Ⓓ Ⓔ	10. Ⓐ Ⓑ Ⓒ Ⓓ Ⓔ	10. Ⓐ Ⓑ Ⓒ Ⓓ Ⓔ
11. Ⓐ Ⓑ Ⓒ Ⓓ Ⓔ	11. Ⓐ Ⓑ Ⓒ Ⓓ Ⓔ	11. Ⓐ Ⓑ Ⓒ Ⓓ Ⓔ	11. Ⓐ Ⓑ Ⓒ Ⓓ Ⓔ	11. Ⓐ Ⓑ Ⓒ Ⓓ Ⓔ	11. Ⓐ Ⓑ Ⓒ Ⓓ Ⓔ	11. Ⓐ Ⓑ Ⓒ Ⓓ Ⓔ
12. Ⓐ Ⓑ Ⓒ Ⓓ Ⓔ	12. Ⓐ Ⓑ Ⓒ Ⓓ Ⓔ	12. Ⓐ Ⓑ Ⓒ Ⓓ Ⓔ	12. Ⓐ Ⓑ Ⓒ Ⓓ Ⓔ	12. Ⓐ Ⓑ Ⓒ Ⓓ Ⓔ	12. Ⓐ Ⓑ Ⓒ Ⓓ Ⓔ	12. Ⓐ Ⓑ Ⓒ Ⓓ Ⓔ
13. Ⓐ Ⓑ Ⓒ Ⓓ Ⓔ	13. Ⓐ Ⓑ Ⓒ Ⓓ Ⓔ	13. Ⓐ Ⓑ Ⓒ Ⓓ Ⓔ	13. Ⓐ Ⓑ Ⓒ Ⓓ Ⓔ	13. Ⓐ Ⓑ Ⓒ Ⓓ Ⓔ	13. Ⓐ Ⓑ Ⓒ Ⓓ Ⓔ	13. Ⓐ Ⓑ Ⓒ Ⓓ Ⓔ
14. Ⓐ Ⓑ Ⓒ Ⓓ Ⓔ	14. Ⓐ Ⓑ Ⓒ Ⓓ Ⓔ	14. Ⓐ Ⓑ Ⓒ Ⓓ Ⓔ	14. Ⓐ Ⓑ Ⓒ Ⓓ Ⓔ	14. Ⓐ Ⓑ Ⓒ Ⓓ Ⓔ	14. Ⓐ Ⓑ Ⓒ Ⓓ Ⓔ	14. Ⓐ Ⓑ Ⓒ Ⓓ Ⓔ
15. Ⓐ Ⓑ Ⓒ Ⓓ Ⓔ	15. Ⓐ Ⓑ Ⓒ Ⓓ Ⓔ	15. Ⓐ Ⓑ Ⓒ Ⓓ Ⓔ	15. Ⓐ Ⓑ Ⓒ Ⓓ Ⓔ	15. Ⓐ Ⓑ Ⓒ Ⓓ Ⓔ	15. Ⓐ Ⓑ Ⓒ Ⓓ Ⓔ	15. Ⓐ Ⓑ Ⓒ Ⓓ Ⓔ
16. Ⓐ Ⓑ Ⓒ Ⓓ Ⓔ	16. Ⓐ Ⓑ Ⓒ Ⓓ Ⓔ	16. Ⓐ Ⓑ Ⓒ Ⓓ Ⓔ	16. Ⓐ Ⓑ Ⓒ Ⓓ Ⓔ	16. Ⓐ Ⓑ Ⓒ Ⓓ Ⓔ	16. Ⓐ Ⓑ Ⓒ Ⓓ Ⓔ	16. Ⓐ Ⓑ Ⓒ Ⓓ Ⓔ
17. Ⓐ Ⓑ Ⓒ Ⓓ Ⓔ	17. Ⓐ Ⓑ Ⓒ Ⓓ Ⓔ	17. Ⓐ Ⓑ Ⓒ Ⓓ Ⓔ	17. Ⓐ Ⓑ Ⓒ Ⓓ Ⓔ	17. Ⓐ Ⓑ Ⓒ Ⓓ Ⓔ	17. Ⓐ Ⓑ Ⓒ Ⓓ Ⓔ	17. Ⓐ Ⓑ Ⓒ Ⓓ Ⓔ
18. Ⓐ Ⓑ Ⓒ Ⓓ Ⓔ	18. Ⓐ Ⓑ Ⓒ Ⓓ Ⓔ	18. Ⓐ Ⓑ Ⓒ Ⓓ Ⓔ	18. Ⓐ Ⓑ Ⓒ Ⓓ Ⓔ	18. Ⓐ Ⓑ Ⓒ Ⓓ Ⓔ	18. Ⓐ Ⓑ Ⓒ Ⓓ Ⓔ	18. Ⓐ Ⓑ Ⓒ Ⓓ Ⓔ
19. Ⓐ Ⓑ Ⓒ Ⓓ Ⓔ	19. Ⓐ Ⓑ Ⓒ Ⓓ Ⓔ	19. Ⓐ Ⓑ Ⓒ Ⓓ Ⓔ	19. Ⓐ Ⓑ Ⓒ Ⓓ Ⓔ	19. Ⓐ Ⓑ Ⓒ Ⓓ Ⓔ	19. Ⓐ Ⓑ Ⓒ Ⓓ Ⓔ	19. Ⓐ Ⓑ Ⓒ Ⓓ Ⓔ
20. Ⓐ Ⓑ Ⓒ Ⓓ Ⓔ	20. Ⓐ Ⓑ Ⓒ Ⓓ Ⓔ	20. Ⓐ Ⓑ Ⓒ Ⓓ Ⓔ	20. Ⓐ Ⓑ Ⓒ Ⓓ Ⓔ	20. Ⓐ Ⓑ Ⓒ Ⓓ Ⓔ	20. Ⓐ Ⓑ Ⓒ Ⓓ Ⓔ	20. Ⓐ Ⓑ Ⓒ Ⓓ Ⓔ
21. Ⓐ Ⓑ Ⓒ Ⓓ Ⓔ	21. Ⓐ Ⓑ Ⓒ Ⓓ Ⓔ	21. Ⓐ Ⓑ Ⓒ Ⓓ Ⓔ	21. Ⓐ Ⓑ Ⓒ Ⓓ Ⓔ	21. Ⓐ Ⓑ Ⓒ Ⓓ Ⓔ	21. Ⓐ Ⓑ Ⓒ Ⓓ Ⓔ	21. Ⓐ Ⓑ Ⓒ Ⓓ Ⓔ
22. Ⓐ Ⓑ Ⓒ Ⓓ Ⓔ	22. Ⓐ Ⓑ Ⓒ Ⓓ Ⓔ	22. Ⓐ Ⓑ Ⓒ Ⓓ Ⓔ	22. Ⓐ Ⓑ Ⓒ Ⓓ Ⓔ	22. Ⓐ Ⓑ Ⓒ Ⓓ Ⓔ	22. Ⓐ Ⓑ Ⓒ Ⓓ Ⓔ	22. Ⓐ Ⓑ Ⓒ Ⓓ Ⓔ
23. Ⓐ Ⓑ Ⓒ Ⓓ Ⓔ	23. Ⓐ Ⓑ Ⓒ Ⓓ Ⓔ	23. Ⓐ Ⓑ Ⓒ Ⓓ Ⓔ	23. Ⓐ Ⓑ Ⓒ Ⓓ Ⓔ	23. Ⓐ Ⓑ Ⓒ Ⓓ Ⓔ	23. Ⓐ Ⓑ Ⓒ Ⓓ Ⓔ	23. Ⓐ Ⓑ Ⓒ Ⓓ Ⓔ
24. Ⓐ Ⓑ Ⓒ Ⓓ Ⓔ	24. Ⓐ Ⓑ Ⓒ Ⓓ Ⓔ	24. Ⓐ Ⓑ Ⓒ Ⓓ Ⓔ	24. Ⓐ Ⓑ Ⓒ Ⓓ Ⓔ	24. Ⓐ Ⓑ Ⓒ Ⓓ Ⓔ	24. Ⓐ Ⓑ Ⓒ Ⓓ Ⓔ	24. Ⓐ Ⓑ Ⓒ Ⓓ Ⓔ
25. Ⓐ Ⓑ Ⓒ Ⓓ Ⓔ	25. Ⓐ Ⓑ Ⓒ Ⓓ Ⓔ	25. Ⓐ Ⓑ Ⓒ Ⓓ Ⓔ	25. Ⓐ Ⓑ Ⓒ Ⓓ Ⓔ	25. Ⓐ Ⓑ Ⓒ Ⓓ Ⓔ	25. Ⓐ Ⓑ Ⓒ Ⓓ Ⓔ	25. Ⓐ Ⓑ Ⓒ Ⓓ Ⓔ
26. Ⓐ Ⓑ Ⓒ Ⓓ Ⓔ	26. Ⓐ Ⓑ Ⓒ Ⓓ Ⓔ	26. Ⓐ Ⓑ Ⓒ Ⓓ Ⓔ	26. Ⓐ Ⓑ Ⓒ Ⓓ Ⓔ	26. Ⓐ Ⓑ Ⓒ Ⓓ Ⓔ	26. Ⓐ Ⓑ Ⓒ Ⓓ Ⓔ	26. Ⓐ Ⓑ Ⓒ Ⓓ Ⓔ
27. Ⓐ Ⓑ Ⓒ Ⓓ Ⓔ	27. Ⓐ Ⓑ Ⓒ Ⓓ Ⓔ	27. Ⓐ Ⓑ Ⓒ Ⓓ Ⓔ	27. Ⓐ Ⓑ Ⓒ Ⓓ Ⓔ	27. Ⓐ Ⓑ Ⓒ Ⓓ Ⓔ	27. Ⓐ Ⓑ Ⓒ Ⓓ Ⓔ	27. Ⓐ Ⓑ Ⓒ Ⓓ Ⓔ
28. Ⓐ Ⓑ Ⓒ Ⓓ Ⓔ	28. Ⓐ Ⓑ Ⓒ Ⓓ Ⓔ	28. Ⓐ Ⓑ Ⓒ Ⓓ Ⓔ	28. Ⓐ Ⓑ Ⓒ Ⓓ Ⓔ	28. Ⓐ Ⓑ Ⓒ Ⓓ Ⓔ	28. Ⓐ Ⓑ Ⓒ Ⓓ Ⓔ	28. Ⓐ Ⓑ Ⓒ Ⓓ Ⓔ
29. Ⓐ Ⓑ Ⓒ Ⓓ Ⓔ	29. Ⓐ Ⓑ Ⓒ Ⓓ Ⓔ	29. Ⓐ Ⓑ Ⓒ Ⓓ Ⓔ	29. Ⓐ Ⓑ Ⓒ Ⓓ Ⓔ	29. Ⓐ Ⓑ Ⓒ Ⓓ Ⓔ	29. Ⓐ Ⓑ Ⓒ Ⓓ Ⓔ	29. Ⓐ Ⓑ Ⓒ Ⓓ Ⓔ
30. Ⓐ Ⓑ Ⓒ Ⓓ Ⓔ	30. Ⓐ Ⓑ Ⓒ Ⓓ Ⓔ	30. Ⓐ Ⓑ Ⓒ Ⓓ Ⓔ	30. Ⓐ Ⓑ Ⓒ Ⓓ Ⓔ	30. Ⓐ Ⓑ Ⓒ Ⓓ Ⓔ	30. Ⓐ Ⓑ Ⓒ Ⓓ Ⓔ	30. Ⓐ Ⓑ Ⓒ Ⓓ Ⓔ
31. Ⓐ Ⓑ Ⓒ Ⓓ Ⓔ	31. Ⓐ Ⓑ Ⓒ Ⓓ Ⓔ	31. Ⓐ Ⓑ Ⓒ Ⓓ Ⓔ	31. Ⓐ Ⓑ Ⓒ Ⓓ Ⓔ	31. Ⓐ Ⓑ Ⓒ Ⓓ Ⓔ	31. Ⓐ Ⓑ Ⓒ Ⓓ Ⓔ	31. Ⓐ Ⓑ Ⓒ Ⓓ Ⓔ
32. Ⓐ Ⓑ Ⓒ Ⓓ Ⓔ	32. Ⓐ Ⓑ Ⓒ Ⓓ Ⓔ	32. Ⓐ Ⓑ Ⓒ Ⓓ Ⓔ	32. Ⓐ Ⓑ Ⓒ Ⓓ Ⓔ	32. Ⓐ Ⓑ Ⓒ Ⓓ Ⓔ	32. Ⓐ Ⓑ Ⓒ Ⓓ Ⓔ	32. Ⓐ Ⓑ Ⓒ Ⓓ Ⓔ
33. Ⓐ Ⓑ Ⓒ Ⓓ Ⓔ	33. Ⓐ Ⓑ Ⓒ Ⓓ Ⓔ	33. Ⓐ Ⓑ Ⓒ Ⓓ Ⓔ	33. Ⓐ Ⓑ Ⓒ Ⓓ Ⓔ	33. Ⓐ Ⓑ Ⓒ Ⓓ Ⓔ	33. Ⓐ Ⓑ Ⓒ Ⓓ Ⓔ	33. Ⓐ Ⓑ Ⓒ Ⓓ Ⓔ
34. Ⓐ Ⓑ Ⓒ Ⓓ Ⓔ	34. Ⓐ Ⓑ Ⓒ Ⓓ Ⓔ	34. Ⓐ Ⓑ Ⓒ Ⓓ Ⓔ	34. Ⓐ Ⓑ Ⓒ Ⓓ Ⓔ	34. Ⓐ Ⓑ Ⓒ Ⓓ Ⓔ	34. Ⓐ Ⓑ Ⓒ Ⓓ Ⓔ	34. Ⓐ Ⓑ Ⓒ Ⓓ Ⓔ
35. Ⓐ Ⓑ Ⓒ Ⓓ Ⓔ	35. Ⓐ Ⓑ Ⓒ Ⓓ Ⓔ	35. Ⓐ Ⓑ Ⓒ Ⓓ Ⓔ	35. Ⓐ Ⓑ Ⓒ Ⓓ Ⓔ	35. Ⓐ Ⓑ Ⓒ Ⓓ Ⓔ	35. Ⓐ Ⓑ Ⓒ Ⓓ Ⓔ	35. Ⓐ Ⓑ Ⓒ Ⓓ Ⓔ
36. Ⓐ Ⓑ Ⓒ Ⓓ Ⓔ	36. Ⓐ Ⓑ Ⓒ Ⓓ Ⓔ	36. Ⓐ Ⓑ Ⓒ Ⓓ Ⓔ	36. Ⓐ Ⓑ Ⓒ Ⓓ Ⓔ	36. Ⓐ Ⓑ Ⓒ Ⓓ Ⓔ	36. Ⓐ Ⓑ Ⓒ Ⓓ Ⓔ	36. Ⓐ Ⓑ Ⓒ Ⓓ Ⓔ
37. Ⓐ Ⓑ Ⓒ Ⓓ Ⓔ	37. Ⓐ Ⓑ Ⓒ Ⓓ Ⓔ	37. Ⓐ Ⓑ Ⓒ Ⓓ Ⓔ	37. Ⓐ Ⓑ Ⓒ Ⓓ Ⓔ	37. Ⓐ Ⓑ Ⓒ Ⓓ Ⓔ	37. Ⓐ Ⓑ Ⓒ Ⓓ Ⓔ	37. Ⓐ Ⓑ Ⓒ Ⓓ Ⓔ
38. Ⓐ Ⓑ Ⓒ Ⓓ Ⓔ	38. Ⓐ Ⓑ Ⓒ Ⓓ Ⓔ	38. Ⓐ Ⓑ Ⓒ Ⓓ Ⓔ	38. Ⓐ Ⓑ Ⓒ Ⓓ Ⓔ	38. Ⓐ Ⓑ Ⓒ Ⓓ Ⓔ	38. Ⓐ Ⓑ Ⓒ Ⓓ Ⓔ	38. Ⓐ Ⓑ Ⓒ Ⓓ Ⓔ
39. Ⓐ Ⓑ Ⓒ Ⓓ Ⓔ	39. Ⓐ Ⓑ Ⓒ Ⓓ Ⓔ	39. Ⓐ Ⓑ Ⓒ Ⓓ Ⓔ	39. Ⓐ Ⓑ Ⓒ Ⓓ Ⓔ	39. Ⓐ Ⓑ Ⓒ Ⓓ Ⓔ	39. Ⓐ Ⓑ Ⓒ Ⓓ Ⓔ	39. Ⓐ Ⓑ Ⓒ Ⓓ Ⓔ
40. Ⓐ Ⓑ Ⓒ Ⓓ Ⓔ	40. Ⓐ Ⓑ Ⓒ Ⓓ Ⓔ	40. Ⓐ Ⓑ Ⓒ Ⓓ Ⓔ	40. Ⓐ Ⓑ Ⓒ Ⓓ Ⓔ	40. Ⓐ Ⓑ Ⓒ Ⓓ Ⓔ	40. Ⓐ Ⓑ Ⓒ Ⓓ Ⓔ	40. Ⓐ Ⓑ Ⓒ Ⓓ Ⓔ
41. Ⓐ Ⓑ Ⓒ Ⓓ Ⓔ	41. Ⓐ Ⓑ Ⓒ Ⓓ Ⓔ	41. Ⓐ Ⓑ Ⓒ Ⓓ Ⓔ	41. Ⓐ Ⓑ Ⓒ Ⓓ Ⓔ	41. Ⓐ Ⓑ Ⓒ Ⓓ Ⓔ	41. Ⓐ Ⓑ Ⓒ Ⓓ Ⓔ	41. Ⓐ Ⓑ Ⓒ Ⓓ Ⓔ
42. Ⓐ Ⓑ Ⓒ Ⓓ Ⓔ	42. Ⓐ Ⓑ Ⓒ Ⓓ Ⓔ	42. Ⓐ Ⓑ Ⓒ Ⓓ Ⓔ	42. Ⓐ Ⓑ Ⓒ Ⓓ Ⓔ	42. Ⓐ Ⓑ Ⓒ Ⓓ Ⓔ	42. Ⓐ Ⓑ Ⓒ Ⓓ Ⓔ	42. Ⓐ Ⓑ Ⓒ Ⓓ Ⓔ
43. Ⓐ Ⓑ Ⓒ Ⓓ Ⓔ	43. Ⓐ Ⓑ Ⓒ Ⓓ Ⓔ	43. Ⓐ Ⓑ Ⓒ Ⓓ Ⓔ	43. Ⓐ Ⓑ Ⓒ Ⓓ Ⓔ	43. Ⓐ Ⓑ Ⓒ Ⓓ Ⓔ	43. Ⓐ Ⓑ Ⓒ Ⓓ Ⓔ	43. Ⓐ Ⓑ Ⓒ Ⓓ Ⓔ
44. Ⓐ Ⓑ Ⓒ Ⓓ Ⓔ	44. Ⓐ Ⓑ Ⓒ Ⓓ Ⓔ	44. Ⓐ Ⓑ Ⓒ Ⓓ Ⓔ	44. Ⓐ Ⓑ Ⓒ Ⓓ Ⓔ	44. Ⓐ Ⓑ Ⓒ Ⓓ Ⓔ	44. Ⓐ Ⓑ Ⓒ Ⓓ Ⓔ	44. Ⓐ Ⓑ Ⓒ Ⓓ Ⓔ
45. Ⓐ Ⓑ Ⓒ Ⓓ Ⓔ	45. Ⓐ Ⓑ Ⓒ Ⓓ Ⓔ	45. Ⓐ Ⓑ Ⓒ Ⓓ Ⓔ	45. Ⓐ Ⓑ Ⓒ Ⓓ Ⓔ	45. Ⓐ Ⓑ Ⓒ Ⓓ Ⓔ	45. Ⓐ Ⓑ Ⓒ Ⓓ Ⓔ	45. Ⓐ Ⓑ Ⓒ Ⓓ Ⓔ
46. Ⓐ Ⓑ Ⓒ Ⓓ Ⓔ	46. Ⓐ Ⓑ Ⓒ Ⓓ Ⓔ	46. Ⓐ Ⓑ Ⓒ Ⓓ Ⓔ	46. Ⓐ Ⓑ Ⓒ Ⓓ Ⓔ	46. Ⓐ Ⓑ Ⓒ Ⓓ Ⓔ	46. Ⓐ Ⓑ Ⓒ Ⓓ Ⓔ	46. Ⓐ Ⓑ Ⓒ Ⓓ Ⓔ
47. Ⓐ Ⓑ Ⓒ Ⓓ Ⓔ	47. Ⓐ Ⓑ Ⓒ Ⓓ Ⓔ	47. Ⓐ Ⓑ Ⓒ Ⓓ Ⓔ	47. Ⓐ Ⓑ Ⓒ Ⓓ Ⓔ	47. Ⓐ Ⓑ Ⓒ Ⓓ Ⓔ	47. Ⓐ Ⓑ Ⓒ Ⓓ Ⓔ	47. Ⓐ Ⓑ Ⓒ Ⓓ Ⓔ
48. Ⓐ Ⓑ Ⓒ Ⓓ Ⓔ	48. Ⓐ Ⓑ Ⓒ Ⓓ Ⓔ	48. Ⓐ Ⓑ Ⓒ Ⓓ Ⓔ	48. Ⓐ Ⓑ Ⓒ Ⓓ Ⓔ	48. Ⓐ Ⓑ Ⓒ Ⓓ Ⓔ	48. Ⓐ Ⓑ Ⓒ Ⓓ Ⓔ	48. Ⓐ Ⓑ Ⓒ Ⓓ Ⓔ
49. Ⓐ Ⓑ Ⓒ Ⓓ Ⓔ	49. Ⓐ Ⓑ Ⓒ Ⓓ Ⓔ	49. Ⓐ Ⓑ Ⓒ Ⓓ Ⓔ	49. Ⓐ Ⓑ Ⓒ Ⓓ Ⓔ	49. Ⓐ Ⓑ Ⓒ Ⓓ Ⓔ	49. Ⓐ Ⓑ Ⓒ Ⓓ Ⓔ	49. Ⓐ Ⓑ Ⓒ Ⓓ Ⓔ
50. Ⓐ Ⓑ Ⓒ Ⓓ Ⓔ	50. Ⓐ Ⓑ Ⓒ Ⓓ Ⓔ	50. Ⓐ Ⓑ Ⓒ Ⓓ Ⓔ	50. Ⓐ Ⓑ Ⓒ Ⓓ Ⓔ	50. Ⓐ Ⓑ Ⓒ Ⓓ Ⓔ	50. Ⓐ Ⓑ Ⓒ Ⓓ Ⓔ	50. Ⓐ Ⓑ Ⓒ Ⓓ Ⓔ

FOR ETS USE ONLY	V1R	V2R	VTR	VCS	Q1R	Q2R	QTR	QCS	A1R	A2R	ATR	ACS

GRADUATE RECORD EXAMINATIONS-GENERAL TEST

SIDE 1

(Use for GRE Administrations between 10/1/90 and 9/30/91 only.)

Use only a pencil with a soft, black lead (No. 2 or HB) to complete this answer sheet.
Be sure to fill in completely the space that corresponds to your answer choice.
Completely erase any errors or stray marks.

DO NOT USE INK.

1. NAME

Omit spaces, apostrophes, Jr., II, etc.

Last Name (Family or Surname) - first 15 letters | First Name (Given) - first 12 letters | M.I.

5. P.O. Box or Street Address first 10 characters

Indicate a space in address by leaving a blank box and filling in the corresponding diamond.

6. TITLE CODE

7. TEST NAME:

FORM CODE:

8. TEST BOOK SERIAL NUMBER:

SHADED AREA FOR ETS USE ONLY

9. YOUR NAME:
(Print)

Last Name(Family or Surname) | First Name(Given) | M.I.

MAILING ADDRESS:

P.O. Box or Street Address

City | State or Province

Country | Zip or Postal Code

CENTER:

City | State or Province

Country | Center Number

10. CERTIFICATION STATEMENT

SIGNATURE:

DATE: ___ / ___ / ___
Month   Day   Year

2. DATE OF BIRTH

Month | Day | Year

Jan.
Feb.
Mar.
Apr.
May
June
July
Aug.
Sept.
Oct.
Nov.
Dec.

3. SOCIAL SECURITY NUMBER

4. REGISTRATION NUMBER

540TF30P250e   I.N.275415   Q1868-07

SIDE 2

GENERAL TEST

SIGNATURE:

DO NOT SIGN UNTIL AFTER THE BREAK

IF YOU DO NOT WANT THIS ANSWER SHEET TO BE SCORED

If you want to cancel your scores from this administration, complete A and B below. No record of this test will be sent to your designated recipients, and there will be no scores on your GRE record. You will receive confirmation of this cancellation. Once a score is canceled, it cannot be reinstated.

To cancel your scores from this test administration, you must:

A. fill in both ovals here . . . . . ◯ – ◯

B. sign your name in full below:

BE SURE EACH MARK IS DARK AND COMPLETELY FILLS THE INTENDED SPACE AS ILLUSTRATED HERE: ●.
YOU MAY FIND MORE RESPONSE SPACES THAN YOU NEED. IF SO, PLEASE LEAVE THEM BLANK.

SECTION 1	SECTION 2	SECTION 3	SECTION 4	SECTION 5	SECTION 6	SECTION 7
1. Ⓐ Ⓑ Ⓒ Ⓓ Ⓔ	1. Ⓐ Ⓑ Ⓒ Ⓓ Ⓔ	1. Ⓐ Ⓑ Ⓒ Ⓓ Ⓔ	1. Ⓐ Ⓑ Ⓒ Ⓓ Ⓔ	1. Ⓐ Ⓑ Ⓒ Ⓓ Ⓔ	1. Ⓐ Ⓑ Ⓒ Ⓓ Ⓔ	1. Ⓐ Ⓑ Ⓒ Ⓓ Ⓔ
2. Ⓐ Ⓑ Ⓒ Ⓓ Ⓔ	2. Ⓐ Ⓑ Ⓒ Ⓓ Ⓔ	2. Ⓐ Ⓑ Ⓒ Ⓓ Ⓔ	2. Ⓐ Ⓑ Ⓒ Ⓓ Ⓔ	2. Ⓐ Ⓑ Ⓒ Ⓓ Ⓔ	2. Ⓐ Ⓑ Ⓒ Ⓓ Ⓔ	2. Ⓐ Ⓑ Ⓒ Ⓓ Ⓔ
3. Ⓐ Ⓑ Ⓒ Ⓓ Ⓔ	3. Ⓐ Ⓑ Ⓒ Ⓓ Ⓔ	3. Ⓐ Ⓑ Ⓒ Ⓓ Ⓔ	3. Ⓐ Ⓑ Ⓒ Ⓓ Ⓔ	3. Ⓐ Ⓑ Ⓒ Ⓓ Ⓔ	3. Ⓐ Ⓑ Ⓒ Ⓓ Ⓔ	3. Ⓐ Ⓑ Ⓒ Ⓓ Ⓔ
4. Ⓐ Ⓑ Ⓒ Ⓓ Ⓔ	4. Ⓐ Ⓑ Ⓒ Ⓓ Ⓔ	4. Ⓐ Ⓑ Ⓒ Ⓓ Ⓔ	4. Ⓐ Ⓑ Ⓒ Ⓓ Ⓔ	4. Ⓐ Ⓑ Ⓒ Ⓓ Ⓔ	4. Ⓐ Ⓑ Ⓒ Ⓓ Ⓔ	4. Ⓐ Ⓑ Ⓒ Ⓓ Ⓔ
5. Ⓐ Ⓑ Ⓒ Ⓓ Ⓔ	5. Ⓐ Ⓑ Ⓒ Ⓓ Ⓔ	5. Ⓐ Ⓑ Ⓒ Ⓓ Ⓔ	5. Ⓐ Ⓑ Ⓒ Ⓓ Ⓔ	5. Ⓐ Ⓑ Ⓒ Ⓓ Ⓔ	5. Ⓐ Ⓑ Ⓒ Ⓓ Ⓔ	5. Ⓐ Ⓑ Ⓒ Ⓓ Ⓔ
6. Ⓐ Ⓑ Ⓒ Ⓓ Ⓔ	6. Ⓐ Ⓑ Ⓒ Ⓓ Ⓔ	6. Ⓐ Ⓑ Ⓒ Ⓓ Ⓔ	6. Ⓐ Ⓑ Ⓒ Ⓓ Ⓔ	6. Ⓐ Ⓑ Ⓒ Ⓓ Ⓔ	6. Ⓐ Ⓑ Ⓒ Ⓓ Ⓔ	6. Ⓐ Ⓑ Ⓒ Ⓓ Ⓔ
7. Ⓐ Ⓑ Ⓒ Ⓓ Ⓔ	7. Ⓐ Ⓑ Ⓒ Ⓓ Ⓔ	7. Ⓐ Ⓑ Ⓒ Ⓓ Ⓔ	7. Ⓐ Ⓑ Ⓒ Ⓓ Ⓔ	7. Ⓐ Ⓑ Ⓒ Ⓓ Ⓔ	7. Ⓐ Ⓑ Ⓒ Ⓓ Ⓔ	7. Ⓐ Ⓑ Ⓒ Ⓓ Ⓔ
8. Ⓐ Ⓑ Ⓒ Ⓓ Ⓔ	8. Ⓐ Ⓑ Ⓒ Ⓓ Ⓔ	8. Ⓐ Ⓑ Ⓒ Ⓓ Ⓔ	8. Ⓐ Ⓑ Ⓒ Ⓓ Ⓔ	8. Ⓐ Ⓑ Ⓒ Ⓓ Ⓔ	8. Ⓐ Ⓑ Ⓒ Ⓓ Ⓔ	8. Ⓐ Ⓑ Ⓒ Ⓓ Ⓔ
9. Ⓐ Ⓑ Ⓒ Ⓓ Ⓔ	9. Ⓐ Ⓑ Ⓒ Ⓓ Ⓔ	9. Ⓐ Ⓑ Ⓒ Ⓓ Ⓔ	9. Ⓐ Ⓑ Ⓒ Ⓓ Ⓔ	9. Ⓐ Ⓑ Ⓒ Ⓓ Ⓔ	9. Ⓐ Ⓑ Ⓒ Ⓓ Ⓔ	9. Ⓐ Ⓑ Ⓒ Ⓓ Ⓔ
10. Ⓐ Ⓑ Ⓒ Ⓓ Ⓔ	10. Ⓐ Ⓑ Ⓒ Ⓓ Ⓔ	10. Ⓐ Ⓑ Ⓒ Ⓓ Ⓔ	10. Ⓐ Ⓑ Ⓒ Ⓓ Ⓔ	10. Ⓐ Ⓑ Ⓒ Ⓓ Ⓔ	10. Ⓐ Ⓑ Ⓒ Ⓓ Ⓔ	10. Ⓐ Ⓑ Ⓒ Ⓓ Ⓔ
11. Ⓐ Ⓑ Ⓒ Ⓓ Ⓔ	11. Ⓐ Ⓑ Ⓒ Ⓓ Ⓔ	11. Ⓐ Ⓑ Ⓒ Ⓓ Ⓔ	11. Ⓐ Ⓑ Ⓒ Ⓓ Ⓔ	11. Ⓐ Ⓑ Ⓒ Ⓓ Ⓔ	11. Ⓐ Ⓑ Ⓒ Ⓓ Ⓔ	11. Ⓐ Ⓑ Ⓒ Ⓓ Ⓔ
12. Ⓐ Ⓑ Ⓒ Ⓓ Ⓔ	12. Ⓐ Ⓑ Ⓒ Ⓓ Ⓔ	12. Ⓐ Ⓑ Ⓒ Ⓓ Ⓔ	12. Ⓐ Ⓑ Ⓒ Ⓓ Ⓔ	12. Ⓐ Ⓑ Ⓒ Ⓓ Ⓔ	12. Ⓐ Ⓑ Ⓒ Ⓓ Ⓔ	12. Ⓐ Ⓑ Ⓒ Ⓓ Ⓔ
13. Ⓐ Ⓑ Ⓒ Ⓓ Ⓔ	13. Ⓐ Ⓑ Ⓒ Ⓓ Ⓔ	13. Ⓐ Ⓑ Ⓒ Ⓓ Ⓔ	13. Ⓐ Ⓑ Ⓒ Ⓓ Ⓔ	13. Ⓐ Ⓑ Ⓒ Ⓓ Ⓔ	13. Ⓐ Ⓑ Ⓒ Ⓓ Ⓔ	13. Ⓐ Ⓑ Ⓒ Ⓓ Ⓔ
14. Ⓐ Ⓑ Ⓒ Ⓓ Ⓔ	14. Ⓐ Ⓑ Ⓒ Ⓓ Ⓔ	14. Ⓐ Ⓑ Ⓒ Ⓓ Ⓔ	14. Ⓐ Ⓑ Ⓒ Ⓓ Ⓔ	14. Ⓐ Ⓑ Ⓒ Ⓓ Ⓔ	14. Ⓐ Ⓑ Ⓒ Ⓓ Ⓔ	14. Ⓐ Ⓑ Ⓒ Ⓓ Ⓔ
15. Ⓐ Ⓑ Ⓒ Ⓓ Ⓔ	15. Ⓐ Ⓑ Ⓒ Ⓓ Ⓔ	15. Ⓐ Ⓑ Ⓒ Ⓓ Ⓔ	15. Ⓐ Ⓑ Ⓒ Ⓓ Ⓔ	15. Ⓐ Ⓑ Ⓒ Ⓓ Ⓔ	15. Ⓐ Ⓑ Ⓒ Ⓓ Ⓔ	15. Ⓐ Ⓑ Ⓒ Ⓓ Ⓔ
16. Ⓐ Ⓑ Ⓒ Ⓓ Ⓔ	16. Ⓐ Ⓑ Ⓒ Ⓓ Ⓔ	16. Ⓐ Ⓑ Ⓒ Ⓓ Ⓔ	16. Ⓐ Ⓑ Ⓒ Ⓓ Ⓔ	16. Ⓐ Ⓑ Ⓒ Ⓓ Ⓔ	16. Ⓐ Ⓑ Ⓒ Ⓓ Ⓔ	16. Ⓐ Ⓑ Ⓒ Ⓓ Ⓔ
17. Ⓐ Ⓑ Ⓒ Ⓓ Ⓔ	17. Ⓐ Ⓑ Ⓒ Ⓓ Ⓔ	17. Ⓐ Ⓑ Ⓒ Ⓓ Ⓔ	17. Ⓐ Ⓑ Ⓒ Ⓓ Ⓔ	17. Ⓐ Ⓑ Ⓒ Ⓓ Ⓔ	17. Ⓐ Ⓑ Ⓒ Ⓓ Ⓔ	17. Ⓐ Ⓑ Ⓒ Ⓓ Ⓔ
18. Ⓐ Ⓑ Ⓒ Ⓓ Ⓔ	18. Ⓐ Ⓑ Ⓒ Ⓓ Ⓔ	18. Ⓐ Ⓑ Ⓒ Ⓓ Ⓔ	18. Ⓐ Ⓑ Ⓒ Ⓓ Ⓔ	18. Ⓐ Ⓑ Ⓒ Ⓓ Ⓔ	18. Ⓐ Ⓑ Ⓒ Ⓓ Ⓔ	18. Ⓐ Ⓑ Ⓒ Ⓓ Ⓔ
19. Ⓐ Ⓑ Ⓒ Ⓓ Ⓔ	19. Ⓐ Ⓑ Ⓒ Ⓓ Ⓔ	19. Ⓐ Ⓑ Ⓒ Ⓓ Ⓔ	19. Ⓐ Ⓑ Ⓒ Ⓓ Ⓔ	19. Ⓐ Ⓑ Ⓒ Ⓓ Ⓔ	19. Ⓐ Ⓑ Ⓒ Ⓓ Ⓔ	19. Ⓐ Ⓑ Ⓒ Ⓓ Ⓔ
20. Ⓐ Ⓑ Ⓒ Ⓓ Ⓔ	20. Ⓐ Ⓑ Ⓒ Ⓓ Ⓔ	20. Ⓐ Ⓑ Ⓒ Ⓓ Ⓔ	20. Ⓐ Ⓑ Ⓒ Ⓓ Ⓔ	20. Ⓐ Ⓑ Ⓒ Ⓓ Ⓔ	20. Ⓐ Ⓑ Ⓒ Ⓓ Ⓔ	20. Ⓐ Ⓑ Ⓒ Ⓓ Ⓔ
21. Ⓐ Ⓑ Ⓒ Ⓓ Ⓔ	21. Ⓐ Ⓑ Ⓒ Ⓓ Ⓔ	21. Ⓐ Ⓑ Ⓒ Ⓓ Ⓔ	21. Ⓐ Ⓑ Ⓒ Ⓓ Ⓔ	21. Ⓐ Ⓑ Ⓒ Ⓓ Ⓔ	21. Ⓐ Ⓑ Ⓒ Ⓓ Ⓔ	21. Ⓐ Ⓑ Ⓒ Ⓓ Ⓔ
22. Ⓐ Ⓑ Ⓒ Ⓓ Ⓔ	22. Ⓐ Ⓑ Ⓒ Ⓓ Ⓔ	22. Ⓐ Ⓑ Ⓒ Ⓓ Ⓔ	22. Ⓐ Ⓑ Ⓒ Ⓓ Ⓔ	22. Ⓐ Ⓑ Ⓒ Ⓓ Ⓔ	22. Ⓐ Ⓑ Ⓒ Ⓓ Ⓔ	22. Ⓐ Ⓑ Ⓒ Ⓓ Ⓔ
23. Ⓐ Ⓑ Ⓒ Ⓓ Ⓔ	23. Ⓐ Ⓑ Ⓒ Ⓓ Ⓔ	23. Ⓐ Ⓑ Ⓒ Ⓓ Ⓔ	23. Ⓐ Ⓑ Ⓒ Ⓓ Ⓔ	23. Ⓐ Ⓑ Ⓒ Ⓓ Ⓔ	23. Ⓐ Ⓑ Ⓒ Ⓓ Ⓔ	23. Ⓐ Ⓑ Ⓒ Ⓓ Ⓔ
24. Ⓐ Ⓑ Ⓒ Ⓓ Ⓔ	24. Ⓐ Ⓑ Ⓒ Ⓓ Ⓔ	24. Ⓐ Ⓑ Ⓒ Ⓓ Ⓔ	24. Ⓐ Ⓑ Ⓒ Ⓓ Ⓔ	24. Ⓐ Ⓑ Ⓒ Ⓓ Ⓔ	24. Ⓐ Ⓑ Ⓒ Ⓓ Ⓔ	24. Ⓐ Ⓑ Ⓒ Ⓓ Ⓔ
25. Ⓐ Ⓑ Ⓒ Ⓓ Ⓔ	25. Ⓐ Ⓑ Ⓒ Ⓓ Ⓔ	25. Ⓐ Ⓑ Ⓒ Ⓓ Ⓔ	25. Ⓐ Ⓑ Ⓒ Ⓓ Ⓔ	25. Ⓐ Ⓑ Ⓒ Ⓓ Ⓔ	25. Ⓐ Ⓑ Ⓒ Ⓓ Ⓔ	25. Ⓐ Ⓑ Ⓒ Ⓓ Ⓔ
26. Ⓐ Ⓑ Ⓒ Ⓓ Ⓔ	26. Ⓐ Ⓑ Ⓒ Ⓓ Ⓔ	26. Ⓐ Ⓑ Ⓒ Ⓓ Ⓔ	26. Ⓐ Ⓑ Ⓒ Ⓓ Ⓔ	26. Ⓐ Ⓑ Ⓒ Ⓓ Ⓔ	26. Ⓐ Ⓑ Ⓒ Ⓓ Ⓔ	26. Ⓐ Ⓑ Ⓒ Ⓓ Ⓔ
27. Ⓐ Ⓑ Ⓒ Ⓓ Ⓔ	27. Ⓐ Ⓑ Ⓒ Ⓓ Ⓔ	27. Ⓐ Ⓑ Ⓒ Ⓓ Ⓔ	27. Ⓐ Ⓑ Ⓒ Ⓓ Ⓔ	27. Ⓐ Ⓑ Ⓒ Ⓓ Ⓔ	27. Ⓐ Ⓑ Ⓒ Ⓓ Ⓔ	27. Ⓐ Ⓑ Ⓒ Ⓓ Ⓔ
28. Ⓐ Ⓑ Ⓒ Ⓓ Ⓔ	28. Ⓐ Ⓑ Ⓒ Ⓓ Ⓔ	28. Ⓐ Ⓑ Ⓒ Ⓓ Ⓔ	28. Ⓐ Ⓑ Ⓒ Ⓓ Ⓔ	28. Ⓐ Ⓑ Ⓒ Ⓓ Ⓔ	28. Ⓐ Ⓑ Ⓒ Ⓓ Ⓔ	28. Ⓐ Ⓑ Ⓒ Ⓓ Ⓔ
29. Ⓐ Ⓑ Ⓒ Ⓓ Ⓔ	29. Ⓐ Ⓑ Ⓒ Ⓓ Ⓔ	29. Ⓐ Ⓑ Ⓒ Ⓓ Ⓔ	29. Ⓐ Ⓑ Ⓒ Ⓓ Ⓔ	29. Ⓐ Ⓑ Ⓒ Ⓓ Ⓔ	29. Ⓐ Ⓑ Ⓒ Ⓓ Ⓔ	29. Ⓐ Ⓑ Ⓒ Ⓓ Ⓔ
30. Ⓐ Ⓑ Ⓒ Ⓓ Ⓔ	30. Ⓐ Ⓑ Ⓒ Ⓓ Ⓔ	30. Ⓐ Ⓑ Ⓒ Ⓓ Ⓔ	30. Ⓐ Ⓑ Ⓒ Ⓓ Ⓔ	30. Ⓐ Ⓑ Ⓒ Ⓓ Ⓔ	30. Ⓐ Ⓑ Ⓒ Ⓓ Ⓔ	30. Ⓐ Ⓑ Ⓒ Ⓓ Ⓔ
31. Ⓐ Ⓑ Ⓒ Ⓓ Ⓔ	31. Ⓐ Ⓑ Ⓒ Ⓓ Ⓔ	31. Ⓐ Ⓑ Ⓒ Ⓓ Ⓔ	31. Ⓐ Ⓑ Ⓒ Ⓓ Ⓔ	31. Ⓐ Ⓑ Ⓒ Ⓓ Ⓔ	31. Ⓐ Ⓑ Ⓒ Ⓓ Ⓔ	31. Ⓐ Ⓑ Ⓒ Ⓓ Ⓔ
32. Ⓐ Ⓑ Ⓒ Ⓓ Ⓔ	32. Ⓐ Ⓑ Ⓒ Ⓓ Ⓔ	32. Ⓐ Ⓑ Ⓒ Ⓓ Ⓔ	32. Ⓐ Ⓑ Ⓒ Ⓓ Ⓔ	32. Ⓐ Ⓑ Ⓒ Ⓓ Ⓔ	32. Ⓐ Ⓑ Ⓒ Ⓓ Ⓔ	32. Ⓐ Ⓑ Ⓒ Ⓓ Ⓔ
33. Ⓐ Ⓑ Ⓒ Ⓓ Ⓔ	33. Ⓐ Ⓑ Ⓒ Ⓓ Ⓔ	33. Ⓐ Ⓑ Ⓒ Ⓓ Ⓔ	33. Ⓐ Ⓑ Ⓒ Ⓓ Ⓔ	33. Ⓐ Ⓑ Ⓒ Ⓓ Ⓔ	33. Ⓐ Ⓑ Ⓒ Ⓓ Ⓔ	33. Ⓐ Ⓑ Ⓒ Ⓓ Ⓔ
34. Ⓐ Ⓑ Ⓒ Ⓓ Ⓔ	34. Ⓐ Ⓑ Ⓒ Ⓓ Ⓔ	34. Ⓐ Ⓑ Ⓒ Ⓓ Ⓔ	34. Ⓐ Ⓑ Ⓒ Ⓓ Ⓔ	34. Ⓐ Ⓑ Ⓒ Ⓓ Ⓔ	34. Ⓐ Ⓑ Ⓒ Ⓓ Ⓔ	34. Ⓐ Ⓑ Ⓒ Ⓓ Ⓔ
35. Ⓐ Ⓑ Ⓒ Ⓓ Ⓔ	35. Ⓐ Ⓑ Ⓒ Ⓓ Ⓔ	35. Ⓐ Ⓑ Ⓒ Ⓓ Ⓔ	35. Ⓐ Ⓑ Ⓒ Ⓓ Ⓔ	35. Ⓐ Ⓑ Ⓒ Ⓓ Ⓔ	35. Ⓐ Ⓑ Ⓒ Ⓓ Ⓔ	35. Ⓐ Ⓑ Ⓒ Ⓓ Ⓔ
36. Ⓐ Ⓑ Ⓒ Ⓓ Ⓔ	36. Ⓐ Ⓑ Ⓒ Ⓓ Ⓔ	36. Ⓐ Ⓑ Ⓒ Ⓓ Ⓔ	36. Ⓐ Ⓑ Ⓒ Ⓓ Ⓔ	36. Ⓐ Ⓑ Ⓒ Ⓓ Ⓔ	36. Ⓐ Ⓑ Ⓒ Ⓓ Ⓔ	36. Ⓐ Ⓑ Ⓒ Ⓓ Ⓔ
37. Ⓐ Ⓑ Ⓒ Ⓓ Ⓔ	37. Ⓐ Ⓑ Ⓒ Ⓓ Ⓔ	37. Ⓐ Ⓑ Ⓒ Ⓓ Ⓔ	37. Ⓐ Ⓑ Ⓒ Ⓓ Ⓔ	37. Ⓐ Ⓑ Ⓒ Ⓓ Ⓔ	37. Ⓐ Ⓑ Ⓒ Ⓓ Ⓔ	37. Ⓐ Ⓑ Ⓒ Ⓓ Ⓔ
38. Ⓐ Ⓑ Ⓒ Ⓓ Ⓔ	38. Ⓐ Ⓑ Ⓒ Ⓓ Ⓔ	38. Ⓐ Ⓑ Ⓒ Ⓓ Ⓔ	38. Ⓐ Ⓑ Ⓒ Ⓓ Ⓔ	38. Ⓐ Ⓑ Ⓒ Ⓓ Ⓔ	38. Ⓐ Ⓑ Ⓒ Ⓓ Ⓔ	38. Ⓐ Ⓑ Ⓒ Ⓓ Ⓔ
39. Ⓐ Ⓑ Ⓒ Ⓓ Ⓔ	39. Ⓐ Ⓑ Ⓒ Ⓓ Ⓔ	39. Ⓐ Ⓑ Ⓒ Ⓓ Ⓔ	39. Ⓐ Ⓑ Ⓒ Ⓓ Ⓔ	39. Ⓐ Ⓑ Ⓒ Ⓓ Ⓔ	39. Ⓐ Ⓑ Ⓒ Ⓓ Ⓔ	39. Ⓐ Ⓑ Ⓒ Ⓓ Ⓔ
40. Ⓐ Ⓑ Ⓒ Ⓓ Ⓔ	40. Ⓐ Ⓑ Ⓒ Ⓓ Ⓔ	40. Ⓐ Ⓑ Ⓒ Ⓓ Ⓔ	40. Ⓐ Ⓑ Ⓒ Ⓓ Ⓔ	40. Ⓐ Ⓑ Ⓒ Ⓓ Ⓔ	40. Ⓐ Ⓑ Ⓒ Ⓓ Ⓔ	40. Ⓐ Ⓑ Ⓒ Ⓓ Ⓔ
41. Ⓐ Ⓑ Ⓒ Ⓓ Ⓔ	41. Ⓐ Ⓑ Ⓒ Ⓓ Ⓔ	41. Ⓐ Ⓑ Ⓒ Ⓓ Ⓔ	41. Ⓐ Ⓑ Ⓒ Ⓓ Ⓔ	41. Ⓐ Ⓑ Ⓒ Ⓓ Ⓔ	41. Ⓐ Ⓑ Ⓒ Ⓓ Ⓔ	41. Ⓐ Ⓑ Ⓒ Ⓓ Ⓔ
42. Ⓐ Ⓑ Ⓒ Ⓓ Ⓔ	42. Ⓐ Ⓑ Ⓒ Ⓓ Ⓔ	42. Ⓐ Ⓑ Ⓒ Ⓓ Ⓔ	42. Ⓐ Ⓑ Ⓒ Ⓓ Ⓔ	42. Ⓐ Ⓑ Ⓒ Ⓓ Ⓔ	42. Ⓐ Ⓑ Ⓒ Ⓓ Ⓔ	42. Ⓐ Ⓑ Ⓒ Ⓓ Ⓔ
43. Ⓐ Ⓑ Ⓒ Ⓓ Ⓔ	43. Ⓐ Ⓑ Ⓒ Ⓓ Ⓔ	43. Ⓐ Ⓑ Ⓒ Ⓓ Ⓔ	43. Ⓐ Ⓑ Ⓒ Ⓓ Ⓔ	43. Ⓐ Ⓑ Ⓒ Ⓓ Ⓔ	43. Ⓐ Ⓑ Ⓒ Ⓓ Ⓔ	43. Ⓐ Ⓑ Ⓒ Ⓓ Ⓔ
44. Ⓐ Ⓑ Ⓒ Ⓓ Ⓔ	44. Ⓐ Ⓑ Ⓒ Ⓓ Ⓔ	44. Ⓐ Ⓑ Ⓒ Ⓓ Ⓔ	44. Ⓐ Ⓑ Ⓒ Ⓓ Ⓔ	44. Ⓐ Ⓑ Ⓒ Ⓓ Ⓔ	44. Ⓐ Ⓑ Ⓒ Ⓓ Ⓔ	44. Ⓐ Ⓑ Ⓒ Ⓓ Ⓔ
45. Ⓐ Ⓑ Ⓒ Ⓓ Ⓔ	45. Ⓐ Ⓑ Ⓒ Ⓓ Ⓔ	45. Ⓐ Ⓑ Ⓒ Ⓓ Ⓔ	45. Ⓐ Ⓑ Ⓒ Ⓓ Ⓔ	45. Ⓐ Ⓑ Ⓒ Ⓓ Ⓔ	45. Ⓐ Ⓑ Ⓒ Ⓓ Ⓔ	45. Ⓐ Ⓑ Ⓒ Ⓓ Ⓔ
46. Ⓐ Ⓑ Ⓒ Ⓓ Ⓔ	46. Ⓐ Ⓑ Ⓒ Ⓓ Ⓔ	46. Ⓐ Ⓑ Ⓒ Ⓓ Ⓔ	46. Ⓐ Ⓑ Ⓒ Ⓓ Ⓔ	46. Ⓐ Ⓑ Ⓒ Ⓓ Ⓔ	46. Ⓐ Ⓑ Ⓒ Ⓓ Ⓔ	46. Ⓐ Ⓑ Ⓒ Ⓓ Ⓔ
47. Ⓐ Ⓑ Ⓒ Ⓓ Ⓔ	47. Ⓐ Ⓑ Ⓒ Ⓓ Ⓔ	47. Ⓐ Ⓑ Ⓒ Ⓓ Ⓔ	47. Ⓐ Ⓑ Ⓒ Ⓓ Ⓔ	47. Ⓐ Ⓑ Ⓒ Ⓓ Ⓔ	47. Ⓐ Ⓑ Ⓒ Ⓓ Ⓔ	47. Ⓐ Ⓑ Ⓒ Ⓓ Ⓔ
48. Ⓐ Ⓑ Ⓒ Ⓓ Ⓔ	48. Ⓐ Ⓑ Ⓒ Ⓓ Ⓔ	48. Ⓐ Ⓑ Ⓒ Ⓓ Ⓔ	48. Ⓐ Ⓑ Ⓒ Ⓓ Ⓔ	48. Ⓐ Ⓑ Ⓒ Ⓓ Ⓔ	48. Ⓐ Ⓑ Ⓒ Ⓓ Ⓔ	48. Ⓐ Ⓑ Ⓒ Ⓓ Ⓔ
49. Ⓐ Ⓑ Ⓒ Ⓓ Ⓔ	49. Ⓐ Ⓑ Ⓒ Ⓓ Ⓔ	49. Ⓐ Ⓑ Ⓒ Ⓓ Ⓔ	49. Ⓐ Ⓑ Ⓒ Ⓓ Ⓔ	49. Ⓐ Ⓑ Ⓒ Ⓓ Ⓔ	49. Ⓐ Ⓑ Ⓒ Ⓓ Ⓔ	49. Ⓐ Ⓑ Ⓒ Ⓓ Ⓔ
50. Ⓐ Ⓑ Ⓒ Ⓓ Ⓔ	50. Ⓐ Ⓑ Ⓒ Ⓓ Ⓔ	50. Ⓐ Ⓑ Ⓒ Ⓓ Ⓔ	50. Ⓐ Ⓑ Ⓒ Ⓓ Ⓔ	50. Ⓐ Ⓑ Ⓒ Ⓓ Ⓔ	50. Ⓐ Ⓑ Ⓒ Ⓓ Ⓔ	50. Ⓐ Ⓑ Ⓒ Ⓓ Ⓔ

FOR ETS USE ONLY	V1R	V2R	VTR	VCS	Q1R	Q2R	QTR	QCS	A1R	A2R	ATR	ACS

GRE® PUBLICATIONS ORDER FORM
1990-91

Graduate Record Examinations
Educational Testing Service
P.O. Box 6014
Princeton, NJ 08541-6014

P-60

Item Number	Publication	Price*	No. of Copies	Amount	Total
	Practice Test Books (540-01)				
241245	†Practicing to Take the GRE General Test—No. 8	$12.00			
241235	Practicing to Take the GRE General Test—No. 7	10.00			
241241	†Practicing to Take the GRE Biology Test–2nd Edition	11.00			
241242	†Practicing to Take the GRE Chemistry Test–2nd Edition	11.00			
241247	Practicing to Take the GRE Computer Science Test	9.00			
241218	Practicing to Take the GRE Economics Test	9.00			
241236	Practicing to Take the GRE Education Test–2nd Edition	11.00			
241237	Practicing to Take the GRE Engineering Test–2nd Edition	11.00			
241227	Practicing to Take the GRE Geology Test	9.00			
241219	Practicing to Take the GRE History Test	9.00			
241243	†Practicing to Take the GRE Literature in English Test—2nd Edition	11.00			
241228	Practicing to Take the GRE Mathematics Test	9.00			
241244	Practicing to Take the GRE Revised Music Test	9.00			
241246	Practicing to Take the GRE Physics Test	9.00			
241234	Practicing to Take the GRE Political Science Test	9.00			
241238	Practicing to Take the GRE Psychology Test–2nd Edition	11.00			
241229	Practicing to Take the GRE Sociology Test	9.00			
	Software Editions (540-07)				
299623	†Practicing to Take the GRE General Test—No. 7, Apple Macintosh Software Edition Version 2.1	70.00			
299624	†Practicing to Take the GRE General Test—No. 7, IBM Software Edition Version 2.1	70.00			
	Directory of Graduate Programs (540-99)				
252025	Volume A—Agriculture, Biological Sciences, Psychology, Health Sciences, and Home Economics	14.00			
252026	Volume B—Arts and Humanities	14.00			
252027	Volume C—Physical Sciences, Mathematics, and Engineering	14.00			
252028	Volume D—Social Sciences and Education	14.00			

* **Postage: In North America, U.S. Territories, and APO addresses,** postage and handling to a single address is included in the price of the publication.
   To all other locations (airmail only) for postage and handling to a single address, add $4 for the first book ordered and $2 for each additional book. Add $10 for each software edition ordered.

† Available September 1990.

● Allow three to four weeks for delivery.

● Payment should be made by check or money order drawn on a U.S. bank, U.S. Postal Money Order, UNESCO Coupons, or current International Postal Reply Coupons.

● *Orders received without payment or a purchase order will be returned.*

TYPE OR PRINT CLEARLY BELOW. DO NOT DETACH THESE MAILING LABELS.

➡ POSTAGE 540-52

Make your remittance payable to Graduate Record Examinations.

⬆ TOTAL ⬆ AMOUNT ENCLOSED

ETS use only

Graduate Record Examinations
Educational Testing Service
P.O. Box 6014
Princeton, NJ 08541-6014

TO: _____

_____

_____

_____

Graduate Record Examinations
Educational Testing Service
P.O. Box 6014
Princeton, NJ 08541-6014

TO: _____

_____

_____

_____